Images of the Plains

Images of the Plains

The Role of Human Nature in Settlement

edited by Brian W. Blouet *and* Merlin P. Lawson

University of Nebraska Press • Lincoln

Publishers on the Plains
UNP

Library of Congress Cataloging in Publication Data

Main entry under title:

Images of the plains.

   Papers presented at the conference held Apr. 30–May 1, 1973
at the University of Nebraska—Lincoln.
   Includes bibliographies.
   1. Great Plains—Congresses. 2. Hewes, Leslie.
I. Blouet, Brian W., 1936–   ed. II. Lawson,
Merlin P., 1941–   ed. III. Nebraska. University.
F591.I42   917.8'03   74–76130
ISBN 0–8032–0839–1

CONTENTS

PART 5: THE DESERT AND THE GARDEN

PART 6: ADAPTATIONS TO REALITY

PREFACE

The essays in this volume are drawn from those presented at the "Images of the Plains" conference, which was held on April 30 and May 1, 1973, at the Nebraska Center for Continuing Education on the East Campus of the University of Nebraska–Lincoln. The idea of holding such a conference was developed at a meeting of historical geographers at the National Archives, Washington, D.C., in November, 1971, at which time Andrew H. Clark, Herman Friis, Martyn Bowden, and John Allen indicated vigorous support for the symposium. Subsequently Dean Melvin D. George of our College of Arts and Sciences gave substantive aid, the University of Nebraska Press responded readily to the suggestion of a volume on the plains, and E. N. Thompson of the Cooper Foundation, Lincoln, Nebraska, made arrangements to underwrite a portion of the publication costs of this book. Howard Hines of the National Science Foundation encouraged us to seek support from that organization.

As organizers and editors we are grateful to our fellow members of the program committee: Marvin Kivett, director, Nebraska State Historical Society; G. Malcolm Lewis, Department of Geography, University of Sheffield, England; Jonathan Levine, Department of History, University of Pittsburgh; Frederick Luebke, Department of History, University of Nebraska–Lincoln; and John Warkentin, Department of Geography, York University, Canada. They gave much valuable aid and counsel. For chairing sessions and for notable contributions to the conference, we wish to thank Warren Caldwell, John Ewers, Dale Henning, Benjamin Rader, Roger Nichols, Thomas Saarinen, Gordon Nelson, Walter Kollmorgen, Michael Williams, Homer Socolofsky, Philip Tideman, Donald Meinig, and James H. Zumberge, chancellor of the University of Nebraska–Lincoln.

We owe a collective debt to our colleagues in the Department of Geography, who in so many ways offered help and encouragement. We should particularly like to thank Donald Wilhite for acting as local arrangements secretary and Mildred Kohler for her assistance with a myriad of administrative tasks.

The symposium and this volume of essays were inspired by our desire to honor the contributions of Dr. Leslie Hewes to scholarship concerned with the plains region over the last three decades. Dr. Hewes came to the University of Nebraska in 1945 and served as chairman of the Department of Geography from 1946 to 1968. He retired from the university, while still an active teacher and publishing scholar, in the summer of 1974. Most of us connected with the symposium have long shared scholarly interests with Dr. Hewes, many as students or colleagues. On behalf of all the participants in the symposium and the contributors to this volume, we offer our thanks to Dr. Leslie Hewes for the contributions he has made to North American scholarship during the course of his distinguished career.

BRIAN W. BLOUET
MERLIN P. LAWSON

University of Nebraska–Lincoln

FOREWORD

The Great Plains: Perception by Any Name

Andrew Hill Clark
University of Wisconsin

Although the essays in this volume range over a rather broad spectrum of interests, as symposium papers often do, the title, *Images of the Plains,* is entirely appropriate. The concern of the contributing scholars was with the sources of imagery of the Great Plains, with the processes of image formation, and, to a somewhat lesser degree, with the behavioral implications of different kinds of images. Because the papers all arose out of the active research interests of individual scholars a certain unevenness was inevitable, but it is balanced by a freshness of observation, a crispness of insight, and a robustness of criticism that the more disciplined structure of a single-minded approach might well have lacked.

Among the contributions there is a good deal of attention to the images developed out of experiences and reports of fur traders, of both military and civil government-sponsored explorations for a variety of purposes, and of the presettlement (or predisposal) evaluations of official land surveyors. There are assessments of images believed to have been held by indigenous inhabitants before and after European contact, and by the earliest Spanish visitors; there are attempts to make a separate evaluation of image making in the northern (essentially Canadian) plains; there are reports on the activities of the promoters, propagandists, and publicists; there are descriptions of and judgments about the cultural and geographical diversity of origin of the perceivers; there are discussions of land acquisition and utilization and its relation to perception; and there are some systematic analyses of diaries and letters from two relatively massive population movements across the plains in the middle of the nineteenth century—those of the gold rushers and the Mormons. Scattered through, as a sort of sauce for this scholarly potpourri, are references to images of fauna and flora, and consideration of assumptions about the relationship of climatic variables to plant cover and land use. In conclusion, there is a most interesting and timely centenary review of John Wesley Powell's assessments of and prescriptions for the plains by Leslie Hewes.

Inevitably one asks for more, but curiosity quickly reveals vistas that would engross a dozen symposia or volumes of this kind. Certainly the beginnings made here in the analysis of image formation and of behavioral responses thereto deserve extensive elaboration and implementation. It would be broadly useful if the insights gained from this sort of attention to the plains could be applied not only to other areas with problems of limited or variable soil moisture, but perhaps to quite different kinds of regions, such as the Canadian North. In that arctic and subarctic expanse one may not face the "garden-desert" antithesis that has become almost a banality in the historiographic discussion of imagery of the plains, but very clearly, the North too is a land where one man's "myth" is forever rubbing shoulders with another's "reality."

It is to be hoped that future scholarship will include more "humanistic" contributions evaluating the impact on image making of imaginative literature, landscape painting, and photography. We may hope too that more attention will be given to the twentieth century and to the ways in which the images and image making of the nineteenth, on which most attention at the symposium was concentrated, may have altered through time, and the significance of such shifts to changing human behavior. Further, we should warmly welcome more work on the sociopsychological implications of low population densities and extreme rural settlement dispersal—particularly, perhaps, for the women of the plains' ranches and farms.

Only the most cursory glance through the literature turned up the following identifications, definitions, explanations, or surrogates of *perception* or *image* as applied to one or another part of the Great Plains: *recognition, delimitation, use, examination, appraisal, impression, description, evaluation,* and *assessment.* However, a major achievement of the symposium was a strict economy in the use of novel or esoteric terminology. Roughly three-fourths of the participants might fit into the elastic rubric of *historical geographers* and it would have been all too easy for them to have bogged down in the use of the terms *image* and *perception* in the way we have done in the past over *landscape, human ecology,* and *sequant occupance,* all of which remain to this day ambiguous or poorly defined so that one seeks to improve communication by avoiding them rather than using them. It would surely be an intellectual disaster if we were to face a future analytical and exegetical literature that could rival in volume the massive results of the dialogue that raged for so long over *landschaft* and *landscape.*

Of course there is wide variety among perceptions, so perhaps the differences deserve variety in labeling. But each of the alternatives carries its own load of color and bias in the minds of its users. Until the symbolic logicians

develop an entirely neutral system of terminology—which in the present state of semantic theory will not be soon—we have to live with the problem, but it is well to remind ourselves that the concepts of *image* and *perception* are far from precise. Moreover, as any geographer or historian who must depend for his evidence upon a great range of quality and kind in past perceptions and perceivers is only too keenly aware, such images always come through screens or filters that easily mask or distort inherent characteristics.

The process of central interest that is implicit in all the papers of this volume, and explicit in many, is that of image making, and it may be useful as an introduction to the collection to discuss a few distinct types of the models through which the images are formed, disseminated, or received. Most of such models used in the following papers are at least intended to be "functional" (or "objective" or "scientific" or whatever); that is, they have been conceived in terms of measurement or some other disciplined or objectively evaluable observation of social, economic, or biophysical phenomena (conditions, processes, organization, etc.). Perhaps one should add, "or upon reasoned hypotheses as to what such scientifically ordered observations might have revealed if they could have been undertaken"!

It must be conceded at once that there are various distinctly nonfunctional models of image making, and had any of the papers explored imaginative literature or other regional artistic interpretations, we might have been involved with one or another of these. For example, the existentialist model of image making is developed from the position that man experiences the world not only by observation through whatever filters are interposed, but also through such emotions as love, hate, and envy. Emotion, in this view, is seen as a particular vehicle of perception—as a fundamental way of apprehending the world. As Yi-Fu Tuan has pointed out in his discussion of the problem, love sees beauty in a plain face or a plain landscape, and grapes that one cannot reach are perceived as green and unripe regardless of other information about them. As a major interpreter of Sartre has put it:

"We operate upon the world, we feel moved by the world, we perceive the world. All these things happen together" (Tuan 1972). In such a view no amount of analysis ever can succeed in transforming these into, or in isolating them as, discrete experiences.

We must let our existentialist model serve as a lone example of the nonfunctional type and turn quickly to some of the kinds of models of image making that have been, or might have been, employed in the symposium papers. One of the first ways of looking at functional models might be to consider a pair representing, first, the system of biophysical processes in the physical setting and, second, the system of cultural occupation and utilization. Where the two systems interlock and impinge on one another is where the fun begins for the environmental anthropologist, the cultural ecologist, the geographical historian, and the historical geographer.

Perhaps more closely relevant to our concerns in this symposium is a second pair of models of regional image making. The first would be based on second-hand reports, rumors, fancies, hopes, and fears by people outside of the region and the second on the experiences of those who actually had been there for longer or shorter periods. The imagery resulting from the first of these was enormously important in influencing decisions, individual and corporate, about ventures to enter, to cross, or to utilize the plains. Moreover, it sometimes may have provided a special filter in the feedback mechanism of the reverse model of the development of imagery of the plains, the transformation of first-hand experience into perception. It well might be supposed that the second of this pair of models, that of direct image formation, would provide more accurate results than the synthesis of second-hand accounts, dreams, or myopic visions filtered through uncounted and diverse screens of prejudice, romanticism, special pleading, public policy, or downright chicanery. Yet the plains were geographically so diverse in character—even within the most limited of hundreds of definitions of circumscriptions—and, at any place, varied so much through time in climate and all of climate's camp followers of

soil moisture, plants, and animals that such transformations of experience into the images of perception gave results as diverse as the environments themselves.

A brief introduction of this kind is no place to expand on these two models, which I see as rather like a pair of "up" and "down" escalators crossing each other and, thus, perhaps not interacting very much; but I suspect that if we even can separate the two resulting kinds of images into distinct "in" and "out" baskets, so to speak, we shall understand a good deal more about individual and group behavior in relation to the plains, whether by those within them as actors on the scene or by outsiders. The latter might have included a party being made up in a Philadelphia tavern to cross the continent to the California gold fields; speculators in a Paris stock market as money was hazarded to build a railroad across the plains; or perhaps someone in a Glasgow counting house deciding to risk a block of life's savings in the plains' cattle industry.

Another double-model approach to the development of the imagery of the plains arises from the rather obvious circumstance that people often generalize images either from the part to the whole or the other way around. Certainly the plains often have been perceived as a segment of a larger whole, be it "the Frontier," "the West," "the Great American Desert," "the Western Interior Grassland," "the Great Central Lowland," the collective trans-Mississippi drainage basins, or what you will. What is important is that attempts to characterize the greater wholes necessarily gloss over individual peculiarities, and clearly, there are attributes of those larger wholes which are not very apt in relation to many parts of the Great Plains, taken alone. In fact, Walter Prescott Webb may have fallen into the trap of considering the plains as part of such an omnibus concept of "the Frontier," and so, all the generally accepted Turnerian frontier attributes were applied to all parts of the region.

The other side of the coin, of course, is that characteristics of some of the better-known or more highly publicized parts of the plains are easily assumed to apply everywhere from the Ozarks to the Front Range, from the Manitoba escarpment to the Canadian Rockies, and from the Edwards Plateau to the Peace River country. The most popular vulgar error of this kind, undoubtedly, is to apply to the Great Plains, generally, imagery derived from the Llano Estacado or the High Plains as a whole; for example, such statements as, "We get a very good picture of the pre-European, pre-horse, pre-gun Indian economies of the Great Plains from the accounts of the Coronado expedition." This is a particularly interesting one because, if the maker were sophisticated enough to realize its implications, it might have some merit as an arguable proposition. Nevertheless, in almost all cases, it is the simple error of generalizing from the part to the whole. The most serious danger of all is that what is absorbed through the partial model into the general image often feeds back into other partial models and turns up in the creation of images where it is entirely inappropriate.

Another rather obvious double model of image making is that resulting from the transect of the plains by the international boundary. In considering the present areas of the United States and Canada as a unit, two basic models of regionalization are constantly blurring each other's images. The continental biophysical regionalizations have predominantly north-south orientations. In contrast, the politico-cultural ones, of which the 49th parallel is the major symbol in our area, have markedly east-west trends. However, the interpretative problems can become quite complex. American scholarly consideration of Appalachia as a cultural region, for example, usually ignores the rather obvious parallels between the Appalachian roughlands south and west of the Hudson, stretching from the Catskills to Birmingham, and those to the north and east reaching through the highlands of New England, the Gaspé Peninsula, and the three Canadian maritime provinces to the island of Newfoundland. Curiously, we face a reverse problem with regard to the plains—instead of ignoring physical and cultural similarities between the national segments of a sup-

ranational biophysical region, we may have overemphasized them.

To cite only one example of problems created by the boundary, the writer has been as guilty as any of the rather pedantic complaint about the use of *prairie* as a rubric for all three of the provinces of Canada's western interior. The problem has been widely discussed. To begin with, open grassland of any kind constitutes a distinctly minor part of the area of the three provinces as they have existed since 1905 and 1912. Morevoer, in that open grassland, true "tall grass" prairie—as defined by the grassland ecologists—is very limited in extent as compared with "mid," or "mixed," and "short" grass areas. The one stretch of the ecologists' prairie that is to be found in Canada's western interior lies entirely in Manitoba, south of the Assiniboine and between the Red River and the Manitoba escarpment, a small area of some 2,500 square miles, only a little larger indeed than Canada's tiny smallest province of Prince Edward Island. Nevertheless, since Professor Spry intends the title of her paper to comprehend all of the parklands and open grasslands of the three provinces, whatever the height of the grass, I would strongly defend her title. This is what most Canadians, even those who live far away, mean by "prairie" and it is in these areas that the vast preponderance of the people of Canada's western interior live. In that sense they *are* the "prairie provinces"; and although they contain a sizable chunk of the continental Great Plains region, and that chunk has much in common with one or another part of the American plains, there is much about the Canadian plains that is distinctive, as this "prairie" image suggests. The differences are in part natural (involving such things as meridional climate, vegetation, and soil-character gradients and glacial debris), in part a matter of cultural history (pre-European, fur trade, and settlement), and in part a matter of the two different sovereignties.

The final pair of models presents the contrast between an image of the plains as a relatively static entity over long periods and an image of a region in which biophysical and cultural systems are in more or less rapid processes of change. Of course it is possible that the plains did change more in the last three-quarters of the nineteenth century, both north and south of the 49th parallel, than they changed before or since, at least during the last ten thousand years. Indeed, it may be that those of us who like to think of historical geography in terms of "changing geographies" and "geographic change" occasionally may become victims of the implications of our own terminology. But the potentialities for change should always be considered. It is perhaps worth a warning that we should not assume that categories of models of image making contain only pairs, trios, or quartets. The writer remembers setting as an exercise for a class, many years ago, "The Great Plains As Seen by _____ ," and the blanks were filled in with as many groups as there were students in the class. We must have covered most of the ways of image making described above without mentioning either of the rubrics *model* or *perception*.

It may be useful to consider two examples of perception problems from the long cultural history of the region. Some twelve to fifteen thousand years ago, give or take a thousand years or two, or a little special pleading here and there, men first made their way across ice-free surfaces from the Yukon Valley and became the first humans to enter the plains region. Although Pleistocene geomorphologists and glaciologists are having some difficulty in providing us with either a more or less continuous tundra surface between the late Wisconsin cordilleran and continental ice sheets or a series of interaccessible ice-free mountain valleys, one or the other appears to be necessary to explain the spoor of *Homo sapiens* in the territory of the present United States. Eurasian Upper Paleolithic men, lately out of Siberia, would not and could not have crossed a thousand miles of sterile ice just to see if the tundra on the other side of the glacier was greener. Their food supply, on the hoof, had to have vegetation on which to graze or browse. And most of us are convinced that northern Pacific, Arctic, and northern Atlantic shorelines were similarly impassable and

their coastal waters impossible for people without boats.

A substantial variety of interpretations allows us great breadth of assumptions as to what the climate, flora, and fauna of the plains may have been like at that time between the Missouri Coteau and the Rockies in the present Dakotas-Montana area. If we postulate a tundra belt (as perhaps we must) it may have been narrow; between it and relatively open grassland somewhere farther south some woodland—perhaps a shrubby parkland of discontinuous clumps—may have intervened. Assuming that the first human invasion of the plains was by men of a culture with many centuries or millennia of adaptation to the hunting of large game, adapted, in turn, to the tundra, it is quite possible that the initial perception of all but the northernmost belt of ice-free land, close to the ice edge, was of an unfriendly, perhaps almost uninhabitable, area. We are constantly advised that Paleolithic man was anything but innovative and venturesome and that significant changes developed not through decades or centuries but through tens of millennia. But I think that it is also possible that the wealth of big game known to have populated the probably brushy and grassy expanses of the present central and southern plains made the territory almost immediately attractive. Elephant, bison, camel, horse, tapir, and sloth (the inventory is familiar enough) could be hunted in much the same way as the woolly mammoth and caribou. The kinds of food, clothing, and shelter provided would have been much the same. And the climate certainly would have been warmer. Although the analogy may not be particularly useful, people moving from the Canadian Great Plains to Victoria, San Francisco, San Diego, or Miami rarely are reported to suffer any acute discomfort from the milder January weather. My guess is that, by the speed of diffusion of the Paleo-Indian big-game hunters suggested by archeological finds to date, we may infer a perception of a substantially improved milieu which also gave the advantage of increased fertility rates and survival spans.

It has become a banality to say that the

Spanish perception of the plains resulting from the first European contact of the Coronado expedition was very negative because the object of the whole operation, to discover sources or artifacts of precious metals, was so completely unfulfilled. But this is only to place all the landscapes of the present United States in the same Spanish basket. Most of the experience of the contemporaneous De Sota expeditions was in quite different ecological circumstances, but they too reported a desert—so far as gold and silver were concerned. Had the Spanish sought a location for a North American *mesta* with as much determination as they devoted to the conquest of Mexico or Peru, the transhumant possibilities between the plains, the mountains, the intermontane parks, the breaks of the plains, and the Texas prairies surely might have attracted them. But despite the lack of treasure and despite their failure to attempt to exploit the grass resource, the Spaniards well may have had a long-term positive image of the plains. After all, they held the outpost on the Rio Grande and expanded later into California and Texas largely to preserve a buffer posture against English, French, and Russians. The emptiness of the plains improved their regional insulating properties, and no doubt the Spanish were pleased that the French and English images of the plains were primarily as areas to get through to furs or through which furs might be brought to them. As the Plains Indians became more formidable with the acquisition of horses, this again was only to the Spanish advantage, if it helped keep the English and French adventurers out of the region. These two examples, of course, indicate the danger of an essentially structuralist model of imagery which postulates that images must have been either quite positive or quite negative. I suppose that they usually ranged through a rather wide spectrum of attraction, indifference, and repulsion.

Despite the wealth of material in print about so many aspects of the Great Plains, it is clear that this volume is a pioneering venture in opening the discussion of the behavioral implications of the varied imagery of the plains and of the motley processes of image making that spawned them.

REFERENCE

Tuan, Yi-Fu.
1972. Structuralism, existentialism, and environmental perception. *Environment and Behavior* 4: 319–31.

PART 1
Exploratory Images of the Plains

Exploration and the Creation of Geographical Images of the Great Plains

Comments on the Role of Subjectivity

John L. Allen
University of Connecticut

Of all the processes that have been instrumental in shaping patterns of belief about the nature and content of the Great Plains from the time of the Spanish Entrada to the late nineteenth century, none have been quite as important as geographical exploration. Whether motivated by the desire to open up new territory for trade, exploitation, or settlement, impelled by scientific curiosity, or stimulated by the incentive of bridging the gap across an unknown territory to known regions that lay beyond (Wright 1961, p. xvii), explorers acquired and provided the bulk of the data from which images of the plains were created. A number of studies have discussed the nature of this data acquisition and transmission and the character of the resultant images (Allen 1971 and 1972; Bowden 1969 and 1971; Lawson 1972; Lewis 1965). But little has been done on the process of image formation itself as related to exploration. It is the purpose of this paper to suggest how such studies might be carried out by using a simple explanatory/descriptive model of that process by which exploratory data are translated into geographical images.

The central questions implied in any attempt to analyze the process of image formation from exploratory information revolve around the nature of the data and how they became a part of the geographical lore from which images are formed. It must be known, for example, whether the exploratory data is mostly empirical—that is, derived from actual field observations by explorers and capable of being evaluated in the light of what is presently accepted as geographic reality—or whether it is largely nonempirical—that is, not necessarily derived from direct observation by an explorer and not evaluated in terms of current reality but in terms of levels of accuracy and reliability as they are perceived by or acceptable to the explorer and his contemporaries (Allen 1972, p. 14). It must be further known to what extent subjective or imaginative elements are present in either the recording or the interpreting of exploratory data. Since virtually all geographical lore is some mixture of empirical and nonempirical data (Lowenthal 1961; Yi-Fu Tuan 1967) and since neither the recording nor the interpreting of that data can be fully objective (Wright 1947), it follows that the processes by which images are formed must be, at least partially, subjective.

Of all regions of the United States and Canada, the Great Plains seem to be the most appropriate laboratory for the investigation of this subjectivity in the creation of images from exploratory data. For plains exploration has traditionally been "programmed" by subjective influences, the plains themselves have been the most subjectively evaluated region, and the images of the plains, derived more from subjective interpretations of geographical lore than from rational analysis of empirical data, have been the most characterized by clashing and oversimplified themes.

THE PROCESS OF IMAGE FORMATION: A SYSTEMS MODEL

In trying to assess the role of subjectivity in the creation of images of the plains from exploratory data, it may be convenient to borrow some concepts and terminology from general systems theory and view image formation as a simple process-response system (Chorley and Kennedy 1971, pp. 126–59). The purpose in defining such a system is to identify the "relationships between a process and the forms resulting from it" (Chorley and Kennedy 1971, p. 9)—in this case, the process being that of image formation and the forms being the images themselves. As in the case of a physical process-response system, the system of image formation consists of four major components: an input, a regulator, a subsystem comprised of a simple morphological system with positive and negative looped feedbacks, and an output (fig. 1). The flow through the system is comprised of geographical information rather than the mass or energy flow characteristic of physical systems. The input component is made up of preexploratory information; the regulator is the exploratory process itself, along with the data it adds to the information flow; the morphological subsystem consists of a "grey box" of image formation; and the output is the image which has been created. The nature of the subjective influences in each of these components will be discussed separately.[1]

The Input: Geographical Information

As the primal source of energy which sets the system in motion, the input factor of geographical information is of critical importance for understanding the process of image formation, particularly if the content of information prior to an exploration can be evaluated in both the quantitative terms of the sheer amount of data and the qualitative terms of the relative proportions of empirical and nonempirical data. In some cases, the nature of the ultimate output of the system (the resultant images) may be conditioned more by the quan-

---

1. It ought to be noted, however, that a view of one part of the system by itself is inconsistent with the concept of the system—in which it is impossible to think of one component without automatically thinking of all the others. I separate the components here simply for the purposes of explanation.

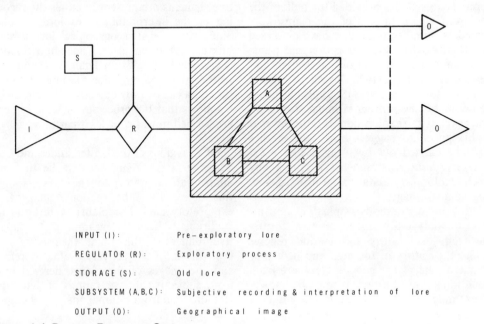

INPUT (I):	Pre-exploratory lore
REGULATOR (R):	Exploratory process
STORAGE (S):	Old lore
SUBSYSTEM (A,B,C):	Subjective recording & interpretation of lore
OUTPUT (O):	Geographical image

Figure 1 A Process-Response System

tity or quality of the lore in the input than by any other factors within the system. Thus, even though the regulatory functions of the exploratory process may be quite objective and "scientific" and the operations of the subsystem of image formation remarkably free from the subjective influences of greed, ambition, desire, etc., the consequent images may be crammed with subjectivity. This seems to be particularly true when the input factor is dominated by myths or legends which have persisted over a long period of time. A good case in point is the immediate process of image formation among the sixteenth-century Spanish in North America following the initial exploration by Coronado into the plains.

By the end of the first four decades of the sixteenth century, the lands of Terra Florida lying north of the Gulf of Mexico and including much of the Great Plains region were, for the Spanish, an empirical unknown. But the geographical imagination needs neither experience nor empirical data to create information, and as a result of the infusion of the mythical element of the Seven Cities from Iberian folklore, rumors of interior provinces of great wealth from gullible travelers such as Cabeza da Vaca, and conjectural half-truths from self-serving priests like Fray Marcos de Niza, a body of geographical lore, almost totally nonempirical in content, was developed (DeVoto 1952, pp. 11–46). At the core of this information, shining forth with remarkable clarity, was the myth of Cibola, a vast interior region of wealth and beauty granted to Francisco de Coronado to "explore and conquer" (Hammond and Rey 1940, pp. 83–86).

In the years 1540–41, Coronado and his army of conquest explored north and east from New Spain as far as central Kansas chasing the mirage of Cibola which, during the journey, was transformed into the myth of Quivira. Coronado did not find the golden lands but he did add significantly to the store of empirical data on the Great Plains. Few expeditions in North American exploratory history were better led and few explorers maintained such a "critical intelligence supported by exact knowledge" (DeVoto 1952, p. 46), even while leading an expedition based on a mirage. Coronado and his chroniclers reported what they saw with surprising clear-

ness, and although those who read his accounts were men of their time and could not, therefore, escape certain distortions, the interpretations of Coronado's data were remarkably objective.

In spite of these facts, however, Spanish images of the plains for years after Coronado were still flavored more with the mythical element of the Seven Cities than they were with the sound, empirical data on the resources, population, and potential of the plains with which he had returned (Clissold 1961). In the informational input, the nonempirical data was weighted more heavily than the empirical, and where few Spanish minds retained the words of Pedro de Castenada, Coronado's chronicler, that the expedition had found "a good land to settle in," many remembered his brief comment about "that better land we did not see" (Hammond and Rey 1940, p. 194). The Seven Cities did not disappear from the Spanish images but only shifted location; other Spanish sought them (or desired to) after Coronado and it was not until the end of the sixteenth century and Juan de Onate's colonization of New Mexico that they faded from their once dominant position.

The Regulator: Exploratory Process

Just as the regulator in the physical process-response system operates either to divert a part of the energy flow into storage or to create a "throughput" of energy into the morphological subsystem, so does the regulator (exploratory process) in the image-formation system function as a "valve." Some preexploratory data may be diverted by this valve into storage, where it either remains indefinitely or is used in some later process of image formation. Other preexploratory information, along with the increments added by the exploratory process itself,[2] may be channeled into the "grey box" of image formation. In those cases where no new significant information has been added

2. In a physical system, an addition of mass or energy would require an additional input factor. Rather than keeping the analogy "pure," I have omitted this additional factor and simply viewed an increase in the flow as being inherent in the regulator.

by exploration, the normal flow is most likely into storage or, diverted around the subsystem of new image formation, directly into an output. If, on the other hand, the exploratory process contributes significantly to the quantity of information, then the throughput type of flow will prevail. It should be clear that by controlling the information flow, the exploratory process becomes a major determinant of the functioning of the entire system.

John K. Wright (1961, p. xvii) has suggested that exploratory processes can be broken down into two basic categories, both of which are quite applicable to the exploration of the Great Plains. The first type is that of discovery —"the urge to open up the unknown for exploitation or trade, conquest or settlement, or for the satisfaction of curiosity, idle or scientific"—and is typical of much of plains exploration, for example, the expedition of the Mallet brothers along the lower Platte, the ventures of the French fur traders up the Missouri, the explorations of Zebulon Pike across the southern plains, Stephen Long through the central plains, John Fremont to the upper Platte in 1842, and the "great reconnaissance" of the Corps of Topographical Engineers in the 1850s. Scarcely less important is Wright's second category of "gap-bridging"—"the urge to establish contacts *across* the unknown, friendly or hostile, with other centers of civilization or wealth or power that lie beyond." Representative of this genre are the explorations of Lewis and Clark in search of an all-water passage across the continent, of the Astorians in their quest for a path to the gateway of the Columbia, and of the railroad surveyors in their reconnaissance of prospective routes for transcontinental railway routes to the Pacific.

In each of these cases, the motive for exploration (often derived subjectively) programmed the nature of the exploratory process, which in turn regulated the quantity and quality of the throughput of both preexploratory data and the incremental geographical lore. Thus the exploratory operations of Louisiana fur traders such as Jacques d'Eglise, Jean Truteau, and Antoine Tabeau, concerned primarily with the navigability of plains rivers as they provided access to the fur-rich regions of the interior, allowed a throughput of data dominated by preexploratory information on river navigability. Even the new lore contributed by their explorations was more heavily imbued with commentary on navigational hazards and impediments than with other geographical references to the plains. Consequently, the flow of information from the early Saint Louis fur trade created images in the late eighteenth century in which such features as the climate, soils, and topography of the region were much less important than they might otherwise have been (Nasatir, 1952).

In a similar vein, the gap-bridging exploration of Lewis and Clark, motivated by the twin desiderata of the water passage to the Pacific and the confirmation of the Jeffersonian ideal of the garden of the interior, did little to divert the positive preexploratory data on the Passage and the Garden. Moreover, even though Lewis and Clark added data on the plains which, in qualitative and quantitative terms, went far beyond that contributed by earlier explorers, the regulatory functioning of their exploration accentuated those aspects of the data that supported the images of Passage and Garden. As a result, many American images of the plains after Lewis and Clark were, for a time at least, quite similar to what they had been before.

Conversely, the "massive scientific inventory . . . of the Great Western Reconnaissance" (Goetzmann 1966, p. 302) of the 1850s, motivated by the need for a total geographic inventory of the plains that would be of use to westward-bound Americans, dammed up the flow of much inaccurate preexploratory data through the system while adding, in an almost Humboldtean fashion, quite reliable information on virtually the total physical environment of the region. And while the reconnaissance did little to resolve the fundamental ambiguity of the conflict between the simplistic Garden and Desert images, views of the plains after the 1850s were never the same as they had been before the process of scientific exploration had performed its vital regulatory function in the informational flow.

The Morphological Subsystem: Image Formation

Although each of the above components of the system is important for the process of image formation, neither is of as great a consequence as the morphological subsystem within which the throughput of information is converted into the output of an image. Such subsystems are normally explained in terms of both the morphological variables which comprise their structure and the interrelationships between those variables. For purposes of simplicity, however, the morphological subsystem here may be viewed as a "grey box" in which each of the sets of important variables is examined while the nature of the connections between those sets (the positive and negative feedback loops) which control the internal operations of the subsystem is ignored (Chorley and Kennedy 1971, p. 7). As a further simplification, only the three sets of variables which seem to be the most critical for the role of subjectivity in image formation will be considered—even though a detailed exposition of the subsystem would normally include an almost infinite number of variables, given the tremendous complexity of the image-formation process.

The first set of variables in the subsystem relates to the subjective recording of exploratory data or writing exploratory accounts. It may be most clearly seen in those instances where established theories or concepts so dominate an explorer's approach to his field observation that what he actually sees and what he thinks he sees are considerably different things. Meriwether Lewis, for example, adhered to the Jeffersonian version of the Louisiana chroniclers' Garden concept of the interior and subsequently described the portion of the plains drained by the Missouri as "one of the fairest portions of the globe . . . fertile, well-watered, and intersected by such a number of navigable streams" (Jackson 1962, p. 223). But Henry Marie Brackenridge, observing the same territory less than half a decade later, noted that it was characterized by "extensive tracts of moving sands similar to those of the African deserts" (Brackenridge 1814, p.

29). "The country can scarcely be said to admit of settlements," he added, and it is clear that Brackenridge, although admittedly having had access to the same preexploratory information as Lewis (Brackenridge 1814, p. 5), was not as heavily influenced by the Jeffersonian concept of the Garden. On the other hand, his traveling companion John Bradbury (an English botanist and, interestingly, an acquaintance and correspondent of Jefferson's), viewing the same region during the same season and at the same time, disagreed with Brackenridge's assessment: "In process of time, it will not only be peopled and cultivated, but . . . will be one of the most beautiful countries in the world" (Bradbury 1819, p. 267). To what extent can these contradictory reports be attributed to variations in the observers' acceptance of the preexploratory lore, concepts, and theories available to them?

Distortions in the recording of exploratory data may also occur as a result of an explorer's teleological leanings, his desire for personal gain, his devotion to national achievement and ambition, or some combination thereof. In a recent study, Merlin Lawson (1972) has pointed out the relationship between such factors and the final reporting procedures for Zebulon Pike's 1806–1807 exploration of the Arkansas basin. On the eve of Pike's expedition, he apparently possessed an optimistic point of view about the potential of the southwestern portions of Louisiana Territory. This optimism did not disappear during Pike's field experience, for in his daily journals he consistently referred to the plains as "prairie"—a term which he equated with the English "natural meadow" (Jackson 1965, p. 223)—and, in fact, only used the term "desert" once in his field journals to describe a small area in the vicinity of the Great Bend of the Arkansas (Lawson 1972, p. 61). Four years later, however, in the published version of his journals, Pike included the following familiar passage often cited by those who see in Pike's account the seed of the Desert myth (Alford 1969): "These vast plains of the western hemisphere, may become in time equally celebrated as the sandy deserts of Africa; for I saw in my route, in various places, tracts of many leagues, where the wind had thrown up the sand, in all the fanciful forms of the ocean's rolling wave, and on which not a speck of vegetable matter existed" (Pike, in Jackson 1966, p. 27).

Lawson has concluded that the inclusion of this passage, so disjunctive in terms of Pike's preexploratory image and apparent field experience, might be most logically explained by examining Pike's possible connection with the Wilkinson-Burr scheme to separate the southwestern portion of Louisiana Territory from the United States. Perhaps as a wish to dissociate himself entirely from Wilkinson (whose enthusiastic views on southwestern Louisiana had formed a major motivating factor in Pike's exploration), Pike reversed his field, toned down his initial favorable impressions of the region, and publicly summarized his opinion of the plains in language acceptable to Jeffersonian Republicans: "Our citizens being so prone to rambling and extending themselves, on the frontiers, will, through necessity, be constrained to limit their extent on the west, to the borders of the Missouri and Mississippi" (Pike, in Jackson 1966, p. 28).[3] In its final form, designed for public consumption, the report of Pike's exploration contained a classic example of the subjective influence of political and personal considerations.

Although the subjective recording of exploratory data is certainly a key factor in determining the nature of resultant images, it is probably less important than the subjective interpretation of exploratory data. Thus, the second major set of variables in the morphological subsystem includes those subjective elements which affect the interpretation of exploratory accounts and data by the various constituencies within the society to whom

the accounts become available. Like explorers themselves, members of a society who interpret exploratory data may have theoretical or abstract concepts that are too strong to be eradicated by accounts which contradict those concepts or may consciously or unconsciously distort data because of personal or national goals. This is particularly true when the character of plains images in the nineteenth century is considered, given the century-long, emotionally charged debates over the economic potential of the region, often generated by those who used exploratory data to support old theories (or myths) or to further self-serving personal or national interests.

Thomas Hart Benton, for example, envisaging himself as the major prophet of expansionism and proponent of the Passage to India, went directly against the bulk of the exploratory data from which his knowledge of the plains was derived to proclaim that the plains rivers—shallow, sluggish, and unnavigable in most of the exploratory literature—were potentially great avenues of commerce: "what the Euphrates, the Oxus, the Phasis, and the Cyrus were to the ancient Romans, lines of communication with eastern Asia, and channels for that rich commerce which, for forty centuries, has created so much wealth and power wherever it has flowed" (Benton, in Smith 1950, p. 27). Similarly, William Gilpin, heir to Benton's geopolitics (Lewis 1966), used physiographic data from exploratory records to develop his "isothermal zodiac"—a regionally chauvinistic theory designed to prove that the star of the West would rise in ascendancy over the star of the East and that the organic whole of the western interior would give birth to the "permanent mistress of the world" (Smith 1950, p. 43).

Perhaps one of the most illustrative examples of subjective interpretations of exploration's records, however, occurred later in the nineteenth century in the form of a bitter controversy between Desert and Garden advocates over the agricultural potential and value of the portion of the plains traversed by the route of the Northern Pacific Railroad west of the Missouri. In 1874, a sour and embittered U.S. Army officer, Brevet Major General Wil-

---

3. It may seem inconsistent, in view of the agrarian tradition of Jeffersonian Republicanism and the Jeffersonian concept of the West as Garden, to say that this statement was acceptable to Jeffersonians. However, Pike's statement echoed one made by Jefferson himself about preserving Louisiana. Garden though it was, Jefferson preferred to have it unoccupied until the lands east of the Mississippi were filled with the independent farmers he believed to be the backbone of the republican system of government.

liam B. Hazen (then commander of Fort Buford in Dakota Territory), wrote a letter to the *New York Tribune* entitled "The Northern Pacific Railroad Country" in which the claim was put forth that the Great Plains region was almost totally useless (Stewart 1968). "This country will not produce the fruits and cereals of the East," wrote Hazen, "for want of moisture, and can in no way be artificially irrigated, and will not, in our day and generation, sell for one penny an acre, except through fraud or ignorance" (Hazen, in Stewart 1968, p. 40). As basis for this contention, Hazen cited the exploratory accounts of men like John Frémont, Isaac Stevens, and Ferdinand V. Hayden—all of whom had been relatively optimistic in their estimations of the economic potential of the Plains. The reasons for Hazen's extraction of a few unfavorable remarks from reports that were generally enthusiastic are uncertain. Possibly they stemmed from a desire to protect investors or settlers against unwise investments; more probably, however, they emerged out of the dissatisfaction and frustration of an ambitious officer stuck with a frontier post, anger at the Northern Pacific Railroad over a fancied personal slight, and a wish "to bring his name before the American public" (Stewart 1968, p. 252).

Whatever his reasons for writing the letter, Hazen's statements stirred up a hornet's nest of reaction, both favorable and unfavorable, to his conclusions. The reaction to Hazen's letter was also based largely on data derived from exploration, particularly the reports of the Pacific Railroad surveys, and was every bit as subjective as the work that had stimulated the controversy (Dillon 1967). Supporters of Hazen called the plains "A Dead Sea transfixed in solution by a fiery sun, and baked into sterility!" (Bickham 1879, p. 41), while detractors like General George Armstrong Custer, backed by evidence from "scientific" explorers such as Hayden, claimed that the northern plains were fit for nearly every conceivable type of agricultural pursuit (Stewart 1968, pp. 78–113). As settlers moved into the northern plains and were, by and large, successful, the controversy died down (Kollmorgen 1969). Before it expired, however, it had provided a

near-perfect example of both the essential ambiguity of American images of the plains and of the subjectivity in interpreting exploratory data as well.

Even though strong preexploratory theories and concepts may be absent and desires for personal and/or national gains may be submerged, there is a third type of subjectivity which will continue to influence image formation. This final set of variables in the morphological subsystem is much harder to isolate than the sets of variables relating to recording or interpretation of exploratory data. It consists of levels of subjectivity, as yet poorly understood, that are inherent in virtually all phases of data acquisition, transmission, and translation—irrespective of the presence or absence of other subjective elements. Typical of this third set of variables are such things as the difficulties involved in adjusting the scale of a region explored with the scale of preexploratory images of the area or the problems encountered in translating the horizontal perspectives of field observations into the vertical perspectives of maps or mental pictures of the area. In many cases, this final type of subjectivity takes the form of "expanding the known to fill the unknown," that is, using either empirical or nonempirical data to fill in those blank spaces which are intolerable to the geographical imagination (Allen 1972).

Could any explorer like John Frémont, crossing the plains along single traverse lines that were narrow indeed when compared to the scope of the region itself, report with any hope of complete objectivity on anything but the thin strips of territory he had actually seen? Could any American of the last half of the 1840s, regardless of his awareness or experience or prejudices, have viewed the charts showing Frémont's tracks across the plains without consciously or unconsciously filling the white spaces between the traverse lines with features derived subjectively? Can anyone at all—even today's trained geographer or historian—read the accounts of Frémont's travels without shaping from the data in those accounts sets of images which may not be fully consistent with reality, either as it was understood in Frémont's time or as it is understood today? It is doubtful whether any but negative responses can be made to these questions. It is just as questionable whether the consequences (images) of any exploration of the plains can be fully and properly assessed without reference to subjectivity, that capacity of the human mind which, in Milton's words, "misjoyning shapes, Wilde work produces oft."

The Output: Images of the Plains

It is beyond the scope of this paper to comment at length on the nature of images of the plains. It may be sufficient to say that the output from the process-response system of image formation, because of the subjectivity within the system, can never be anything but subjective itself. Going slightly farther, it might be said that the nature of the subjectivity in the images might best be measured by analyzing in detail the processes by which they have been shaped. Some studies have suggested, for example, that "elite" and "folk" images of the plains in the nineteenth century were considerably different from one another (Bowden 1969). Such differences indicate that the systems of image formation were dissimilar, for as in any process-response system, variations in input, regulator, and morphological subsystems will create variations in the output.

In our examination of images of the plains, should we not focus on these variations first and on the process through which they operate rather than beginning with the resultant images? Should we not concentrate on the subjective influences within the system of image formation of those clashing and oversimplified themes which have conditioned the recording and interpretation of exploratory data? The themes are many:

localism vs. nationalism or, as the case may be, internationalism; practicality vs. theory; science vs. common sense; private interests vs. broad public policy; settlers vs. soldiers; and soldiers in turn vs. politicians; white men vs. Indians; East vs. West; and in the broadest sense a clash of contrasting images of the West vastly oversimplified—the

Garden (meaning a belief in the economic potential of the West) and the Desert (meaning the belief that the West was a land of scarcity that would take centuries to develop). [Goetzmann 1966, p. 305]

Each of the themes helped to "program" the consequences of exploration for the creation of geographical images. We can comprehend neither those consequences nor the images themselves without a prior understanding of the subjective influence of the themes in the system of image formation.

REFERENCES CITED

Alford, T. L.
    1969.   The West as a desert in American thought prior to Long's 1819–1820 expedition. *Journal of the West* 8:515–25.
Allen, John L.
    1971.   Geographical knowledge and American images of the Louisiana Territory. *Western Historical Quarterly* 2:151–70.
    1972.   An analysis of the exploratory process: The Lewis and Clark Expedition of 1804–1806. *Geographical Review* 62:13–39.
Bickham, William D.
    1879.   *From Ohio to the Rocky Mountains.* Dayton: Journal Book & Job Printing House.
Bowden, Martyn J.
    1969.   The perception of the western interior of the United States, 1800–1870: A problem in historical geosophy. *Proceedings of the Association of American Geographers* 1:16–21.
    1971.   The Great American Desert and the American frontier, 1800–1882: Popular images of the plains. In *Anonymous Americans: Explorations in nineteenth century social history,* ed. K. Haraven, pp. 48–79. Englewood Cliffs, N.J.: Prentice-Hall.
Brackenridge, Henry M.
    1814.   *Views of Louisiana.* 1962. Chicago: Quadrangle Books, Inc. Bradbury, John.
    1819.   *Travels in the interior of America.* 1904. Cleveland: Arthur H. Clark Co.
Chorley, Richard J., and Kennedy, Barbara.
    1971.   *Physical geography: A systems approach.* London: Prentice-Hall.
Clissold, Stephen.
    1961.   *The Seven Cities of Cibola.* New York: C. N. Potter, Inc.

DeVoto, Bernard.
1952. *Course of empire.* Boston: Houghton-Mifflin Co.

Dillon, Richard H.
1967. Stephen Long's Great American Desert. *Proceedings of the American Philosophical Society* 111:93–108.

Goetzmann, William H.
1966. *Exploration and empire.* New York: Alfred A. Knopf.

Hammond, George P. and Rey, Agapito.
1940. *Narratives of the Coronado expedition, 1540–42.* Albuquerque: University of New Mexico Press.

Jackson, Donald.
1962. *Letters of the Lewis and Clark Expedition.* Urbana: University of Illinois Press.
1965. *Journals of Zebulon Montgomery Pike.* Vol. 1. Norman: University of Oklahoma Press.
1966. *Journals of Zebulon Montgomery Pike.* Vol. 2. Norman: University of Oklahoma Press.

Kollmorgen, Walter M.
1969. The woodsman's assaults on the domain of the cattleman. *Annals of the Association of American Geographers* 59:215–39.

Lawson, Merlin P.
1972. A behavioristic interpretation of Pike's geographical knowledge of the interior of Louisiana. *Great Plains–Rocky Mountain Geographical Journal* 1:58–64.

Lewis, G. Malcolm.
1965. Three centuries of desert concepts in the cis–Rocky Mountain West. *Journal of the West* 4:457–68.
1966. William Gilpin and the concept of the Great Plains region. *Annals of the Association of American Geographers* 56:33–51.

Lowenthal, David.
1961. Geography, experience, and imagination: Towards a geographical epistemology. *Annals of the Association of American Geographers* 51:241–60.

Nasatir, Abraham P.
1952. *Before Lewis and Clark.* St. Louis: St. Louis Historical Documents Foundation.

Smith, Henry Nash.
1950. *Virgin land: The American West as symbol and myth.* New York: Vintage Books.

Stewart, Edgar I.
1968. *Penny-an-acre empire in the West.* Norman: University of Oklahoma Press.

Tuan, Yi-Fu.
1967. Attitudes toward environment: Themes and approaches. In *Environmental Perception and Behavior,* ed. David Lowenthal, pp. 4–17. Chicago: University of Chicago Department of Geography Research Papers.

Wright, John Kirtland.
1947. Terrae incognitae: The place of the imagination in geography. *Annals of the Association of American Geographers* 37:1–15.
1961. Introduction to the Torchbook Edition of *A history of exploration,* by Sir Percy Sykes. New York: Harper Torchbooks.

Some Early Euro-American Percepts of the Great Plains and Their Influence on Anthropological Thinking

Waldo R. Wedel
Smithsonian Institution

Depending largely on the particular viewpoint of the observer, the Great Plains area has been defined in many ways. As an ethnographic culture area, it was long ago delineated by Wissler (1914, p. 466 and pl. 33) as extending from the mouth of the Missouri River westward beyond Great Salt Lake, south to the Rio Grande, and north beyond the Saskatchewan River. Archeologically, in what was probably the first published application of Mason's (1896) culture-area concept to the study of American antiquities, Holmes (1914, p. 430 and pl. 32) combined the Great Plains with the northern Rocky Mountains, eliminated the Missouri River trench in Nebraska and the Dakotas, and added a corridor running west to the California border. In his initial presentation of the culture-area concept Mason stated that the "plains of the Great West have constituted a definite culture area characterized, among other things, by . . . a piedmont sloping down to the immense prairies of the Missouri, the Platte, and the Arkansas; temperate climate," If the upper Saskatchewan is added to Mason's list of streams, this is an acceptable delineation—that is to say, it roughly fits the anthropogeographic biases that I have developed from more than four decades of archeological research including studies of the short-grass plains or steppe of the west and the adjoining tall-grass prairie on the east.

The southern sections of the plains area came under Spanish scrutiny in the mid–sixteenth century, and by the early eighteenth century there were Spanish names for streams and other geographic features as far north as the Platte (Thomas 1935). French traders from Canada were active in the eastern sectors in the seventeenth century and on into the eighteenth. Anglo-American interest began toward the end of the eighteenth century, increasing sharply during the nineteenth century and thereafter. Of primary interest here are the early Spanish impressions of the plains, the contrasting percepts developed by the Anglo-Americans, and the manner in which the latter particularly affected anthropological thought regarding the length and nature of the aboriginal human occupancy of the plains.

For Euro-Americans, first-hand knowledge concerning the Great Plains began with the Coronado expedition to Quivira in 1540–41. Coronado himself seems to have been impressed with what he saw, notably with the extent of the plains—"so vast that in my travels I did not reach their end, although I marched over them for more than 300 leagues." He also remarked the great abundance of the wild cattle, that is, the bison: "It would be impossible to estimate their numbers for in traveling over the plains, there was not a single day, until my return, that I lost sight of them" (Hammond and Rey 1940, p. 186 ff.). On the Llano Estacado, he commented further on "plains as bare of landmarks as if we were surrounded by the sea. Here the guides lost their bearings because there is nowhere a stone, hill, tree, bush, or anything of the sort;" but there were "many excellent pastures with fine grass." On the debit side, Coronado noted that he "suffered greatly from lack of water on finding myself in those endless plains. Many times I drank some which was so bad that it tasted more like slime than water." Beyond these "barren lands," when he finally reached Quivira around the great bend of the Arkansas and eastward, he noted that the "soil itself is the most suitable that has been found for growing all the products of Spain, for, besides being rich and black, it is well watered by arroyos, springs, and rivers. I found plums like those of Spain, nuts, fine sweet grapes, and mulberries."

As to the human occupants of the plains, the Spanish were disappointed and disillusioned with their relative poverty and lack of material wealth. Because the accounts are based largely on eyewitness observations and concern people and lands utterly unaffected by prior white contact, they are of prime interest, nevertheless. In the buffalo plains, people called Querechos roamed after the bison, "go[ing] about like nomads with their tents and with packs of dogs harnessed with little pads, pack-saddles, and girths . . . hunting and dressing skins to take to the pueblos to sell in the winter, since they go to spend the winter there . . . some to the pueblos of Pecos, others to Quivira. . . . They are very skillful in the use of signs. They dry their meat in the sun."

Sixty years after Coronado, in June, 1601, another major Spanish expedition led by Don Juan de Oñate, governor of New Mexico, made the long trek to Quivira, probably on the Arkansas River downstream from the locality reached by Coronado. Approaching the buffalo plains via the Canadian River, Oñate (Hammond and Rey 1953, p. 748 ff.) spoke of the "very extensive and delightful plains" to which they had come; "wherever we went the land looked better," he said; and it "was also rich in fruits, particularly of infinite varieties of plums," growing on small trees with "the fruit more numerous than the leaves. . . . Hardly a day passed that we failed to find

groves of them, or grapevines, which, even when found in remote places, produced sweet and tasty grapes." The herds of bison were still a source of wonder, because "we found so many of them that it will be difficult for anyone who has not seen them to believe it, for, according to the guess of everyone in the army, wherever we went we saw as many cattle every day as one finds on the largest cattle ranches in New Spain. They were so tame that unless chased or frightened they stood still and did not run away." These lands were also "inhabited by people of the Apache nation, who are the masters of the plains. They have no permanent settlement or homes, but follow the cattle as they roam about."

By the first quarter of the eighteenth century, some notable changes had taken place. Now the Spanish were dealing in part with semisedentary Indians who were attempting maize-growing in the western plains. These were the Cuartelejo and other Apache tribes or bands, who had come under increasing pressure from the Comanches and Utes out of the Colorado Rockies. In 1706, on his way from Santa Fe to El Cuartelejo in eastern Colorado, Ulibarri reported (Thomas 1935, p. 64) cornplanting Apaches on the Purgatoire. At El Cuartelejo, in eastern Colorado or western Kansas (Thomas 1935, pp. 68, 264; Wedel 1959, p. 467; Bowman 1969), Ulibarri observed (Thomas 1935, p. 72) "the great fertility of the land and its good climate, for at the end of July they had gathered crops of Indian corn, watermelons, pumpkins, and kidney beans. It was believed that crops of wheat /in case sowed/ would be ready before the day of San Juan. So that because of the fertility of the land, the docility of the people, and the abundance of herds of buffalo, and other game, the propagation of our holy Catholic faith could be advanced very much."

By 1715, however, the Spanish in Santa Fe expressed concern about surface water deficiencies and the difficulties in following a planned course of march without guides and in the absence of landmarks on the plains. By 1720, when the establishing of a presidio at El Cuartelejo was being considered, Captain Naranjo, who had been there, argued (ibid., p.

157) that "the vicinity of El Cuartelejo is not appropriate nor has it the conveniences which are necessary to establish either a presidio or a settlement. ... These accommodations are only seasonal because there is little water and no wood so that after harvesting their crops, the Indians leave the spot."

At El Cuartelejo, the Cuartelejo Apache settlements alluded to were clearly scattered on small stream valleys in what is today the High Plains region. Suitable valleys, with restricted but arable bottomlands, perennial springs and seeps, and other natural attractions for people content with an austere subsistence economy are scattered throughout the High Plains of western Kansas, eastern Colorado, and beyond to the north and south. It seems clear that the High Plains were being utilized by the early historic Plains Apache groups for seasonal residence; that their activities included limited food-producing as well as food-collecting, and in some cases practising irrigation learned from the Pueblos; and that this utilization can be documented by Spanish eyewitness records.

In the vanguard of American exploration of the western plains was New Jersey-born Lt. Zebulon M. Pike. In 1810, he wrote feelingly in an oft-quoted statement on the future prospects for the western plains and prairies: "Numerous have been the hypotheses formed by various naturalists, to account for the vast tract of untimbered country which lies between the waters of the Missouri, Mississippi, and the western Ocean, from the mouth of the latter river to the 48° north latitude. ... here a barren soil, parched and dried up for eight months in the year, presents neither moisture nor nutrition sufficient to nourish the timber. These vast plains of the western hemisphere, may become in time equally celebrated as the sandy deserts of Africa."

In his disdain for the western prairies and plains, Pike was reflecting a point of view that was to dominate the easterner's thinking about the grasslands for many years to come. In the report on his 1819–20 expedition to the Rocky Mountains (James 1823), Major Stephen H. Long echoed Pike's sentiments and provided cartographic support for the desert thesis by labeling the region east of the Rockies, south of the Platte, north of Red River, and west of the great bend of the Arkansas—roughly beyond the 99th or 100th meridian—the Great American Desert. On that 1823 map, immediately south of the 40th parallel in present eastern Colorado and northwestern Kansas, is a revealing legend: "The Great Desert is frequented by roving bands of Indians who have no fixed place of residence but roam from place to place in quest of game." Here there is no hint of the maize-growing Apaches who had seasonally resided in select localities in the High Plains in the early eighteenth century, according to the Spanish.

Army officers on western assignments were not alone in these adverse judgments concerning the plains. In 1856, Secretary Joseph Henry of the Smithsonian Institution wrote (Henry 1858) that "the whole space to the west, between the 98th meridian and the Rocky Mountains, denominated the Great American Plains, is a barren waste, over which the eye may roam to the extent of the visible horizon with scarcely an object to break the monotony. ... the entire region west of the 98th degree of west longitude, is a country of comparatively little value to the agriculturist."

Omitting numerous other evaluations (e.g., Fitzpatrick 1847, p. 238 and 1853, p. 365; Emory 1857, p. 47; Hind 1860), we can accept the position reached by Lewis (1965, p. 9) to the effect that after the 1850s, "the term 'Great Plains' was to be associated with several regional concepts but the area to which it referred was never again to be thought of as a vast, useless, and unbroken desert."

Excepting, we may suggest, by the anthropologists. Writing in eastern Kansas Territory in 1859, Lewis Henry Morgan (White 1959, pp. 41–42) noted that "before the discovery of the country by Columbus, and before the Indian was possessed of any domestic animal, the prairie must have been an intolerable country to him. ... The prairie is not congenial to the Indian, and is only made tolerable to him by the possession of the horse and the rifle."

Two years later, on the Red River of the North, he wrote (ibid., pp. 118–119), "From the Rio Grande to the Mississippi it is on the whole a poor country for the Indian without the horse. . . . East of the great range of the Rocky Mountains from Mexico to Peace River, we have the prairie in the interior of the continent, a country incapable of occupation to any considerable extent without the horse."

And finally, at Saint Joseph on the Lower Missouri in 1862 (ibid., p. 141), Morgan commented, "There is some game besides the buffalo almost all the way across the prairie, but without the horse, it would be extremely difficult for an Indian band to migrate across it."

Morgan's pronouncements of 1859–62 placed an early stamp of anthropological approval on the old notion, not even yet wholly dispelled, that the western plains were unfit for human use except as a region to be crossed as quickly as possible. Although Morgan's comments were not published until much later, the view they reflected became so firmly embedded in anthropological thinking that until perhaps four decades ago, the existence of prehistoric Indian remains left by maize-growing, pottery-making semisedentary peoples in the plains one to two hundred miles and more west of the Missouri River was doubted by many professionals. In 1914, for example, after a reconnaissance among the pithouse ruins and mounds along the Missouri between Omaha and Leavenworth, and after considering Gilder's Nebraska "loess man," Fowke (1922, p. 160) concluded that "any estimate of age must be only a guess at the best, but it is a safe guess that no earthwork, mound, lodge site, or human bone along this part of the Missouri River has been here as long as ten centuries."

A few years previously, Wissler (1908, p. 201) had postulated a "prehistoric uninhabited region in the western part of the Missouri-Saskatchewan area" but at the same time noted the inadequacies of the archeological record; and he later (Wissler 1914, p. 485) pointed out the cultural-historical significance in Coronado's reports of the dog-nomads. Fourteen years after Wissler, Kroeber (1928, pp. 394–5; 1939, pp. 76, 78; 1948, p. 823) observed that the "largely negative results of archeology indicate the Plains as only sparsely

or intermittently inhabited for a long time. The population was probably in the main a Woodland one along the eastern margin." He went on to suggest that "the Plains traits that have historic depth . . . seem Woodland, and date from the time when such Plains culture as there was constituted a margin at the fringe of a natural area."

Kroeber, I think, misjudged the true significance of the "largely negative results of archeology," but he correctly inferred the nature of some of the older occupations as since partially revealed by archeology. As to the origins of Plains culture, to the extent that it included primary reliance on the bison for subsistence, high development of skin-working, portable conical skin dwellings, dog traction, sign language, etc., it cannot be accurately assessed as of eastern Woodland origin; and, as Lowie (1955) has cogently argued, the Plains culture was something more than "only a fading-out fringe of the Eastern culture (Kroeber 1948, p. 823)." The ethnohistoric record and archeology both suggest that Caldwell's (1962, p. 292) allusion to "an impoverished bison-hunting economy" in Coronado's time, and Service's (1963, p. 114) characterization of the Plains hunters as "merely marginal nomads, . . . ekeing out a precarious and poverty-stricken existence" are both ineptly phrased value-judgments. I suggest that *austere,* meaning severely simple and unadorned, is preferable to "impoverished," with its connotation of a depleted or weakened lifeway.

Our sampling of contemporary opinions above, admittedly incomplete, nevertheless illustrates the point this paper is making. The early Spanish accounts succinctly record the changing lifeways of Plains Indians who, first as dog-using, herd-following, bison hunters—or dog-nomads (Gunnerson 1956)—and later as seasonal maize-growers and big-game hunters, were able to utilize appropriate portions of the short-grass country—but not necessarily on a year-around basis any more than did the historic horse Indians (Wedel 1963 and references), who, like the bison herds, sought the shelter and comparative security of timbered stream valleys and mountain districts in winter and in droughty seasons.

By the time the Americans arrived, two centuries and more later, the seasonally occupied Indian communities in the High Plains of eastern Colorado and western Kansas, where they had been visited by Ulibarri, Valverde, and others, had been given up, and only the mounted buffalo hunters and war-bonneted raiders of history and romance occupied the region. Whether this abandonment reflected growing pressures from the Comanches on the west, the adversities of a capricious climate and deteriorating environment, or a combination of these and other factors is not yet clear. It was only natural, I suppose, that the Americans, already repelled by the dry and treeless appearance of the land, and imbued with the easterner's notions that agriculture was feasible only on ground which had been cleared of forest, should conclude that the western plains were of no possible use for agricultural man, particularly if they traveled through the region at times other than during its vernal exuberance.

The region disparaged by Pike, Morgan, Henry, and others in the nineteenth century, whether they set its eastern edge at the Mississippi-Missouri or the 98th meridian or some other arbitrary line, included extensive tracts where a subsistence economy based in part on maize-growing was entirely feasible, even if a commercial economy was not. So it was that when systematic archeology on a sustained basis began in the trans-Missouri area in the 1920s and the 1930s, it soon became clear that the previous ethnological analyses of its prehistory and the concept of a prehistoric uninhabited region were in need of revision (Strong 1933, 1935). The remains of earthlodge villages now known to date from about A.D. 1000 or before up to the early nineteenth century, and distributed from Kansas River up the Missouri through the Dakotas and on many of its major tributaries two hundred miles and more to the west, have been convincingly demonstrated. So also has the existence yet farther west of eighteenth-century Apache communities associated with irrigation works, pottery, domestic crops, etc., including the western Kansas localities reported by the Spanish (Wedel 1959, pp. 422, 589; Wedel 1961, p. 111;

Gunnerson 1960). For the late prehistoric (eleventh- to thirteenth-century) Upper Republican maize-growers whose numerous settlements in the loess plains continue in diminishing numbers along the creek valleys west into Colorado, there is still no clear evidence of crop-raising in the High Plains of eastern Colorado (Wood 1971); but further south, along the Canadian and North Canadian rivers, the slabhouse builders of the Panhandle aspect seem to have extended their settlements and maize-growing farther west than did their contemporaries and immediate predecessors in the north (Wendorf 1960). Still earlier, Woodland cultural remains (around A.D. 900 and before) and those of the Archaic hunters and gatherers of two to six thousand years ago, occur widely all through the plains region. And finally, scattered from Texas to Saskatchewan and Manitoba, there are the remains of the early big-game hunters who, as makers of the Folsom, Plainview, Hell Gap, and other distinctive weapon points, pursued giant bison nine to ten thousand years ago and, as Clovis point makers, hunted mammoth on the plains from eleven to twelve thousand years ago. The fact that some of the older sites are coming to light only after extensive dislocation and alteration of the land surface by natural or other agencies—erosion, road building, land leveling, dam construction, and so on—is evidence that drastic changes have taken place in the environmental settings since man first came into the western plains and that these, too, have contributed significantly to the "largely negative" results of archeology in past years.

Because the plains area from the standpoint of climate is on the borderland of successful corn-growing without specialized techniques, there is a correlation between the distribution through time of aboriginal cultures based in part on maize-growing and the natural environmental sections. Very roughly, it appears that Plains Indian subsistence economies based in substantial part on gardening can be expected to occur about as far west as the mapped limits of the tall grass (Shantz and Zon 1924, fig. 2), except in the north, where the Missouri valley in the Dakotas must be added. One or two thousand years ago that line might well have been drawn differently. Beyond that general line in many parts of the plains, as Bowman (1972) has persuasively argued in an important contribution to central plains prehistory and aboriginal ecology, the obstacles to year-round human occupation are formidable indeed. In the west, the wild plant food resources and small game on which a forager type of subsistence economy might have been based when the bison were unavailable may not have been present in adequate quantities to serve as a dietary mainstay under a climatic regime like the present or that of the past half-millenium since the arrival of the white man.

With respect to perceptions of the plains as the home of man, it is perhaps worth noting that for each of the native lifeways briefly enumerated in a previous paragraph for various periods of prehistory, the archeologist has necessarily formulated an image of the landscape which differs from that of the present or of a hundred years ago. Equally, no two scholars, even if they are working the same area, are likely to have identical images regarding the contemporary setting of their constructs. What you have been getting here is a set of images developed by one archeologist over a succession of years and from varied experiences in different parts of the plains region.

Since 1930, a major obstacle to anthropological thinking about the plains—the image of the region as uninhabitable by man in prehorse days—has finally been demolished. A continuous and uninterrupted occupation by native man is not demonstrable at this time, and perhaps never will be. A priori, it seems likely that some sections were suited only to transient residence and much larger sections may have been unusable during some of the major drought periods for which there is growing evidence (Wedel 1941, 1953; Bryson, Baerreis, and Wendland 1970; Lehmer 1970). But to the archeologist the question is no longer whether, but how and by what adaptive mechanisms and at what periods of time, man was in the area. Facing these hydra-headed concerns, we must realize that such solutions as may emerge will acquire validity in propor-

tion as they bring to bear all of the other applicable disciplines of natural history— ethnozoology, ethnobotany, geology, geomorphology, and climatology, to name a few of the more obvious. Only through such an interdisciplinary attack, closely linked to a critical analysis of the history and ethnohistory of the region, will we be able to work out a more accurate and meaningful story or, if you prefer, a more appropriate series of images of man in the Great Plains and of his periodic readjustments to the ever changing environmental circumstances with which he has been confronted.

BIBLIOGRAPHY

Abert, Lt. J. W.
1848.   Notes of Lieutenant J. W. Abert. In notes of a military reconnaissance from Fort Leavenworth, in Missouri, to San Diego, in California, including part of the Arkansas, del Norte, and Gila rivers, by Lt. Col. W. H. Emory. U.S., *House, Executive Document no. 41,* 30th Cong., 1st sess., pp. 386–414.

Baerreis, David A., and Bryson, Reid A.
1965.   Historical climatology and the southern plains: A preliminary statement. *Oklahoma Anthropological Society Bulletin,* 13:69–75.

Bowman, Peter W.
1969.   Some observations on Ulibarri's route and the location of Santo Domingo of El Cuartelejo. *Kansas Anthropological Association Newsletter,* vol. 14, nos. 4 & 5.
1972.   Weather in the west central plains and its significance in archeology. *Kansas Anthropological Association Newsletter,* vol. 18, nos. 1 & 2, pp. 1–32.

Bryson, Reid A., Baerreis, David A., and Wendland, Wayne M.
1970.   The character of late-glacial and postglacial climatic changes. In *Pleistocene and Recent environments of the central Great Plains,* ed. W. Dort, Jr., and J. K. Jones, Jr., pp. 53–74. Lawrence: University Press of Kansas.

Caldwell, Joseph R.
1962.   Eastern North America. In *Courses toward urban life,* ed. R. J. Braidwood, and G. R. Willey, pp. 288–308. Viking Fund Publications in Anthropology, no. 32.

Carleton, Lt. J. Henry.
1943.   A dragoon campaign to the Rocky

Mountains in 1845. Edited by Louis Pelzer. Chicago: Prairie Logbooks.

Emory, W. H.
1848. Notes of a military reconnaissance, from Fort Leavenworth, in Missouri, to San Diego, in California, including parts of the Arkansas, del Norte, and Gila Rivers [made in 1846–47]. U.S., *Senate Executive Document no. 7,* 30th Cong., 1st sess.
1857. Report on the United States and Mexican boundary survey [1855,] vol. 1. U.S., *House Executive Document no. 135,* 34th Cong., 1st sess.

Fitzpatrick, Thomas
1847. Appendix to the report . . . [pp. 238–249]. Report of the Commissioner of Indian Affairs for the year 1847. U.S., *House Executive Document no. 8,* 30th Cong., 1st sess. (War Dept., Cong. Ser. no. 503).
1853. Reports accompanying the annual report . . . no. 44 [pp. 359–371]. Report of the Commissioner of Indian Affairs for the year 1853. U.S., *House Executive Document no. 1,* 33rd Cong., 1st sess. (Interior Dept., Cong. Ser. no. 690, 710).

Fowke, Gerard.
1922. Explorations along the Missouri River Bluffs in Kansas and Nebraska. *Bureau of American Ethnology Bulletin 76*:151–60.

Frémont, J. C.
1845. Report of the exploring expedition to the Rocky Mountains in the year 1842, and to Oregon and California in the years 1843–1844. U.S., *House Executive Document no. 166,* 28th Cong., 2nd sess.

Gregg, Josiah.
1954. *Commerce of the prairies.* Edited by Max L. Moorhead. Norman: University of Oklahoma Press.

Gunnerson, Dolores A.
1956. The southern Athabascans: Their arrival in the Southwest. *El Palacio* 63:346–65.

Gunnerson, James H.
1960. An introduction to Plains Apache archeology: The Dismal River Aspect. *Bureau of American Ethnology Bulletin 173, Anthropological Papers, no. 58.* Washington, D.C.

Hammond, George P., and Rey, Agapito.
1940. *Narratives of the Coronado Expedition.* Coronado Historical Series, vol. 2. Albuquerque: University of New Mexico.
1953. *Don Juan de Oñate, Colonizer of New Mexico, 1595–1628.* Coronado Cuarto Centennial Publications, 1540–1940, vols. 5 & 6. Albuquerque.

1966. *The rediscovery of New Mexico, 1580–1594.* Coronado Historical Series, vol. 3. Albuquerque: University of New Mexico.

Henry, Joseph.
1858. Meteorology in its connection with agriculture. In *Agricultural Report of the U.S. Patent Office, 1856,* pp. 455–92. Washington, D.C.

Hind, Henry Youle.
1860. *Narrative of the Canadian Red River exploring expedition of 1857 and of the Assiniboine and Saskatchewan exploring expedition of 1858.* 2 vols. London.

Holmes, William H.
1914. Areas of American culture characterization tentatively outlined as an aid in the study of antiquities. *American Anthropologist,* 16:413–46.

James, Edwin.
1823. *Account of an expedition from Pittsburgh to the Rocky Mountains, performed in the years 1819–20 . . . under the command of Major Stephen H. Long.* 2 vols. Philadelphia.

Johnston, Col. Joseph E.
1932. Surveying the southern boundary line of Kansas [1857], from the private journal of Col. Joseph E. Johnston. Ed. Nyle H. Miller, *Kansas Historical Quarterly,* 1:104–39.

Kroeber, Alfred L.
1928. Native culture of the Southwest. *University of California Publications in American Archaeology and Ethnology,* 23:375–98.
1939. Cultural and natural areas of native North America. *University of California Publications in American Archeology and Ethnology,* vol. 38., (whole volume, 242 pp).
1948. *Anthropology,* Rev. ed. New York: Harcourt, Brace & Co.

Lehmer, Donald J.
1970. Climate and culture history in the Middle Missouri valley. In *Pleistocene and recent environments of the central Great Plains,* ed. W. Dort, Jr., and J. K. Jones, Jr., pp. 117–29. Lawrence: University Press of Kansas.

Lewis, G. Malcolm.
1965. Early American exploration and the cis–Rocky Mountain desert, 1803–1823. *Great Plains Journal,* 5:1–11.
1966. William Gilpin and the concept of the Great Plains region. *Annals of the Association of American Geographers,* 56:33–51.

Lewis, Meriwether, and Clark, William.
1904–1905. *Original journals of the Lewis and Clark expedition, 1804–1806,* ed. R. G. Thwaites, vols. 1–8. New York.

Lowie, Robert H.
1954. *Indians of the Plains.* Anthropological Handbook no. 1, American Museum of Natural History. New York.
1955. Reflections on the Plains Indians. *Anthropological Quarterly,* (formerly *Primitive Man*), vol 28 (n.s. 3), pp. 63–86.
Mason, Otis T.
1896. Influence of environment upon human industries or arts. In *Annual Report of the Smithsonian Institution, 1895,* pp. 639–65.
Pike, Zebulon M.
1810. *An account of expeditions to the sources of the Mississippi, and through the western parts of Louisiana, to the sources of the Arkansaw, Kans, La Platte, and Pierre Jaun, rivers; performed by order of the government of the United States during the years 1805, 1806, and 1807, and a tour through the interior parts of New Spain, when conducted through these provinces.* Philadelphia: C. & A. Conrad & Co.
Service, Elman R.
1963. *Profiles in ethnology.* New York: Harper & Row.
Shantz, H. L., and Zon, Raphael.
1924. *The natural vegetation of the United States. Atlas of American Agriculture.* Washington, D.C.: U.S. Dept. of Agriculture.
Smith, Harlan I.
1910. An unknown field in American archeology. *Bulletin of the American Geographical Society,* 42(July):511–20.
Strong, William Duncan.
1933. The plains culture area in the light of archeology. *American Anthropologist,* 35:271–87.
1935. *An introduction to Nebraska archeology.* Smithsonian Miscellaneous Collections, vol. 93, no. 10.
Thomas, A. B.
1935. *After Coronado: Spanish exploration northeast of New Mexico, 1696–1727.* Norman: University of Oklahoma Press.
Tyrrell, J. B., ed.
1916. *David Thompson's narrative of his explorations in western America, 1784–1812.* Toronto: Champlain Society.

Wedel, Waldo R.
1941. Environment and native subsistence economies in the central Great Plains. Smithsonian Miscellaneous Collections, vol. 101, no. 3, 29 pp.
1953. Some aspects of human ecology in the central Plains. *American Anthropologist,* 55(October):499–514.
1959. An introduction to Kansas archeology. *Bureau of American Ethnology Bulletin 174,* (whole volume).
1961. *Prehistoric man on the Great Plains.* Norman: University of Oklahoma Press.
1963. The High Plains and their utilization by the Indian. *American Antiquity,* 29:1–16.
Wendorf, Fred.
1960. The archaeology of northeastern New Mexico. *El Palacio,* 67:55–65.
Wendorf, Fred, and Hester, James J.
1962. Early man's utilization of the Great Plains environment. *American Antiquity,* 28:159–71.
Wheat, Joe Ben.
1972. The Olsen-Chubbuck site, a paleo-Indian bison kill. *American Antiquity,* 37:1–180, (Memoir No. 26).
White, L. A., ed.
1959. *Lewis Henry Morgan: The Indian journals, 1859–62.* Ann Arbor: University of Michigan Press.
Wislizenus, A.
1848. Memoir of a tour to northern Mexico. U.S., *Senate Miscellaneous Document no. 26,* 30th Cong., 1st sess.
Wissler, Clark.
1908. Ethnographical problems of the Missouri Saskatchewan area. *American Anthropologist,* 10:197–207.
1914. Material cultures of the North American Indians. *American Anthropologist,* 16:447–505.
Wood, W. Raymond.
1971. Pottery sites near Limon, Colo. *Southwestern Lore,* 37:53–82.

PART 2
Resource Evaluation in the Prefrontier West

The Recognition and Delimitation
of the Northern Interior Grasslands
during the Eighteenth Century

G. Malcolm Lewis
University of Sheffield, England

This volume consists of papers which consider some of the many images of the plains. It therefore presupposes that North America contains an area which is or was distinguishable from the rest of the continent by the images that it has generated in men's minds, a presupposition which raises questions concerning images in general, the nature of the area, and the motives of those who have experienced it. After a brief consideration of the process by which images of regions develop, this paper traces and attempts to explain the emergence of images of the northern part of the interior grasslands in the minds of those who experienced the area during the eighteenth century. Finally, it examines the influence of the boldest of these images.

Images of Regions

In contrast to a given phenomenon (P) in the world outside a specific senser's (s) mind, it is useful to distinquish between several types of image to which it can give rise.

Instant Image (A). An instantaneous representation of P or B (Recalled Image, as defined below) in the mind via the senses. It is unique because no two sensers ever sense a given phenomenon in the same way and a specific senser never re-senses a given phenomenon in the same way. Therefore, every instant image of a given phenomenon is a distortion such that: $A \neq P$

Recalled Image (B). A mental copy of A or C (Message Image, as defined below), recollected in the mind in the absence of sensory stimulus from the original P. It is distorted by the complex environmental and mental processes operating during the interval between sensing and recollection such that: $B \neq P$

Message Image (C). A visual, aural, tactile, or olfactory image, transmitted from senser (s) to receiver (r) across space or through time. While ultimately derived from P, a message image must exist in one of forms A or B before it can be transmitted and it is therefore distorted before transmission. Furthermore, additional distortions occur during transmission and again during reception, when the receiver converts the image into a new form of A.

$$C_r \neq C_s \neq (A_s \text{ or } B_s) \neq P$$

In practice, images of the real world rarely derive from a single phenomenon but from groups of associated phenomena. In the geographer's ordering of phenomena, two of the most important of these groupings are associations of images of phenomena at given locations (L) and associations of images of contiguous locations possessing similar associations of phenomena into regions (R).

$$L = \sum_{i=1}^{n} P_i$$

and

$$R = \sum_{j=1}^{n} L_j$$

23

Because the three types of images recognized thus far are derived from a consideration of what happens when a specific senser receives, recollects, and recreates images of a given phenomenon, they fail to provide a basis for understanding why, over a period of time, groups of sensers may develop a distinctive group image of a set of associated phenomena. For example, in the case of the image of a major region, the locations are too widespread for them to have been sensed as instant images by a specific senser (except by recently developed remote sensing techniques) and too numerous to have been sensed over a period of time for recollection by a specific senser as a set of recalled images. In order to begin to understand this eminently geographical process, it is useful to recognize two further types of images.

Apperceptive Image (D). A conceptually related group of B-type images to which further A or B images either passively intrude or are actively added. In the former case, the new images infiltrate into the senser's consciousness and compel attention upon themselves because they relate to the existing D image. In the active case, the senser consciously seeks new images and assimilates them into a D image standing in readiness (Jung 1924, p. 524).

$$D = \sum_{i=1}^{n} A_i + \sum_{j=1}^{n} B_j + \sum_{k=1}^{n} C_k$$

Stereotype Image (E). A preconceived representation in the mind of a group of phenomena, which remains unmodified in form (but may change in strength) with each subsequent sensing of phenomena from within the group.

$$E = E + \left(\sum_{i=1}^{n} A_i + \sum_{j=1}^{n} B_j + \sum_{k=1}^{n} C_k \right)$$

Images of regions are of the D or E type, although they must be transmitted in form C. In the D type, the component A and B images are areally grouped and related. During the emergence of a D-type image of a region, the apperception process is dominantly passive, but at a later stage in development, it becomes increasingly active, and with heightened awareness on the part of the senser, it is more likely to be transformed into a message image. Once in this form, it is likely to be translated by receivers into a stereotype image.

Inevitably, any study of images must be based on the evidence of message images, from which it may be possible to make inferences about types A, B, D, and E. In this particular study the message images have been transmitted through time as writings and maps in either manuscript or published forms. They will not, however, be referred to as message images but, with varying degrees of inference, as instant (A), recalled (B), apperceptive (D), or stereotype (E) images.

The First White Sensers

The images generated in the minds of the earliest European and colonial explorers by the landscapes and perceived resources of what was later to be thought of as the Great Plains region would seem to have been of the instant type. Little is known about these pre-nineteenth-century soldiers, missionaries, traders, and trappers or how they sensed the environment, what they thought, what they learned from the Indians, and what they communicated to each other in conversation. However, their journals present a series of instant images which, other than that they are usually presented in a chronological sequence, are unrelated and frequently unrelatable. Positions, distances, and routes are only vaguely given, there is little indication of pattern, generalizations are few, and examples of regionalization are even fewer. These instant images incorporate only those "relevant" elements of the environment relating to the well-being of the traveler or the purpose of the journey. Relevant elements are amplified but almost everything else appears to have been filtered out in the perception process (A), lost in the process of recall (B), or suppressed in the course of transmission (C). After spending the winters of 1784 to 1787 on the upper North Saskatchewan, Edward Umfreville (1790, p. 167), a shrewd but bitter critic of his former employer, the Hudson's Bay Company, observed that "unfortunately those mercantile gentlemen who have hitherto been sent into the Terra incognita have been so very intent upon the pecuniary emoluments arising from the trade they are engaged in, as entirely to neglect every effort to obtain a knowledge of the country and its productions." For the most part, these men were not the conscious fashioners of apperceptive images but the first white receivers of instant images.

What can be learned from the instant images of two hundred years ago that have been communicated to us? Before trying to answer this question it is necessary to realize that in bringing consciousness to bear on the images of others one is creating in one's own mind a new order of images. These will not, indeed cannot, be congruous with the images from which they are derived because of the twin biases inherent in the inevitably selective approach and the unrepresentative nature of the evidence. (Nothing is known about the images generated in the minds of most of those who experienced the plains during this period, either because they were never converted into permanent messages or because the messages have been lost.)

The first white men to enter this part of the continent were, for the most part, intelligent and observant, but relatively uneducated. They knew little about the area as a whole when they first approached it and they had limited opportunity for establishing what was known to others. With but few exceptions, they had no training in or need for systematic record keeping, and what reports were made tended to become effectively lost in government or company archives or to be published without acknowledgment, in abbreviated and distorted form, in the maps and atlases of the commercial ateliers or the voluminous compilations of travel writers. The bringing together of early images of the various parts of the plains *sensu lato* was inevitably limited by the fact that the initial approaches into the area were launched from four quite different directions by men of three different language and culture groups from three (and, after the American Revolution, four) major nation states. First the Spaniards, then the French and British, and finally the Canadians and Americans had specific objectives of which,

except for the early Spaniards, the search for furs was paramount (fig. 1).

The early Spaniards approached the area from the shrub and dry grasslands to the southwest, via the needleleaf forests of the southern Rocky Mountains; the French, and later, the Spaniards, Canadians, and Americans, from the mixed and broadleaf forests with prairie openings to the east; and the British, from the tundra and needleleaf forests to the northeast, via the transition zone of aspen groves and grassy openings. With the exception of the early Spaniards, they almost all traveled by canoe. Hence, they followed the main valleys, along·the floors of which the galeria forests penetrate for hundreds of miles into and, in some cases, across the plains. Characteristically, the floodplains are a hundred or more feet below the level of the grassy interfluvial plains, from which they are usually separated by steep bluffs, and the two are therefore only rarely intervisible. The interior grasslands contained fewer commercially desirable fur-bearing animals than the surrounding forests and consequently the area was less attractive, many traders stopping short of or merely skirting it. The beaver was a partial but significant exception, being present in floodplain forests and absent from the interfluvial plains. For the most part, those who went in search of the beaver had no cause or wish to leave these valleys. To do so was fraught with dangers: in winter, the sudden blizzard and the near absence of natural shelter and fuel; in summer, the scarcity of water and the risk from fires; and at all seasons, the absence of natural protection from marauders and competitors. The need to leave the valleys was restricted to the occasions when traders traveled with or in search of Indians, when they had cause to cross from one valley system to another, or when they wished to reach the Rocky Mountains from a river system having its source within the plains. Not surprisingly, therefore, like the old freighters of the plains of a century later, whom Samuel Aughey (1880, p. 11) met in the years after the Civil War, many of them failed to recognize the dual character of the area "because they had followed the valleys." When they did leave the valleys they received instant images which in

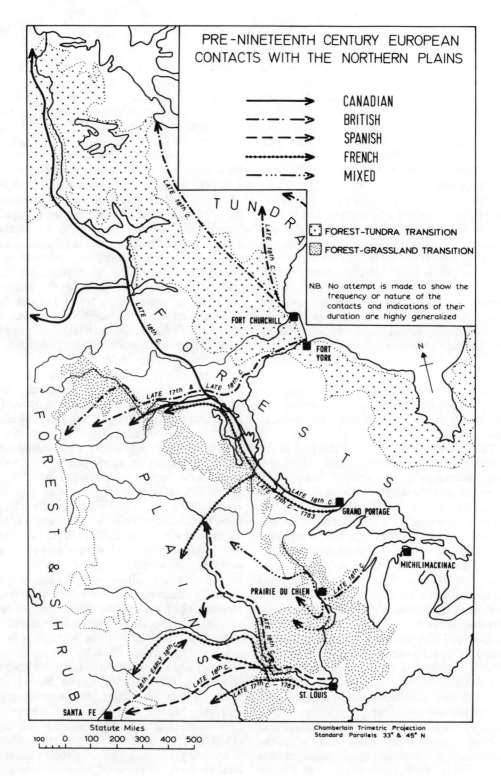

PRE-NINETEENTH CENTURY EUROPEAN
CONTACTS WITH THE NORTHERN PLAINS

CANADIAN
BRITISH
SPANISH
FRENCH
MIXED

☐ FOREST-TUNDRA TRANSITION
▨ FOREST-GRASSLAND TRANSITION

N.B. No attempt is made to show the
frequency or nature of the
contacts and indications of their
duration are highly generalized

TUNDRA

LATE 18th C.

LATE 18th C.

LATE 18th C.

FORT CHURCHILL

FORT
YORK

N

F O R E S T S

LATE 17th &
LATE 18th C.

LATE 17th C. – 1763
LATE 18th C.

GRAND PORTAGE

F O R E S T   &   S H R U B

P L A I N S

MICHILIMACKINAC

LATE 18th C.

PRAIRIE DU CHIEN

LATE
18th C.

18th – EARLY 18th C.

LATE 18th c.

LATE 17th C. – 1763

ST. LOUIS

SANTA FE

Statute Miles
100   0   100 200 300 400 500

Chamberlain Trimetric Projection
Standard Parallels 33° & 45° N

Figure 1

many cases they seem to have considered exceptional, whereas had their travels been along random routes these would have been seen to be the norm.

Instant Images

The earliest known images of any part of the northern interior grasslands are in the journal of Henry Kelsey (1691, M, pp. 1–16) who in 1690 and 1691, only six years after he had joined the Hudson's Bay Company as a boy apprentice, penetrated further inland from Hudson Bay than any previous European. In 1690 he may not have penetrated beyond the transition zone of aspen groves and grassy openings to the west of Lakes Winnipegosis and Manitoba, but in the summer of the following year he almost certainly moved out onto the wheatgrass prairies, somewhere to the southeast of present-day Saskatoon (fig. 2). The style of Kelsey's journal for 1690 is closer to Geoffrey Chaucer's than subsequent explorers', but that for the following year is less poetic and the account is arranged chronologically. An analysis of the relevant parts of the journal reveals that Kelsey's images of the lands beyond the aspen groves and grassy openings included most of the elements which were to recur in eighteenth-century accounts of other parts of the interior grasslands. He remarked on the abrupt edges to the woods, the scarcity of water, absence of trees, abundance of buffalo, the shortness of the grass, and, in August, the generally barren appearance of the land. By implication, he indicated that the grasslands were devoid of beaver, and in using the term barren he probably implied that the soil was infertile. Of these characteristics, the ones that were to occur most frequently in the instant images of eighteenth-century explorers were the absence of trees, dryness of the ground, scarcity of fresh surface water, shortness of the grass, and the abundance of buffalo and other large herbivorous mammals. Unlike several of the subsequent explorers, Kelsey made no mention of beautiful landscapes, a healthy climate, or the problems consequent upon the absence of wood.

Kelsey used three key terms in conveying instant images of the landscapes of the area beyond the woods: champion land; plain; and barren ground. All were Middle English terms still in common use in late seventeenth-century England. Champion, or champaign, land was any expanse of level, open (unenclosed) country or common land. It was frequently used as the antithesis of mountains and woods. A plain was an extent of level ground or flat meadow land. Barren land was characterized by little or no vegetation. Together, these terms conveyed an image incorporating the following characteristics: absence of trees; a smooth, relatively open aspect; and a soil believed to be infertile on the false premise that if it only supported grass it could not be otherwise. However, the terms were used by Kelsey only in the topographic sense to refer to areas of a few tens of square miles: the largest plain was "about 46 miles over" (1691, M, p. 14). Plain and barren ground were to recur and several other topographical-ecological terms were to be introduced in the course of the eighteenth century, when there was a growing tendency to apply them to larger and larger areas. Most important among the new terms were meadow, prairie, savannah, and desert, but plain continued to be used most frequently, and barren ground persisted. In the sample of journals analyzed, plain was used by all three native Americans (Carver 1766–67, M, p. 23, and 1778, P, p. 80; Henry 1781, M, p. 43, and 1809, P, pp. 264–73; and Pond 1785b, M, fol. 3) (fig. 2) and by six out of nine Britons. The exceptions (Cocking 1773, M, pp. 105–13; Umfreville 1790, P, p. 153; and Graham 1791, M, p. 37) (fig. 2) each used the term barren ground, but as all three had experience of the better known but fundamentally different barren ground (tundra) to the north of the boreal forest, it must be assumed that they used the adjective barren to indicate the absence of trees, the only characteristic which the two environments had in common. Four of the Britons also used the term meadow (Dobbs 1744, P, p. 33; Graham 1791, M, p. 5; Evans 1796–97, M, p. 497; and Mackay 1807, P, pp. 27–37) (fig. 2), but Henday (1754, M, pp. 3–4) adopted the Indian term Muscuty Tuskee,

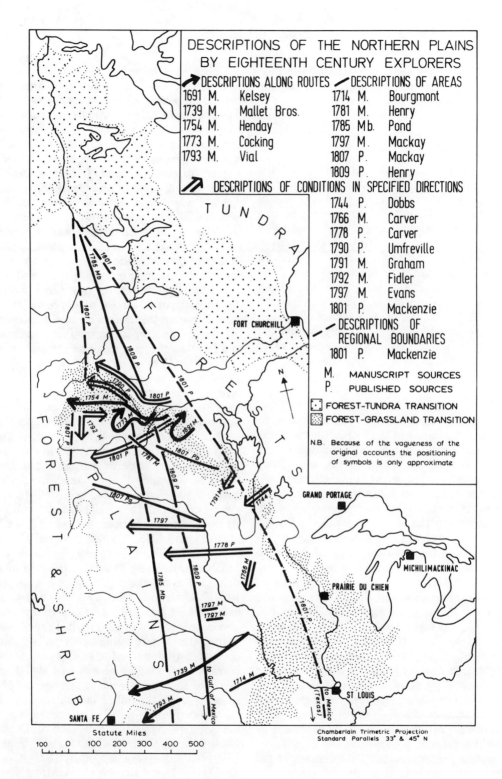

Figure 2

which he interpreted to mean dry inland country but seems likely to have been derived from the two Knisteneux (Cree) words, *mos-ko-se-ah* (grass) and *as-kee* (earth), or grassy ground (Harmon 1820, pp. 385–403). Only Mackay (1797, M) (fig. 2), a Scotsman who was reputedly fluent in both French and Spanish and who at the time was employed by the Spaniards as manager of the Missouri Company's affairs on the upper Missouri, used the term *desert*. Even then, it was only applied to a relatively small area, believed to have been near the northern edge of the Sandhills in present-day Brown County, Nebraska (Diller 1955, p. 127).

The increasing size of the areas to which the terms were applied is more significant than the semantic and cultural differences between terms. Because of the lack of precision in many of the descriptions and the absence of reliable information about latitude, longitude, and drainage networks in the areas described, it is often difficult to determine the extent of the area to which a particular term was applied. However, whereas Kelsey's (1691, M, p. 14) largest plain was only approximately 46 miles across, the "immense plains or meadows" described by Mackenzie (1801, P, pp. 402–3) 110 years later extended southward from "about the junction of the River of the Mountains (Liard River) with Mackenzie's River (62°N), widening as they reach the Red River at its confluence with the Assinboin River, from whence they take a more Southern direction, along the Mississippi towards Mexico" (fig. 2). Kelsey's "plain" was probably less than a thousandth part of Mackenzie's "immense plains." Whereas Kelsey's was an instant image, Mackenzie's was an apperceptive or stereotype image composed mainly of elements derived from the images of other sensers, written retrospectively as part of a short postscript to his journal, and organized in such a way that it related the image geographically to images of adjacent regions: "a broken country composed of lakes, rocks and soil" (the forested, southwestern part of the Laurentian shield) to the northeast and the "Barren Grounds" (tundra) beyond; and a "narrow strip of very marshy, boggy and uneven ground, the outer edge of which produces coal

and bitumen" which was supposed to separate the "immense plains" to the east from the "stony mountains" to the west.

The Emergence of Apperceptive Images

In 1754 Anthony Henday, an Englishman who had joined the Hudson's Bay Company only four years before, was sent into the interior to persuade more Indian tribes to bring pelts direct to Hudson Bay. His journey marked the beginning of the company's attempt to counter the French traders operating from the Great Lakes, which was in part a response to the enquiry by a House of Commons committee in 1749 into the "State and condition of the countries adjoining to Hudson's Bay and of the trade carried on their" (House of Commons 1803). Henday was only the second Briton known to have penetrated as far as the interior grasslands, but he went some five hundred miles farther west than Kelsey, passing through the northern part of the wheatgrass prairies via the valley of the Battle River and crossing the upper Red Deer valley to within sight of the Rocky Mountains. Some seven days before he reached The Pas on the lower Saskatchewan, and while still within the needleleaf forest, he met four canoes of Indians, the leader of which informed him that he was "on the Confines of the dry inland country, called by the Natives the Muscuty Tuskee." (Henday, 1754, M, pp. 3–4) (fig. 2). On August 13 he recorded, "We are now entering the Muscuty plains and shall soon see plenty of Buffalo, and the Archithunue (Blackfeet) Indians hunting them on Horse Back" (p. 15). According to Burpee's reconstruction of the route (Henday 1754–55, M, 1907 ed., p. 328), Henday was then somewhere near present-day Humboldt, Saskatchewan. Seventy-seven days later (October 29) and some 350 to 400 miles farther west by a direct route, Henday (p. 41) recorded that he "Left (the) Muscuty plains." During this period he appears to have been conscious of the magnitude and distinctiveness of this vast area, as in his journal entries for August 31, September 24, and October 5 he records, "We are yet in (the) Muscuty plains" (pp. 20, 28–29, and 131).

Though the interior grasslands obviously

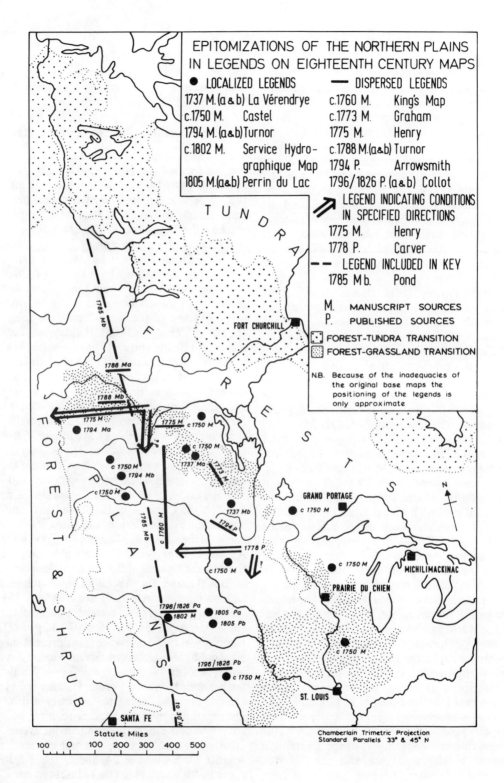

Figure 3

made an impression on Henday he had been led to anticipate them by the Indians and adopted their term when referring to them. He gave no indication of an awareness of their extent towards the south but other evidence suggests that some Indians had apperceptive or stereotype images of a distinctive region extending for a great distance in that direction. Carver (1778, P, p. 80) refers to Indians who "dwell higher up, to the west of the River St. Pierre (Minnesota River), on plains that according to their account, are unbounded; and probably terminate on the coast of the Pacific Ocean" (fig. 2). On the accompanying map of his travels a legend to the west of the River St. Pierre indicates "The Country of the Nadowessie of the Plains / from this place the Plains are unbounded suppos'd to extend to the South Sea" (Carver 1778, P) (fig. 3). In the late eighteenth century *South Sea* and *Pacific Ocean* were synonymous terms, but a manuscript version of Carver's diary refers to "the plains which extend to the South Sea as the savages say" (Carver 1766, M, p. 23) (fig. 2). To the Indians of the interior the South Sea was presumably the Gulf of Mexico, and at least one Indian map indirectly confirms this by indicating that their West Sea was the Pacific Ocean (Auchagach et al. 1728–29). This interpretation has much to recommend it in that it is essentially true, whereas Carver's published version is false. It is unlikely that the Nadowessi (Dakota Indians of the Siouan language family) were ignorant of the forest-covered Rocky Mountains which fell within the territories of their near neighbors. Conversely, it is reasonable to suppose that they were aware that the grasslands and savannahs extended towards a sea to the south.

Most of the legends indicating plainslike conditions on eighteenth-century maps were aligned from west to east, partly because most explorers followed east-west routes and partly because of the convention of orienting maps with north towards the top linked with a natural preference on the part of cartographers for placing legends horizontally. However, a manuscript map from the King's Collection in the British Museum (King's Map c. 1760, M) has the bold legend "Great Meadows" extend-

ing from south to north between 45° and 55° along a meridian approximately halfway between Lake Winnipeg and the Pacific Ocean—that is, through the grasslands of what are now Montana, Alberta, and Saskatchewan (fig. 3). The representation of Lake Winnipeg and adjacent lakes would appear to have been derived from a French manuscript map of 1740 (La Vérendrye Expedition 1740), and the legend concerning the "Suposed ... Mountains of Bright Stones mention'd in the Map of the Indian Ochagach" still further strengthens the conviction that the anonymous compiler (the cartouche is reminiscent of that on John Mitchell's great map of 1755) had seen the Vérendrye papers. The concept of the Great Meadows was almost certainly derived from this or other French sources. The translation of *prairie* into *meadow* on maps published in London during the second half of the eighteenth century must have created false instant images in the minds of those who knew the lush hay fields and water meadows of England. The French priest and cosmographer Father Louis Castel also drew maps influenced by the La Vérendrye expedition. One of these (Castel 1750, M), while containing more errors than the anonymous British map of circa 1760, is of interest in that the term *prairie* occurs fifteen times within the broad area bounded by the western side of Lake Winnipeg, the southern end of Lake Michigan, the northern edge of the Ozarks (possibly) and what would seem to be the eastern front of the Rocky Mountains (fig. 3).

In contrast to the widespread "prairies" on Castel's map and the "Great Meadows" on the King's Map, most of the legends indicating plainslike conditions on eighteenth-century maps were restricted to small areas and reflect instant or recalled images. A map drawn by a member of the La Vérendrye expedition (1737, M, a and b) indicated two apparently smaller "Prairies" to the south of Lac des Prairies (Lake Manitoba) (fig. 3). Graham (c. 1773, M) indicated "Barren Ground. Buffalo Plenty in Winter" in approximately the same area and did so in such a way that it was clear rather than bold (fig. 3). It was the edge of the map and he was probably incorporating information communicated to him at York Fort by Tomison, a Hudson's Bay Company employee who had spent the winter of 1767–68 around the mouths of the Winnipeg and Red rivers and may have gleaned from the Indians some knowledge of the areas beyond. Turnor indicated "Mostly open dry Meadows full of Buffalo and plenty of Wolves" (c. 1788, M, a) to the north of Hudson's House on the North Saskatchewan and "Meadow Country full of Buffalo and Wolves" (c. 1788, M, b) to the south (fig. 3). On a later map he indicated "No woods" (1794, M) between the lower Red Deer valley and the Rocky Mountains (fig. 3). An anonymous French map of the Mississippi now in the Bureau du Service Hydrographique in Paris indicated "Land of moving sand" (Service Hydrographique c. 1802, M) to the north of the fork of the Platte, and a map compiled by Perrin du Lac at about the same time indicated "a great desert of drifting sand without trees, soil, rocks, water or animals of any kind, excepting some little varicoloured turtles" (1805, M, a) and "Sandy rolling country" (1805, M, b) in what are now Brown and Loup counties, Nebraska (Diller 1955, p. 127) (fig. 3). In 1796, Collot commenced a map which, although not published until 1826, was printed in 1804 and indicated "Barren Country covered with an efflorescent Salt" (1796/1826, P, b) to the south of the Republican River (fig. 3).

The Earliest Fully Developed Apperceptive Images

With but one important exception which has still to be described (Pond 1785, M, a, c, and h), Castel's, Collot's, and the King's maps were the only ones to carry legends sufficiently extensive in range and bold in style to suggest apperceptive images, and of these, only Pond's contained the word *plain*. The earliest recorded uses of *Great Plains* as a geographical name as distinct from *plain* as a topographic term are on a manuscript map supposed by A. J. H. Richardson to have been drawn by Alexander Henry the Elder (1775, M.) (fig. 3) and in a letter which Henry wrote to Sir Joseph Banks (1781). In outlining a pos-

sible land route across the continent via the North Saskatchewan he described "the Great Plains . . . which abounds with buffeloes, and supplys the numerous Inhabitants with every thing necessary for food and cloathing" (1781, M, p. 43) (fig. 2). Henry considered that these Great Plains commenced some ten to fifteen leagues above what is now The Pas, Manitoba, and extended westwards to the Stony Mountains. The geographical name Great Plains would seem to have been introduced by British and American fur traders during the last quarter of the eighteenth century. Mackay (1807, P, p. 34), in what is clearly a paraphrase of Evans's journal of 1796–97, referred to "the great plains and prairies" reaching as far west as the Stony Mountains, where the latter (1796–97, M, p. 497) had referred to the "Mountains where the great Meadows and Prairies terminate" (fig. 2). Prior to the late eighteenth century the terms *prairie* and *meadow* had been interchangeable, but the emergence of the name Great Plains marked the beginning of a realization that the grasslands to the west differed from the better-known tall-grass prairies to the east. The fur traders rarely stated what, for them, must have been the obvious and essential differences between the two, but in describing the South Saskatchewan country, Alexander Mackenzie came close to doing so: "The plains are sand and gravel, covered with fine grass, and mixed with a small quantity of vegetable earth [and are] covered with buffaloes, wolves and small foxes." In contrast, the wooded North Saskatchewan was inhabited by "Beaver and other animals, whose furs are valuable [as was the] space of hill country clothed with wood . . . where the plains terminate towards the Rockies" (1801, P, pp. lxviii–lxix) (fig. 2).

Four years after Henry's one-dimensional description of 1781, Peter Pond, another American-born trader, added a second dimension to the Great Plains in a memoir (1785, M, b) which accompanied a remarkable map (1785, M, a). Located on the map approximately halfway between Lake Winnipeg and the Stony Mountains and somewhere between the South Saskatchewan and Qu' Appelle Rivers is the numeral 17, one of twenty-six reference points referred to in the memoir. It indicates "Immense plains, which extend from 30° to 60°N and which are terminated by this enormous chain of mountains" (1785, M, b, fol. 3) (fig. 3). Further south, somewhere between the Red River of the North and the Missouri, the numeral 16 indicates that "One finds here as far as 54° a very fine species of horse, a few mules and donkeys and large herds of buffaloes as far as 63°." A legend placed just to the west of the Mississippi River between its confluence with the Missouri and Ohio indicates "ye eastern boundaries of those immense plains which reaches to the great Mountains." Pond's image of the cis–Rocky Mountain West was clearly of the apperceptive type. Reinterpreting the map in the light of subsequent discoveries it becomes apparent that Pond envisaged an immense region of plains extending from somewhere to the west of Great Slave Lake, south-southeastward for almost 2,500 miles to the Gulf of Mexico. At their widest, in the latitude of Saint Louis, the plains were about 700 miles across.

Pond's image of the Great Plains region is almost certainly the earliest fully developed apperceptive image of the cis–Rocky Mountain West to have been handed down to us, but it was probably not unique. Alexander Henry, whose one-dimensional image of 1781 has already been referred to, was actively engaged as a fur trader from 1761 to 1776. During these years he made observations which he "committed to paper [to] form the subject matter of a book" that was not to be published until more than thirty years later (1809, p. v). Most of the book gives the impression of being based on the journal but some sections are retrospective, incorporating his reflections or information subsequently derived from others. The account of his journey up the Saskatchewan River in the winter of 1775–76 is prefixed with a description clearly indicating Henry's appreciation of the extent of the interior grasslands:

The Plains, or, as the French denominate them, the Prairies, or Meadows, compose an extensive tract of country, which is watered by the Elk, or Athabasca, the Saskatchiwaine, the Red River and others,

and runs southward to the Gulf of Mexico. On my first setting out for the north-west I promised myself to visit this region, and I now prepared to accomplish the undertaking. [1809, P, p. 264; see also fig. 2]

Later on in the book Henry observed that he understood the plains to extend northward as far as 60°N and westward to the Rocky Mountains. Whether this is really what he anticipated toward the end of 1775 or, alternatively, the way he recollected his motives many years later is uncertain. A letter from Crèvecoeur to the Marquis de Castries of March 17, 1785, seems to suggest that Pond may have sent his map of that year to Congress via Henry, in which case the latter must have been aware of Pond's image of the plains at least twenty-four years before his book was published (Pond 1785f). Other sections of the account were written in the present tense and indicate that he was anticipating the Great Plains, whether or not at that time he had any conception of their magnitude. Thus, fifteen days up the Saskatchewan from Cumberland House he noted, "We are now on the Border of the Plains" (Henry 1809, P, p. 269), and two days before reaching Fort des Prairies he observed, "we found the borders of the Plains reaching to the very banks of the river" (1809, P, p. 271). Significantly, in a remarkably well-written book, in which upper-case letters were used in much the same way we would now use them, the region is always referred to as "the Plains" or "the Great Plains" and never as "the plains."

Henry and Pond had certain common characteristics differentiating them from most of the late-eighteenth-century British traders. They both had long experience of various parts of the western interior and of the Indians and traders therein. By 1776 Henry had been in the west for sixteen years and by 1785 Pond had been active in the western fur trade for approximately twenty years, including two seasons on the upper Mississippi and ten to the north of the North Saskatchewan. They had a knowledge of and relationship with the western Indians unequalled by employees of the Hudson's Bay Company. (In aggregate, Kelsey, Henday,

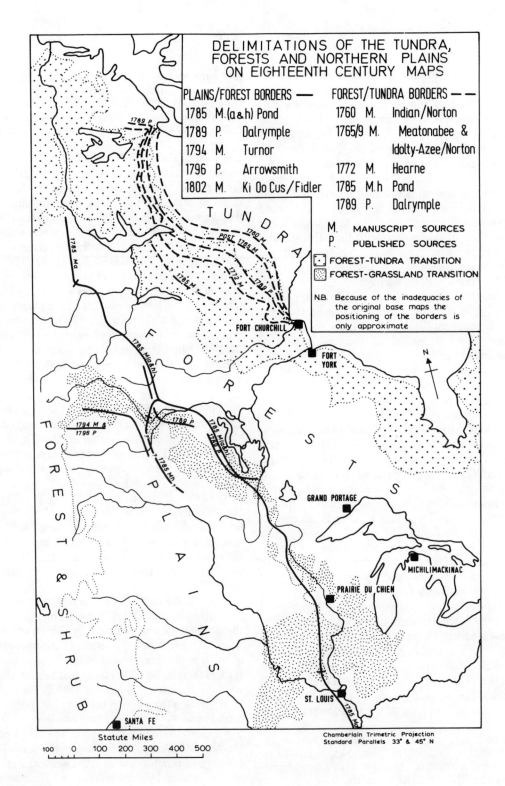

Figure 4

34

Cocking, Tomison, and Turnor spent fewer seasons in the western interior than either Henry or Pond.) On his first journey to the Mississippi, Pond described how Sauk Indians on the Wisconsin portage route "go against the Indians on the Miseure and west of that. Sometimes they Go Near St. Fee in New Mexico and Bring with them Spanish Horseis" (Pond post 1800, p. 249). Pond and Henry also had experience of various western trading posts and made a wider range of contacts with other traders than the Hudson's Bay Company employees operating from the isolated posts at York, Churchill, and Severn. Like Carver before him, Pond knew Prairie du Chien, where Canadian, American, and Spanish traders met each spring. He stayed there on at least four occasions between the fall of 1773 and the spring of 1775, and on one of these he records having asked "Meney Questions [of] a french man who Had Bin Long among the Nations on the Misura" (post 1800, p. 254). On another occasion he expressed surprise at the presence of large numbers of traders and Indians "from Eavery Part of the Misseppey . . . Even from Orleans Eight Hundred Leagues Belowe us" (post 1800, p. 251). It seems more than likely that it was in the course of one of these visits to Prairie du Chien that Pond began to receive the first message images from which in due course he was to assemble his apperceptive image of the Great Plains.

Pond's map of 1785 also showed a remarkable boundary, the significance of which has not apparently been recognized hitherto. It is a "Prik'd Line" depicting "ye eastern Boundaries of those immense Plains which reaches to the great Mountains" (1785, M, a) (fig. 4). This approximately 3,000-mile-long boundary, together with the representation on the map of the Stony Mountains to the west and the descriptions in the accompanying memoir, afford conclusive evidence that by 1785 Pond had a fully developed apperceptive image of the interior grasslands as a distinctive region and that he was able to delimit it with remarkable precision. The map terminates at 30°N and hence affords no indication of how Pond would have delimited the "immense plains" to the south. Otherwise the "ring" is complete,

except to the southwest, where there is a break in the Stony Mountains in the vicinity of Santa Fe, and in the extreme north, where the plains apparently link with what the memoir describes as "regions . . . full of immense plains, where there is neither wood or grass" (1785, M, b, fol. 3), that is, the barren grounds, or tundra.

Before assessing the significance of Pond's attempt to delimit the "immense plains," it is relevant to note that he had personally crossed the boundary at least four times on the Saint Peter (Minnesota) River between 1773 and 1775 and at least twice to the west of Lake Winnipegosis in the winter of 1775–76. Furthermore, he would seem to have traded with Indians within 50 to 150 miles of it during at least six winters between 1776 and 1784: twice near the forks of the Saskatchewan; once on and twice to the south of Lake Athabasca; and once on Lac Ile-a-la-Crosse. Pond doubtless delimited the eastern edge of the "immense plains," in part at least, on the basis of his own observations. However, there is evidence that Indians were capable of drawing similar boundaries on maps. Peter Fidler's copy of a map drawn for him at Chesterfield House early in 1802 by Ki Oo Cus (the Little Bear), a Blackfoot chief, shows approximately 400 miles of the "woods edge" extending eastward from the Rocky Mountains to the lower Battle valley and south towards the South Saskatchewan (Ki Oo Cus 1802, M) (fig. 4). Even more significantly, the more than 1,500-mile-long boundary between the forest and tundra from York Fort to the lower Coppermine valley, as it appeared on Samuel Hearne's map of the area to the west of Hudson Bay (Hearne 1772, M), can be shown to have antecedents in two maps drawn by Moses Norton (fig. 4), the bastard son by an Indian of a former governor of Fort Prince of Wales. The first of these (Indian/Norton 1760, M) was "laid down on Ind'n information" and the second (Meatonabee and Idolty-Azee/Norton 1765–69, M) was "a Draught brought by two Northern Indian Leaders Call'd Meatonabee and Idolty-Azee." It was Meatonabee who subsequently led Hearne from Fort Prince of Wales to the Coppermine estuary in 1770–72, informing him in advance of the strategic significance of this boundary. During the first winter Meatonabee deliberately kept the party just inside the woods' edge, where there was shelter and plenty of deer. Following a period of waiting, they moved north into the barren grounds on May 22 and, after a dash to the Coopermine estuary, returned south to reach the shelter of the woods on November 10. Similarly, the Indians on the northern and eastern edge of the interior grasslands were conscious of the significance of the boundary. In the absence of mountains, sea coasts, and major lakes, it was the main landmark between the widely spaced valleys. However, the woods' edge was something more than a navigator's landmark; it marked the boundary between environments necessitating different modes of life and travel. While the woods were the source of numerous Indian needs, the grassy plains were the habitat of what, for many Indians, was the most important need of all: the buffalo. Leaving the woods for the plains was an experience to be anticipated, planned for, and even feared: in the absence of trees, kindling wood and tent poles had to be carried; in order to guarantee fresh water at nightly camp sites, circuitous routes had to be followed, such that a day's journey could be considerably longer or shorter than an ideal march; to afford shelter against sudden blizzards, the ideal route in winter was never far from the shelter of a valley or clump of trees; in a dry season it was necessary to be wary of grass fires to windward and in a wet season, when naturally induced fires were rare, it was essential to conceal camp fires, which at night would announce the existence of a camp to other Indians within a radius of several tens of miles. Conversely, leaving the plains for the woods or for the mountains to the west was an occasion to be anticipated with a mixture of relief and fear of concealed dangers. For these reasons, it would have been surprising if Indians had not had a fairly clear image of the position and pattern of the woods' edge. It seems reasonable, therefore, to infer that, in delimiting the edge of the "immense plains," Pond supplemented his own observations with information derived from Indians and or other traders.

Just as it is impossible to be sure how Pond obtained and compiled the evidence upon which to delimit the eastern edge of the "immense plains," so it is uncertain as to why he attempted the delimitation. However, there is circumstantial evidence in the remarks which accompany the Crèvecoeur version of the "Congress" map suggesting that Pond recognized it as the western boundary of the area in which beaver were plentiful. In the first of twenty-six remarks he observed that "the greater part of the region situated to the east of the great Plains in the vicinity of latitude 49°N [could] well be called the Region of the Beaver" and, in the third remark, that to the north of 54°N in general and beyond 58°N in particular the natives during the winter spent "their time hunting the Beaver" in order to barter the pelts with the English traders (Pond 1785, M, b, fol. 1). Conversely, to the west of the boundary, he observed that "a very fine species of horse, (and) a few mules and donkeys" were to be found as far as 54°N and "large herds of buffaloes as far as 63°N" (1785 M, b, fol. 3). However, there was no mention of beaver, which, by implication, were rare or absent.

The Communication of Pond's Apperceptive Image

There can be no doubt that by 1785 Pond had a well-developed apperceptive image of the "immense plains" or that his map quickly became accessible to a wide range of persons potentially capable of promoting the image. It is therefore of interest to examine the extent to which they did so.

At some date between January 11 and March 1, 1785, the map and accompanying remarks were presented to the Continental Congress in New York, though there is apparently no official record of this and the original versions do not appear to have survived (Wagner 1955, p. 28 and Richardson c. 1953, p. 6). On March 1, 1785, the map and accompanying remarks were copied for or by (probably the latter) Michel Guillaume Jean de Crèvecoeur (better known as Hector St. John de Crèvecoeur, the noted essayist) (Pond 1785,

M, a [rough version,] b, and c), the French consul in New York. Soon afterwards they were copied by or for Francois, Marquis de Barbé-Marbois, the French consul general who had followed Congress from Philadelphia to New York (Pond 1785d and g). Subsequently, the Crèvecoeur and Barbé-Marbois copies were transmitted to France, where the former was transcribed by Jean Denis Barbié du Bocage, the eminent cartographer who at various times held senior positions in the Bibliothèque du roi, Ministère des affaires étrangères, Ministère de l'intérieur, and Faculté des lettres de l'académie de Paris (Pond 1785a [neat version]). Sometime before April 4, 1785, Pond presented a similar map to Lieutenant Governor Hamilton of Quebec, who forwarded an exquisitely redrawn version of the same to Lord Sydney, secretary of state with responsibility for the colonies (Pond 1785h). In an interview with Pond, Hamilton "collected . . . some remarks on the country . . . explored," which he promised to transmit to Lord Sydney when he had had time to digest them but which apparently were not sent (Hamilton 1785). Hence, within less than three months, Pond's map and notes were presented to or came into the possession of British, French, and American officials. Of the four nations with active interests in the interior of North America, only Spain would seem to have lacked an opportunity to familiarize itself with them.

Each of the maps of 1785 apparently depicted the eastern boundary of the Great Plains, though on the "Hamilton" version its significance was missed because of the absence of remarks. The "Congress" map and those copied from it would appear to have had no influence in the United States or France. Though Barbié du Bocage later redrew the Crèvecoeur version of the "Congress" map (Pond 1785, M, a [neat version]) it is unlikely that it was available in Paris at the time at which he was revising and augmenting D'Anville's "Hemisphère Occidental ou du Nouveau Monde . . ." (Barbié du Bocage 1786). A version of the map presented to Hamilton would appear to have been known in London as "the map of the Canadian Traders," proba-

bly because it was referred to by Pond on April 18, 1785, in a memorial presented to Hamilton on behalf of the North West Company, in which he was a partner (Pond 1785e). William Faden, geographer to George III, gave a version of this map to Alexander Dalrymple, hydrographer to the East India Company, who referred to two versions of the map in a memoir explaining the construction of his "Map of the lands around the North Pole" (Dalrymple 1789a, pp. 4 and 8). In a rigorous attempt to assess the accuracy of latitudes and longitudes on various maps of the Canadian Arctic, Dalrymple made numerous detailed references to the "map of the Canadian traders," from which it is clear that it was a version of the "Hamilton" map (Dalrymple 1789a, pp. 5, 8, 10, and 12). Dalrymple could not have seen a copy of Pond's remarks (as indicated above, Hamilton may never have recorded them) because on "Map of the lands around the North Pole" (1789b, P,) he indicated part of Pond's eastern boundary of the Great Plains (fig. 4) but referred to it in the accompanying memoir as "a track" (1789a, pp. 11–12). The map containing this misrepresentation of part of the boundary was apparently the only published version of Pond's attempt at regionalization. To a casual user of the map it would have been visually recessive and meaningless, while to a careful reader of the accompanying memoir it would have been interpreted as a track. No one could possibly have appreciated its true significance, and on Dalrymple's map of the following year it did not even appear (Dalrymple 1790).

Other British cartographers would also seem to have seen versions of the "Hamilton" map. Aaron Arrowsmith's "Chart of the world . . .," as published in 1790, represented the area between Lakes Athabasca and Winnipeg in a manner very similar to Pond's (Arrowsmith 1790). In a memoir accompanying his "Map of the world . . ." of 1794, Arrowsmith acknowledged 632 maps presented to him by Dalrymple and referred to two manuscript maps showing the "Tracks and settlements of the Canadian Traders in the interior parts of the country" (Arrowsmith 1794a, pp. 19 and 21). There are slight indications on this map that Arrowsmith incorporated certain information from Pond, and "Great Plains" are indicated in the watershed area between the Missouri, Red, and Minnesota rivers (1794, P, b). However, although the 1796 edition of Arrowsmith's great map of North America (1796, P) showed the woods' edge to the east and west of the Red Deer (fig. 4) as described by Fidler and mapped by Turnor (1794, M), none of his maps ever portrayed Pond's boundary.

In discussing the conflicting evidence concerning the latitude of the coast to the north, John Meares also referred to charts "made by the Canadian traders." According to Meares, Pond placed the coast in 65°N and the Canadian traders in 68°30' (1790, p. xlix). The former latitude agrees with all the known Pond maps of 1785 and the latter with a later Pond map, of which there are two known versions signed by him, in July, 1787, and December 6 of the same year (Pond 1787a and b). However, the official copy which was sent to London on November 23, 1790, had not been received by January 4, 1791 (Dorchester 1790), and Meares must have used another version in writing his *Voyages . . .*, the preface of which is dated November 16, 1790. According to Meares, Pond's "account" (presumably a reference to the 1785 map) placing the shore in 65°N was "in everybody's hand" (1790, p. lxi). However, although Meares's own "A chart of the interior part of North America . . ." (1790, facing p. viii) has several features in common with the "Hamilton" map, neither he nor anyone else would appear to have published Pond's boundary of the "immense plains."

There would seem to be no doubt that between approximately 1786 and 1794 copies of Hamilton's version of Pond's map were in circulation in London. The surviving version contains a stippled line extending from a point immediately west of the Mississippi at 45°N to a point west of Lake Athabasca (Pond 1785, M, h). This coincides almost exactly with the line labeled "eastern Boundaries of those immense Plains" on the Crèvecoeur versions of the "Congress" map, except that on the latter

it extends some 4° farther north and 5° farther south (fig. 4). Unlike the "Congress" map, the "Hamilton" map does not place a legend on the line, but it does have a series of points located along it labeled A1–A13. This is one of seven systems of points (A, B, D, E, H, K, and L) embracing thirty-eight individual points presumably relating to the remarks which Hamilton intended to write. There is no evidence that Dalrymple, Arrowsmith, or Meares derived any information from these points, and from this it would seem that the version(s) of the map to which they had access either lacked them or did not have any accompanying notes. This would explain the complete failure of these cartographers to convey anything of Pond's apperceptive image of the Great Plains. However, this, or a very similar image, did appear in a somewhat distorted and diminished literary form in Alexander Mackenzie's *Voyages . . .*

Mackenzie's published journal terminates somewhat abruptly after the entry for August 24, 1793, and is followed by a "short geographical view of the country" to the north of 45°N (1801, p. 397). This contains several remarkably bold attempts at regionalization, some of which coincide with information on the "Hamilton" map. This is in no way surprising, as Mackenzie had spent some time with Pond at Athabasca in 1787, when both were members of the North West Company. During this period Pond is believed to have given Mackenzie a copy of his 1787 map (Pond 1787 a and b) to deliver to the empress of Russia when he reached that country (Wagner 1955, p. 17). Finally, as Arrowsmith is known to have had access to a manuscript copy of Mackenzie's journals at least seven years before they were published (Arrowsmith 1794a, p. 21), it is equally likely that Mackenzie knew of the two maps of the Canadian traders to which Arrowsmith referred. As indicated above, one of these was almost certainly the "Hamilton" map or a version thereof.

According to Mackenzie, the eastern edge of the "immense plains, or meadows" extended from "a point about the junction of the River of the Mountains with Mackenzie's

River ... widening East and South [to] the Red River at its confluence with the Assinboin River, from whence [it] takes a more Southern direction, along the Mississippi towards Mexico" (1801, P, p. 402) (fig. 2). The northern terminus of this boundary is not far from its position on the "Hamilton" map and its intersection with the Assinboin and Red Rivers at their confluence coincides exactly. Between the Rocky Mountains and the "immense plains" Mackenzie (1801, P, p. 402) described "a narrow strip of very marshy, boggy and uneven ground, the outer (eastern) edge of which produces coal and bitumen" stretching from the Mackenzie River in latitude 66°N southward as far as the South Saskatchewan. As evidence, Mackenzie cited his own observations and those of Fidler farther south; but in the Crèvecoeur notes to his copy of the "Congress" map, bitumen springs were referred to by Pond as close to the eastern boundary of the Plains (Pond 1785b, fol. 3). More significantly, the Plains boundary on the "Hamilton" map bifurcates in the watershed area between the Saskatchewan and Beaver river drainage. Although the western branch of the boundary extends south only as far as the North Saskatchewan, it is aligned with a series of four points (H1–H4), the line of which is parallel to the Rocky Mountains and extends as far south as the headwaters of the Rib (Souris?) River. Mackenzie was certainly describing what physiographers now recognize as the dissected lands of the Alberta-Missouri Plateau. It could well be that this image was in part received from Pond and that the latter attempted to incorporate it on the map and in the evidence he gave to Hamilton. Whether or not Mackenzie obtained the image from Pond, its presentation lacked impact and occupied less than a page towards the end of a more than four-hundred-page book and was not indicated on the accompanying map. As such, it represented the last weak expression of an image which through observation and communication with the Indians had taken shape in the minds of fur traders during the first three-quarters of the eighteenth century and attained its fullest graphical expression in Pond's maps of 1785 and 1787.

Summary and Conclusions

During the past two and a half centuries the cis–Rocky Mountain West has generated distinctive images in the minds of several groups of people: Amerindians; fur traders; explorers; the first permanent white settlers; scientists; native whites; and outsiders (Lewis 1966). Each group's image incorporated the distinctive elements of the environmental system as perceived by the more discerning members of the group.

The Amerindians' image would seem to have associated grass and a near absence of trees (the Muscuty Tuskee of the Crees) with a way of life which minimized the consequences of a distinctive set of environmental hazards and optimized the utilization of the buffalo. Because most of the Indians were migratory and also knew (or knew of) the adjacent forests or mountains, this was probably a fairly widely held image. However, it was predominantly an image of a landscape or set of landscape types. While many Indians knew the extent of the grasslands in a given direction and while some could delimit long stretches of the woods' edge, images of the grasslands as a circumscribed region would seem to have been weak.

Between approximately 1735 and 1785, the fur traders' images of the cis–Rocky Mountain West quickly passed through several developmental stages. The first instant images of landscapes that were markedly different from any of the better-known landscape types to the east and northeast were presented in terms of misleading analogs with landscapes in Europe. However, as a few traders obtained experience of various parts of the interior grasslands, they developed apperceptive images of larger areas. With the rapid growth in the demand for beaver there was a consequent increase in the number of traders and trappers and in the variety of interests involved in the trade. A few of the more perceptive traders developed a continental perspective which enabled them to develop the trade and compete with others in relation to the perceived location of the resource. Passively or actively, a few Canadian traders developed an apperceptive image of an area which they called the Great Plains and delimited as a region. For them, its distinctive landscapes were of negative significance in that they were the manifestations of an environmental system which, in relation to the forests to the east and north, supported relatively few beaver. For a decade or two after approximately 1770 this regional image would seem to have been part of a steering mechanism directing the search for furs around the northern edge of the grasslands.

The Canadian traders' image of a Great Plains region was not effectively communicated and was probably unknown to the American explorers of the cis–Rocky Mountain West in the first quarter of the nineteenth century. Not surprisingly, therefore, the Americans perceived similar landscapes in a different way and developed an apperceptive image to which they gave the name Great American Desert (Lewis 1965). Unlike the fur-traders' image of the Great Plains, this later image was widely publicized and developed into a powerful stereotype image which was not to disappear until after the Civil War.

That three quite different groups of people during the century and a half prior to permanent white settlement should have independently developed images of a distinctive set of environments, that at least two of these had a fairly clear idea of the geographical extent of these environments, and that each gave geographical names to the area characterized by them constitutes empirical evidence as to the reality of a distinctive natural region. Each group perceived certain characteristics of the environmental system which were of significance to them and associated these with the landscapes which were the manifestations of that system. However, these apperceptive images did not relate to areas which were congruous in extent. Neither were they dominant images: most who experienced the area had far clearer images of nodes (e. g., trading posts, fording places, and isolated buttes) and of networks (e. g., rivers, trails, and wagon roads). Indeed, probably only a small proportion of each group developed or shared images of the region. They had emerged somewhat passively in the consciousness of the more perceptive members of each group and were not, as Harvey would seem to assume, "the end-result of a whole chain of evaluative decisions" (1969, p. 271). They were first and foremost images and only secondarily concepts. However, as images which were subsequently promoted as stereotypes, they may subsequently have influenced the decisions of those nineteenth-century scientists who, in the course of "systematically" subdividing North America into "topical" regions, almost inevitably recognized a Great Plains region.

Acknowledgments

The author wishes to acknowledge financial support from the University of Sheffield through Research Fund Grants 859 and 987. He also wishes to thank the Hudson's Bay Company for permission to publish information from several documents in the company's archives and Mrs. J. Craig, the company's archivist, for invaluable help in tracing maps and other documents. Numerous other people gave assistance, but above all, the author wishes to record his indebtedness to his colleague, Miss J. Margaret Wilkes, for her diligence and intuition in tracing sources and for her candid criticism in commenting on the paper in its penultimate form.

BIBLIOGRAPHY

Citations in the text containing the letters P (published) or M (manuscript) refer to descriptions, epitomizations or delimitations indicated on figures 2, 3, or 4. However, they are not distinguished in this way in the following bibliography.

Arrowsmith, Aaron.
1790. *A chart of the world upon Mercator's projection, shewing all the new discoveries . . .* London: Aaron Arrowsmith.
1794*a*. *A companion to a map of the world.* London: George Biggs for the author.
1794*b*. *Map of the world on a globular projection, . . .* London: Aaron Arrowsmith.
1796. *A map exhibiting all the new discoveries in the interior part of North America . . . with additions to 1796.* London: Aaron Arrowsmith.
Auchagach, Tacchigic, La Marteblanche, et al.
1728–29. *Course des rivières, et fleuve, courant*

a l'ouest du nord du Lac Superieur . . . Paris. Dépôt des Cartes et Plans de la Marine. Service Hydrographique, Bibliothèque, 4044 B, no. 84. Reproduced in Warkentin and Ruggles, 1970, p. 73.

Aughey, Samuel.
1880. *Sketches of the physical geography and geology of Nebraska.* Omaha: Daily Republican Book and Job Office.

Barbié du Bocage, Jean D. 1786. Hemisphere occidental ou du Nouveau Monde public sons les auspices de Monseigneur Louis Philippe duc d'Orleans, Premier Prince du Sang par le Sr. D'Anville . . . revu et augmenté des nouvelles decouvertes en 1786 par M. Barbié du Bocage. Map no. 2 in Anville, Jean B. D. d', *Atlas General.* Paris, 1727–86.

Bourgmont, Etienne Veniard du.
1714. Exacte Description de la Louisiane. Paris. Archives Nationales, Colonies, C13, vol. 1, fol. 346–56. English translation edited by Marcel Giraud, *Bulletin of the Missouri Historical Society* 15 (1958): 8–19.

Carver, Jonathan.
1766–67. Journals of travels, and The same journal put by the author into a form which he intended for publication with several additions . . . London. British Museum Additional Manuscript 8950.
1778. *Travels through the interior parts of North America in the years 1766, 1767, and 1768.* London: Printed for the author. Contains a Plan of Captain Carver's travels in the interior parts of North America in 1766 and 1767.

Castel, Le Père Louis B.
c. 1750. A map of North America, in Papiers du Pere Castel sur le passage de la mer d'Ouest en Asie, avec des letters de Missionaires sur cet sujet. Paris. Bibliothèque National. Fonds Francais, 13, 373–1 and 2. Reproduced in Warkentin and Ruggles, 1970, p. 127.

Cocking, Matthew.
1773. Matthew Cocking's journal. In Lawrence J. Burpee, ed., *Proceedings and Transactions of the Royal Society of Canada* 2 (3rd series, 1908, sec. 2): 89–121.

Collot, George H. Victor.
1796/1826. Map of the Missouri; of the higher parts of the Mississippi; and of the elevated plain, where the waters divide, which run eastward into the River St. Lawrence; north east into Hudson's Bay; north north west into the Frozen Sea; and south into the Gulf of Mexico, in *Voyage dans l'Amérique Septentrionale* . . . Paris: A. Bertrand.

Dalrymple, Alexander.
1789*a.* *Memoir of a map of the lands around the North Pole.* London: George Bigg.
1789*b.* *Map of the lands around the North Pole by Dalrymple.* London: Alexander Dalrymple.
1790. *A map of Hudson's Bay and of the rivers and lakes between the Atlantick and Pacifick Oceans by Dalrymple 1790.* London: W. Harrison.

Diller, Aubrey.
1955. James Mackay's journey in Nebraska in 1796. *Nebraska History* 36: 123–28.

Dobbs, Arthur.
1744. *An account of the countries adjoining to Hudson's Bay in the north-west part of America* . . . London: J. Robinson.

Dorchester.
1790. Letter from Lord Dorchester, governor of Quebec, to Lord Grenville, secretary of state for the home department, Quebec, November 23, 1790. London. Public Record Office. C. O. 42/73. fol. 1–2.

Evans, John T.
1796–97. Mr. Evans' journal. From extracts published in Nasatir 1952, vol. 2, pp. 495–99.

Graham, Andrew.
1773. A plan of part of Hudson's Bay, and rivers, communicating with York Fort and Severn. London. Hudson's Bay Company Archives. G. 2/17. Transcript in Warkentin and Ruggles 1970, p. 95.
1791. Observations on Hudson's Bay. Twenty five years in the Company's service. Fifteen years as chief factor at Severn, York and Churchill settlements. Edited by Glyndwr Williams. *Publication of Hudson's Bay Record Society,* vol. 27. London, 1969.

Hamilton, Henry.
1785. Letter from Henry Hamilton, Lieutenant governor of Quebec, to Lord Sydney, secretary of state for the home department, Quebec, April 9, 1785. London. Public Record Office. C.O. 42/47. fol. 667–68.

Harmon, Daniel W.
1820. A specimen of the Cree or Knisteneux tongue. *A journal of voyages and travels . . . ,* pp. 385–403. Andover, Mass: Flagg and Gould.

Harvey, David.
1969. *Explanation in geography.* London: Edward Arnold.

Hearne, Samuel.
1772. A map of part of the inland country to the N. W. of Prince of Wales Fort. London. Hudson's Bay Company Archives. G. 2/10.

Henday, Anthony.
  1754–55. The journal of Anthony Henday copied in 1792 by Andrew Graham. London. Hudson's Bay Company Archives. E. 2/11. Published version edited by Lawrence J. Burpee, in *Proceedings and Transactions of the Royal Society of Canada* 1 (3rd series, 1907, sec. 2): 307–64.
Henry, Alexander, the Elder.
  1775. (Untitled pen-and-ink map of Lake Winnipeg and the lands to the north and west.) Ann Arbor. University of Michigan, William L. Clements Library. Manuscript map 147.
  1781. Letter written by Alexander Henry to Sir Joseph Banks, Montreal, October 18, 1781. London. British Museum of Natural History. Sir Joseph Banks' Correspondence, MS., vol. 2 (1781–83), pp. 39–51.
  1809. *Travels and adventures in Canada and the Indian territories between 1760 and 1776.* New York: I. Riley.
House of Commons.
  1803. *Reports from committees of the House of Commons.* Miscellaneous subjects for 1738–65, Vol. 2. London: Reprinted by order of the House.
Indian/Norton, Moses.
  1760. Moses Norton's drt. of the northern parts of Hudson's Bay laid down on ind'n information and brot home by him anno. 1760. London. Hudson's Bay Company Archives. G. 2/8.
Jung, Carl G.
  1924. *Psychological types or the psychology of individuation.* Translated by H. Godwin Baynes. London: Kegan Paul, French, Trubner, & Co.
Kelsey, Henry.
  1691. A journal of a voyage and journey undertaken by Henry Kellsey, to discover, and endeavour to bring to a commerce, the Naywatamee Poets. In *The Kelsey papers,* edited by Arthur G. Doughty and Chester B. Martin. Ottawa: Public Archives of Canada and Public Record Office of Northern Ireland, 1929. Two other versions of the journal were published in *Report from the committee of the House of Commons appointed to enquire into the state and condition of the countries adjoining to Hudson's Bay, and of the trade carried on there.* Reported by Lord Strange, April 24, 1749.
King's Map.
  c. 1760. Map of the northern parts of America. London. British Museum. Map Room, King's Collection cxix.
Ki Oo Cus/Fidler, Peter
  1802. (Untitled map of the upper Missouri and upper South Saskatchewan basins drawn by Peter Fidler from a draft by Ki Oo Cus), in Fidler's journal of exploration and survey, 1789–1804, vol. 2, pp. 206–7. London. Hudson's Bay Company Archives. E. 3/2.
Lewis, G. Malcolm.
  1965. Early American exploration and the cis-Rocky Mountain desert, 1803–1823. *Great Plains Journal* 5: 1–11.
  1966. Regional ideas and reality in the cis-Rocky Mountain West. *Transactions and Papers of the Institute of British Geographers* 38: 135–150.
Mackay, James.
  1797. (Untitled and undated pen and ink manuscript map, with French legends, embracing the territory from Lake Superior to the Pacific Ocean and between the 50th and 60th parallels of latitude.) Once thought to have been by John T. Evans (see Annie H. Abel, A new Lewis and Clark map, *Geographical Review* 1: 329–45, map facing p. 344.), this map has since been convincingly attributed to Mackay (see Aubrey Diller, Maps of the Missouri River before Lewis and Clark, in *Studies and essays in the history of science and learning offered in homage to George Sarton,* edited by Montagne F. A. Montagu [New York: Printed privately, 1946]).
  1807. Extracts from the manuscript journal of James M'Kay. *Medical Repository,* hexade 2, vol. 4, pp. 27–37. Reprinted in Nasatir 1952, vol. 2, pp. 490–99.
Mackenzie, Alexander.
  1801. *Voyages from Montreal, on the River St. Laurence through the continent of North America.* London and Edinburg: T. Cadell & W. Davies, Cobbett & Morgan, & W. Crouch.
Mallet, Pierre, and Mallet, Paul.
  1739. Journal. Paris. Archives Nationales. Colonies, C13, vol. 4, fol. 228–31. Translated in part by Henri Folmer in "The Mallet Expedition of 1739 through Nebraska, Kansas and Colorado to Santa Fé," *Colorado Magazine* 16 (1939): 161–73.
Meares, John.
  1790. A chart of the interior part of North America . . ., in *Voyages made in the years 1788 and 1789 from China to the north west coast of America* . . . London: Logographic Press.
Meatonabee and Idotly-Azee/Norton, Moses.
  1765–69. Draught brought by two northern Indian leaders call'd Meatonabee and Idotly-Azee of ye country to ye northward of Churchill river viz. Hudson's Bay. London. Hudson's Bay Company Archives. G. 2/27.
Mitchell, John.
  1755. *A map of the British and French domin-*

ions in North America . . . London: Published by the author.

Nasatir, Abraham P.
1952. *Before Lewis and Clark: Documents illustrating the history of the Missouri, 1785–1804.* 2 vols. St. Louis: St. Louis Historical Documents Foundation.

Perrin du Lac, Francois.
1805. Carte du Missouri Levée ou rectifee dans tout son etendue, in *Voyage dans les deux Louisianes, et chez les nations sauvages du Missouri, par les États-Unis, l'Ohio et les provinces qui le bordent en 1801, 1802, et 1803* . . . Paris: Capelle et Renaud. Map reproduced in Wheat 1957, vol. 1, facing p. 160.

Pond, Peter.
1785*a*. Copy of a map presented to the Congres by Peter Pond a native of Milford in the State of Connecticut. London. British Museum Additional Manuscript 15,332 c (rough version, probably traced by Crèvecoeur) and 15,332 d (neat version, redrawn by J. D. Barbié du Bocage).
1785*b*. Amerique Septentrionale. Remarques sur la carte presentée au Congrés le ler Mars 1785. London. British Museum. Additional Manuscript 15,332 e. Published as Appendix B in Gordon C. Davidson, *The North West Company.* University of California Publication in History, no. 12. Berkeley, 1918. These Remarques were almost certainly sent by Crèvecoeur to Louise Alexandre duc de la Roche Guyon et de La Rochefoucauld d' Anville to accompany the map referred to in the letter of March 17, 1785, from Crèvecoeur to Castries (Paris, Archives des Affaires Étrangères, Correspondance des Consuls, Etat Unis, New York, vol. 1, carton number 2532, folios 47–51).
1785*c*. Copy of a map presented to the Congres by Peter Pond of Milford, in the State of Connecticut. Paris. Bibliothèque du Service Hydrographique de la Marine. MS. 4044-B, no. 30. Reproduced in Wagner 1955, map 1.
1785*d*. Partie nord de l'Amerique Septrentrionale appelie depuis Nouvelle Bretagne. Paris. Ministère des Affaires Étrangères. Service Géographique, no. 7430. Reproduced as F 29-1-1 in Louis C. Karpinski, *Maps of the United States in the Principal European Archives* (Ann Arbor, 1930).
1785*e*. To the Honorable Henry Hamilton Esq. Lieutenant Governor and Commander in Chief in and over the Province of Quebec and frontiers thereof in America. . . . The memoir of Peter Pond on behalf of the North West Company in which he is a partner. Quebec, April 18, 1785.

London. Public Record Office. C.O. 42/47, fols. 649–51.
1785*f*. Letter from Crèvecoeur, French Consul in New York, to the Marquis de Castries, Minister of Marine, March 17, 1785, referring to a map of the far Northwest of which he had forwarded a copy to Louise Alexandre duc de la Roche Guyon et de La Rochefoucauld d'Anville. Paris. Archives des Affaires Étrangères. Correspondence des Consuls, Ètat Unis, New York, vol. 1, carton no. 2,532, fols. 47–51.
1785*g*. References to Peter Pond's map, accompanying dispatch no. 424 from M. de Marbois, New York, May 16, 1785. Paris. Ministère des Affaires Etrangères. Service Géographique, no. 7430.
1785*h*. (Map without title of the region from Hudson Bay to the Pacific Ocean and from Lake Michigan to the Arctic Ocean.) London. Public Record Office. MPG. 425.
1787*a*. (An untitled map copied from an original by Peter Pond dated Araubascha, July 1787.) Ottawa. Public Archives of Canada. National Map Collection, V2/700—1787.
1787*b*. (An untitled map, generally known as "the tin-case map" copied from an original by Peter Pond dated Araubaska, December 6, 1787.) London. Public Record Office. C.O. 700. America N. & S. 49.
Post 1800. (Untitled manuscript journal of Peter Pond's activities before 1775.) New Haven. Yale University Library. Published in 1906 in *Connecticut Magazine* 10: 239–59.

Richardson, A. J. H.
c. 1953. Peter Pond's maps, an undated letter from Richardson, head of the Map Division of the Public Archives of Canada, to Henry R. Wagner. Berkeley. Bancroft Library. MS. C—B 849, carton 5, in folder labeled "Notes from other sources concerning Peter Pond, Northwest Passage etc."

Service Hydrographique.
c. 1802. Carte du Mississippi et des ses embranchemens. Paris. Bureau du Service Hydrographique. C-4044. Reproduced in Wheat, 1957, vol. 1, facing p. 164.

Turnor, Philip
c. 1788. Chart of lakes and rivers in North America by Philip Turnor, those shaded are from actual surveys and others from Canadian and Indian information. London. Hudson's Bay Company Archives. G.2/13. This map was reproduced without acknowledgement in Joseph B. Tyrell, ed., *Journals of Samuel Hearne and Philip*

Turnor, Publication of the Champlain Society, vol. 21, Toronto, 1934 (folded in pocket).

1794. To the Honourable the Governor, Deputy Governor, and Committee of the Hudson's Bay Company this map of Hudson's Bay and the rivers and lakes between the Atlantick and Pacifick Oceans is most humbly inscribed by their most obedient and dutiful servant Philip Turnor. London. Hudson's Bay Company Archives. G.2/32.

Umfreville, Edward.
1790. *The present state of Hudson's Bay containing a full description of the settlement and the adjacent country; and likewise of the fur trade.* London: Charles Walker.

La Vérendrye Expedition.
1737. Carte contenante les nouvelles découvertes de L' ouest en Canada, mers, rivières, lacs, etc nations qui y habittent en l'anneé 1737. . . . Quebec. Seminary. Original manuscript. Reproduced in Warkentin and Ruggles 1970, p. 81.

1740. Carte contenant les nouvelle dé couvertes de l'ouest en Canada, lac rivieres et nations qui y habittent en l'anneé 1740. Paris. Dépôt des Cartes et Plans de la Marine. Service Hydrographique, Bibliothèque. 4044B, piece no. 23. Reproduced in Warkentin and Ruggles, 1970, p. 83.

Vial, Pedro.
1793. Diary. Mexico City. Archivo Generaly Público de la Nación. Provincias Internas, vol. 102, no. 2, fols. 214–24. This version of the diary of Vial's journey from Santa Fé to Saint Louis and return is translated in Noel M. Loomis and Abraham P. Nasatir, *Pedro Vial and the roads to Santa Fé.* Norman: University of Oklahoma Press, 1967, pp. 372–80 and 397–405.

Wagner, Henry R.
1955. *Peter Pond: Fur trader and explorer.* Yale University Library Western Historical Series, no. 2. New Haven, Conn.

Warkentin, John, and Ruggles, Richard I.
1970. *Historical Atlas of Manitoba: A selection of facsimile maps, plans and sketches from 1612 to 1969.* Winnipeg: Historical & Scientific Society of Manitoba.

Wheat, Carl I.
1957. *Mapping the transmississippi West, 1540–1861.* Vol. 1. *The Spanish entrada to the Louisiana Purchase, 1540–1804.* San Francisco: Institute of Historical Cartography.

Images of the Northern Great Plains
from the Fur Trade, 1807–43

David J. Wishart
Beloit College, Wisconsin

It would surprise most persons to realize how quickly a neglected core of fact gathers the mold of myth.
                                   Coues, in Larpenteur 1898, xvi

Despite the penetration of even the most inaccessible areas of the Great Plains by trappers and traders in the first four decades of the nineteenth century, the area remained to all but these privileged few unknown except in the framework of publicized images. Such regional images are founded upon patterns of belief about the nature and content of the land which may be far removed from geographic reality (Wright 1947). The *nature* of an area may be understood to represent the physical framework of climate, physiography, and vegetation, and its *content* includes the indigenous population, the animal life and appraisals of the resource base (Allen 1972). In the annals of the fur trade there are innumerable (but scattered) references to the nature and content of the northern Great Plains, and such favorite topics as the apparent flatness of the plains, the impression of aridity (especially on the western margins), the lack of trees, the large herds of buffalo, and the dubious prospects of the area for permanent settlement seem to have played a major role in the formation of its regional image during the period of the fur trade (1807 to 1843).

This was an extensive stage of occupance, spreading a thin veneer over the northern Great Plains and only in the vicinity of the trading posts creating a distinctive cultural landscape. It was an intermediate stage in the formation of the regional images of the northern Great Plains. The trappers and traders often adopted and elaborated the impressions of the explorers Lewis and Clark, Pike, and Long, who had made intermittent contact with the Great Plains in the first two decades of the nineteenth century. These images were only dispelled in the era of permanent settlement after 1854. It is impossible to ascertain the regional images that were held by the common trapper and trader. It is estimated that one thousand men sought a living in the fur trade on the upper Missouri in the 1820s (*Missouri Intelligencer,* September 17, 1822). In addition, some six hundred trappers were employed in the Rocky Mountains in the halcyon years of the early 1830s (Missouri Historical Society [3b]; Russell 1965, p. 3). Yet very few of these men recorded their impressions, and those who did aspire to publication were the literary cream of the fur trade and probably unrepresentative of the whole.

The sources of information must, therefore, be approached with caution. Fur trappers such as William H. Ashley and travelers with the fur trade such as William Marshall Anderson and Prince Maximilian left valuable diaries recorded in the field (Missouri Historical Society [1]; Anderson 1967; Maximilian 1905). Their regional images, however, were often based on preconceived notions formed when they read the account of Stephen Long's expedition or possibly the narratives of Washington Irving (James 1822–23; Irving 1886, 1909). Even the Missouri newspapers which publicized the information of the geography of the Great Plains relied on information from the gentlemen of the fur trade (William Ashley was a particularly prolific contributor) and so perpetuated elitist images. It was only after retirement from the field that trappers from the rank and file published their narratives, which then suffered from factual inaccuracies and again incorporated the prevailing regional images. One final reservation needs to be stressed. Often the regional images were actually impressions of a traverse across the plains (such as the Platte and Missouri routeways) which were expanded to categorize the whole. Consequently, these regional images emerging from the fur trade contained a high level of subjectivity resulting from the intellectual and environmental backgrounds of the observers and from the locational aspects of the fur trade.

With these reservations in mind it is possible to discern a number of regional images of the northern Great Plains that were projected from the fur trade. Four evolving images of the nature and content of this area may be gleaned from the trappers' diaries, the trading post journals, the newspaper accounts of the fur trade, and the narratives of the trappers. The plains are represented variously as a wilderness unsuitable for permanent settlement, a "land to cross" in order to reach more promising pastures, a potential grazing region, and, in a limited sense, an agricultural region.

The physical setting is that portion of the Great Plains bounded on the south by the Platte River, on the east and north by the Missouri River and its tributaries, and on the west by the Rocky Mountains. This area and the adjacent Rocky Mountains formed the hinterland of Saint Louis when the fur trade was at a zenith, and from 1807 to 1843 the fur trapper or trader was its sole white occupant.

The trade was organized as two subsystems, both aligned to Saint Louis, but each with its own form of spatial organization. In the

mountains the fur trade developed in the early 1820s with beaver the most important fur-bearing animal and the "rendezvous" as the focal point of organization. The system on the Missouri River was operated through trading posts and depended to a great extent on buffalo robes traded from Indians and moved by water to Saint Louis. In the initial stage of activity (following the return of Lewis and Clark with news of abundant fur resources and trading Indians) the economic sphere of Saint Louis reached to the lower Platte River; trade was conducted with the Pawnee, Omaha, and Otoe Indians through a post at the Council Bluffs, and occasional traders would venture farther upstream to do business with the Sioux (fig. 1). Farther up the Missouri River the Mandan Indians had previous trade connections with the North West Company, but the total number of American traders on the river at this early period (1807–1808) did not exceed fifty men (Missouri Historical Society [4c]). Little was being added to the existing geographic knowledge that had stemmed from the Lewis and Clark expedition (Allen 1972).

A massive expansion of operations and associated geographic knowledge came with the Manuel Lisa's Missouri Fur Company, formed in 1808 with 150 men. According to Thomas Biddle, an authority on the fur trade, Lisa's objectives were to monopolize the trade of the lower Missouri from a post at the Council Bluffs and to send a large party to trap the fabled riches of Blackfoot and Crow country at the headwaters of the Missouri and Yellowstone rivers (Missouri Historical Society [4a]). Trading posts were subsequently established at the junction of the Yellowstone and Bighorn rivers (Fort Raymond) and at the Three Forks of the Missouri in an attempt to divert the Blackfoot trade from the Hudson's Bay Company (fig. 2). The trappers scoured the land from these posts eastward to the Tongue River, westward to the mountains, and as far south as the Wind River. They may even have passed through South Pass, but very little information of this area was transmitted to the public. George Drouillard left two extremely valuable maps of Yellowstone country which demonstrate an accurate grasp of its geography, but for the most part the information was retained by the trappers (Wheat 1957–63, vol. 2, p. 52). Continual harassment from the Blackfoot Indians and the disruption of trading conditions on the upper Missouri caused by the conflict with Great Britain resulted in a withdrawal of trading operations to the accessible reaches of the lower river. Biddle was of the opinion that the fur trade from 1812 to 1819 was "of little importance from a pecuniary point of view" (Missouri Historical Society [4a]).

It was only after 1819 with the restoration of settled conditions and a speculative boom in Saint Louis that the fur trade expanded its operations to cover the entire northern Great Plains (fig. 3). Trading posts proliferated on the Missouri River system, first under the control of the Columbia Fur Company with its major depot at Fort Tecumseh, and then, after 1827, under the virtual monopoly of the Upper Missouri Outfit of the American Fur Company. The "Company" established its central depots, Forts Pierre and Union, at the two most strategic locations on the Missouri River, and regional posts such as Forts Cass, Clark, and Mackenzie were founded to serve the trading Indians. Lower down the hierarchy were numerous seasonal trading posts, or often a trader would simply accompany the Indians on the forays for buffalo robes. There is no doubt that the entire diverse area of the central and northern plains become familiar to the traders in the following two decades, but for the most part their knowledge did not find its way to the American public. Some information was passed along indirectly, and later, through the narratives and letters of travelers like Maximilian and Audubon (Maximilian 1905; Audubon 1965).

Most of the knowledge about the Great Plains from 1820 to 1840 resulted from the development of the Platte overland route to the mountains. William H. Ashley pioneered this arterial and engineered the trapping system in the mountains in 1823–24, and in following years the annual trade caravans (of fifty to one hundred men) made the journey to the rendezvous. The result was a proliferation of observations in newspapers and journals of this one rather atypical swath across the plains. It was natural for the travelers to project their impressions of the Platte valley to cover the unseen portions of the Great Plains. This, of course, remains the case today. Occasionally other routes were used to and from the mountains (for example, the Bighorn River), but large areas of the plains such as the Sandhills saw little traffic and earned even less renown.

The travelers' favorable impressions of the Great Plains declined in proportion to distance traveled westward along the Platte River or northward up the Missouri River as the familiar landscape of the Midwest gave way to the increasing aridity of the plains. Maximilian, a traveler with the fur traders on the steamboat *Yellowstone* in 1833, used the fashionable comparison with the deserts of Africa and wrote that "Savannahs or grassy plains" aptly described the country of the lower Missouri but not "the dry sterile tracts of the northwest" in the vicinity of Fort Union (Maximilian 1905, vol. 1, p. 266). Maximilian's journals were not translated into English until 1843, and even then they probably only spread the desert image among the educated elite (as did Long's observations two decades before). However, a letter by Audubon (who traveled up the Missouri River in 1843) found its way into the Saint Louis newspapers, indicating that the desert image was getting some publicity. With his steamboat grounded on a sandbar below Fort Pierre, Audubon wrote, "The prairies around us are the most arid and dismal you can conceive of. In fact, these prairies (so called) look more like great deserts. Notwithstanding you seldom look upon them without seeing multitudes of buffaloes" (*Missouri Republican*, July 14, 1843). Obviously these travelers had preconceived notions of the geography of the Great Plains, but equally valid is the fact that they were extracting many of their ideas from conversations with the fur traders. Audubon's statement also exhibits the dual image of the plains as a wasteland and as a pastoral region, supporting vast herds of buffalo.

In a similar manner the easterly portions of the overland route to the mountains evoked a

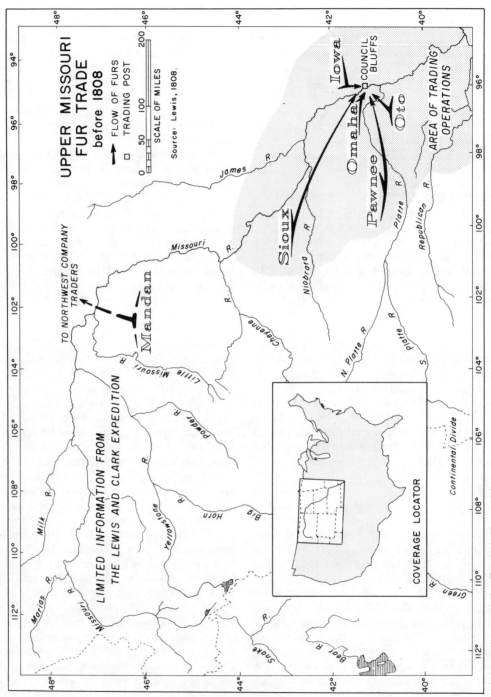

Figure 1 Upper Missouri Fur Trade before 1808

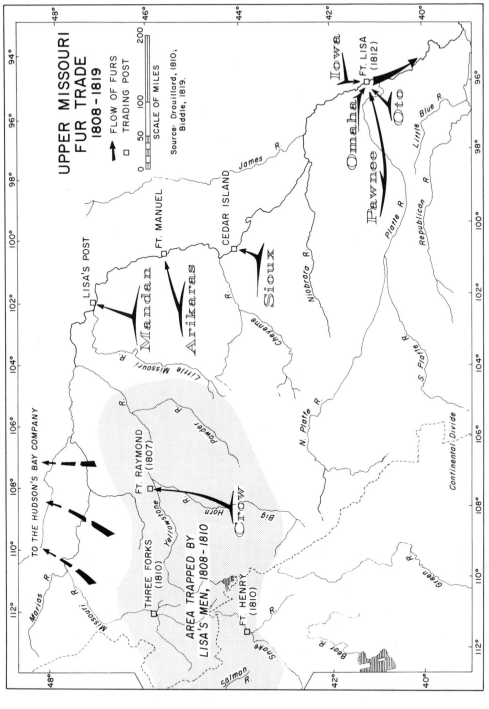

Figure 2 Upper Missouri Fur Trade, 1808–19

very favorable response from the trappers and travelers. Osborne Russell, for example, traveling westward with Nathaniel Wyeth's party in 1834, recalled "beautiful verdant and widely extended prairie" on the route up the Platte to the Grand Island (Russell 1965, p. 2). In similar vein, William Marshall Anderson who accompanied William L. Sublette's party to the 1833 rendezvous, frequently recorded in his diary "beautiful and fertile pastures" along the Big Blue River (Anderson 1967, p. 78). It is significant not only that a familiar type of landscape was breeding a favorable response but that the travelers were fresh on the trail and had not yet encountered the monotony and hardships to come. Moreover, the overland journeys commenced in early summer when the grasslands were at their aesthetic best. By the time the caravans reached the western plains (in July and August) the vegetative growth cycle had ceased and a picture of severe aridity was presented.

It was in the vicinity of the Grand Island that the impressions of the plains became less favorable. Indeed, with reference to Walter Prescott Webb's renowned cultural break at the 98th meridian, this area may be termed a "perceptual faultline" (Webb 1931). Anderson lamented the flatness of the land and the absence of trees, "save here and there a cottonwood near the banks or some wood in the Platte (to a forest-born Kentuckian they are scarcely more entitled to the name of trees than a hemp stalk)" (Anderson 1967, p. 111). On the north fork of the Platte the favorable term *Prairies* gave way to what the trapper Zenas Leonard described as "sand plains where there was scarcely a spear of grass to be seen" (Leonard 1959, p. 7). Both Stephen Long and Washington Irving had told the public to expect "the great steppes of Asia" and this area seemed to fit the role of the Great American Desert admirably. Moreover, at this stage of the journey the trappers were anticipating the profits to be made in the mountains, and in this respect the plains seemed to be a "fur desert."

Because of the monotony of this plains traverse, certain landmarks gained much more distinction in the trappers' journals than they

merited. Just as our mental maps of today's cities are orientated by prominent landscape features, so outstanding topographical features along the Platte route—the Grand Island, Chimney Rock, Red Buttes—were emphasized in the trappers' journals, while the remainder of the route (and, by inference, all the Great Plains) was dismissed as flat, monotonous, treeless, and unhabitable. These biased accounts of the geography of the plains were transmitted to the local press in many instances. Warren Ferris's "Life in the Rocky Mountains" was serialized in Buffalo's *Western Literary Messenger* from 1842 to 1844; Zenas Leonard's "Narrative" was published in Pennsylvania's *Clearfield Republican* in 1838; and William Marshall Anderson aired his views of "Scenes in the West" in the *American Turf Register* in 1837 (Ferris 1940, p. xix; Leonard 1959, p. xxi; Anderson 1967, pp. 237–45).

It is apparent that the trappers who left literary records thought that the plains were indeed uninhabitable for any permanent purpose. William H. Ashley (who shows in his diary that he had read the account of Long's expedition) wrote from the Green River in the winter of 1824–25 that "from this place to Plumb Point [Lexington] on the River Platt the proportion of [potential] arable land . . . is so inconsiderable, that the whole country may be considered of no value for the purpose of agriculture" (Missouri Historical Society [1]). This desert image persisted in the trappers' accounts. Rufus Sage, an extremely perceptive observer and writer, traveled westward with Lancaster Lupton's party in 1841 and concluded, "That this section of the country should ever become inhabited by civilized man, except in the vicinity of large water courses is an idea too preposterous to be entertained for a single moment" (Sage 1956, pp. 160–62). Sage's narrative was first published in 1846 and his ideas (and map) owe much to the accounts of the Long and Fremont expeditions. This is particularly evident when Sage theorized that the plains grassland was a subclimax vegetation caused by natural fires and burning by the Indians. Ezekial Williams is also credited with similar insight into the

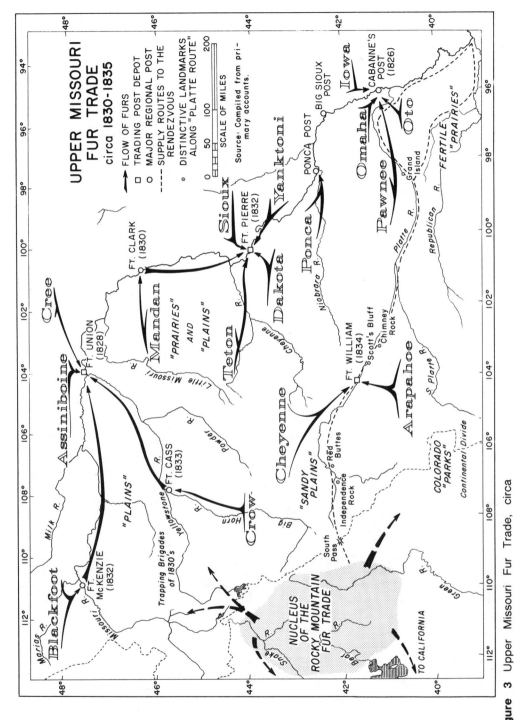

Figure 3 Upper Missouri Fur Trade, circa 1830–35

origin of the plains grassland, although Coyner's biography of this trapper is something less than gospel truth. Williams observed, "The opinion generally entertained by those persons who reside in the great prairies of the West is that they are formed by the fires by which they are overrun each autumn. . . . In all low places, such as ravines, hollows and river bottoms and small valleys, where the dampness of the soil and vegetation is such as to check the progress of the great fires, there and only there is timber to be found" (Williams 1969, pp. 56–57). This theory had received attention in the 1820s further eastward in Illinois and it was natural for the trappers to reveal it as an original explanation of the plains vegetation (Brown 1948, pp. 210–11). It is interesting to note, however, that all the journals of the trading posts record the frequency of prairie fires most often started by Indians for the purpose of military strategy.

It has been suggested that the Missouri newspapers did not adhere to the stereotyped desert image of the plains, but rather they depicted a more realistic, diverse portrait based on feedback from the trappers (Bowden 1969, p. 19; DeVoto 1947, p. 3). This does not seem to have been the case. In the Missouri newspapers the Great Plains became a "region to cross," a natural routeway to the mountains and the Pacific Northwest. The journeys of William H. Ashley evoked great attention from the Missouri press. The Platte route was publicized as "so broad and easy a way that thousands may travel it in safety" (*St. Louis Enquirer*, March 11, 1826). Following Ashley's triumphant return from the mountains in October, 1826 (with 123 packs of beaver), the newspapers again promoted the idealistic view of the Platte routeway: "It has proved that overland expeditions in large bodies may be made to that remote region without the necessity of transporting provisions for man or beast. . . . The animals keeping their strength and flesh on the grass they found . . . , buffalo furnished the principal food. . . . Water of the best quality was met with every day" (*Missouri Herald and St. Louis Advertiser*, November 8, 1826). So the image was cast of a level and open routeway, "better for carriages than any

turnpike road in the United States" (ibid.). This was indeed an erroneous representation of the ease of transportation of the Platte route, and when Captain Bonneville did take the first wagons to the 1832 rendezvous he encountered severe problems on the north fork of the Platte (Missouri Historical Society [3a]).

At the same time the Missouri newspapers were doing nothing to dispel the desert image of the plains. The same issue of the *St. Louis Enquirer* noted above observed that "The sterility of the country generally is almost incredible . . . and no district of the country visited by General Ashley, or of which he obtained satisfactory information, offers inducements to civilized people sufficient to justify the expectation of permanent settlement." A more thorough examination of the Missouri newspapers would be necessary to prove the point conclusively, but from a limited survey it does not seem that they were publicizing accurate, detailed knowledge of the geography of the Great Plains.

Many of the trappers were struck by the potential of the plains as a grazing region, although none took the observation to its logical conclusion and suggested its suitability for cattle. The animal ecology of the Great Plains was perhaps its most widely publicized characteristic. For example, Anderson's *National Turf Register* articles took as their subject the animals of the "boundless prairie" (Anderson 1967, pp. 237–45). He had observed "tens of thousands" of buffalo near the forks of the Platte in 1834 and was "confident that providence has provided pasturage for them even if they were tenfold increased" (ibid., p. 94). Jedediah Smith, on his way to the Yellowstone in 1822, saw "ten thousands of Buffalo that seemed sufficiently numerous to eat everything like vegetation from the face of the earth in a single week," but as an afterthought he appreciated how the "rich, undulating prairie" could support such herds (Morgan 1964*b*, p. 14).

The trappers were certain that by 1830 the buffalo, like the beaver, were diminishing rapidly. Anderson summarized the situation in 1834: "Conversation was had upon the subject of the diminution of the buffalo which several of the oldest mountaineers pronounced to be very considerable. This led to an enquiry as to the number of robes traded of the Indian Tribes by the American Fur Company, which seems to be enormous. Mr. Fontenelle, lately of said company, told me that three years ago there was traded from the Sioux fifty thousand robes" (Anderson 1967, p. 178). Even at this early date a vacuum was being created for grazing animals on the northern plains and it is possible that some of the roots of the pastoral image of the Great Plains were to be found in the statements of the fur trappers. It was, however, only after 1850 with the writing of William Gilpen that the practicability of the pastoral image became apparent.

The Missouri River trading posts were also filters of information about the Great Plains. The traders' journals describe an extremely harsh environment where problems of food supply and the difficulties of operating an economic system dependent on tenuous transportation lines and the whims of the trading Indians were the dominant issues. It is not surprising, therefore, that the impressions of the plains that emerge from the journals are very unfavorable.

Every winter brought the threat of famine. Francis Chardon at Fort Clark recorded his annual complaint in January of 1836, lamenting that "our prospect for winter is now gloomy in the extreme. I have concluded to send all my horses and hunters to make a living in the Prairies—or starve as fate may direct" (Chardon, 1932, p. 54). Even in the summer of 1833 William Laidlaw was faced with food shortage at Fort Pierre because "there are no buffaloes nearer than 5 or 11 days maybe and owing to the scarcity of meat nearby all our provisions of flour and pork has been consumed" (Missouri Historical Society [2]). Mostly it was the same loneliness that brought despair to the plains settlers a half century later that caused the traders to malign the northern plains. Chardon frequently referred to his harsh state of existence, and especially toward the end of the long winter he became "extremely lonesome and low spirited gazing around on this dreary savage waste" (Chardon, 1932, p. 58). These views were transmit-

ted in letters and also in conversations with Missouri River travelers (such as Maximilian and Audubon), so they were by no means limited to the company records.

Yet equally apparent to the travelers was the fact that the fur traders were managing to cultivate the land around the posts to a limited degree. There was no question of agricultural self-sufficiency on the upper Missouri (such as that achieved by the Hudson's Bay Company in the Pacific Northwest), but with their cornfields, vegetable gardens, and livestock the trading posts advertised the possibility of a later agricultural development. The problems of agriculture in an area of periodic drought and a short growing season were quickly encountered, particularly at the posts above Fort Pierre. In 1823 Major Henry experimented with corn at the mouth of the Yellowstone, "but the ground was so dry it did not even swell or rot" (Missouri Historical Society [4b]). At Fort Union it was found that oats, corn, potatoes, and most garden vegetables would grow well in favorable seasons, but because of grasshoppers and drought only one good year from every three could be expected (Denig 1961, p. 68). At the nearby opposition post, Fort William, Robert Campbell concluded that there was not sufficient moisture to raise vegetables and grass (Campbell 1963–64, p. 213). Lower down the river at Forts Clark and Pierre and particularly at the Council Bluffs post a very successful agricultural system based on garden vegetables, corn, and livestock was operated. It is probable that these initial enterprises (along with farming by the Indians and cultivation at the military posts) served to demonstrate the potential of the eastern Great Plains for agriculture.

There were, therefore, a number of images of the geography of the Great Plains emerging from the fur trade. Only a minority of the trappers and traders expressed their views in print, and mostly they were incorporating preconceived notions into their descriptions. Despite the intricate practical knowledge of the West that the fur traders and trappers developed in the pursuance of their occupation, it is apparent that Goetzmann was correct in deemphasizing their role in spreading geographical knowledge (Goetzmann 1959, passim). The Great American Desert image was strengthened in the fur trade records if not in name then by inference and reference to treelessness and desolation. The Missouri newspapers further publicized this image and gave a great deal of attention to the Great Plains as a transit region. It seems, however, that the fur traders realized the potential of the "prairies" for grazing, and by their attempts at cultivation they were illustrating the possibilities of future agriculture on the eastern margins of the plains. In 1840 the Great Plains was predominately a region to cross and in which a permanent settlement was not likely, but the seeds of new appraisals of the land were sown and later stages of occupancy would prove their worth.

REFERENCES CITED

ARCHIVAL SOURCES

Missouri Historical Society, Saint Louis.
(1)   William H. Ashley Papers, including diary, 1823–24.
(2)   Chouteau Collection. Letter from William Laidlaw to Pierre Chouteau, Jr., n.d. Fort Pierre Letterbook.
(3)   Fur Trade Envelope.
       (a) Official Report of Captain Benjamin L. Bonneville, 1833–35.
       (b) Letter from William Gordon to Lewis Cass, Secretary of War, October 8, 1831.
(4)   Indian Trade Papers.
       (a) Letter from Thomas Biddle to Col. Henry Atkinson, Camp Missouri on the Missouri River, 1819.
       (b) Letter from H. Leavenworth to Maj. Gen. A. McComb, December 20, 1823.
       (c) Licenses granted to Meriwether Lewis to trade and hunt with the Indians from April 1 to September 30, 1808.

NEWSPAPERS

Missouri Herald and St. Louis Advertiser. November 8, 1826.
Missouri Intelligencer (Saint Louis). September 17, 1822.
Missouri Republican (Saint Louis). July 14, 1843.
St. Louis Enquirer. March 11, 1826.

BOOKS AND ARTICLES

Allen, John L.
1972. An analysis of the exploratory process: The Lewis and Clark Expedition of 1804–1806. *Geographical Review* 62: 13–39.
Anderson, William M.
1967. *The Rocky Mountain Journals of William Marshall Anderson: The West in 1834.* Edited by Dale L. Morgan and Eleanor T. Harris. San Marino, Calif.: Huntington Library.
Audubon, John J.
1965. *Audubon in the West.* Edited by John F. McDermott. Norman: University of Oklahoma Press.
Bowden, Martyn J.
1969. The perception of the western interior of the United States, 1800–1870: A problem in historical geosophy. *Proceedings of the Association of American Geographers* 1: 16–21.
Brown, Ralph H.
1948. *Historical geography of the United States.* New York: Harcourt, Brace & World.
Campbell, Robert.
1963–64. The private journal of Robert Campbell. Edited by George R. Brooks. *Bulletin of the Missouri Historical Society* 20: 3–24, 107–18.
Chardon, Francis A.
1932. *Chardon's journal at Fort Clark, 1834–1839.* Edited by Ann H. Abel. Pierre, S. Dak.: n.p.
Denig, Edwin T.
1961. *Five Indian tribes of the upper Missouri* ... Edited by John C. Ewers. Norman: University of Oklahoma Press.
DeVoto, Bernard.
1947. *Across the wide Missouri.* Boston: Houghton Mifflin Co.
Ferris, Warren A.
1940. *Life in the Rocky Mountains* ... Edited by Paul C. Phillips. Denver: Old West Publishing Co.
Geotzmann, William H.
1959. *Army exploration in the American West, 1803–1863.* New Haven: Yale University Press.
Irving, Washington.
1886. *The adventures of Captain Bonneville.* New York: John B. Alden. First published Philadelphia, 1837.
1909. *Astoria.* New York: Century Co. First published Philadelphia, 1836.
James, Edwin.
1822–23. *Account of an expedition from Pittsburgh to the Rocky Mountains, performed in the years 1819 and '20 ... under the command of Stephen H. Long.* Philadelphia: n.p.

Larpenteur, Charles.
 1898.   *Forty years a fur trader on the upper Missouri . . . 1833–1872.* Edited by Elliot Coues. 2 vols. New York: Francis P. Harper.
Leonard, Zenas.
 1959.   *Adventures of Zenas Leonard, fur trader.* Edited by John C. Ewers. Norman: University of Oklahoma Press. First published in 1839.
Lewis, G. Malcolm.
 1966.   William Gilpen and the concept of the Great Plains region. *Annals of the Association of American Geographers* 56: 31–51.
Maximilian, Prince of Wied-Neuwied.
 1905.   *Travels in the interior of North America, 1832–1834.* Edited by Reuben G. Thwaites. 3 vols. Cleveland: Arthur H. Clark Co. First published London, 1843.
Morgan, Dale L.
 1964*a*.   *Jedediah Smith and the opening of the West.* Lincoln: University of Nebraska Press.
Morgan, Dale L., ed.
 1964*b*.   *The West of William Ashley, 1822–1838.* Denver: Old West Printing Co.
Russell, Osborne.
 1965.   *Journal of a trapper . . . 1834–1843.* Lin-

coln: University of Nebraska Press. Edited by Aubrey L. Haines. First published in the 1840s.
Sage, Rufus B.
 1956.   *Scenes in the Rocky Mountains . . . 1836–1837.* Edited by LeRoy R. Hafen and Ann W. Hafen. 2 vols. Glendale, Calif.: Arthur H. Clark Co. First published Philadelphia, 1846.
Webb, Walter P.
 1931.   *The Great Plains.* Boston: Ginn and Co.
Wheat, Carl I.
 1957–63.   *Mapping the transmississippi West, 1540–1861.* 5 vols. San Francisco: Institute of Historical Cartography.
Williams, Ezekial.
 1969.   *The lost trappers: A collection of interesting scenes and events in the Rocky Mountains.* Edited by David H. Coyner. Glorietta, N. Mex.: Rio Grande Press. First published Cincinnati, 1847.
Wright, John K.
 1947.   Terrae incognitae: The place of imagination in geography. *Annals of the Association of American Geographers* 37: 1–15.

PART 3
Government Appraisers on the Western Frontier

The Role of the United States Topographical Engineers in Compiling a Cartographic Image of the Plains Region

Herman R. Friis

The National Archives, Washington, D.C.

The initial official predecessor of the Topographical Bureau was the office of the geographer of the roads and surveyor general of the Continental army, established in July, 1777, in the headquarters of General George Washington (Heusser 1966). Some 150 maps were prepared under Robert Erskine and his successor Simeon DeWitt and their staff during the Revolutionary War (fig. 1). With the end of hostilities in 1783 and the nearly complete dissolution of the army, employment of the small body of "geographers" attached to the general staff was terminated. Lacking a permanent central topographic mapping unit, the federal government, usually the War Department, accomplished such requisite mapping programs as were required by letting them out on contract to civilian surveyors, cartographers, and draftsmen, generally under the supervision of the few topographical engineers in the army (Friis 1958, 1965, 1867a). This was the modus operandi until the establishment of the Topographical Bureau in Washington City in 1818.

It is perhaps ironic that in the moment of maximum need during this country's initial period of geographical exploration west of the Mississippi River following the Louisiana Purchase in 1803, President Jefferson did not have a central topographical corps to tap for well-qualified topographer-cartographers. It is, however, significant to point out that in 1802 Jefferson had established the military academy at West Point and that in subsequent years geography, terrain description, and topographical engineering were subjects in the curriculum (Friis 1967[a]). Indeed, between the War of 1812 and the creation of the Topographical Bureau in 1818, some 10 percent or more of the graduates were trained in the Academy as topographical engineers (Friis 1967a; Heitman 1903).

Lacking well-qualified topographical engineer officers, Jefferson (Martin 1952) nonetheless did successfully press for geographical exploration and mapping of the trans-Mississippi West (Billington 1967; Brebner 1933; Brown 1948; Burpee 1914; Camp 1953; Diller 1944; Ehrenberg 1971a). He was aware of the extensive terra incognita that appeared as a nearly blank area on Arrowsmith's *Map of North America* published in 1801, a copy of which, with other geographical works, he had in his library (fig. 2). As president, he was of course privy to a variety of geographic intelligence about the region in government offices and had obtained information from Alexander von Humboldt during his visit to Washington City in 1804 (Friis 1959, 1960–62; Shapley, 1943). One of Jefferson's primary geographical interests (Surface 1909) following the Louisiana Purchase was the hydrographic pattern on the plains, particularly that of the Red River of the South and of the Missouri River in the north and its destination to the Pacific Coast (Whittington 1927).

We do not have time here to detail the several pioneering fact-gathering expeditions that Jefferson sent into and across the plains between 1803 and 1806, though we should note them briefly and show representative examples of their extant cartographic products (Jefferson 1806). One of the most significant of these was that by Lieutenant Zebulon Montgomery Pike (D. Jackson 1966a, 1966b) from Saint Louis, Missouri, up the Mississippi River in search of its headwaters (fig. 3). He did not reach the headwaters, but the map of his route of survey drafted from his survey notes by Anthony Nau is a landmark in the early history of our exploration of the West.

Pike was recalled to Saint Louis early in 1806. In July he and twenty men under orders proceeded west and south across the plains to the Rocky Mountains and then southwest toward Santa Fe on an exploring expedition. Pike and his party observed and, in a rather elementary way, described and sketched many features. In his survey field notes is a crude sketch of the terrain he viewed from the western fringe of the plains along their contact with the Rocky Mountain front (fig. 4).

The expeditions of Captains Meriwether Lewis and William Clark between 1804 and 1806 from the Mississippi River to the Pacific Ocean and the return gave Jefferson a large volume of invaluable information including, especially, the pattern of the principal rivers in the northern plains, particularly the Missouri River (Allen 1971, 1972; Biddle 1814; Coues 1876; Cutright 1969; Ehrenberg 1971b; Friis 1954; Hamilton 1934; D. Jackson 1962; Thwaites 1904–1905; U.S. Congress 1832–61). In the recently found journal of the Missouri River survey to the Mandan villages in the Great Bend are notes and rather elementary maps (Osgood 1964) (fig. 5). Lewis sent these items, a general map of western North America compiled by Clark, and other records down the Missouri to Jefferson in the spring of 1805.

Jefferson received these items, including a "Chart of the Missouri . . . " and the general map by Clark, possibly by July 13. Of particular interest is Clark's general map, the basic ingredients of which were projected by Nicho-

las King in 1803 for use by Lewis and Clark and which was to be corrected and modified as field information justified. Albert Gallatin, in his letter to Jefferson dated Washington, March 14, 1803, notes that he had King "project a blank map to extend from 88° to 126° West longitude from Greenwich & from 30° to 55° North latitude" (D. Jackson 1962, pp. 27–28). He further mentions the various sources King used in projecting the outline and the principal rivers. The general map that Clark sent to Jefferson appears to have been this map with requisite annotations and modifications (Ehrenberg 1969; Friis 1954). Interestingly, Secretary of War Dearborn apparently had King make four copies of the map received in July, 1805, one of which he preserved in the archives of the War Department (fig. 6). Here is perhaps our first official map, however inaccurate, of the plains region, made in part from field surveys.

In 1804–1806, Jefferson sent William Hunter and George Dunbar to explore and survey the Red River of the South and its tributary, the Washita (Cox 1905, 1946; Dunbar and Hunter 1832; Dunbar 1904; McDermott 1959, 1963). Nicholas King in Washington City compiled a large-scale map of these rivers from Dunbar's survey field notes (fig. 7).

In 1806 Thomas Freeman and Captain Sparks, in command of an expedition, surveyed the Red River and its tributaries westward across the southern plains to a point 635 miles above its mouth. Nicholas King, in 1806, compiled a map of this reconnaissance from Freeman's survey field notes (fig. 8).

Unfortunately, as quickly as these systematically planned projects began, so indeed they were quickly closed out by 1807. With Jefferson's official retirement from the scene in 1809, the federal government had relatively few officials with the foresight to recognize the significance of the West to the future development of the United States.

During the period of our brief review to 1860 the contribution of the military academy at West Point to the training of topographical engineer officers for surveys in our West was large. It was therefore only natural that they should play leading roles in the creation and the development of the Topographical Bureau, beginning in 1818 (Beers 1935, 1942; Cullum 1891; Dupuy 1951; Friis 1958; U.S. Superintendent of Documents 1911).

THE TOPOGRAPHICAL BUREAU: 1818–38

It is of particular interest to note here that in 1818, Major Isaac Roberdeau, in charge of the newly created Topographical Bureau, copied, possibly with some modification, a map of the American West entitled "Sketch of the Western Part of the Continent of North America, between Latitudes 35° and 52°N" (fig. 9). This map, in the archives of the Topographical Bureau, appears to bear every evidence of the draftsmanship of Roberdeau, who indeed is noted in the caption as its delineator. This, then, is the first of a succession of composite maps of the American West, including the plains, prepared in the bureau as representative of the state of cartographical knowledge at selected moments in time to 1857. Significantly, these composite maps, through 1857, delineate the image of the plains through the professional eyes of competent topographical engineers with field experience in the West (Claussen and Friis 1941; Goetzmann 1959, 1966; Hartwell 1911; Hasse 1899; Wheat 1957–63).

Major Stephen H. Long's reconnaissance surveys of the Missouri-Mississippi waterways in 1817 convinced him of the need of a scientific approach to establishing a network of astronomical and geodetic observations, describing the environment, and mapping the terrain. In his letter of March 15, 1817, to President James Monroe, Long proposed building a steamboat for expediting his reconnaissance (Chittenden 1903, 1936). John C. Calhoun, secretary of war, late in 1817 directed Long to organize and command an expedition which was to "explore the country between the Mississippi and the Rocky Mountains [and explore] the Missouri and its principal branches, and then in succession, Red River, Arkansas, and Mississippi, above the mouth of the Missouri" (James 1823, vol. 1, p. 3).

This expedition was popularly referred to as the "Yellowstone Expedition" because it was originally authorized to ascend the Missouri and Yellowstone rivers and establish new posts along the way (Thwaites 1904–1907). However, the panic of 1819 curbed the primary objectives. Long's earlier explorations as a topographical engineer, his professional know-how, and his confidence in the steamboat for river travel were a substantial background for adequate planning. During the winter of 1818–19, Long selected his military assistants, his scientists, and his crew. He also prepared the design and specifications of his steamboat, the *Western Engineer,* which was built in the boat yards in Pittsburgh. The design of this fire-spouting, dragon-like ship of the plains was intended in part to awe and subdue the natives as Long's men worked their way up the Missouri River (fig. 10a). The route of the expedition and the topographic information acquired during reconnaissance up the Missouri River to near present-day Council Bluffs and then west overland to ascend the Platte River to its source, the exploration of the plains and the headwaters of the rivers at the base of the Rocky Mountains, and the return to Saint Louis by the Arkansas and Red rivers during 1819–20 have been described in detail in several publications and may be found in the official records (Fuller and Hafen 1957). A military force under Colonel Henry Atkinson, in the summer of 1819, marched north from Saint Louis to establish a winter quarters, named Engineer Cantonment for the expedition, a short distance west across the river from present-day Council Bluffs. Lieutenant Andrew Talcott, a topographical engineer, drafted a map of this very early United States encampment in the plains, which later became a historic departure point for migrations west (fig. 11).

A large fund of field-derived terrain information was obtained. After the return of the expedition in 1820 many of the records were made available to Dr. Edwin James for use in preparing the official narrative report (James 1823). Significantly, Long was given responsibility for the cartographic efforts, which included the compilation of a large map of the United States between Washington City and the Rocky Mountains (fig. 12). This map was compiled in the Topographical Bureau from the field data and a variety of other sources (Friis 1967*b*). It is of interest to note that this large detailed manuscript map in the National Archives has rarely been referred to, whereas the very small-scale map in the James publication has been used as the Long map (fig. 13). The two maps are surprisingly different. The Long map may indeed have been the first map of the American West compiled in and by the Topographical Bureau.

During the 1830s the Topographical Bureau initiated a program of topographical investigations of the extensive plains area to the base of the western mountains. One of the earliest of these was Lieutenant James Allen and Henry R. Schoolcraft's expedition in search of the headwaters of the Mississippi and west toward the Red River of the North (Allen and Schoolcraft 1835; Boutwell 1902; Ehrenberg 1968; U.S. Congress 1834). A map of this region was compiled for and published with the report (fig. 14).

Perhaps the first government-sponsored geotopographical survey into the plains was that made by George W. Featherstonhaugh, an English geologist, in the employ of the Topographical Bureau (Featherstonhaugh 1835, 1836). In 1834 and 1835 he made extensive surveys of the area between the Saint Peter, Red, and Missouri rivers (Ehrenberg 1968). Several detailed topographic maps were compiled from field survey for publication with his report (fig. 15).

During the summers of 1834 and 1835, Colonel Henry Dodge made a comprehensive reconnaissance of the "Indian frontier," which then included the plains between Fort Leavenworth and the Rocky Mountains (Dodge 1836; U.S. Congress 1836). Though this survey was primarily to observe the lands of the Comanches and Pawnees, it did map the general area between the Red and Canadian rivers west to the Wichita Mountains (fig. 16). These are but several examples of a large number of records of the field work and the cartographic compilations of the bureau during the twenty years following its inception.

THE CORPS OF TOPOGRAPHICAL ENGINEERS: 1838–60

In 1838 the Topographical Bureau was reorganized with considerably expanded functions in civil and internal improvements and was renamed the Corps of Topographical Engineers. Its activities in the West were accelerated, particularly in geographical exploration and surveying and mapping (Gilbert 1933). Colonel John J. Abert continued as officer-in-charge until 1863 (Friis and Claussen 1941).

The key to detailed geographical exploration of the West for the purpose of identifying and describing primary lines of mobility was the availability of accurate knowledge of the composition and arrangement of the principal physiographic features, especially the passes and the interfluves (Brown 1930, 1948; Gilbert 1929, 1933; Goetzmann 1959). By 1840 the major breaks in the Rocky Mountain front leading from the plains into the interior were well, though not accurately, known. An excellent example of the detailed cartographic information about one of these passes, South Pass, is the relief map by Captain Washington Hood (fig. 17). He was a topographical engineer and compiled it from survey field notes and sketch maps in the military headquarters in Independence, Missouri, in 1839.

Joseph N. Nicollet (Bray 1969; Gallaher 1945; Winchell 1891), a French topographer-geographer, came to the United States in the mid-1830s "for the purpose of making a scientific tour." The high quality of Nicollet's work so impressed Colonel John J. Abert, chief of the Corps of Topographical Engineers, that he was commissioned to explore, survey, and map extensively in the Missouri River drainage basin and produce a large-scale map of the region (Ehrenberg 1968, 1971*a*; Nicollet 1843*a*, 1843*b*). During 1838 and 1839 Nicollet, with the capable assistance of Lieutenant John C. Frémont, completed extensive surveys and over a period of several years finished the compilation of two large manuscript maps (fig. 18). Nicollet's report is filled with a wealth of information about the physical and cultural features of the landscape by a scientist with a keen sense for analytical description. Nicollet and Frémont's "Map of the Hydrographical Basin of the Upper Mississippi River . . . ," a significant contribution to the cartographic image of the northern plains, was accomplished by Frémont under the ever exacting supervision of Nicollet. The two maps were printed for publication in Congressional Documents (Nicollet 1843*a,* 1843*b*). These manuscript compilations in the National Archives reveal the cartographic technique used in compilation. This was valuable training for Frémont in planning for his subsequent transcontinental western explorations (Bigelow 1856; Carey 1931; Dellenbaugh 1914; J. B. Frémont 1891; J. C. Frémont 1887).

Perhaps the single most significant series of topographical reconnaissances of the 1840s were four undertaken by Lieutenant John C. Frémont (Hine 1962; Nevins 1955). His reasonably accurate observations and broad interpretations of the landscape and his cartographic contributions were both timely and facilitative, coming as they did on the eve of the great migrations of the 1840s and 1850s (Gudde and Gudde 1958; Jackson and Spence 1970). Though most of his reconnaissances covered the regions west of the plains, each began from bases along the eastern margins of that region and maps were made of the plains during the travel westward and the return. Let us briefly refer to two of them as examples.

With Frémont's published report and journal of his first expedition in 1843 in the country lying between the Missouri River and the Rocky Mountains (Frémont 1843, 1845*a,* 1845*b,* 1848) is a relief map of the region on a scale of 1:1,000,000 (fig. 19). A manuscript copy of this map is among the archives of the Corps of Topographical Engineers. On it are recorded not only the elements of terrain as surveyed but distribution of Indian tribes, routes of other surveys, and contemporary toponymics.

The historic Oregon Road, which nature endowed and Frémont mapped westward from Independence, Missouri, in 1846, became a highway of unparalleled importance to the development of the new image and to the settlement of the West (Frémont 1845*a,* 1845*b;*

Mattes 1969). Frémont's detailed large-scale map of the road was of inestimable value to settlers and travelers alike. Sheet 1 covers the route from near Independence westward across the plains to the headwaters of the Little Blue River in about longitude 98°30'W(fig. 20).

A second transcontinental route to the Pacific Coast led from Fort Leavenworth in eastern Kansas to San Diego, California, by way of El Paso, Texas (Emory 1848). In 1846–47 Lieutenant William H. Emory conducted a reconnaissance along this route, which included collecting and identifying materials in the natural sciences, observing weather, climate, and astronomical and geographical phenomena, and mapping the terrain (Hafen and Rister 1941). The principal results of this survey were expressed as detailed reports by the scientists and as a series of overlapping sheets, together comprising a large-scale topographic map. An example of the cartographic description of the terrain is shown on this portion of a sheet of Emory's final manuscript compilations of the entire route of survey (fig. 21).

During the decade of the 1840s the United States Army, particularly the Topographical Bureau, emphasized its field operations west of the Mississippi River (Friis 1967*c*). The large majority of these expeditions were primarily responsible for a progressive, systematic survey of the plains, the Rocky Mountains, and the vast interior that spread west toward the sea. In 1850 the Topographical Bureau compiled and published a relief map of "The United States and Their Territories Between the Mississippi and the Pacific Ocean," based on the most authentic information available in the files of the federal government (fig. 22). Most of the available usable information consisted of field survey reports and maps of topographical engineer officers and others that were on file in the archives of that agency, a few representative examples of which we have just discussed. A portion of the manuscript compilation of this map covering the plains reveals the quality and composition of the cartographic technique employed (fig. 23). It was of course immediately obvious that large portions of the West in 1850 were inadequately explored and erroneously mapped. This map pointed up the needs for and ushered in a new era of intensive exploration and mapping, especially by the Topographical Bureau. This was the official cartographic image of the West in 1850, perhaps the first reasonably accurate map of the broad physiographic features (Friis 1967c). The rather rapid increase in universal interest in the American West, clearly sharpened by the discovery of extensive mineral deposits and by proof, as in the Mormon oases and in the Willamette Valley settlements, that rich agricultural potentialities existed, presaged a new and a highly productive era of geographical exploration—a response to the increasing tempo of requests for more accurate topographic intelligence, especially along the routes of maximum travel.

During the decade of the 1850s the federal government initiated a major program of systematic exploration and mapping of the West (Friis 1958, 1965, 1967c). This program included especially: exploration to determine in accurate detail the precise location, extent, and composition of the primary landform features; exploration and surveys of the principal river systems; and exploration and surveys for civilian and military transportation routes, including, significantly, the most practicable routes for a transcontinental railroad. Let us briefly describe a few of the most representative examples as they cover the plains.

In 1852 Captain Randolph B. Marcy led a reconnaissance up the Red River to its source. Dr. G. G. Shumard accompanied the expedition as surgeon and geologist. The official report (Marcy 1853) is especially well illustrated and includes two large-scale maps (fig. 24).

Lieutenant Gouverneur K. Warren, one of the most productive and outstanding professional United States topographical engineers of the nineteenth century, was responsible during the 1850s for a succession of detailed surveys in the West. One of these, from May through September, 1855, required extensive topographic reconnaissance of the northern plains. Warren left Saint Louis, ascended the Missouri to Fort Pierre, crossed the plains to Fort Kearney, and then mapped extensively in this large region preparatory to compiling a large-scale map of the northern third of the plains (fig. 25). In 1856 and 1857, Warren returned to mapping in the Dakotas, Nebraska, and south into Kansas.

Warren's notebooks and journal accounts are clearly written and filled with sketch maps of the routes of his travels. For example, the sketch on page 71 of one of his notebooks includes the notation "place where somebody cursed about the crossing" (fig. 26).

Warren's notebooks, as indeed many of his other records, reflect his personality and his wit. This is well illustrated in the sketch he made during his 1855 summer survey on the plains. Perhaps this is a kind of self-portrait, appropriately entitled "Bug Catching" (fig. 27).

Much of Warren's summer of 1856 was spent in a detailed reconnaissance of the Missouri River from the northern boundary of Kansas to a place sixty-two miles above Fort Union in Montana (Chittenden 1903, 1936; Warren, 1856, 1859b). This survey resulted in a compilation of a forty-four-sheet topographic map of the river on a scale of one and a half inches to the mile. One of these sheets covers the area vicinal to Sailor Island in Latitude 43°32'N; Longitude 99°28'W (fig. 28).

During the 1850s much of the cartographic work of the Corps of Topographical Engineers had been extended into the regions west of the plains and included important roles in the explorations and surveys for Pacific railroad routes. Some topographical engineer officers, notably Warren and Abbot, were assigned to the Office of Explorations and Surveys in Washington, in which maps were compiled for the railroad surveys reports.

THE OFFICE OF EXPLORATIONS AND SURVEYS, 1853–61

The call for a transcontinental railroad between the Mississippi River and the Pacific, a whisper in the 1830s, a promise and a hope in the 1840s, became a national issue of formidable proportions by the early 1850s (Albright 1921; Taft 1951; Secretary of War 1854–55 and 1859–60). In 1853, Congress authorized the secretary of war to undertake a systematic survey along each of four east-west routes from the Mississippi River to the Pacific Ocean to determine the best, most practicable route for a railroad (fig. 29). A fifth route was to be run in California. These reconnaissance surveys constituted the government's first concerted attempt at comprehensive and systematic geographical information of the American West along predetermined belts of latitude. The resulting terrain information made possible the first reasonably accurate topographic map of the country west of the Mississippi River. Significantly, the reports, sketches, survey field notebooks, meteorological, astronomical, and other observations, numerous field-made maps, and a variety of topographical, geological, and other scientific information comprise a remarkable reservoir of information about the area for the period of 1853 to 1857 (Friis 1970; Taft 1951).

In addition to the military and their civilian assistants, each survey party included botanists, topographers, geologists, civil engineers, surveyors, astronomers, naturalists, meteorologists, and artists. At convenient intervals each survey party, as it progressed west from an eastern starting point, transmitted to Washington the products of the group's field work. The secretary of war, who was given responsibility for the operation, established the Office of Explorations and Surveys in the Winder Building in Washington, staffed with topographical engineers, cartographers, and draftsmen, mostly from the Corps of Topographical Engineers.

In addition to the collection of the archives or records of the office that is in the National Archives, the United States Congress published in thirteen volumes as official documents the reports, maps, illustrations, and other results of these surveys (Albright 1921; Hartwell 1911; Taft 1951; Secretary of War 1854–55 and 1859–60). These are a fundamental source of information on the historical geography of the plains at mid-century.

Governor Isaac I. Stevens (Meinig 1955), in charge of the northernmost survey west from Saint Paul to Puget Sound during the period 1853–55, and his assistants prepared reports, maps, profiles, and illustrations that were published in several volumes (vols. 12 and 13) of the Congressional Documents (Secretary of War 1859 and 1860). Among the remarkable colored and black and white lithographic landscape views sketched by J. M. Stanley, artist on the expedition, is a view of "Sheyenne" River in present eastern North Dakota in which the party bivouaced and carried out surveys and observations on July 8, 1855 (fig.30). Two days later the party surveyed in the nearby region of Lake Jessie (fig. 31). In this illustration of the landscape Stanley includes the large herd of buffalo that excited the interest of the party.

The manuscript compilation of successive sheets of the topographic map of the route of survey from Saint Paul to Puget Sound on a scale of twenty miles to one inch includes a large fund of landscape information. An example is "Sheet No. 1, St. Paul to Riviere des Lacs . . . drawn by John Lambert, Topographer of the Expedition." The preceding illustrations are of landscapes slightly left of the central part of the sheet (fig. 32). One of the most important products of this office was a terrain map of the United States west of the Mississippi River (fig. 33). Lieutenant Gouverneur K. Warren was in charge (Warren 1859 a). Published on a scale of 1:3,000,000, or about fifty miles to one inch, and measuring four feet by three and a half feet, this was indeed a new and relatively accurate map. Warren notes in his remarks on the compilation of the map that only cartographic and topographic information judged to be accurate was used and that therefore there are extensive blank areas. Compilation of this map was accomplished as a large number of matching sheets, each of which covered areas to be compiled by the cartographer by a series of graticule reductions. The painstakingly exacting draftsmanship used by the chief cartographers, Edwin Freyhold and Henry L. Abbott, in preparing final copy for the engravers is illustrated by the compilation sheet covering the central Rocky Mountains and adjoining plains region of the upper Arkansas River (fig. 34). This terrain map includes settlements, forts, and distribution of Indian tribes; routes of military and civilian expeditions and reconnaissance parties; a wealth of contemporary toponymics; roads and territorial and state boundaries; and names of geographical features. It represents the new look of the macromorphology of the geographical landscape of our West generally and the plains specifically—a new image, if you will, at mid-century.

We have shown but a representative few of the large volume of journals, survey field notebooks, field and compiled maps, and reports and correspondence that are in the National Archives. They are indeed a treasure trove to those of us whose special interest is historical geography and the cartography of the plains.

LIST OF ILLUSTRATIONS

The following are descriptions of the illustrations used in this article. All records in the National Archives are noted as NA. All other sources are identified specifically. (The editors appreciate that not all of the originals of the illustrations are of such quality as to be reproduced with great clarity. However, the whole sequence has been included to provide a guide to this corpus of cartographic source material.)

Figure 1. Map of "Survey of Morristown, [N.J.] by Chain only [Dec. 17, 1779?] . . . No. 105, by Rt Erskine." Scale 6 chains to 1 inch. Dimensions 5 X 7¼ inches. MS map in ink on paper. In New York Historical Society, New York City.

Figure 2. "Map Exhibiting All the New Discoveries in the Interior Parts of North America . . . ," published in London with additions to 1802 by Aaron Arrowsmith. Scale approx. 1 inch to 70 miles. Dimensions 48½ X 57 inches. Printed map in color on paper. Reference Collection in the Cartographic Archives Division, NA.

Figure 3. "A Sketch of the Mississipi [sic] . . . Taken from the notes of Lieutenant Zebulon Montgomery Pike . . . 1805 and 1806 . . . by Anthony Nau Sworn Interpreter of the French Language. Territory of Louisiana." Scale of 10 miles to 1 inch. Dimensions 39 X 32 inches. MS map in color on paper. Records of the Office of the Chief of Engineers, Map M34, NA.

Figure 4. Pike's sketch of the Pikes Peak–Pueblo–Canon City Region, Colorado, in his notebook of 1806, including a separate sketch of Pikes Peak. No scale is given. Dimensions 12½ X 15 inches. MS map in ink on paper. Records of the Adjutant General's Office, NA.

Figure 5. Map of ancient fortification adjoining and including the Missouri River, September 1, 1804, with William Clark's field notes of September 1 through 2, 1804. Sketch map without scale. Dimensions of pages of survey notebook 8½ X 11½ inches. Original MS is on paper in the Western Americana Collection in Sterling Library at Yale University, New Haven, Conn. Published in Ernest Staples Osgood, *The Field Notes of Captain William Clark, 1803–1805* (New Haven, Conn.: Yale University Press, 1964), p. 291.

Figure 6. "A map of Part of the Continent of North America . . . Copied by Nicholas King, 1806." Scale approx. 1 inch to 35 miles. Dimensions 43⅛ X 30 inches. MS map in ink on paper. Records of the Office of the Chief of Engineers, Map Ama 21, NA.

Figure 7. "Map of the Washita River in Louisiana . . . Laid down from the Journal and Survey of Mr. Dunbar, in the year 1804 by Nichs. King." Scale approx. 1 inch to 4 miles. Dimensions 39½ X 79½ inches. MS map in color on paper. Records of the Office of the Chief of Engineers, Map M35, NA.

Figure 8. "Map of the Red River in Louisiana from Natchitoches to the Coashatay Village. Protracted from the Courses and Distances given in Mr. Thos. Freeman's Journal of a Survey thereof made in June 1806 by Nichs. King." Scale approx. 1 inch to 1 mile. Dimensions 33 X 10½ inches. MS map in ink and color on paper. Records of the Office of the Chief of Engineers, Map M33-1, NA.

Figure 9. "Sketch [map] of the Western part of the continent of North America between Latitudes 35° and 52°N . . . Gen. Land Office, 21 Jan. 1818 signed Josiah Meigs . . . [Isaac] Roberdeau, U. S. T[opographical] Engineers, del. 1818." Scale 1 inch to approx. 46 miles. Dimensions 29½ X 51 inches. MS map in color on paper. Records of the Office of the Chief of Engineers, Map Ama 6, NA.

Figure 10a. "The Western Engineer," a print of Mr. Ismaert's drawing of the boat used on the Missouri River by the S. H. Long expedition from Pittsburgh to the Rocky Mountains, 1819–20. It was executed according to printed descriptions of the boat by Mr. Ismaert in 1948. A print of the drawing, measuring 11 X 13¾ inches, is in the Academy of Natural Sciences in Philadelphia.

Figure 10b. A contemporary, perhaps more accurate, on-the-spot sketch of the *Western Engineer* by Titian Ramsay Peale, a member of the Long expedition. This sketch may have been made by Peale at Engineer Cantonment. See Jessie Poesche, "Titian Ramsay Peale . . . 1799–1885," *Memoirs of the American Philosophical Society* 52 (1961): 29.

Figure 11. "Map of the Missouri Bottom," with insets showing the location and environment of

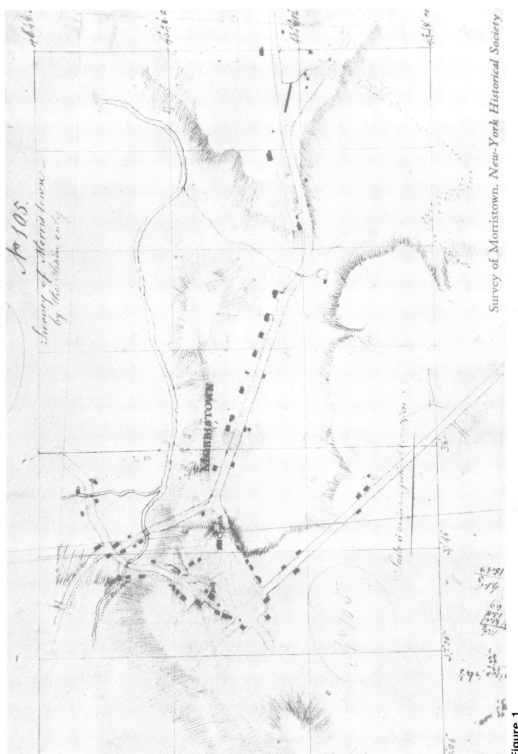

Survey of Morristown. New-York Historical Society

Figure 1

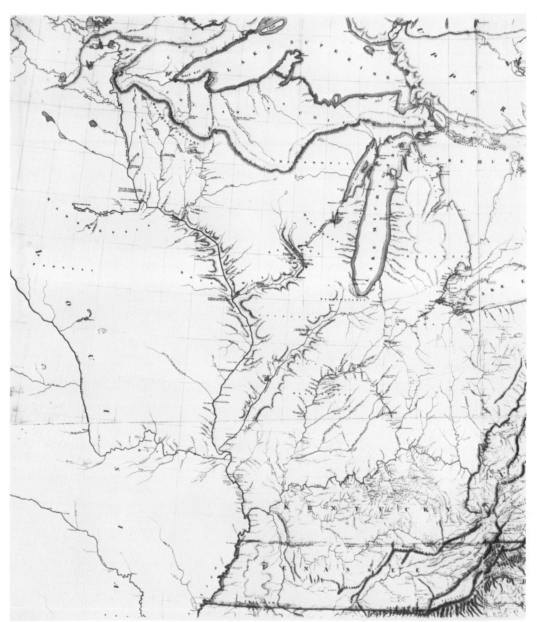

Figure 2

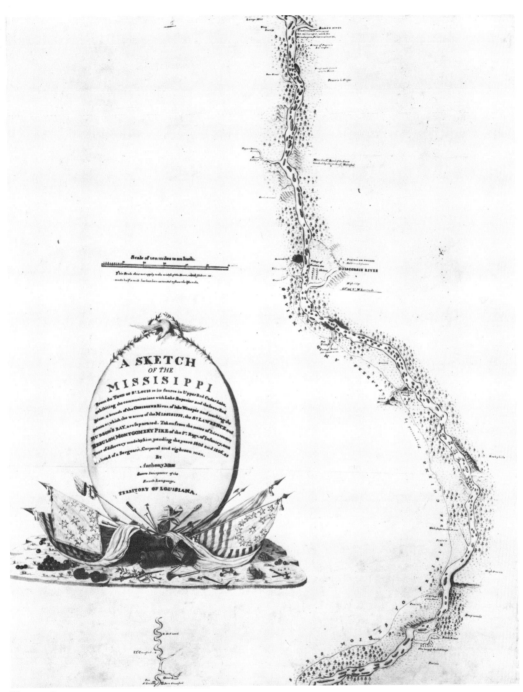

Figure 3

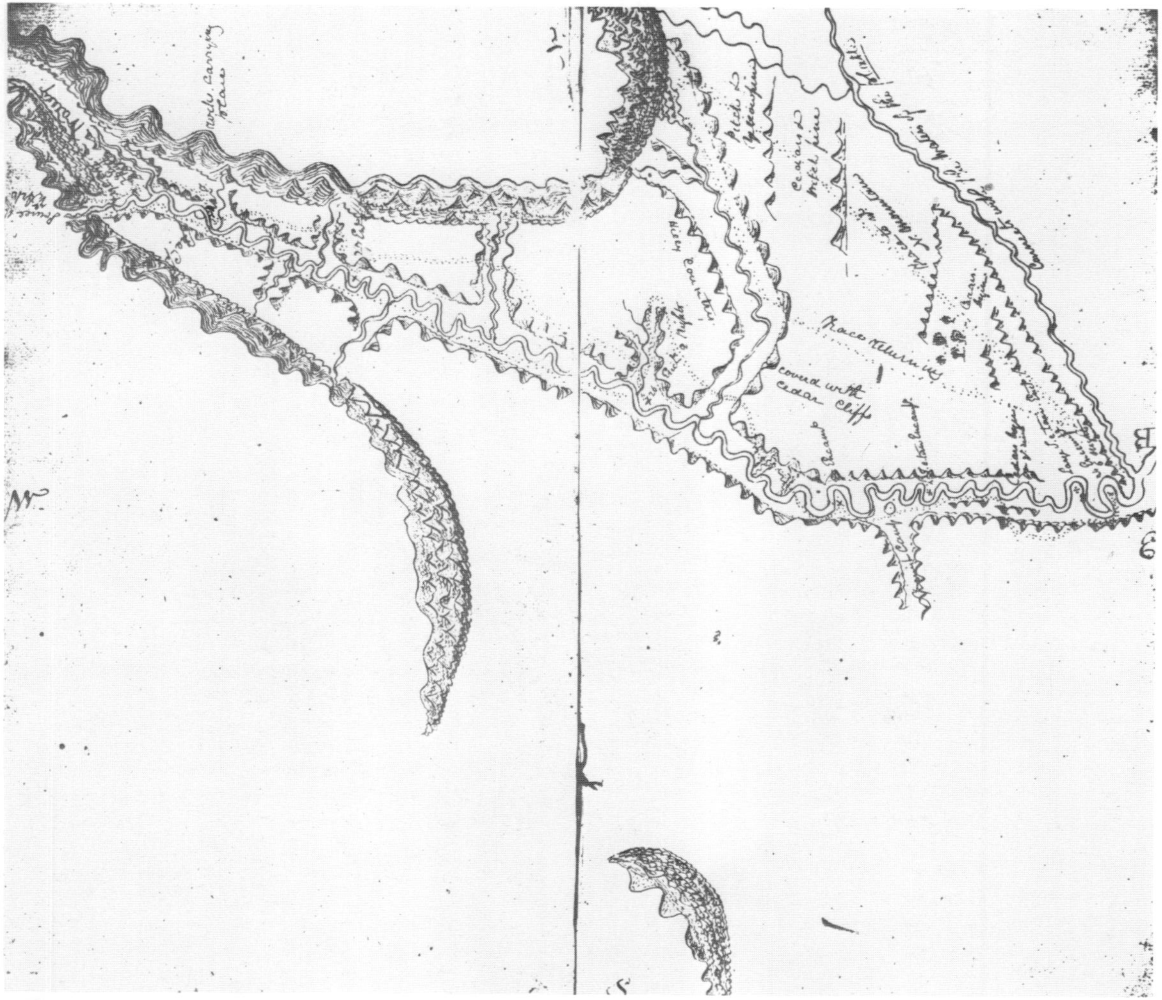

Figure 4

Figure 5

Figure 6

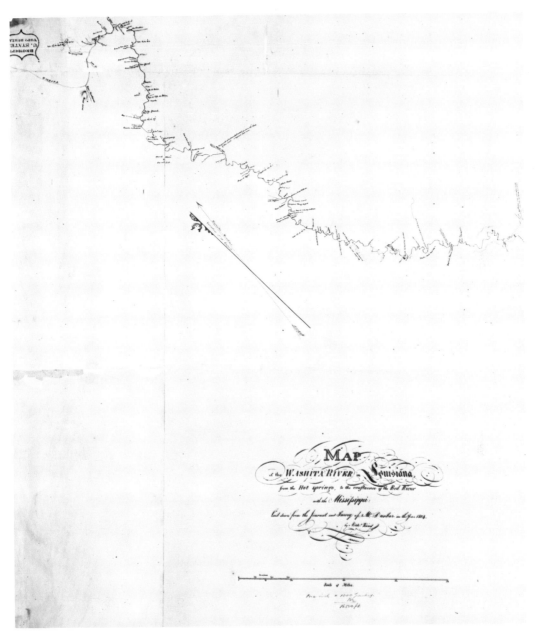

Figure 7

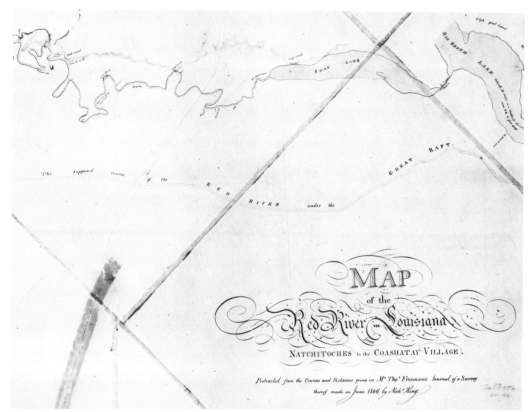

Figure 8

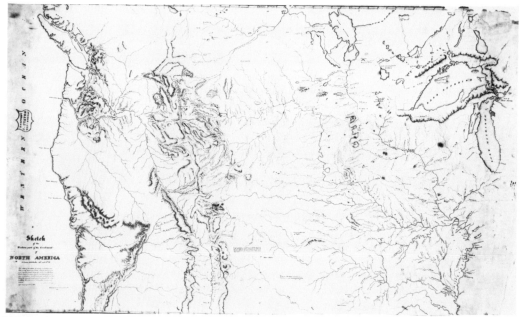

Figure 9

Figure 10A

Figure 10B

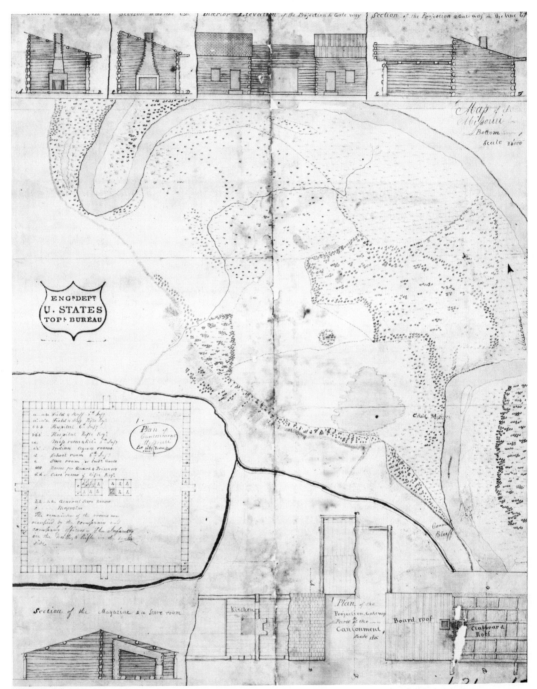

Figure 11

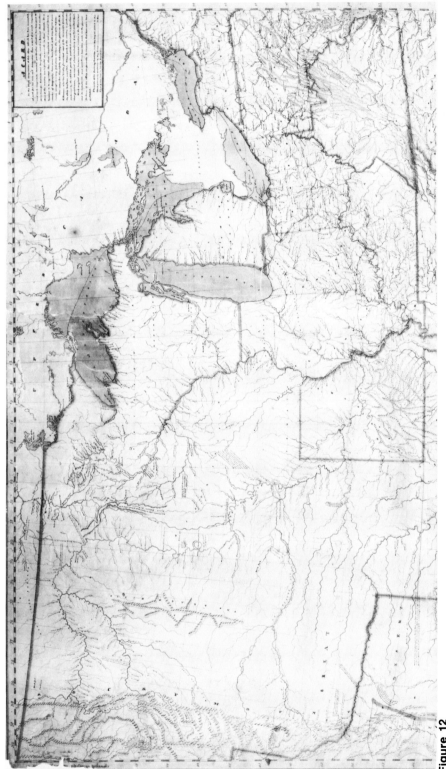

Figure 12

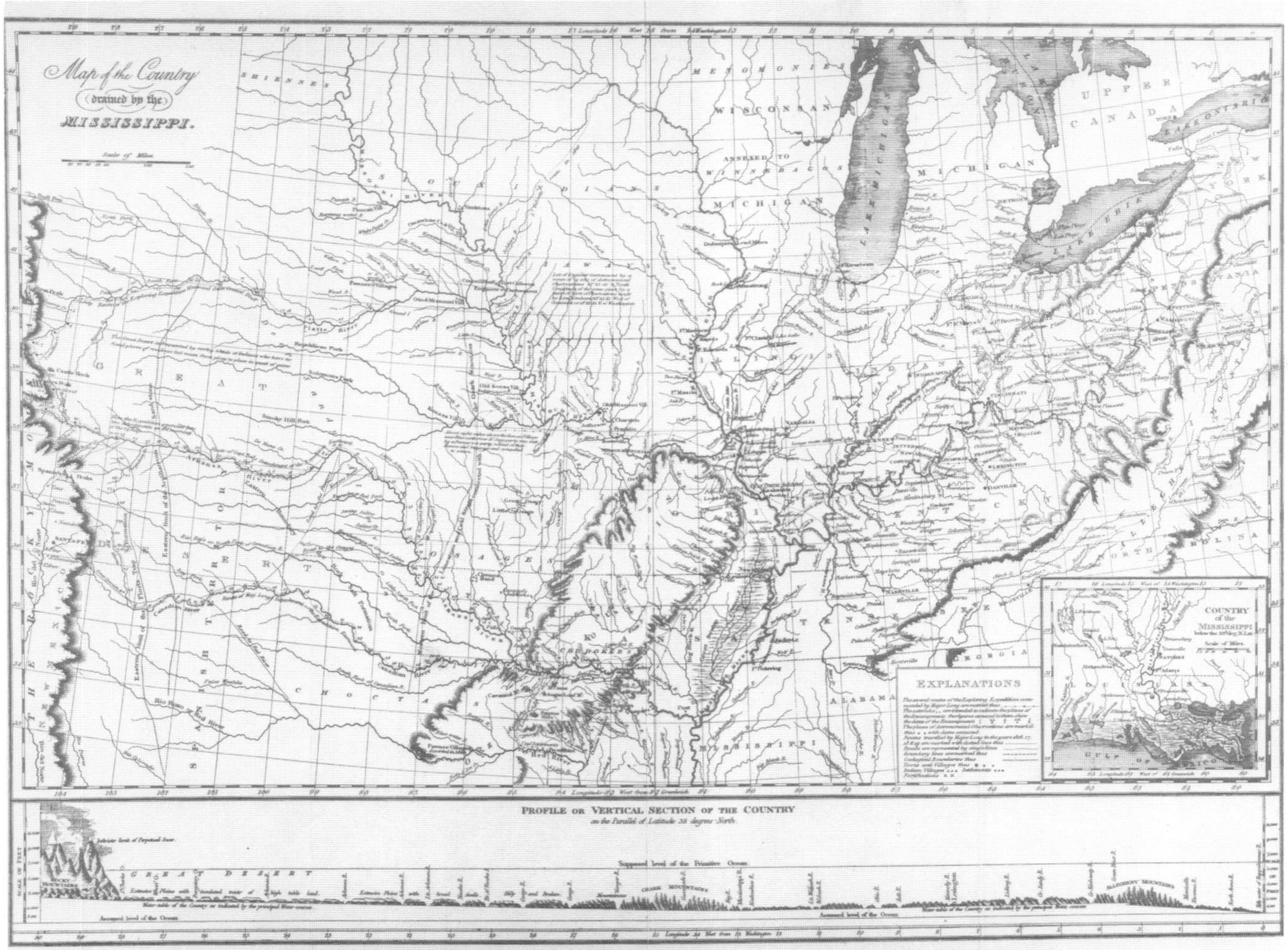
Map of the Country
drained by the
MISSISSIPPI.
EXPLANATIONS
COUNTRY
of the
MISSISSIPPI
PROFILE OR VERTICAL SECTION OF THE COUNTRY
on the Parallel of Latitude 38 degrees North.

Figure 13

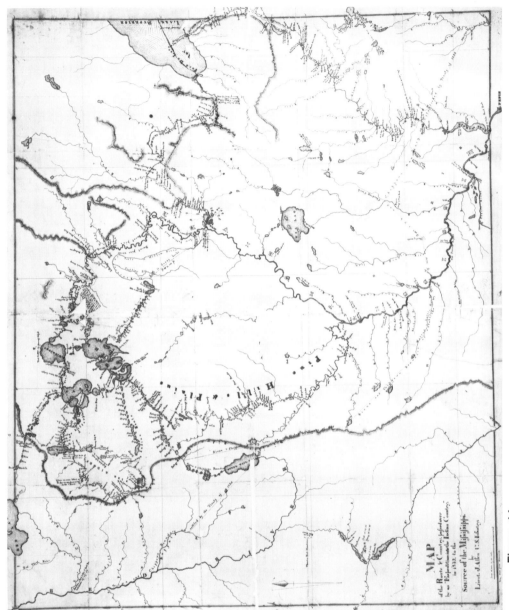

MAP
of the Route & Country, explored
by an Expedition into the Indian Country
in 1832, to the
Source of the Mississippi
by
Lieut. J. Allen U.S.Infantry

Figure 14

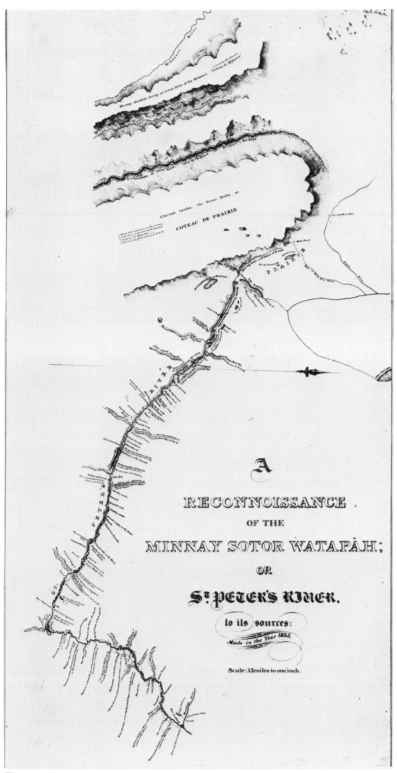

Figure 15

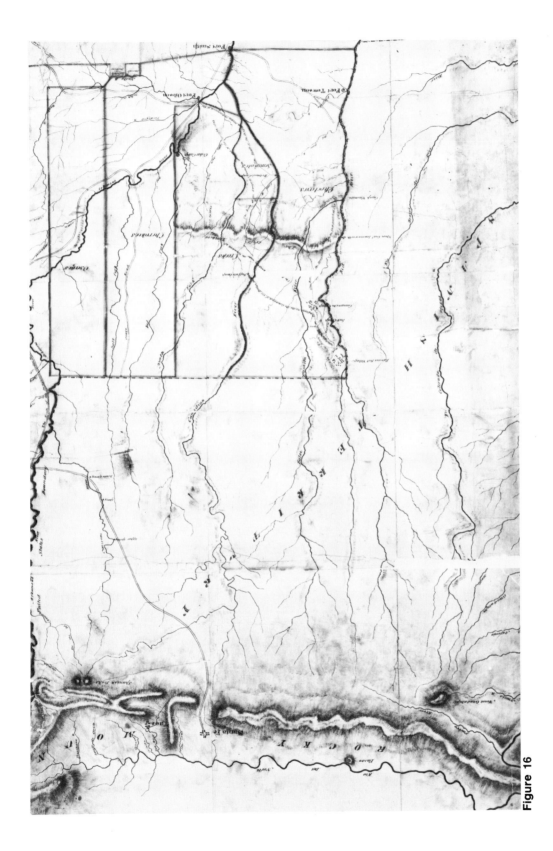

Figure 16

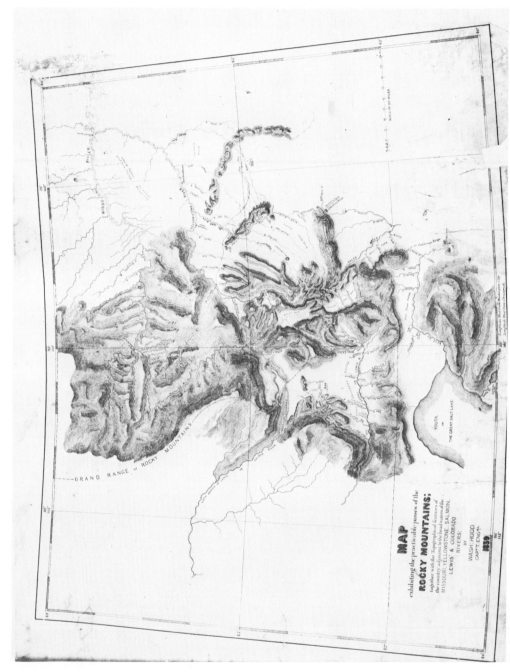

MAP

exhibiting the practicable passes of the

ROCKY MOUNTAINS;

together with the Topographical features of
the country adjacent to the head waters of the
MISSOURI, YELLOWSTONE, SALMON,
LEWIS & COLORADO
RIVERS;

BY

WASH: HOOD
CAPT. ENG'S.

1839

Figure 17

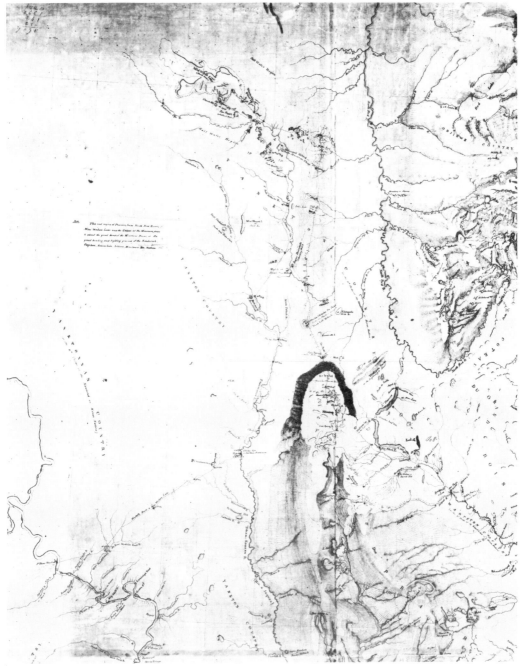

Figure 18

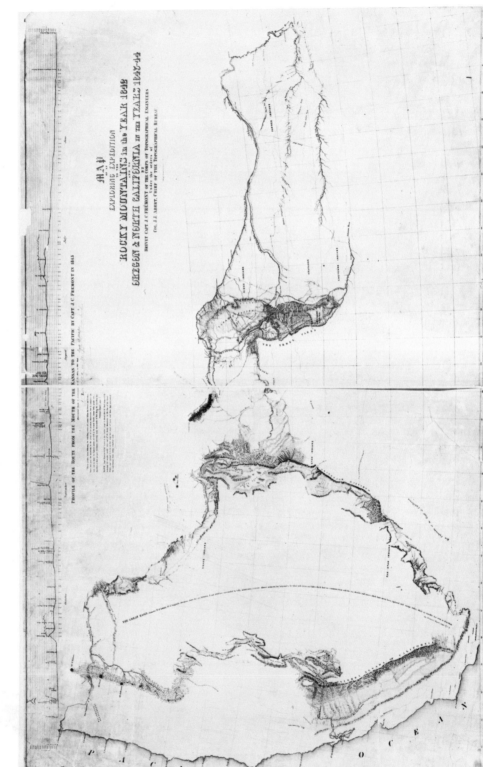

Figure 19

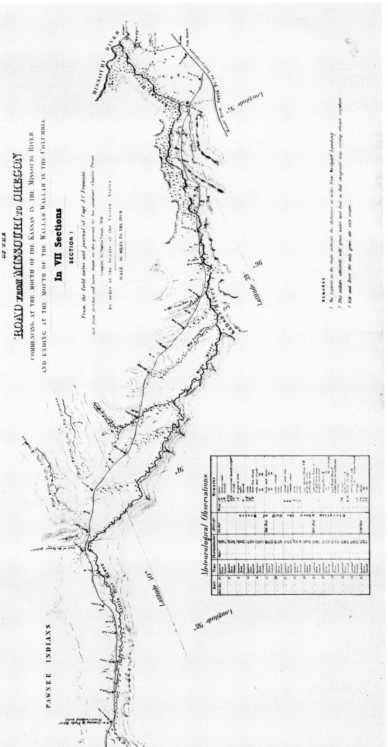

Figure 20

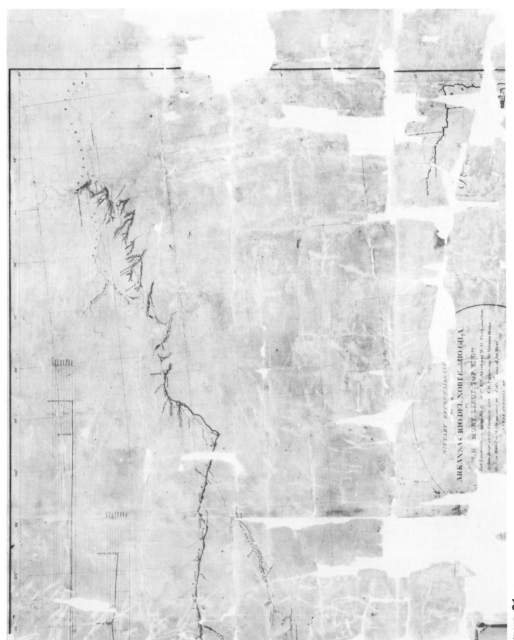

Figure 21

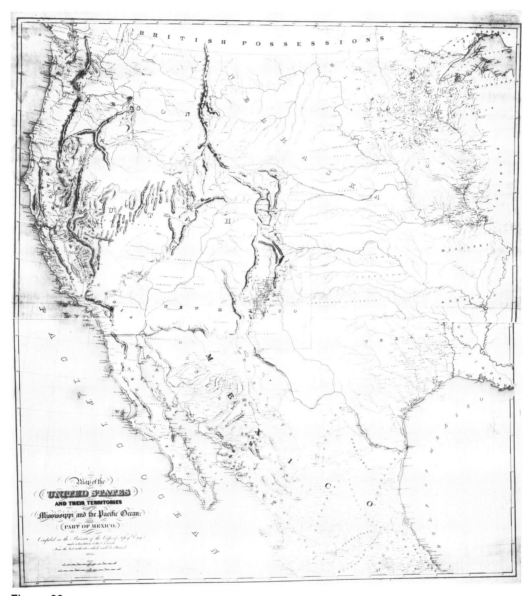

Figure 22

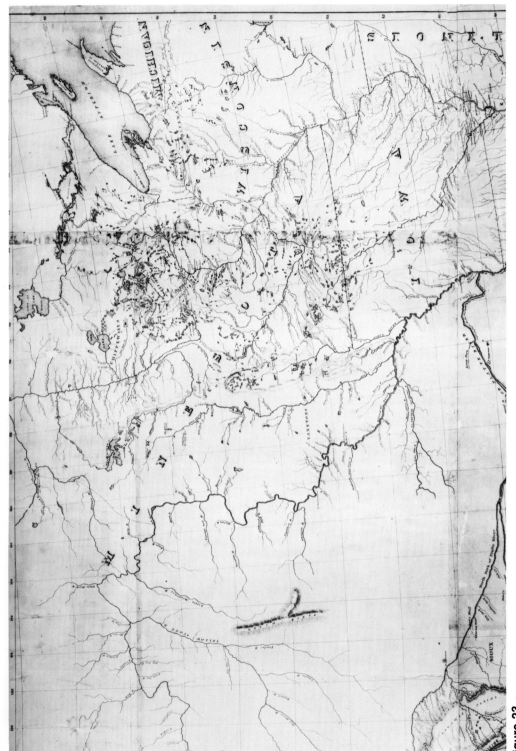

Figure 23

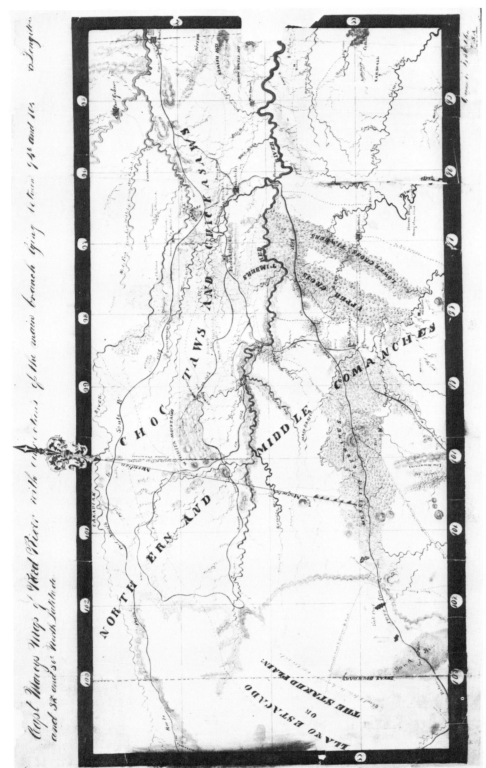

Figure 24

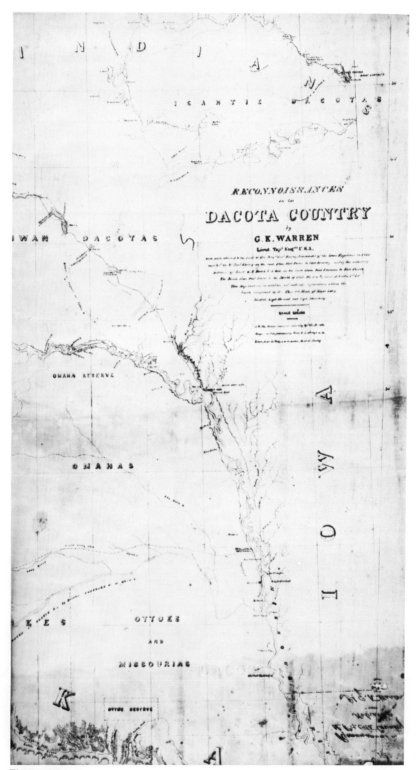

Figure 25

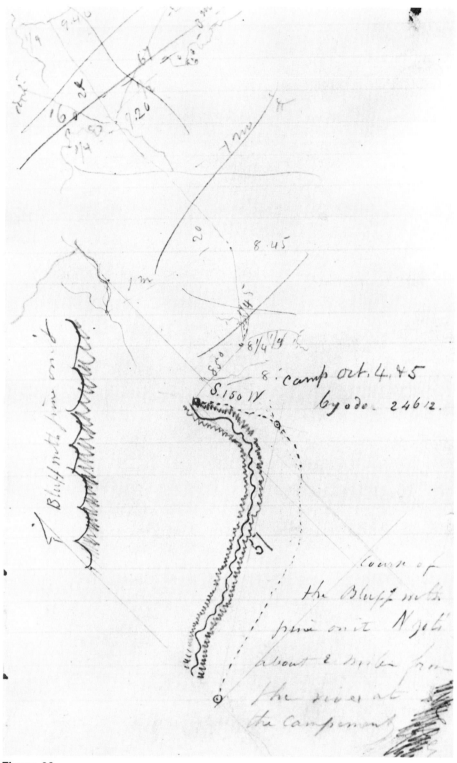

Figure 26

Figure 27

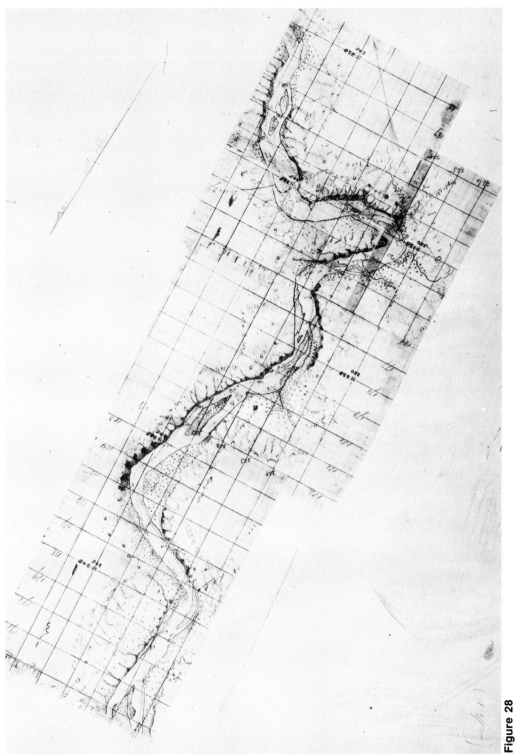

Figure 28

MAP OF ROUTES
FOR A
PACIFIC RAILROAD
Compiled to accompany the Report of the
HON. JEFFERSON DAVIS, SEC. OF WAR
In Office of P. R. R. Surveys
1855.

Figure 29

Figure 30

Figure 31

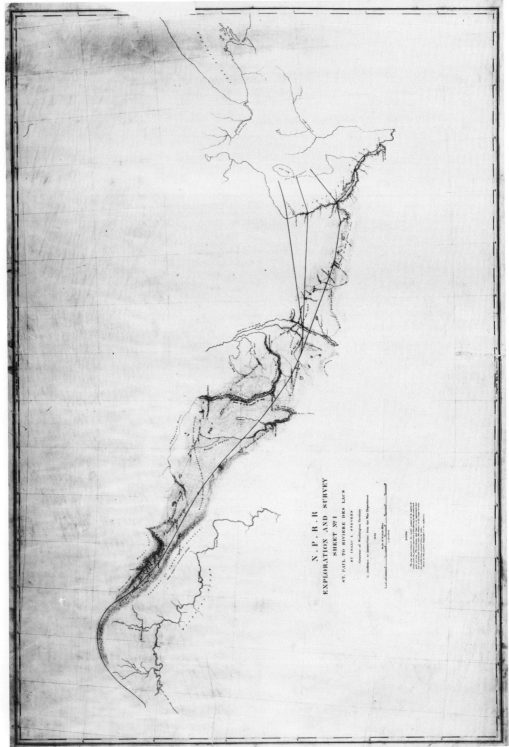

N. P. R. R
EXPLORATION AND SURVEY
SHEET Nº 1
ST. PAUL TO RIVIERE DES LACS
BY ISAAC I. STEVENS
Governor of Washington Territory

Figure 32

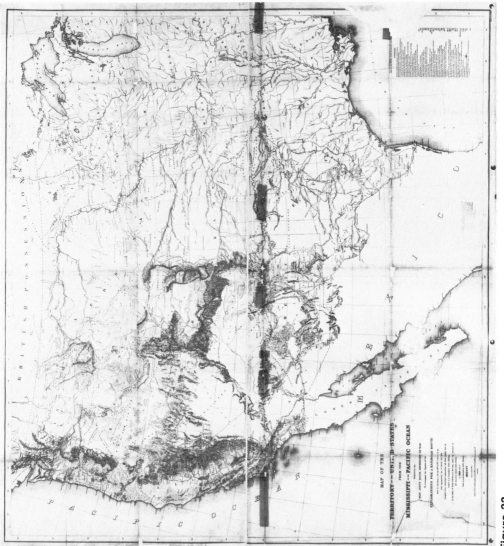

Figure 33

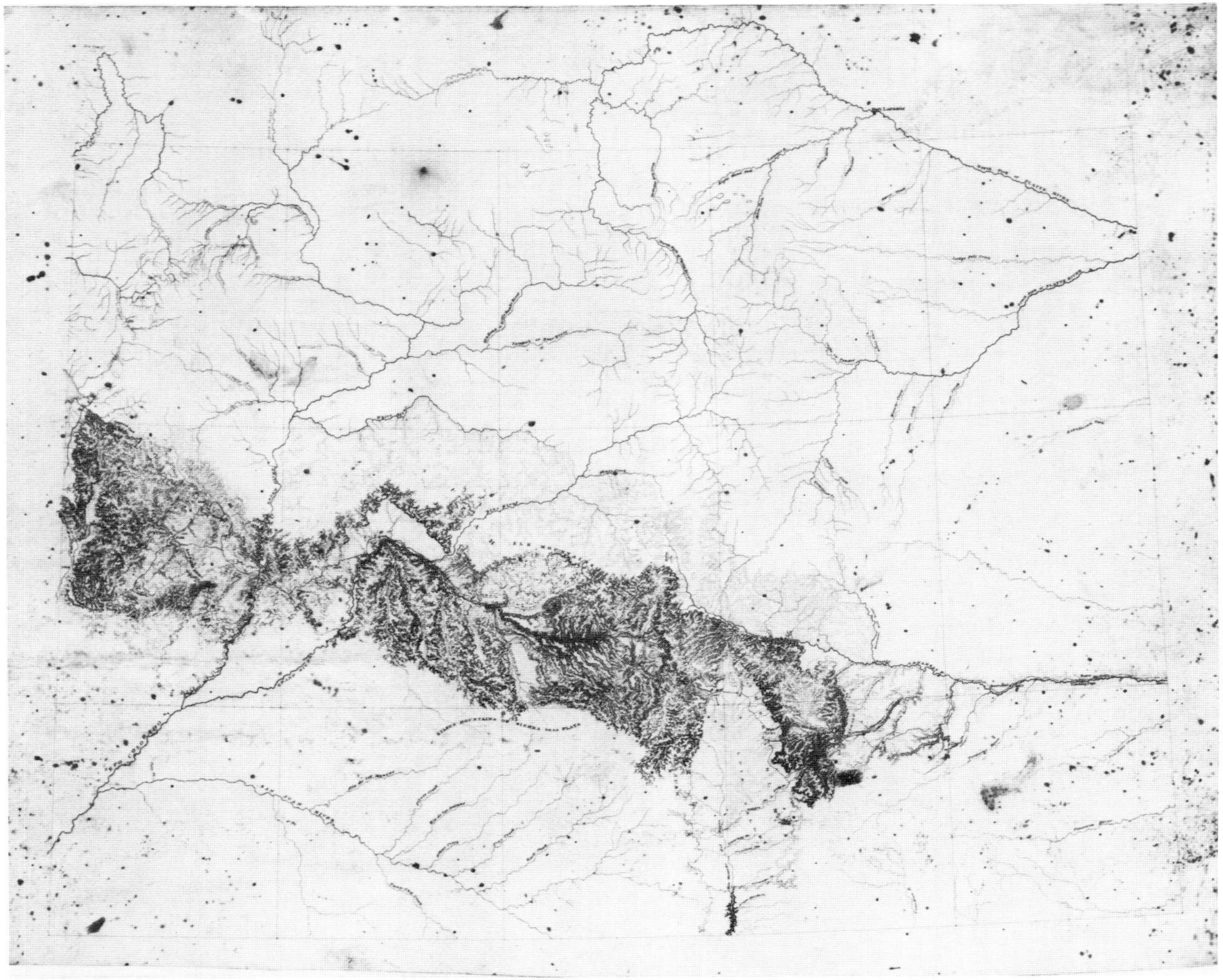

Figure 34

Cantonment Missouri (Engineer Cantonment) above Council Bluff on the Missouri River, by Lieut. Andrew Talcott, 1819. Scale 1:24,000. Dimensions 23 × 19 inches. MS map in color on paper. Records of the Office of the Chief of Engineers, Map Drawer 131, Sheet 17, NA.

Figure 12. Upper half of the "Map of the Country situated between the Meridian of Washington City and the Rocky Mountains exhibiting the route of the late Exploring Expedition commanded by Maj. Long, together with other recent surveys and explorations by himself and others . . ." Scale 1 inch to 36 miles. Dimensions 44½ × 56 inches. MS in ink and tinted shades on paper. Records of the Office of the Chief of Engineers, Map US62, NA.

Figure 13. "Map of the Country drained by the Mississippi." Scale approx. 80 miles to 1 inch. Dimensions 17 × 22 inches. Printed map on paper. A frontispiece to vol. 1 of Edwin James (comp.), *Account of an Expedition from Pittsburgh to the Rocky Mountains performed in the years 1819, 1820, . . . under the command of Maj. S. H. Long, of the U.S. Top. Engineers . . .*, 3 vols. (London, 1823).

Figure 14. "Map of the Route & Country, passed over by an 'Expedition into the Indian Country' in 1832, to the Source of the Mississippi, by Lieut. J. Allen, U.S. Infantry." Scale 1 inch to 11½ miles. Dimensions 29½ × 37 inches. MS map in ink on paper. Records of the Office of the Chief of Engineers, Misc. 13, NA.

Figure 15. Map of "A Reconnaissance of the Minnay Sotor Watapah; or St. Peter's River, to its sources: Made in the Year 1835," by G. W. Featherstonhaugh. Scale 1 inch to 15 miles. Dimensions 34 × 17 inches. MS map in ink on paper. Records of the Office of the Chief of Engineers, Map Misc. 14=1, NA.

Figure 16. Map of the plains region between the Rio Colorado in Texas and the Nebraska–South Dakota boundary and between the meridian of Fort Leavenworth on the east and the Rocky Mountains on the west, showing especially Indian cessions, reservations, and lands held, and the principal elements of terrain and hydrography. "By Lieut. Steen of the United States Dragoons commanded by Col. Henry Dodge." Scale 20 miles to 1 inch. Dimensions 45½ × 36 inches. MS map in ink and color wash on paper. Records of the Office of the Chief of Engineers, Map Q14, NA.

Figure 17. "Map exhibiting the practicable passes of the Rocky Mountains; together with the topographical features of the country adjacent to the headwaters of the Missouri, Yellowstone, Salmon, Lewis' and Colorado Rivers: By Wash. Hood, Capt. T. Engrs., 1839." Scale 1 inch to 43 miles. Dimen-

sions 16½ × 22 inches. MS map in color on paper. Records of the Office of the Chief of Engineers, Map U.S. 110, NA.

Figure 18. Western half of the "Map of the Hydrographical Basin of the Upper Mississippi River. From Astronomical observations, Survey and information by I. [J.] N. Nicollet [in the years 1836–40]." Scale 1 inch to 9½ miles. Dimensions 75 × 61 inches (4 sections). MS map in ink and pencil on paper. Records of the Office of the Chief of Engineers, Map U.S. 131–1, NA. For a reduced published edition, see U.S. 26th Cong., 2d sess., *Senate Executive Doc. 237*, Serial 243 (Washington, D.C., 1843), opp. p. 96.

Figure 19. "Map of an Exploring Expedition to the Rocky Mountains in the Year 1842 and to Oregon & North California in the Years 1843–44, by Brevet Capt. J. C. Frémont of the Corps of Topographical Engineers . . ." Scale 1 inch to 35 miles. Dimensions 32 × 26 inches. Printed map on paper. Records of the Office of the Chief of Engineers, Map U.S. 130, NA.

Figure 20. "Topographical Map of the Road from Missouri to Oregon commencing at the mouth of the Kansas in the Missouri River and ending at the mouth of the Wallah Wallah in the Columbia. In VII Sections. Section I, From the field notes and journal of Capt. J. C. Frémont . . ." Scale 10 miles to 1 inch. Dimensions 15½ × 24½ inches. Printed map on paper. Records of the Office of the Chief of Engineers, Map U.S. 155, NA.

Figure 21. Part of the northeastern corner of the map of the "Military Reconnaissance of the Arkansas, Rio Del Norte and Rio Gila by W. H. Emory, Lieut. Top. Engrs. Fort Leavenworth to Santa Fea, by Lieut. J. W. Abert and W. G. Peck, . . . Drawn by Joseph Welch . . . 1847." Scale 1 inch to 24 stat. miles. MS map in ink on paper. Records of the Office of the Chief of Engineers, U.S. 147–1, NA.

Figure 22. "Map of the United States and Their Territories between the Mississippi and the Pacific Ocean and of part of Mexico, Compiled in the Bureau of the Corps of Topog'l. Engs. under Resolution of the U.S. Senate, From the best authorities which could be obtained, 1850." Scale 1 inch to 48 miles. Dimensions 48 × 42 inches. Printed map on paper. Records of the Office of the Chief of Engineers, Map U.S. 152, NA.

Figure 23. Northeast quadrant of "A map of the United States and Their Territories between the Mississippi and the Pacific and of a part of Mexico. Compiled in the Bureau of the Corps of Topographical Engineers, . . . [1850]." Scale approx. 1 inch to 22 miles. Dimensions 62 × 82 inches. MS map in ink on paper. Records of the Office of the Chief of Engineers, Map U.S. 150, NA.

Figure 24. "Capt. Marcys Map of Red River with corrections of the main branch lying between 94° and 104° West Longitude, and 32° and 36° North Latitude [ca. 1852]." Scale approx. 1 inch to 25 miles. Dimensions 14½ X 25½ inches. MS map in ink on paper. Records of the Office of the Chief of Engineers, Map Q74, NA.

Figure 25. Eastern third section of "Reconnoissances [sic] in the Dakota Country by G. K. Warren, Lieut. Top'l Engrs, U.S.A. ... [1885]." Scale 1:600,000. Dimensions 37 X 60 inches. MS map in ink on paper. Records of the Office of the Chief of Engineers, Map Q57-1, NA.

Figure 26. Pencil sketch made by G. K. Warren in his survey field notebook during his "Reconnaissance from Ft. Laramie to Camp of Oct. 5th & 6th on White River, ... in Nebraska, in 1855." Scale very large. Dimensions 6½ X 4 inches. MS in pencil on paper. Records of the Office of the Chief of Engineers, Q579, no. 50, NA.

Figure 27. "Bug Catching," a sketch in pencil included in a survey field notebook in the hand of Lt. G. K. Warren, 1857, during his surveys in the Dakota Country. Dimensions 6½ X 4 inches. MS in pencil on paper. Records of the Office of the Chief of Engineers, Q579, no. 53, NA.

Figure 28. Part of a field survey sheet of the Missouri River in the vicinity of Sailor Island (Lat. 43°32'N, Long. 99°28'W), sheet 17, in "Original sketches of a Reconnaissance of the Missouri River from the Northern Boundary of Kansas to a part sixty-two miles above Fort Union, made during the Summer of 1855 and 1856 by Lieut. G. K. Warren, U.S. Top'l Eng'rs ... " Scale 1½ inch to 1 mile. Dimensions of sheet 39 X 27 inches. MS map in pencil on paper. Records of the Office of the Chief of Engineers, Q579-17, NA.

Figure 29. "Map of [the United States West of the Mississippi River showing] Routes for a Pacific Railroad, compiled to accompany the Report of the Hon. Jefferson Davis, Sec. of War, in Office of P. R. R. Surveys, 1855 ... G. K. Warren." Scale 1 inch to 100 miles. Dimensions 22½ X 24½ inches. Printed map on paper. Records of the Office of the Secretary of the Interior, General maps. Pacific Railroad Surveys, NA.

Figure 30. "Sheyenne River [Dakota Territory, 1853], J. M. Stanley, Del. ... Sarony, Major & Knapp, Liths. 449 Broadway, N.Y." Dimensions 8 ½ X 11½ inches. Lithographic print in color. Published in "General Report by Isaac I. Stevens," *Reports of the Explorations and Surveys to Ascertain a Most Practicable and Economical Route for a Railroad from the Mississippi River to the Pacific Ocean*

... 1853–5, vol. 12, book 1 (Washington, D.C.: 1860), pl. 9, opp. p. 58, NA.

Figure 31. "Herd of Bison, near Lake Jessie [Dakota Territory, 1853], J. M. Stanley, Del. ... Sarony, Major & Knapp, Liths. 449 Broadway, N.Y." Dimensions 8½ X 11½ inches. Lithographic print in color. Published in "General Report by Isaac I. Stevens," *Reports of the Explorations and Surveys to Ascertain a Most Practicable and Economical Route for a Railroad from the Mississippi River to the Pacific Ocean ... 1853–5,* vol. 12, book 1 (Washington, D.C.: 1860), pl. 10, opp. p. 59, NA.

Figure 32. "N. P. R. R. Exploration and Survey [Map] Sheet No. 1, St. Paul to Riviere des Lacs, By Isaac I. Stevens, Governor of Washington Territory. In obedience to instructions from the War Department, 1853 ... Drawn by John Lambert, Topographer of the exploration." Scale 1 inch to 22 miles. Dimensions 27 X 39½ inches. MS map in ink on paper. Records of the Office of the Secretary of the Interior, Maps, Records near the 47th and 49th Parallels, NA.

Figure 33. "Map of the Territory of the United States from the Mississippi to the Pacific Ocean. Ordered by the Hon. Jeff'n Davis, Secretary of War, to accompany the Reports of the Explorations for a Railroad Route ... Compiled from authorized explorations and other reliable data by Lieut. G. K. Warren, Top'l Engineers, 1854–5–6–7." Scale 1 inch to 50 miles. Dimensions 44 X 48½ inches. Printed map in ink on paper. Records of the Department of the Interior, Pacific Railroad Surveys, Published Map Series, General, NA.

Figure 34. Portion (36° to 42°N; 102° to 108°30') of a section of a manuscript compilation prepared presumably in the Office of Explorations and Surveys in Washington, D.C., during 1853–57 for use in engraving for the "Map of Territory of the United States from the Mississippi to the Pacific Ocean. Ordered by the Hon. Jeff'n Davis, ... To accompany the Reports of the Explorations for a Railroad Route ... by Lieut. G. K. Warren, Top'l Engineers, 1854–5–6–7." Scale approx. 1 inch to 40 miles. Dimensions 10½ X 13 inches. MS map in pencil and ink on paper. Records of the Department of the Interior, Pacific Railroad Surveys, MS General Map, folder 2, NA.

RELEVANT RECORDS IN THE NATIONAL ARCHIVES

The following are the principal groups of records in the National Archives in Washington, D.C., in which there is a significant resource of official records bearing on the general subject of this paper. They are listed in order by Record Group (RG) and by subgroup (a, b, etc.) in each instance as the potential volume merits. There are available in the Central Research Room of the National Archives various inventories, lists, and other finding aids and detailed identification and accession inventories.

RG39 Records of the Bureau of Accounts (Treasury)
   a. Division of Bookkeeping and Warrants
RG46 Records of the United States Senate
   a. Legislative (A)
   b. Executive (B)
   c. Records of the Office of the Secretary (D)
RG48 General Records of the Department of the Interior
   a. Lands and Railroads Division (1849–1907)
   b. Office of Explorations and Surveys for Pacific Railroads (1851–62)
RG75 Records of the Bureau of Indian Affairs
   a. Letters Received, 1806–60
   b. Copies of Letters Sent, 1807–60
   c. Central Map Files, 1790–1860
RG76 Records of Boundary and Claims Commissions and Arbitrations
   a. United States and Canada (Northern) Boundary, 1814–60
   b. United States and Texas Boundary, 1838
   c. United States and Mexico Boundary, 1848–60
RG77 Records of the Office of the Chief of Engineers
   a. General Correspondence, 1789–1870
   b. Reports, 1842–85
   c. Returns, 1832–1916
   d. Issuances, 1811–1941
   e. Papers of Engineer Officers and Others, 1803–1907
   f. Field Notes and Observations, 1793–1916
   g. Cartographic Records, Headquarters Map Files, 1783–1960
   h. Cartographic Records, Fortifications Map Files, 1783–1960
RG92 Records of the Office of the Quartermaster General
   a. Central Records, 1792–1926
   b. Records of Officers, 1826–1916

   c. Cartographic Records, 1783–1860
RG93 War Department Collection of Revolutionary War Records
   a. Record Books of the Revolutionary War, 1776–83, entries to Geographer, Robert Erskine, Simeon DeWitt, Thomas Hutchins
   b. Records of General or Varied Content Documenting Revolutionary War Activities, 1775–83
   c. Records Relating to Military Organization and Service, 1775–83
RG94 Records of the Adjutant General's Office, 1780s–1917
   a. Cartographic Records Relating to Army Explorations in the Western United States, 1853–60
   b. Records Relating to the United States Military Academy, 1803–60
   c. Records of the Military Reservation Division, 1800–60
RG98 Records of the United States Army Commands, 1784–1821
   a. Records of Army Posts, 1840–60
   b. Records of Geographical Commands, 1813–60
RG107 Records of the Office of the Secretary of War
   a. Secretary of War, Correspondence Books, 1800–60
   b. Secretary of War, Letters Received, 1793–1860
   c. Secretary of War, Copies of Letters Sent, 1800–1809
   d. Secretary of War, Copies of Miscellaneous Letters Sent, 1800–1809
RG108 Headquarters of the Army
RG233 Records of the United States House of Representatives
   This voluminous body of records is arranged by Congress and Session and thereunder by major functions of the House generally, including Records of Legislative Proceedings and Records of the Office of the Clerk, 1789–1860.

PUBLISHED FINDING AIDS TO RECORDS IN THE NATIONAL ARCHIVES

The following finding aids published by the National Archives include references to records of particular research value to the historical geography and cartography of the plains. The entries with an asterisk before them are out of print but may be available in reference libraries.

*Guide to the Records in the National Archives, 1948. 684 pp.

Preliminary Inventories:

*17. Adjutant General's Office, 1949. 149 pp.
*23. United States Senate, 1950. 284 pp.
 81. Cartographic Records of the Office of the Secretary of the Interior, 1955. 11 pp.
113. House of Representatives, 1959. 587 pp. 2 vols.
114. War Department Collection of Revolutionary Records, 1962. 40 pp.
136. Records of the United States and Mexican Claims Commission, 1962. 51 pp.
163. Bureau of Indian Affairs, 1965. 2 vols.

Special Lists:

13. Cartographic Records of the Bureau of Indian Affairs, 1954. 127 pp.
19. Cartographic Records of the General Land Office, 1964. 202 pp.

REFERENCES CITED

The following published or printed references have been useful in the preparation of this paper. Many are the official published reports and maps. There is of course an additional large number of relevant publications.

Albright, George L.
  1921. *Official explorations for Pacific railroads.* Berkeley: University of California Press.
Allen, James, and Schoolcraft, H. R.
  1835. A map and report of Lieut. J. Allen and H. B. [sic] Schoolcraft's visit to the northwest Indians in 1832. U.S. Congress, 1st sess. *House Doc. 323,* Serial 257, pp. 1–68.
Allen, John L.
  1971. Lewis and Clark on the upper Missouri: Decision at the Marias. *Montana: The Magazine of Western History* 21(3): 2–17.
Allen, John L.
  1972. An analysis of the exploratory process: The Lewis and Clark Expedition of 1804–1806. *Geographical Review* 62:13–39.

Beers, Henry P.
  1935. *The western military frontier, 1815–1846.* Philadelphia: Published privately.
Beers, Henry P.
  1942. A history of the U.S. Topographical Engineers, 1813–1863. *The Military Engineer* 34: 287–91, 348–52.
Biddle, Nicholas, ed.
  1814. *History of the expedition under the command of Captains Lewis and Clark, . . . 1804–5–6 . . .* 2 vols. Philadephia: London et al.
Bigelow, John.
  1856. *Memoir of the life and public services of John Charles Frémont. . . .* New York: Derby & Jackson.
Billington, Ray A.
  1967. *Westward expansion: A history of the American frontier.* New York: Macmillan Co.
Boutwell, William T.
  1902. Schoolcraft's exploration tour of 1832. *Minnesota Historical Society Collections* 1: 121–40.
Bray, Martha C.
  1969. Joseph Nicolas Nicollet, geographer. In *Frenchmen and French ways in the Mississippi Valley,* edited by John Francis McDermott, pp. 29–55. Urbana: University of Illinois Press.
Brebner, John B.
  1933. *The explorers of North America, 1492–1806.* New York: Macmillan Co.
Brown, Ralph H.
  1930. Trans-montane routes in Colorado. *Economic Geography* 4: 412–24.
  1948. *Historical geography of the United States.* New York: Harcourt, Brace.
Burpee, Lawrence J.
  1914. *Pathfinders of the Great Plains: Chronicle of La Vérendrye and his sons.* Toronto: Brook & Co.
Camp, Charles L.
  1953. *Henry R. Wagner's "The Plains and the Rockies": A bibliography of original narratives of travel and adventure, 1800–1860.* Columbus, Ohio: Long's College Book Co.
Carey, Charles H.
  1931. *The journals of Theodore Talbot, 1843 and 1849–52, with the Fremont Expedition of 1843 . . .* Portland, Ore.: Metropolitan Press.
Chittenden, Hiram M.
  1903. *History of early steamboat navigation on the Missouri River, . . .* New York: F. P. Harper.
  1936. *The American fur trade and the Far West: A history of the Missouri Valley and the Rocky Mountains . . .* New York: R. R. Wilson, Inc.

Claussen, Martin P., and Friis, Herman R., comps.
  1941.   *Descriptive catalog of maps published by Congress, 1817–1843.* Washington, D.C.: Published privately.
Coues, Elliott.
  1876.   An account of the various publications relating to the travels of Lewis and Clark. *Bulletin of the Geological and Geographical Survey of the Territories,* ser. 2, no. 6, pp. 417–44.
Cox, Isaac J.
  1905.   The exploration of the Louisiana frontier, 1803–1806. *American Historical Association Annual Report for 1904,* pp. 149–74.
  1946.   An early explorer of the Louisiana Purchase. *American Philosophical Society Library Bulletin* 4:73–77.
Cullum, George W.
  1891.   *Biographical register of the officers and graduates of the U.S. Military Academy . . . , 1802 to 1890.* 3 vols. Boston: Houghton, Mifflin & Co.
Cutright, Paul R.
  1969.   *Lewis and Clark, pioneering naturalists.* Urbana: University of Illinois Press.
Dellenbaugh, Frederick S.
  1914.   *Frémont and '49.* New York: G. P. Putnam's Sons.
Diller, Aubrey.
  1944.   Maps of the Missouri River before Lewis and Clark. In *Studies and essays . . . in homage to George Sarton,* edited by M. F. Ashley Montagu, pp. 505–19. New York: Schuman.
Dodge, Henry.
  1836.   . . . a report of the expedition of the dragoons, under the command of Colonel Henry Dodge to the Rocky Mountains, during the summer of 1835, etc. U.S. 24th Congress, 1st sess. *House Doc. 181,* Serial 289, pp. 1–37.
Dunbar, William.
  1904.   Journal of a geometrical survey commencing at St. Catherine's landing on the east shore of the Mississippi descending to the mouth of the red river, and thence ascending that river, the black river and river of the Washita . . . In *Documents relating to the purchase and exploration of Louisiana.* Boston: Houghton, Mifflin & Co.
Dunbar, William, and Hunter, George.
  1832.   Observations made in a voyage, commencing at St. Catherine's landing, . . . and the Washita River, extracted from the Journals of William Dunbar, Esquire, and Dr. Hunter. *American State Papers: Indian Affairs,* 1: 731–43.
Dupuy, Richard E.
  1951.   *Men of West Point: The first 150 years of the United States Military Academy.* New York: Sloane.
Ehrenberg, Ralph E.
  1968.   Cartographic records of the Red River region in the National Archives. *Red River Valley Historian* 2:5–7.
  1969.   Nicholas King: The first surveyor of the City of Washington, 1803–1812. *Records of the Columbia Historical Society,* vol. 1969–70, pp. 31–65.
  1971a.   *Exploration, surveying, and mapping records in the national archives: resources for historical geographers.* Washington, D.C.: National Archives.
  1971b.   Our heritage in maps: sketch of part of the Missouri and Yellowstone Rivers with a description of the country. *Prologue: The Journal of the National Archives* 3: 73–79.
Emory, W. H.
  1848.   Notes of a military reconnaissance, from Fort Leavenworth, in Missouri to San Diego, in California, . . . made in 1846–7 . . . U.S. 30th Congress, 1st sess. *House Executive Doc. 41,* Serial 517, pp. 1–134.
Featherstonhaugh, George W.
  1835.   Geological report of an examination made in 1834, of the elevated country between the Missouri and Red Rivers, . . . U.S. Geologist. U.S. 23rd Congress, 2d sess. *House Doc. 151,* Serial 274, pp. 1–97.
  1836.   Report of a geological reconnaissance [*sic*] made in 1835, from the Seat of Government by the way of Green Bay and the Wisconsin Territory, to the Coleau de Prairie, an elevated ridge dividing the Missouri from the St. Peter's River . . . U.S. 24th Congress, 1st sess. *Senate Executive Doc. 333,* Serial 282, pp. 1–168.
Frémont, Jessie B.
  1891.   The origin of the Frémont expeditions. *Century Magazine* 61:768–69.
Frémont, John C.
  1843.   A report on an exploration of the country lying between the Missouri River and the Rocky Mountains on the line of the Kansas and Great Platte Rivers. U.S. 27th Congress, 3rd sess. *Senate Doc. 243,* Serial 416, pp. 1–207.
  1845a.   *Report of the exploring expedition to the Rocky Mountains in the year 1843 and to Oregon and North California in the years 1843–44.* Washington, D.C.: Blair & Rives.
  1845b.   A report of the exploring expedition to Oregon and North California in the years 1843–'44, by Brevet Capt. J. C. Frémont. U.S. 28th Congress, 2d sess. *House Executive Doc. 166,* Serial 467, pp. 103–583.

1848. *Narrative of the exploring expedition to the Rocky Mountains in the year 1842, and to Oregon and North California in the years 1843–44.* Syracuse: Hall & Dickson.

1887. *Memoirs of my life . . . including in the narrative five journeys of western exploration during the years 1842, 1843–4, 1845–7, 1848–9, 1853–4.* Chicago: Bedford, Clarke & Co.

Friis, Herman R.

1954. Cartographic and geographic activities of the Lewis and Clark Expedition. *Journal of the Washington Academy of Science* 44: 338–51.

1958. Highlights in the first hundred years of surveying and mapping and geographical exploration of the United States by the federal government, 1775–1880. *Surveying and Mapping: A Quarterly Journal* 18(2): 186–206.

1959. Alexander von Humboldt's Besuch in den Vereinigten Staaten von Amerika . . . 1804. In *Alexander von Humboldt Studien . . .* edited by Joachim H. Schultze, pp. 142–95. Berlin: Die Gesellschaft für Erdkunde zu Berlin.

1960–62. Alexander von Humboldt's visit to Washington, D.C., June 1 through June 13, 1804. *Records of the Columbia Historical Society, 1960–62,* pp. 1–36.

1965. A brief review of the development and status of geographical and cartographical activities of the United States government: 1776–1818. In *Imago mundi: A review of early cartography,* edited by C. Koeman, pp. 68–80. Amsterdam: N. Israel.

1967a. Highlights of the geographical and cartographical contributions of graduates of the U.S. Military Academy with a specialization as topographical engineers prior to 1860. *Proceedings of the Eighth Annual Meeting of the New York—New Jersey Division of the Association of American Geographers at West Point,* vol. 1, pp. 10–29.

1967b. Stephen H. Long's unpublished manuscript map of the United States compiled in 1820–1822(?). *California Geographer* 8 (1967): 75–87.

1967c. The image of the American West at mid-century (1840–60): A product of scientific geographical exploration by the United States government. In *The Frontier Re-Examined,* edited by John Francis McDermott, pp. 49–63, Urbana: University of Illinois Press.

1970. The documents and reports of the United States Congress: A primary source of information on travel in the West, 1783–1861. In *Travelers on the western frontier,* ed. J. F. McDermott, pp. 112–67. Urbana: University of Illinois Press.

Fuller, Harlin M., and Hafen, LeRoy R., eds.

1957. The journal of Captain John R. Bell, official journalist for the Stephen H. Long Expedition to the Rocky Mountains, 1820. *Far West and the Rockies Historical Series* 6: 1–349.

Gallaher, Ruth A.

1945. J. N. Nicollet, map maker. *Palimpset* 26: 289–302.

Gilbert, Edmund W.

1929. South Pass: A study in the historical geography of the United States. *Scottish Geographical Magazine* 45: 144–54.

1933. *The exploration of western America, 1800–1850: An historical geography.* Cambridge, Eng.: University Press.

Goetzmann, William H.

1959. *Army exploration in the American West, 1803–1863.* New Haven, Conn.: Yale University Press.

1966. *Exploration and empire: The explorer and scientist in the winning of the American West.* New York: Alfred A. Knopf.

Gudde, Erwin G., and Gudde, Elizabeth K., trans. and eds. 1958. *Exploring with Frémont,* by [Charles Preuss.] Norman: University of Oklahoma Press.

Hafen, LeRoy R., and Rister, Carl C.

1941. *Western America: The exploration, settlement, and development of the region beyond the Mississippi.* New York: Prentice-Hall.

Hamilton, R. N.

1934. The early cartography of the Missouri Valley. *American Historical Review* 39: 645–62.

Hartwell, Mary A.

1911. *Checklist of United States public documents, 1789–1909 . . .* Washington, D.C.: GPO.

Hasse, Adelaide R.

1899. *Reports of explorations printed in the documents of the U.S. government: A contribution toward a bibliography.* Washington, D.C.: GPO.

Heitman, Francis B.

1903. *Historical register and dictionary of the United States Army.* 2 vols. Washington, D.C.: GPO.

Heusser, Albert H.

1966. *George Washington's map maker: A biography of Robert Erskine . . .* New Brunswick, N.J.: Rutgers University Press.

Hine, Robert V.

1962. *Edward Kern and American expansion.* New Haven, Conn.: Yale University Press.

Jackson, Donald D., ed.

1962. *Letters of the Lewis and Clark Expedition, with related documents, 1783–1854.* Urbana: University of Illinois Press.

1966*a*. Maps of the Pike expeditions. In *Journals with letters and related documents, Zebulon Montgomery Pike,* vol. 1, pp. 451–62. Norman: University of Oklahoma Press.

1966*b*. *Journals, with letters and related documents, Zebulon Montgomery Pike.* 2 vols. Norman: University of Oklahoma Press.

Jackson, Donald, and Spence, Mary Lee, eds.

1970. *The expeditions of John Charles Frémont.* Vol. 1. *Travels from 1838 to 1844, with a portfolio of maps.* Urbana: University of Illinois Press.

Jackson, William T.

1952. *Wagon roads west: A study of federal road surveys and construction in the trans-Mississippi West, 1846–1896.* Berkeley: University of California Press.

James, Edwin, comp.

1823. *Account of expedition to the Rocky Mountains, performed in the years 1819 and '20 . . .* 2 vols. and Atlas. Philadelphia: H. C. Carey & I. Lea.

Jefferson, Thomas.

1806. *Message from the President of the United States communicating discoveries made in exploring the Missouri, Red River, and the Washita, by Captains Lewis and Clark, Doctor Sibley, and Mr. Dunbar.* Washington City.

Kelsay, Laura E.

1971. *Cartographic records in the National Archives relating to Indians in the United States.* Washington, D.C.: National Archives.

Marcy, Randolph B.

1853. Exploration of the Red River of Louisiana in the year 1852. U.S. 32d Congress, 2d sess. *Senate Executive Doc. 54,* Serial 666, pp. 1–320.

1856. Report of an expedition to the sources of the Brazos and Big Wichita rivers, during the summer of 1854. U.S. 34th Congress, 1st sess. *Senate Executive Doc. 60,* Serial 821, pp. 1–48.

Martin, Edwin T.

1952. *Thomas Jefferson: Scientist.* New York: H. Schuman.

Mattes, Merrill J.

1969. *The Great Platte River Road.* Lincoln: Nebraska State Historical Society.

McDermott, John F.

1959. The western journals of George Hunter, 1796–1805. *Proceedings of the American Philosophical Society* 103: 770–73.

1963. The western journals of Dr. George Hunter, 1796–1805. *Transactions of the American Philosophical Society . . . ,* N.S. vol. 53(4), pp. 1–133.

1967. *The frontier re-examined.* Urbana: University of Illinois Press.

1969. *Frenchmen and French ways in the Mississippi Valley.* Urbana: University of Illinois Press.

McDermott, John F., ed.

1970. *Travelers on the Western Frontier.* Urbana: University of Illinois Press.

Meinig, Donald.

1955. Isaac Stevens: Practical geographer of the early Northwest. *Geographical Review* 45: 542–58.

Meisel, Max.

1926. *A bibliography of American natural history: The pioneer century, 1769–1865.* 3 vols. New York: Premier Publishing Co.

Michler, N. H., et al.

1850. Reconnaissance of routes from San Antonio to El Paso. U.S. 31st Congress, 1st sess. *Senate Executive Doc. 64,* Serial 562, pp. 1–54.

Mitchill, Samuel L.

1806. Lewis's map of parts of North-America . . . *Medical Repository,* 2d hex, vol. 3, pp. 315–19.

Nevins, Allan.

1955. *Frémont: Pathmarker of the West.* New York: Longmans, Green.

Nicollet, Joseph N.

1843*a*. [Nicollet] exhibited his original map of the northwestern territory of the United States, made from personal observations, and read an account of his geographical exploration of the sources of the Mississippi. *Proceedings of the American Philosophical Society* 3: 140–42.

1843*b*. Report intended to illustrate a map of the hydrographical basin of the Upper Mississippi River, made by I. [sic] N. Nicollet, while in employ under the Bureau of the Corps of Topographical Engineers. U.S. 26th Congress, 2d sess. *Senate Doc. 237,* Serial 380, pp. 1–237.

Osgood, Ernest S., ed.

1964. *The field notes of Captain William Clark, 1803–1805.* New Haven, Conn.: Yale University Press.

Poore, Ben Perley, comp.

1885. Descriptive catalogue of the government publications of the United States, September 5, 1774–March 4, 1881. U.S. 48th Congress, 2d sess. *Senate Miscellaneous Doc. 67,* Serial 2268.

Riley, Franklin F.

1899. Sir William Dunbar: The pioneer scientist of Mississippi. *Publications of the Mississippi Historical Society* 2: 85–111.

Rowland, Eron, ed.

1930. *Life, letters, and papers of William Dunbar, 1749–1810.* Jackson: Mississippi Historical Society.

Shapley, Harlow.
1943.   Notes on Thomas Jefferson as a natural philosopher. *Proceedings of the American Philosophical Society* 87(1): 234–37.

Surface, Thomas G.
1909.   Thomas Jefferson: A pioneer student of America's geography. *American Geographical Society Bulletin* 41: 743–50.

Taft, Robert.
1951.   The pictorial record of the Old West: XIV. Illustrators of the Pacific Survey Reports. *Kansas Historical Quarterly* 19: 353–80.

Thwaites, Reuben G., ed.
1904–1905.   *Original journals of the Lewis and Clark Expedition, 1804–1806; Printed from the original manuscripts in the library of the American Philosophical Society, . . .* 8 vols. New York: Dodd, Mead & Co.
1904–1907.   *Early western travels, 1748–1846, . . .* 32 vols. Cleveland: A. H. Clark Co.

U.S. Congress.
1832–61.   Lewis and Clark's expedition. *American State Papers: Indian Affairs,* 1: 705–43. U.S. Secretary of War.
1834.   Letter . . . transmitting a map and report of Lieut. Allen and H. B. [sic] Schoolcraft's visit to the northwest Indians in 1832. U.S. 23rd Congress, 1st sess. *House Doc. 323,* Serial 257, pp. 1–68.
1836.   Journal of a march of a detachment of dragoons, under command of Colonel [Henry] Dodge, during the summer of 1835, in a report of the secretary of war dated February 27, 1836. U.S. 24th Congress, 1st sess. *House Doc. 181,* Serial 289, pp. 1–37.

U.S. Superintendent of Documents.
1911.   *Checklist of United States public documents, 1789–1909 . . .* Washington, D. C.

War, Secretary of.
1854–55.   Reports of explorations and surveys, to ascertain the most practicable and economical route for a railroad from the Mississippi River to the Pacific Ocean. Made under the Secretary of War, in 1854–5, . . . U.S. 33rd Congress, 2d sess. *Senate Doc. 78,* vol. 1–11, Serials 758–68. Washington, D.C.
1859–60.   Reports of explorations and surveys, . . . U. S. 36th Congress, 1st sess. *House Executive Doc. 56,* volume 12, pt. 1 and 2, Serials 1054 and 1055.

Warren, G. K.
1856.   Report of Lieutenant G. K. Warren of the United States Topographical Engineer Corps, of his recent exploration of the region of the country between the Missouri and the Platte rivers and the Rocky Mountains with the maps accompanying the same. U.S. 34th Congress, 1st sess. *Senate Executive Doc. 76,* Serial 822, pp. 1–79.
1859*a*.   Memoir to accompany the map of the Territory of the United States from the Mississippi to the Pacific Ocean; giving brief account of each of the exploring expeditions since A.D. 1800 . . . in U.S. War Department, reports of explorations and surveys . . . U.S. 33rd Congress, 2d sess. *Senate Doc. 78,* vol. II, pp. 1–120.
1859*b*.   Explorations in Nebraska [1855–57]. U.S. 35th Congress, 2d sess. *Senate Executive Doc. 1,* Serial 975, pp. 620–70.

Wheat, Carl I.
1957–63.   *Mapping the transmississippi West, 1540–1861.* 5 vols. San Francisco: Institute of Historical Cartography.

Whittington, G. P.
1927.   Dr. John Sibley of Natchitoches, 1757–1837. *Louisiana Historical Quarterly* 10: 463–512.

Winchell, N. H.
1891.   Joseph Nicolas Nicollet, 1786–1843. *American Geologist* 8: 343–52.

Subjective Surveyors

The Appraisal of Farm Lands in Western Canada, 1870–1930

John L. Tyman
Brandon University, Canada

*If gold ruste, **what shall iren** do?*
*For if a preest **be foul**, on whom we truste,*
*No wonder is **a lewd man** to ruste.*
  Geoffrey Chaucer, *The Canterbury Tales*
  (ca. 1390)

A century ago on the Canadian prairies, while the advocates of settlement in "Palliser's triangle" battled with those who clung to the "fertile belt," while "Professor" Macoun pronounced in confidence and "Yowl" Hind cried out in rage, surveyors were at work assessing the suitability of individual townships and sections. Their purpose in so doing was to provide a thorough inventory of the agricultural resources of the interior as a guide to future settlement. The question was, how much faith should a would-be pioneer place in such an assessment? How much could he? And how much did he? (Tyman 1972).

VESTED INTERESTS

Needless to say, by no means everyone was interested in complete objectivity. Those receiving large grants of land from the Crown, for one reason or another, had occasion sometimes to view the land with their own interests in mind. Best known, of course, is the case of the Canadian Pacific Railway; but there were other bodies which benefited from assessments similarly biased in their favor. This is true, for example, of the Provincial Government of Manitoba in its search for "Swamp Lands."

CPR Lands

Under the terms of its contract with the dominion government the Canadian Pacific Railway, in selecting its subsidy of 25 million acres, was not bound to accept any land which was not "fairly fit for settlement" (Statutes of Canada, 1881). Within the main line belt which paralleled the transcontinental railway, the bulk of the land which was rejected lay west of the Missouri Coteau, in the short-grass country. Further east, though, in fairly well-watered areas, many sections were also rejected.

Even a very generalized representation of the distribution of unacceptable quarter sections reveals the dominance of physical criteria. In southwest Manitoba, for example (fig. 1), rejection of land was common even close to the railway in areas which were sandy or marshy, or had definite topographic limitations associated with the degree of dissection or the frequency of sloughs.

Detailed study, however, of actual sales records (Glenbow Archives) suggests that other factors were considered also, since the aim of selection in this case was not land classification but land sale. The earliest official lists of lands accepted and lands rejected were compiled after the Manitoba land boom of 1881–82 (Canadian Sessional Papers, 1885). A total of 8,854 quarter sections had been examined in western Manitoba to December 29,

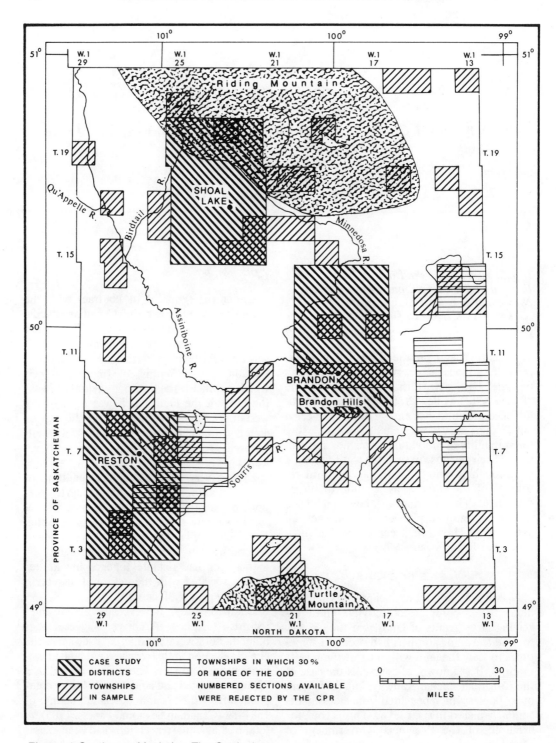

Figure 1 Southwest Manitoba: The Study Area

1884, and 15 percent of these were rejected. All of those rejected, however, had been offered for sale in 1882. In fact, there are instances of lands being sold in 1882 but later rejected by the company on the failure of the sales contracts relating thereto. Conversely, of the 1,298 quarter sections rejected in southwest Manitoba in 1884, 80 were accepted in 1888—at a time, presumably, when the standards for selection had necessarily been lowered (Canadian Sessional Papers, 1889).

Swamp Lands

The "Better Terms Act" of 1885 provided that all Crown Lands in Manitoba which could be shown to be "Swamp Lands" would be transferred to the province "and enure wholly to its benefit and uses." The term *swamp,* however, was open to various interpretations.

The Canadian government, as usual, followed the American precedent, specifying "all legal sub-divisions the greater part of which are subject to overflow and thereby rendered unfit for cultivation" (Canadian Orders in Council, 1886). Selections were to be made by two surveyors appointed for the purpose and working only in summer, between May 20 and October 1. The cost would be borne by the province. These swamp lands commissioners supplied the minister of the interior with lists of lands selected, and transfers were approved by Order in Council.

It sounds simple enough, but in practice, lands which the commissioners considered to be swampy often appeared to others to be eminently suitable for cultivation. In 1900 the general colonization agent of the dominion government noted that the reports of his local agents and of the swamp lands commissioners were "very conflicting." The provincial commissioners had "selected the land in a wholesale manner, without giving the matter a very close inspection" (Public Archives, [1]). The federal commissioner of immigration (Public Archives, [2]) was more outspoken:

I have no doubt whatsoever that these Swamp Lands Commissioners took lands they were not entitled to. I understand they thought anything that has been flooded any time within the last few years will be considered as swamp lands. In that case, as I am told that nearly all of North Dakota is now under water and the grain sheaves are floating, I presume these would be considered swamp lands.

The Manitoba government actually confided in potential customers that in many cases what were referred to as "swamp lands" were "not swamp lands at all, but are valuable for farming purposes" (Manitoba, 1889). And the truth of these remarks was attested to by many of the Ukranian immigrants coming to Manitoba at the turn of the century. Forced, by their late arrival, to take up lands on the margins of the settled area, they often squatted on lands which they cleared and cultivated, only to discover that the area had been closed to homesteading following selection by the swamp lands commissioners. Just how these "surveyors" were paid is uncertain, but it seems not unreasonable to suggest that they were paid on a commission basis!

THE DOMINION LANDS SURVEY CLASSIFICATION

Where vested interests complicate the issue the anomalous and the subjective are only to be expected. In examining the notebooks of dominion lands surveyors (Manitoba Surveys Branch), however, one assumes a greater measure of objectivity. The rates of pay of surveyors under contract varied, admittedly, in response to differences in the character of the land, but in accordance with vegetation, not soil type. Precision (or a reasonable facsimile thereof) is what one expects of men hired to mark lines upon the ground, of men sworn to accuracy of observation. But they were, in fact, assigned a wide range of tasks, and though they had duly qualified as land surveyors, they were scarcely soil scientists.

The officers of the Dominion Lands Survey inevitably became involved in the debate concerning the agricultural value of western Canada, especially when they began laying out townships in the open prairie along the United

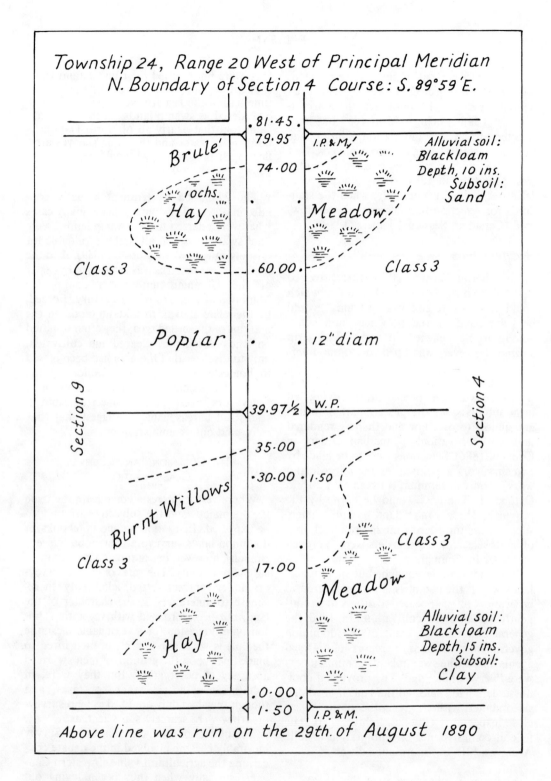

Figure 2 Page from DLS Field Notes

78

States border. At the close of 1879, for example, the surveyor general reported:

> The surveys made during the past season go to show that previously held estimates of quantities of first-class arable land in any given part of the territory, have been within the mark. Districts hitherto roughly classified as inferior, prove to be but partly so, and those defined as fertile areas, have their limits more extended the fuller our information becomes. As a particular instance may be cited the so-called "infertile lands of the Souris". . . . The generalization of infertility . . . would be altogether incorrect if used to qualify the country on the lower part of the river's course. [Canadian Sessional Papers, 1880]

The reports on townships surveyed in the Souris and Turtle Mountain districts in 1880 were "favorable in the extreme." Indeed it appeared that the whole country south of the Assiniboine and Qu'Appelle rivers was well suited to settlement, at least as far west as the Missouri Coteau.

Basis of Scheme

In their field notes the surveyors had to indicate "the nature of the soil, classifying it, according to its fitness for agriculture, as first, second, third or fourth rate" (fig. 2). Later editions of the *Manual of Dominion Land Surveys* required also the "depth of loam and kind of subsoil where pits were dug" (fig. 3). However, no indication was given of the criteria to be used in classification, and the related literature is similarly devoid of any systematic guide to the method used.

The "Schedule showing Classification of Land" which accompanies the report of William Pearce's survey of township outlines in 1879 provides some indication of his thoughts on the matter. His percentage figures for "Land Suitable for Cultivation" were obtained by deducting from the whole, areas of "stony" lands, "ponds," "hay land," and "timber" (Canadian Sessional Papers, 1880). Pearce's

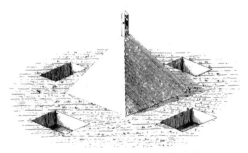

Figure 3 "Ordinary Earth Mound"—with Pits and Post

avoidance of numerical grades, however, precludes any attempt at the correlation of his findings with those of the later subdivision surveys, which were in any case the work of other men.

The usefulness of George Simpson's "section" from Winnipeg to the Rockies is limited for much the same reason, but his report does at least suggest the weight given in classification to the depth of "loam" and the character of the subsoil. On the basis of sixty-one pits, four feet in depth, dug at intervals of twenty miles, he classified the soils of the parkland belt and of the prairie between Elbow and Saskatoon (Canadian Sessional Papers, 1882):

I.   Loam with clay subsoil—
    30 samples, or . . . . . 49.2 per cent
  Loam 16 to 30 inches deep,
    sand subsoil—
    11 samples, or . . . . . 18.0 per cent
  Loam over thin layer of gravel,
    with clay subsoil—
    2 samples, or . . . . 3.3 per cent
        Total . . . . 70.5 per cent
  All the above are first class soils
  for agricultural purposes.

II. Second class—good grazing ground:
  Loam 6 to 16 inches in thickness,
    sand subsoil—
    13 samples, or . . . . . 21.3 per cent
  Loam over gravel or sand—
    2 samples, or . . . . 3.3 per cent
        Total . . . . 24.6 per cent

III. Third class, or sand—
    4 samples, or . . . . 4.9 per cent

Problems of Objectivity

Various writers, including Weir (1961), have noted the difficulties involved in interpreting DLS data on soils. The most interesting observations, though, were those made in 1919 at a minor symposium on land classification (Brenot et al. 1919). At that time a new classification of lands was in course of implementation in readiness for the settlement of returned war veterans, and it was suggested that use might be made of the records of the original survey. In reply it was noted that "when the surveyor's field notes were made up, he hadn't in view so much the recording of information sufficient for an accurate land classification as he did the return of field notes of high accuracy in measurement." His chief objective had been "accuracy and economy of surveys. Data of an engineering or economic nature was of secondary importance and visions of future development didn't haunt him."

In short, although the appearance of the soil and of the plant cover were undoubtedly taken into account when the land was graded during subdivision, in the final analysis much depended on the outlook and experience (or lack of it) of the surveyor himself and also, possibly, on the date of the survey. In later life William Pearce (1914) commended the early surveyors (himself included?) for "the honesty and truthfulness of their reports of the country, and accuracy of work," without which "settlement would have been a miserable failure." However, while there is no reason to doubt their honesty, there is every reason to question their objectivity, even the possibility of the same in the absence of detailed instructions for classification.

Individual Surveyors

The kind of difficulties encountered by surveyors in grading the soil can be imagined from George Stewart's record of the subdivision of Township 19, Range 20 W.1:

The land generally appears to be fair, but owing to the depth of snow that was on the ground at the time the survey was made, good opportunities for observing the soil seldom occurred. . . . I have endeavoured to classify the soils in my field notes to the best of my knowledge.

Personal qualities also proved to be significant. Certain surveyors, for example, were unable ever to bring themselves to grade any land as fourth class: others were grudging in their use of class one. Some were more ready to generalize than others: James Reiffenstein is a good example. His township summaries invariably conclude with a statement that "the soil throughout is of the finest quality" (regardless of vegetation or parent material!) and in his notebooks there is rarely any attempt to differentiate soils within a township. In contrast, Evans and Bolger, George McPhillips, and John Morris took great pains to record even minor differences. Milner Hart had a system all of his own; he seldom assigned unqualified grades, preferring designations such as "1 & 2," "2 & 3."

Though individuals may have been more or

TABLE 1

Percentage Correlation of DLS Classification with Type of
Vegetation, Brandon District

LAND CLASSIFICATION		TYPE OF VEGETATION			
Class	Percentage	Woodland	Scrub	Prairie	Marsh
First	43	53	46	42	11
Second	41	21	41	42	44
Third	14	17	12	14	15
Fourth	2	9	1	2	30

TABLE 2

Percentage Correlation of DLS Classification with Type of Vegetation, Brandon District, Individual Surveyors

SURVEYOR(S)	LAND CLASSIFICATION		TYPE OF VEGETATION		
	Class	%	Woodland	Scrub	Prairie
Hermon and Bolton	First	100	–	100	100
	Second	–	–	–	–
	Third	–	–	–	–
	Fourth	–	–	–	–
Walter and David Beatty	First	30	–	30	33
	Second	50	27	51	50
	Third	20	73	19	17
	Fourth	–	–	–	–
Jean Richard	First	83	76	82	90
	Second	17	24	18	10
	Third	–	–	–	–
	Fourth	–	–	–	–
William Otty	First	51	100	56	45
	Second	29	–	34	30
	Third	20	–	10	25
	Fourth	–	–	–	–
John Otty	First	4	–	1	5
	Second	93	100	98	94
	Third	2	–	–	1
	Fourth	1	–	1	–
George Abrey	First	59	33	28	66
	Second	35	67	57	30
	Third	6	–	15	4
	Fourth	–	–	–	–
Thomas Breen	First	28	–	16	33
	Second	32	6	22	34
	Third	26	22	45	23
	Fourth	14	72	17	10
Joseph Doupe	First	–	–	–	–
	Second	33	–	75	31
	Third	57	–	25	68
	Fourth	10	–	–	1

NOTE: Marshland was excluded because of frequent anomalies occasioned by the small area involved.

less consistent in their interpretation of such criteria as they deemed to be of relevance, it is rare indeed to find surveyors agreeing with one another. This is seen in the sharp divisions obvious in maps of soil grades (figs. 8A and 9A). It is noticeable also from the records of townships reexamined some time after the initial subdivision survey and from repeated differences along township outlines, as between the grades assigned in the block survey and those given during subdivision. For example, S. L. Brabazon, having tried to subdivide

Township 6, Range 25 W.1, in October of 1880 and having been forced to abandon the task because of flooding, tried again in June of 1882. Though conditions were no better then, he was able to lay out a few lines in the eastern part of the township. He graded the soil in twenty-four quarter sections—twenty-two of them as third class and two as fourth. George McPhillips later subdivided almost the entire township during a drier period (in 1884). In the process, he classified all but two of the quarter sections graded as third class by Brabazon—fifteen of them as second class, two as third, and three as fourth. As for block outlines, Pearce classified the southern edge of Township 7, Range 26 W.1, as being everywhere second class, and the eastern edge of Township 10, Range 27 W.1, as third class throughout. With subdivision, though, the former was downgraded (by Evans and Bolger) to third class and the latter upgraded (by James Warren) to a mixture of first and second class land.

INVESTIGATION OF CORRELATIONS

Since the records of the DLS classification are more or less complete, although uneven in quality, it is possible to investigate their basis and subjectivity and their influence on settlement. This was attempted at both township and quarter-section levels, using southwest Manitoba as an example—a region which en-

compasses the transition from damp woodland with heavily leached soils in the north and northeast to drier grasslands with darker soils in the south and southwest. The analysis was based on a random (though balanced) sample of 64 townships and on punch card information for the 10,163 quarter sections in three case study districts (fig. 1).

Three questions were investigated—the relationship of DLS soil categories to (a) the type of vegetation as reported by the surveyors, (b) the grades assigned in subsequent soil surveys, and (c) the date of disposal.

From a visual comparison of figures 4 and 7 a degree of similarity is noticeable in the delineation of subregions, but inconsistencies in grading are every bit as obvious. Of the two main areas of class 1 soils, for example, one belongs to the parkland area north of the Assiniboine and the other to the treeless prairie south of the Souris. The remainder of the prairie was generally rated as second class, and though forested townships in the northwest were graded first class, heavily wooded areas elsewhere were more likely to be ranked as third.

Brandon District

A detailed study of the Brandon District bears this out, though of course it is especially representative of the southern margins of the parkland belt. From table 1 it can be seen that

TABLE 3

DLS Classification, Reston District, Individual Tracts

SURVEYOR(S)	PERCENTAGE PRAIRIE	LAND CLASSIFICATION: PERCENTAGE EACH CLASS			
		First	Second	Third	Fourth
Duncan Sinclair	97	74	26	–	–
S. L. Brabazon	100	42	49	8	1
Evans and Bolger	99	21	56	18	5
James McArthur	96	42	58	–	–
Richard Jephson	100	21	54	25	–
George McPhillips	100	–	91	9	–
William Wagner	99	10	90	–	–
Frederick Wilkins	100	–	4	65	31

the percentage breakdown for scrub and prairie is almost identical with that for the area as a whole and that each was as likely to be graded Class 1 as Class 2. One-half of the woodland was rated first class, but the number of quarters involved, as with the noticeably lower grades assigned to marshland, is probably insufficient to allow for any final statement in this regard.

Table 2 illustrates differences in approach among surveyors. They were dealing with different townships, admittedly, but it is obvious that some were more generous than others. Variations in degree of generalization are also noticeable, as they are on the plat (fig. 8A).

The Canada Land Inventory (fig. 8B) provides a useful means of assessing the DLS classification. It is assumed, of course, that this recent study of "soil capability for agriculture" is more "scientific" and more reliable. In very general terms it can be said that the CLI rates as first class the lacustrine silts on the margins of the former delta (see fig. 6), the alluvial flats adjacent to the Assiniboine, and the till plains to the north (save where these are breached by the valley of the Minnedosa River). Lighter, sandy soils are graded second class, and areas of dune sand or gravel are rated as third class, together with the Brandon Hills. The lowest grades are reserved for the shallow swamp deposits on the eastern margin of the area and for the steepest of valley slopes. The general pattern of soil zones on the DLS plat is remarkably similar to that of the CLI over the townships surveyed in 1880–81 by Abrey, Breen, and Doupe. In the area north of the delta, however, where the CLI detected little variation in soil type, the dominion lands surveyors found scope enough to indulge their individuality.

Reston District

The Reston case study offers an interesting comparison with that of the Brandon District, since the plains west of the Souris were largely devoid of trees. It is obvious that notwithstanding the uniformity of the vegetation cover, the surveyors recognized marked differences in the agricultural value of the land. This is clear from the plat (fig. 9A) and from table 3, both of which again point to differences of opinion among surveyors. The individuality of Frederick Wilkins is especially marked.

When the DLS Classification is compared with that of the Canada Land Inventory (fig. 9B) the uniqueness of Mr. Wilkins's work is still more obvious. He recognized the main differences in soil type but was grudging in his bestowal of grades. The patterns distinguished by Evans and Bolger also agree pretty well with those of the CLI. Overall, though, the DLS grades seem inversely related to those of the later classification. The CLI favored the till plains in the north and west, and the DLS, the lighter soils to the south and east. Weir attributed this in part to the idea that the lighter soils were easier to plow, but it is difficult to square this with the grading of ground moraines north of the Assiniboine.

In the Reston District 168 quarter sections were later rejected by the CPR. Their percentage breakdown by DLS classification is as follows:

Class 1—36%
Class 2—42%
Class 3—17%
Class 4—5%

Dominion lands surveyors and CPR land examiners were not of one mind, obviously.

Southwest Manitoba as a Whole

In conclusion, the relationship of the dominion lands classification to the facts of physical geography can best be illustrated by a comparison of figures 4 and 6, bearing in mind always the need to allow for the individuality of surveyors' reports. The map of grades displays, first, a mildly concentric arrangement in the south, the shallow black soils of the ground moraine grading higher than the wooded soils of Turtle Mountain proper. Secondly, low grades were assigned to the coarse-textured soils of the "sand hills" and to the area of outwash at the mouth of the Qu'Appelle. The adjacent silts with black, medium-textured soils were ranked as first or second class; and

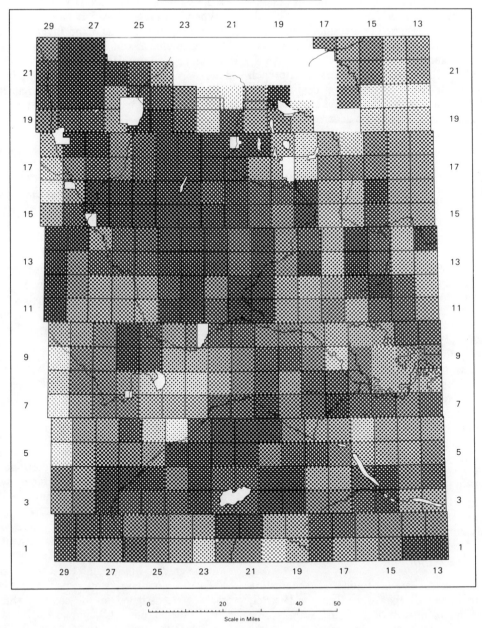

Class 1 .... 46%		Township Mean
		1·0-1·1
		1·2-1·5
Class 2 .... 37%		1·6-1·9
		2·0-2·3
Class 3 .... 14%		2·4-2·8
		2·9-3·2
Class 4 .... 3%		3·3-3·9

Figure 4 Southwest Manitoba: DLS Soil Classification

84

Proportion of Subdivided Area (exc. Reserves)
and Equivalent in Quarter Sections

Townships Each Class			Class Values	
No.	%		%	$\frac{1}{4}$'s
36	10		1-2	0-3
53	15		3-30	4-43
42	12		31-40	44-57
56	16		41-50	58-72
74	21		51-64	73-93
43	12		65-75	94-108
47	13		76-94	109-135

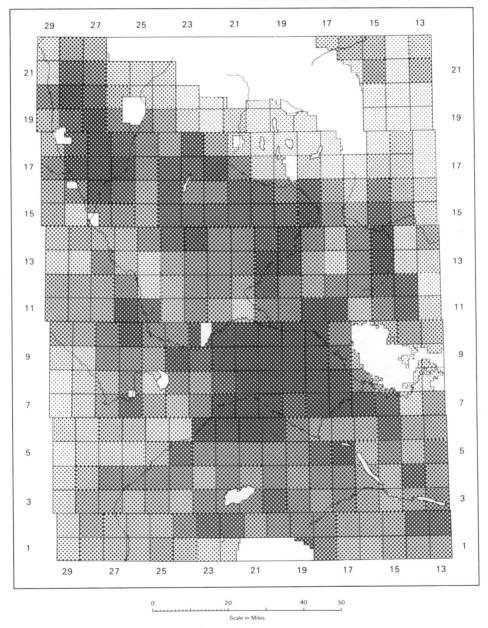

Scale in Miles

Figure 5 Lands Disposed of within Ten Years of
Subdivision

85

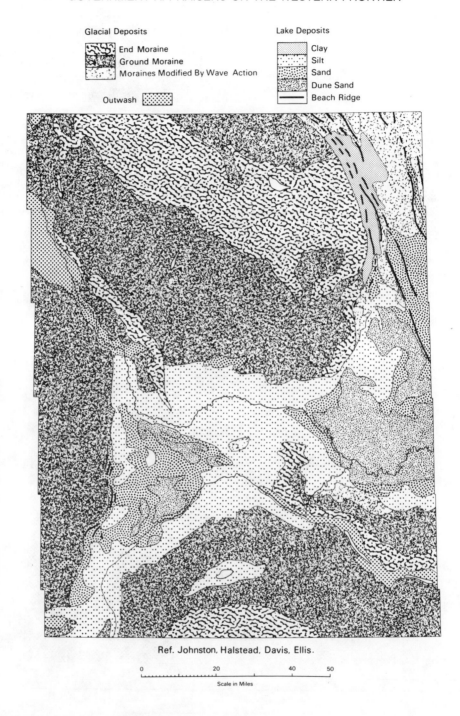

Ref. Johnston, Halstead, Davis, Ellis.

Figure 6 Southwest Manitoba: Surficial Geology

		Percentage Prairie
WOODLAND 17%		0-4
	Admixture of Scrub	5-24
PARKLAND 23%	Scrub Emphasis	25-49
	Grassland Emphasis	50-69
PRAIRIE 60%	Admixture of Scrub	70-94
		95-100

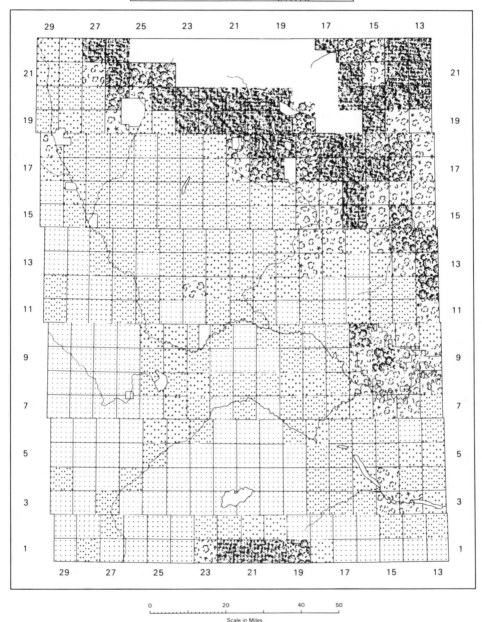

Figure 7 Vegetation prior to Settlement

the boulder clays of the parkland belt, with degrading black earth, were almost everywhere rated first class. The drift-covered areas of the open prairie west and south of the Assiniboine were less favored, Wilkins's townships especially so. Hilly and stony end moraines were assigned lower grades than those given to adjacent areas, the more so since they were often densely wooded, with podzolic characteristics in the north. Poorly drained areas like the northeast were also downgraded.

ATTENTION PAID TO SURVEYORS' REPORTS

To demonstrate the basis of the DLS classification is one thing, albeit unsubstantiated statistically: to establish any kind of causal relationship between DLS classes and the settlement process is an altogether different matter. It is possible again to distinguish broad similarities in the arrangement of zonal boundaries: there are elements common to figures 4 and 5. Most notable are the triangular area between the Souris and the Assiniboine (with its apex west of the Brandon Hills) and the arrangement about Turtle Mountain, the sand hills north of the Assiniboine, and the boundary between the degrading black earths of the parkland and the grey wooded soils further north. It is, however, impossible to establish any precise relationship between soil classification and date of settlement.

Things would be a lot simpler if settlement had always followed hard on the heels of the surveyors, if the surveyor general had been better able to predict the direction and rate of frontier advance. As it is, figure 5 clearly reflects differences in date of subdivision, as between the parkland subdivided in 1872–73 east of Birdtail Creek and the townships surveyed in 1880 between the Assiniboine and the Souris and between the Birdtail on the east and the Assiniboine on the west. Other influences upon lands disposal also complicate the issue —such as vegetation, soil characteristics, type of grant, the evolution of group settlements, and occasional delays in the opening up of subdivided townships.

This is true even at the quarter-section level,

where the miscalculations of the surveyor general are bypassed (in part at least) by investigating correlations *within* townships. Of the two districts referred to above, the Reston area is by far the simplest: all twenty-four townships were surveyed at much the same time and the vegetation cover was, as already noted, almost uniform throughout. A measure of correlation is obvious both from a comparison of the plats (figs. 9A and 9C) and from table 4. Referring again to the Canada Land Inventory, it can be seen that the mediocre soils were settled first and the better grades left till later. This roughly parallels the valuation of the original surveyors, but it could just as well be explained in terms of the chronology of settlement.

In the case of the Brandon District it seemed logical at the outset to examine the sixteen townships subdivided in 1873 (in the pre-Macoun era) separately from those laid out in 1880–81. As things turned out, however, the uneven character of the surveys of 1873 ruled out any possibility of a clear graphical relationship between DLS classification and date of sale or entry (figs. 8A and 8C). Over the area surveyed later it was possible to distinguish common elements in the plats, but since the DLS grades here had more in common with the CLI than with the timing of lands disposal, there was little evidence of any direct causal relationship between the date of settlement and the DLS classification. It was impossible to isolate the impact of the surveyors' grading from the actual capability of the soil (assuming, again, that the Canada Land Inventory does in fact represent an acceptable control). This is borne out by table 4, where the only major departures from the mean in the Brandon area are those noted for lands disposed of more than twenty-five years after subdivision and those on hand in 1930. Since the data for CPR and Dominion Lands refers, of necessity, to the first *completed* sale or homestead entry, the greater proportion of class 3 and 4 lands in the final interval column is again more likely to be a reflection of the actual character of the land than of the surveyor's assessment of the same.

The Settlers' Assessment of Woodland and Prairie

It seems rather that the individual settler or speculator was a law unto himself in regard to the selection of land. There was no end to the amount of advice available, but it was manifestly of varying quality and often contradictory. Thus, Warkentin (1964) observes, "The task of judging how suitable the land was for farming passed from the scientist and the government to the individual settler. . . . The fate of each homestead rested on the wisdom the settler himself had shown in appraising the land." Few pioneers, it seems, were ever inhibited by DLS classifications when selecting a suitable homestead. This was something which later land examiners noted on several occasions. In one township, for example, Brenot (1919) records that "of 43 quarter sections examined from the [DLS] fieldbooks 21 were considered to be too heavily timbered for settlement, 8 might be economically improved, 4 were considered fair for settlement, and 10 suitable. By looking up the disposal sheets it was found that the whole 43 were already taken up."

In making their selection of lands for entry or purchase, individual settlers were inevitably influenced by the continuing discussion of the merits of prairie, parkland, and forest and of the soil types and climatic conditions associated therewith. This can be seen even from a comparison of small-scale maps (figures 5 and 7). The unattractiveness of heavily wooded areas and, to a lesser extent, of the Souris Plains is readily discernible, notwithstanding differences already noted between frontier advance as anticipated by the DLS and the actual sequence of events.

At the quarter-section level there was an obvious correlation in the Brandon District between grassland and lands settled in the 1880s. The Shoal Lake District, however, is more representative of southwest Manitoba as a whole, from the viewpoint both of vegetation and date of settlement. From the plats (figs. 10A and 10C) the delayed occupancy of heavily wooded areas is quite striking. Table 5 em-phasizes this still more and also points to a continuing preference for grassland rather than scrub, albeit grassland in close proximity to a supply of timber: but the influence of communication facilities (fig. 10B) upon the direction of settlement must also be considered.

To Hind (1859) the Souris Plain had seemed "a treeless desert" in no way "fitted for the permanent habitation of civilized man." Macoun (1882) considered it a region "of unsurpassed fertility." In 1881 he declared: "Today South Western Manitoba is called the garden of the Province; five years since it was supposed to be a barren, irreclaimable waste." Those who "made it" on the plains learned firsthand of the advantages which Macoun had proclaimed: in the Dirty Thirties, though, they had cause to remember Palliser and Hind.

REFERENCES CITED

ARCHIVAL SOURCES

Glenbow Foundation Archives, Calgary.
    Land Sales Records of the Canadian Pacific Railway, vols. 75–187.
Manitoba Surveys Branch, Winnipeg.
    Field Notes of the Dominion Lands Survey.
Public Archives of Canada, Ottawa.
    Record Group 15, Series Bla, file 410595(2).
    (1) Speers to Pedley, April 24, 1900.
    (2) McCreary to Turiff, September 8, 1900.

PUBLISHED MATERIAL

Brenot, L.; Fawcett, S. D.; and McElhanney, T. A.
    1919. "Classification of lands." In *Annual report of the Association of Dominion Land Surveyors,* pp. 51–59.
Canadian Orders in Council.
    1886. June 19.
Canadian Sessional Papers.
    1880.   43 Vic., no. 4, pt. II, pp. 6 and 43.
    1882.   45 Vic., no. 18, pp. 88–101.
    1885.   48 Vic., no. 25, pp. 191–98.
    1889.   52 Vic., no. 36, p. 45.
Hind, Henry Youle.
    1859.   *Report of the Assiniboine and Saskatchewan Exploring Expedition.* Toronto: John Lovell.
Macoun, John.
    1882.   *Manitoba and the Great Northwest.* Guelph, Ont.: World Publishing.

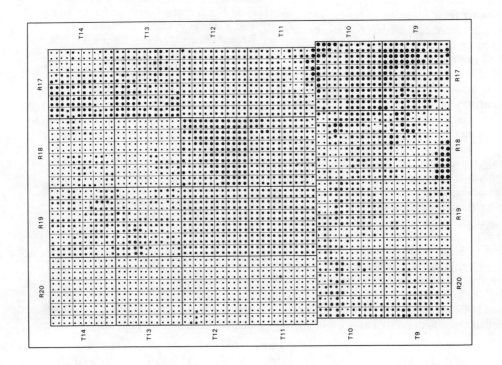

Figure 8 Brandon District: Land Classification and Disposal

Details of Subdivision (73-1873)

A Walter and David Beatty
B Jean Richard
C Hermon and Bolton
D John Otty
E William Otty
F Joseph Doupe
G Thomas Breen
H George Abrey

Scale in Miles

A: Dominion Lands Survey

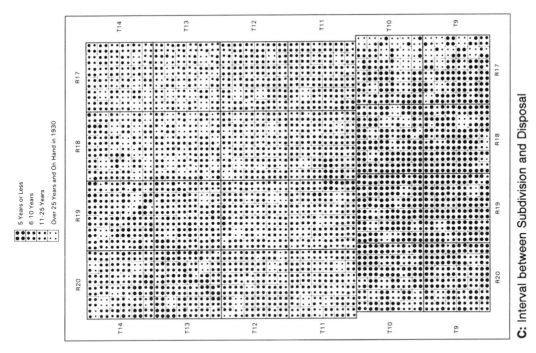

C: Interval between Subdivision and Disposal

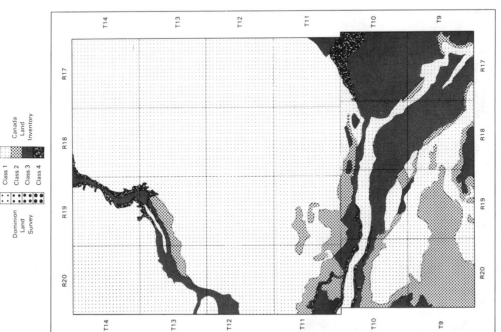

B: Canada Land Inventory (Modified)

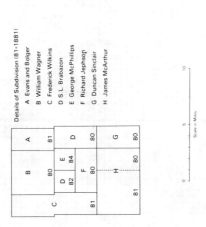

Details of Subdivision (81-1881)

A Evans and Bolger
B William Wagner
C Frederick Wilkins
D S.L. Brabazon
E George McPhillips
F Richard Jephson
G Duncan Sinclair
H James McArthur

Scale in Miles

Figure 9 Reston District: Land Classification and Disposal

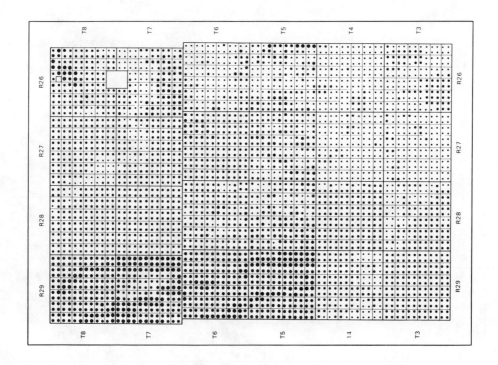

A: Dominion Land Survey

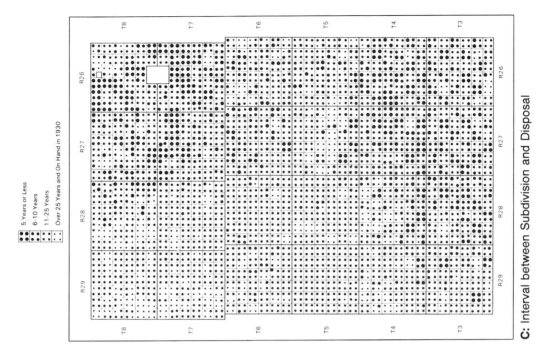

C: Interval between Subdivision and Disposal

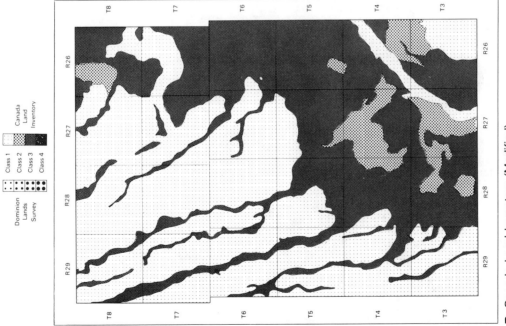

B: Canada Land Inventory (Modified)

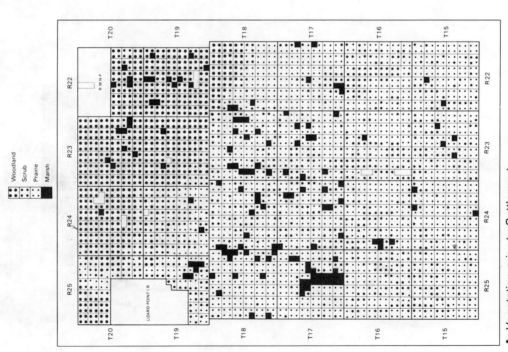

Figure 10 Shoal Lake District

A: Vegetation prior to Settlement

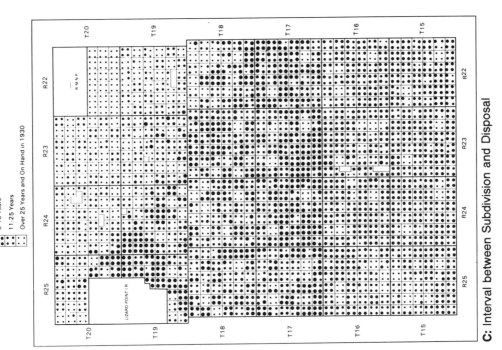

C: Interval between Subdivision and Disposal

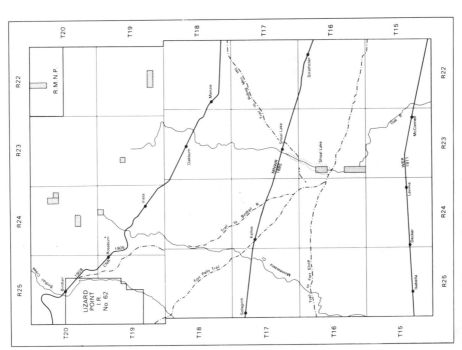

B: Lines of Communication

TABLE 4

Percentage Correlation of DLS Classification with Length of Interval
between Subdivision and Disposal, Reston and Brandon Districts,
1873–1929

LAND CLASSIFICATION		INTERVAL BETWEEN SUBDIVISION AND DISPOSAL			
Class	%	5 Years or Less	6–10 Years	11–25 Years	Over 25 years and On Hand
Reston District					
First	27	47	41	22	15
Second	51	49	50	52	50
Third	16	4	8	19	23
Fourth	6	–	1	7	12
Brandon District					
First	43	51	43	35	37
Second	41	35	46	46	31
Third	14	12	10	17	24
Fourth	2	2	1	2	8

TABLE 5

Percentage Correlation of Vegetation Type with Length of Interval
between Subdivision and Disposal, Brandon and Shoal Lake Districts,
1873–1929

VEGETATION		INTERVAL BETWEEN SUBDIVISION AND DISPOSAL			
Type	%	5 Years or Less	6–10 Years	11–25 Years	Over 25 Years and On Hand
Brandon District					
Woodland	4	2	5	4	7
Scrub	29	17	32	32	42
Prairie	65	79	62	61	48
Marsh	2	2	1	3	3
Shoal Lake District					
Woodland	21	4	1	28	51
Scrub	24	30	26	23	16
Prairie	51	61	70	44	29
Marsh	4	5	3	5	4

Manitoba, Province of.
  1889.   *Manitoba and its resources.*
Pearce, William.
  1914.   "Early surveys and land administration
  in Manitoba." In *Report of the thirty-fourth annual meeting of the Association of Manitoba Land
  Surveyors,* pp. 25–42.
Statutes of Canada.
  1881.   44 Vic., c. 1, s. 11.
Tyman, John.
  1972.   *By section, township, and range: Studies*

in prairie settlement. Brandon, Manitoba: Department of Geography, Brandon University, for
the Assiniboine Historical Society.
Warkentin, John.
  1964.   *The western interior of Canada.* Toronto:
McClelland & Stewart.
Weir, Thomas R.
  1961. "Settlement in southwest Manitoba:
1870–1891." In *Papers read before the Historical
and Scientific Society of Manitoba,* series 3, no.
17, pp. 54–64.

PART 4
Real and Imagined Climatic Hazards

Toward a Geosophic Climate of the Great American Desert

The Plains Climate of the Forty-Niners

Merlin P. Lawson
University of Nebraska

In June, 1844, in commenting on the predilection of easterners to migrate to the West Coast, the editor of the *Missouri Republican* admonished, "No man of information or in his right mind, would think of leaving such a country as this, to wander over a thousand miles of desert and five hundred of mountains to reach such as that." Desert or not, by 1849, with news of the gold discoveries in California and with word of the official cession of California following the Mexican War, masses of pioneers were ready to trek across the continent. Migration estimates of a wave of civilization across the Great American Desert in 1849 place the number of emigrants at approximately thirty thousand.

From the first of May to the first of June, company after company took its departure from the frontier of civilization, till the emigrant trail from Fort Leavenworth, on the Missouri, to Fort Laramie, at the foot of the Rocky Mountains, was one long line of mule-trains and wagons. The rich meadows of the Nebraska, or Platte, were settled for the time, and a single traveler could have journeyed for the space of a thousand miles, as certain of his lodging and regular meals as if he were riding through the old agricultural districts of the Middle States. [Taylor 1862, p. 282]

The excitement of wagon-train organization, the adventure of migrating epic distances in search of a new way of life, the anticipation and anxiety of facing incalculable dangers of the vast continental interior with its diversity of terrain, vegetation, and weather—these were the ingredients of the argonaut's life and the scenes which were to be recorded in the diaries of emigrants or in letters sent east to their friends and families remaining behind. Overland journals as descriptive narratives of travel in the West comprise a significant source of information for contemporary historical interpretations.

The overland narrative, manifested in either a journal or letter, serves the student of western history as an invaluable informational source. Commonly, the historian has emphasized the social, economic, and political ramifications of emigration, minimizing the environmental aspects except where the latter directly influenced the former.

Landforms, soil, vegetation, fauna, weather, and climate are known as they affected individuals, yet surprisingly few, if any, attempts have been made to reconstruct the environmental parameters of the folk experience. Too often, perhaps, the historian "envisions the average overland journal as a wasteland of mileage and weather: 'August 25, 30 miles, some cloudy. August 26, 20 miles today, wind from the Northwest' " (Morgan 1962, p. 71). But taken together and set in a spatial context, the average overland journals can tell us a great

101

deal about the weather and climate of large sections of earth space in particular seasons, often providing detail that no other sources can give. For instance, three of four diaries of travelers widely separated on the Oregon or Santa Fe trails can give us clues as to the types, intensity, distribution, and frequency of weather situations and climatic systems in the central (and perhaps southern) plains in the months of May and June. They can yield much concerning the types of rainfall encountered (frontal or convective), the seasonableness of temperatures, and whether seasonal rainfall was high or low. Weather information for the year 1849 has been gleaned from some thirty-four diaries and collated with the daily records of weather stations peripheral to the region traversed.

The objective of this paper is to reconstruct the real weather and climate of the plains in May and June (and, to a lesser extent, April and July), 1849, as experienced by emigrants and to develop a methodology for the reconstruction of weather situations experienced in the 1840s and 1850s from the diaries and letters of overland travelers. Reconstruction of the real climate will make it possible to establish whether the settlers *actually faced* and saw a *real desert* in 1849 and whether they experienced conditions that they might have interpreted as droughty or relatively dry. The reconstructed climate and environment of "experiences" as relayed by letters and occasionally by diaries can tell us much about the information *that must have molded* the environmental imagery of literate Americans.

The thirty-four diarists were located for each travel day across the plains by reference to fourteen well-known landmarks, and every detail relevant to climatological reconstruction was noted. The diarists, for the purposes of this study, acted as weather recording stations spread across the region, and from this information it is possible to piece together the succession of daily weather and to reconstruct the climate of the late spring and early summer (late April to early June in the east; mid-May to early July in the west beyond Fort Laramie).

Keeping a journal presented many problems for the diarist, and these difficulties limit the comprehensiveness of the record and occasionally produce contradictions. Often those expecting to make daily entries in a journal either found it too difficult to maintain regular notations or became lax as the novelty of the migration was replaced with the reality of monotonous toil. Journals often would not be kept on a daily basis as the rigors of the journey increased. Usually diary entries were made in the evening following the chores while the events of the day were fresh in the mind, but the onset of darkness and fatigue also resulted in morning entries. Writing conditions were invariably difficult, and this makes for illegibility and difficulty of transcription in many cases.

Variations in the hour chosen by diarists to record their experiences account for some diversity of their accounts. Weather descriptions by diarists traveling in the same organization would normally agree on the general conditions, except where a particular storm developed after that day's entry. In that case one diarist writing late in the evening would make special note of the deluge and a second might not mention it at all. The next day, however, the entry commonly would begin, "Owing to the heavy rain of last night, we did not start so early as usual."

There are, of course, problems with diary entries, but they remain an invaluable source for reconstructing the environment and particularly the climate of the plains. As Giffen points out,

If one were to read all the diaries kept by those who negotiated the hazardous trails to California there would be found a certain similarity. By common accord, and certainly by no predestined plan, these travelers were primarily concerned with rain, wind, heat, cold, sickness, and all the other physical aspects of their trek across the plains. Time was another important factor. The hour of breaking camp, the "nooning" and the setting up of a new camp for the night— these hours were usually meticulously recorded as well as daily temperatures. [Giffen 1966, p. 16]

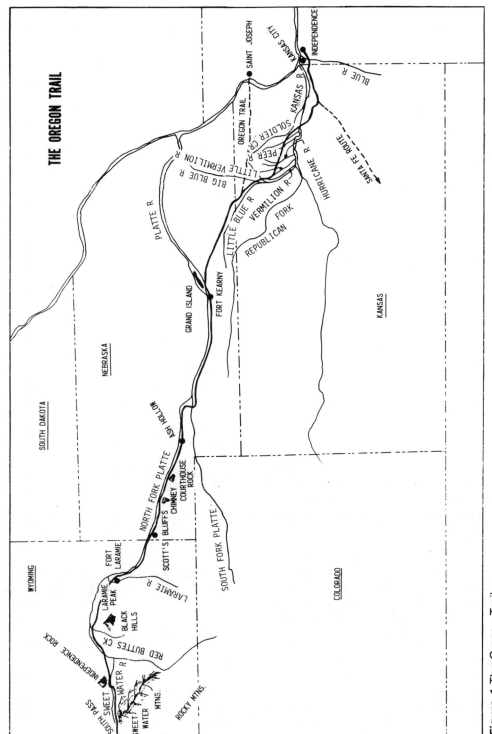

Figure 1 The Oregon Trail

CLIMATIC EXPERIENCES OF THE
FORTY-NINERS:
THE NARRATIVE APPROACH

The organization and preparation for the Great Migration were made final by most wagon-train companies each year at various jumping-off places along the Missouri—Westport, Fort Leavenworth, Saint Joseph, and Council Bluffs (fig. 1). The primary factor regulating the annual exodus was the condition of the grass on the prairies. By the time the grass was sufficiently green to support the animals, snows would be of small consequence and yet the heat of summer would not have dried the intermittent streams of the interior basins.

The spring of 1849 was uncommonly cold and blustery and the grass immature. Those who arrived early at the jumping-off places endured a long, cold, wet sojourn as they unhappily took advantage of the enforced delay by training their team animals on short "shake-down" trips. Experience had shown April 15 to be a good target date for departure. Most emigrants hoped to arrive at the Missouri during the first or second week of that month. They would reach Fort Kearny, by May 15, arrive at Fort Laramie one month later, and enter South Pass by the Fourth of July.

William G. Johnston was among those early arrivals at the jumping-off places. Arriving at Independence in mid-March, he was obliged to spend more than forty nights sleeping in his wagon awaiting a sufficiency of grass on the trail. At first the weather was not unpleasant except for cold nights which produced "a thick coating of ice . . . on the water bucket" (Johnston 1948, p. 12). Cold air dominated through mid-April, accompanied by chilling rains almost every day. Then, on the day normally designated as the starting time for crossing the prairies, a snow shower once again delayed departure. "Whilst at dinner, a blinding snowstorm came up, lasting for an hour. The white robe of snow covering the earth has such a wintry aspect, that we feel a fresh blight is thrown over our prospect for rolling out" (Johnston 1948, p. 17–18).

Although most of the argonauts had arrived at the jumping-off places at least by the beginning of April, many did not leave the East Coast region until mid-April. The members of the Boston-Newton Company delayed their departure to enable one of them to complete his medical degree. "In the end this worked to their advantage, since the grass on the prairies was not high enough to provide forage until the second week in May. However, it was unwise to delay departure too long, for if a party did not reach the mountains before snow started it would be in trouble" (Hannon 1969, p. 34).

Finally, on April 27, 1849, W. Johnston succinctly summarized the long agonizing wait on the weather. "Our march will begin tomorrow. Today ends the sixth week of camp life, attended much of the time with great discomfort, on account of inclement weather, incident to a spring having many of the characteristics of winter" (Johnston 1948, p. 26).

Once under way, however, the early departees found they had not waited long enough for sufficient growth to sustain the vast numbers of animals associated with the emigration. Major Cross recorded, "The cold weather has considerably impeded its growth, and confirmed me in the opinion that the first of May is too soon to leave Missouri, unless you contemplate a rest after arriving on the borders of the Platte" (Settle 1940, p. 53).

The bitterly cold nights persisted throughout most of the time that the pioneers were east of the mountains. Many of the pioneers, including one by the name of Banks, complained about the cold all the way across the plains. Suffering great facial discomfort, he advised "those coming this route to bring court plaster for lips, nose, and perhaps ears; mine sore" (Scamehorn 1965, p. 16). Those remaining in the wagons during the night probably had experiences similar to those of Peter Decker: "Wind blew incessantly last night and today, it rocked my bed (the wagon) like a cradle, and nearly blows one away today" (Giffen 1966, p. 78).

The chilling wind-whipped cold doubtlessly had been expected by the earlier Forty-Niners, although judging from a cursory content analysis of weather notations, they were not pre-

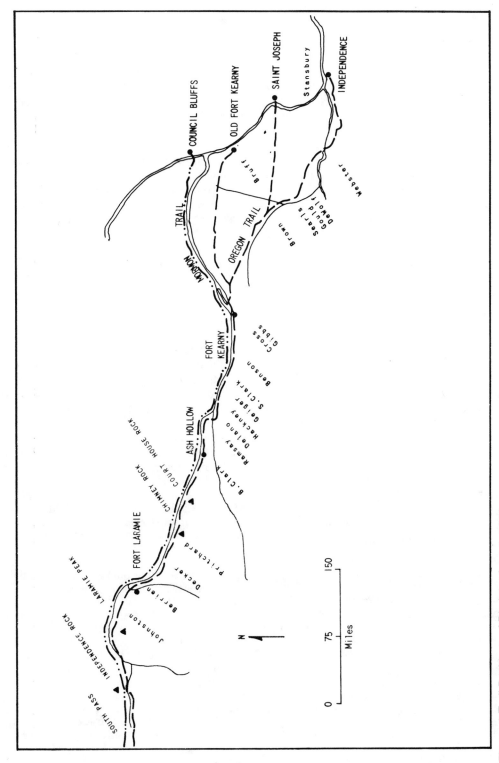

Figure 2 Trail Positions of Diarists: June 1, 1849

105

pared for the inordinately heavy and frequent rains that followed them across the plains. For the first half of the trip to California, the pioneer was not plagued with the supposed drought of a Great American Desert, but by cloudbursts of magnificent proportion, swollen rivers, and inundated fords. Accompanied by brilliant electrical displays, "outrageous" downpours driven by winds of "hurricane force" proved devastating to the frail wagon coverings and pitched tents.

The travelers most severely affected by the "copious effusions" were the lead trains of the season. One of the first wagons to leave Independence was that of William Johnston. The first morning out, his train having "reached the frontier line of Missouri, which marks the separation between civilized and the uncivilized life," he entered in his journal: "A heavy rainstorm coming up, we were compelled for a time to halt; for it came in such gusts, that neither men nor animals could face it; the former took shelter on the lee side of the wagons, and the mules turned their tails to the severe elements" (Johnston 1948, p. 29).

It would take Johnston forty-three days to reach South Pass, and rain fell on twenty-four of those. Like thousands of his fellow Forty-Niners, he was about to wade across the Great American Desert.[1]

Trains departing the vicinity of Saint Joseph at this time were hit with cold, hard-driving rains. It had not rained at all during the third and fourth weeks of April, but once the trains were under way, torrential nocturnal showers baptized the greenhorns.

Supplies and equipment as well as travelers were soaked by the torrential rains. Wet flour and sugar were common even when protected well within the wagons (Brown 1908). Searls records, shortly after leaving Independence,

being "awakened at 2 a.m. by a pelting shower of rain. Books, papers, guns, coats, and baggage of every kind were wet or soiled by the tremendous gale" (1940, p. 12).

The rains surpassed any that could be remembered by the few who had experienced the climate of the region. "We have had much more rain and cold weather than usual at this season on the plains, and has been altogether an unusually wet one, with more rain and cold than ever known" (Wyman 1952, p. 56).

In places the roads were almost impassable. Day after day entries refer to "heavy roads" because of the previous night's rains. Mud, usually three to six inches deep, resulted in loss of footing for the animals, and tremendous quantities of soil stuck to the wheels, binding them tight to the wagon. In the lowland river bottoms, wheels commonly sunk to their hubs in the mire.

Many trains as they neared Fort Kearny began to relax the guard at night because of news that the Indians had moved south. As he went to bed one night (May 29) Joseph Hackney noted in his diary, "the weather looks veary stormy i expect we will catch it before morning" (Page 1930, p. 135). Had he only surmised that the violence of the storm would cause the unguarded cattle to seek shelter, he may have prevented the unfortunate episode which followed:

May 30. Laid by this day last night was one of the stormiest I ever heard tell of the rain fell in torrents and covered the ground a foot deep in water i have seen it rain as hard at home for half an hour but neve seen it pour down by the buckets full for 6 hours incessantly the wind also blew a perfect gale, driving rain through our tents and wagons covers like as though they had been paper theare was not much chance to sleep without you could fancy wet blankets and a torrent of water running under you when we got up in the mornin our cattel wear scattered to the four ends of the earth we started after them and it was ten o'clock before we found all of them some was ten miles off taking the back track every camp that we saw had lost cattel it commenced raining again at noon and it rained till night. [Page 1930, pp, 135–36]

---

1. The concept of "Wading to California" was first introduced by Watson Parker, "Wading to California: The Influence of the Forty-Niners on the Notion of a Great American Desert," *Great Plains Journal* 3 (1964): 35–43. In his article Parker assumes that the notion of the desert existed, concluding that the heavy rains of the season must have done much to dispel such beliefs.

As the storms became more violent, they frequently included the formation of hailstones. On the average, diarists recorded two such storms during their crossing of the plains. All of these storms were located west of Grand Island where the main trail met the Platte River. It appears that near Ash Hollow, the very first emigrants along the trail were unfortunate enough to experience a most devastating hailstorm. William Johnston, who passed the region of the storm five days after it had wreaked havoc on a wagon train, describes what they had encountered.

A number of emigrant trains were passed, among them one called the Platte City Company, commanded by Colonel Ransom; from whom we learned of a hailstorm of considerable violence, encountered on Tuesday last, ten or twelve miles west of Ash Hollow. Their wagon covers and tents had been riddled by hailstones, some of which were of extraordinary size, weighing as much as eight and nine ounces each. The cattle of some emigrant parties were so badly frightened that they ran in various directions for many miles from their owner. When passing the locality where this occurred, we had noticed the ground was tore up, and in places forming large cavities, but were unable to conjecture the cause until learning these facts. We are also able to account for the cold weather which followed the storm we had experienced in the evening referred to but had not been accompanied by hail. [Johnston 1948, pp. 73–74]

Mention is made by a few diarists of whirlwinds, but the nature of such storms is open to conjecture. There can be no doubt, however, that Joseph Berrien, traveling with Colonel Jarrott unmistakably witnessed a tornado from the summit of a hill near present day Brule, Nebraska, on May 19.

A tornado was whirling across the prarie and though there was but little on which to exert its fury still the commotion of the clouds and the immense masses of vapour whirling with inconceivable rapidity . . . while the roaring of the wind could be distinctly heard at 2 miles distance,

furnishing a sight seldom witnessed. After the tornado had passed clouds of grasshoppers fell from the sky. . . . The cloud presented the appearance of a long funnel the small end downwards as black as ink, fortunate for us was it that it did not pass near or over our wagons which had it so occur'd would have been scattered to the four winds of Heaven. [Berrien 1960, p. 302]

Experiences along the Southern Trails

Those departing from Fort Smith had an earlier start, some even leaving the fort in late March. The wet weather had so saturated the "Soft alluvial soil" as to render passage difficult to wagons for 150 miles. Diary entries such as "cooked our supper in a great hurry in the rain" (Powell 1931, p. 23) are common along the Fort Smith trail. Others simply remained in camp, citing in their journal, "the road's a complete bog" (Oliphant 1955, p. 39). Farther south, C. C. Cox, making his way across Texas to El Dorado, noted in his diary, "Our journey . . . was exceedingly toilsome and disagreeable, the recent rains had rendered the road very wet and muddy, and but for the aid of some ox teams that pulled our wagon through the worst places—we possibly would have been there jacking up the wheels till yet" (Martin 1926, p. 38).

The streams encountered along the southern routes demonstrated extreme wetness of the season. Emigrants found the Pecos River to be "full of bank," and the Rio Grande "overflowed to the edge of the mountains" (Bieber 1937, p. 266). Along the Santa Fe Trail, delays were frequent because creeks were "too turbulent and deep to be forded" (Powell 1931, p. 23). There were instances when a party would camp for the night in a seemingly dry location only to be indignantly awakened, like the experience recorded by Charles Pancoast along the Arkansas River near the present Colorado-Kansas state border.

That night, after we were all quietly asleep, there came up a thunder storm. About midnight we were suddenly aroused by the water pouring into our tents. We were in a terrible dilemma: our blankets were afloat, and our cattle in the corral up to their knees in water. If the water increased in depth, we feared that it would soon sweep us and our property into the River. The darkness was intense, relieved only by flashes of lightning; the rain came down in torrents; and we paddled about in the dark, seeking to consult each other in regard to the best course to be pursued. Our Captain and Lieutenant seemed to be paralysed, and hesitated about giving orders. The water rose to two feet in our tents, after which the rain began to moderate; and we spent the balance of the night wading around until a late daybreak enabled us to relieve ourselves of the terrors of the night by driving up on higher land. [Potter 1962, p. 111]

Parker wrote in 1964 that the Forty-Niners "waded to California" (1964, pp. 41–42). The preceeding account suggests this to be true during May and perhaps early June in the eastern plains. But it was hardly their condition later in June and July, as can be demonstrated using a geographic approach to analyzing weather notations of diarists along the plains.

CLIMATIC EXPERIENCES OF THE FORTY-NINERS: THE GEOGRAPHIC APPROACH

To read the accounts of individual travelers in the Missouri country and eastern plains is to agree with Parker's impressionistic conclusion that the argonauts "waded to California." But when the travelers' accounts and their climatic references are set in a spatial context, it becomes clear that their wading was largely restricted to portions of the prairie-plains and that they were fortunate if they had "heavy dews" the remaining months of travel. What follows is an attempt to reconstruct the daily weather and climatic systems that affected the plains between mid-April and mid-July. Only in this way can we establish with any exactitude whether the monthly and seasonal rainfall was above or below average and whether travelers waded across the plains or burnt their soles on the sands of a desert.

The daily weather situations duly noted by

diarists on the trail can serve collectively to facilitate and provide a unique opportunity for identifying the meteorological systems that were affecting their travel. As the earlier departees headed west, with the main wave following two to three weeks later, a meteorological network of sorts began to spread out, ultimately extending the entire width of the plains. The nature of the comments—generally referring to wind velocity with occasional direction, relative daily temperature comparisons, and sky conditions such as degree of cloudiness, rain, or even dustiness—provide the historical climatologist with an acceptable data source which is quite adequate for deducing generalized synoptic patterns prevailing during the peak of migration. Information of this type is particularly appropriate when evaluating the areal extent of the weather situations cited by the travelers. The technique can be applied by researchers to the early 1840s, and certainly to 1845, which is considerably earlier than the establishment of meteorological observations at military posts in the region.

Tabulations of daily weather conditions were constructed by this author from thirty-four diaries of Forty-Niners as they crossed the western interior to the South Pass. The spacing of these records was reasonably well distributed within the overall wave of emigrant passage, facilitating analysis of weather types throughout the critical months of May, June, and the beginning of July (fig. 2).

In general these tabulations indicate that the month of May was associated with an inordinately large number of cold-wave incursions from the northwest, whose intensification was particularly noticeable as they progressed from west to east bringing cold, chilling rains lasting anywhere from one to three days. The rate of frontal movement seems in most cases to have decelerated toward the east, becoming almost stationary on one occasion. Particularly impressive is the fact that surface wind-speeds were extremely high, especially considering the previous lack of exposure to such "hurricanes" by most of the pioneers who were bearing their brunt.

Accompanying these cold winds were relatively short violent thunderstorms, frequently associated with hail development closer to the western margin of the plains. As the frontal system progressed eastward, the chilling rains become more prolonged, occasionally initiating squall lines. As these closely spaced, fast-moving perturbations swept across the plains, the polar front gradually weakened, shifting the track northward as it extended to the east. Thus, fewer frontal storms influenced the regions as far south as Independence.

The first of these storms swept rapidly eastward behind a well-developed fair-weather system that had dominated the region since mid-April. Following the snowfall which dampened the hopes of the first arrivals for getting an early start, cold, dreary winds gave way to warm, pleasant breezes by April 22. Gradually the warm sector moved to the east, as winds intensified. By the last day of April, with strong drying winds having prevailed for more than a week, the winter-killed grasses caught fire and blazed across the prairies in the vicinity of Saint Joseph. At this time, those traveling to the northwest of Independence recorded what appear to be isolated, convectively induced thunderstorms which may or may not have set the prairies on fire. What is certain is that Independence received heavy rain on April 30, but that Saint Joseph (fifty miles away) had a pleasant day. By May 2, a weak but rapidly moving cold front had displaced the warm winds (which presumably had been out of the southwest).[2] A second, more contrasting, cold front followed only two days later, bringing torrential, cold rains throughout the night of May 3, leaving "horses shivering in the cold wind" the following morning. Within two days yet another incursion of polar air triggered widespread rains of considerable amounts. The roads had now become a general quagmire, making travel cumbersome and slow. By the second week of May, the air over the interior was moderating in temperature. Warm cloudless days with rapidly dropping temperatures at night caused by radiational cooling became commonplace. Occasionally this cooling led to showers which

the comprehensive records of that date indicate to have been isolated, yet concentrated in the center of present-day Kansas and Nebraska.

Generally widespread rains had not fallen for more than a week. The roads were now dry and hard. But the new grass lacked water to sustain a growth sufficient for the "scourge" of thousands of grazing animals. By the twelfth, "great clouds of blinding, stifling dust filled the air, covering with a thick coat wagons, mules and men." The vanguards of the migration, who had gambled on finding enough pasturage, were now benefiting from excellent dry road conditions but were seriously concerned about the availability of grass to the west.

Then the much-needed water came in the form of a well-developed, rapidly moving cold front. The nocturnal "heavens hung with black clouds," illuminated by "serpentine streaks" of lightning lasting several hours during the night. To the east, these conditions began later and extended into the following day. Winds were once again "cold," "chilly," and "piercing."

The diarists were well spread out along the trail by this time, with those in the lead pushing two or three days beyond Fort Kearny. The region was now about to come under the influence of a frontal system which appears to have extended along a west-east axis, stagnating for four to five days, presumably as a stationary front. In the third week in May, cold, rainy weather prevailed along most of the Oregon Trail east of the Forks of the Platte. Winds blew incessantly, interspersed with "gloomy," "drizzling" rains which became hard-driving storm cells at times. The prolonged impact of this system brought extreme hardship to the travelers, fatiguing the animals with heavy road conditions, and weakening further the health of the weary emigrants. Unable to secure warmth and shelter, many cholera victims died during this period of inclement weather.

As the stationary system gradually dissipated, hot, sultry air moved into the vicinity of Ash Hollow and Courthouse Rock. That night (May 19) another cold front moved in a wavelike manner from the northwest into the

---

2. This wind direction is neither confirmed nor refuted by any of the available diaries.

plains region. The accompanying rain was torrential; hail fell at Ash Hollow; a "deluge" occurred at the South Platte Ford; and a tornado was sighted near present-day Brule, Nebraska. By early the next morning the fast-moving squall line of showers had passed Kansas Ferry. Two days later a second line of showers swept east, penetrating well to the south. Winds changed to the northeast, bringing cool air and severe showers. Just east of Fort Kearny, S. B. F. Clark experienced violent thunder and lightning with a storm that left six inches of water in his tent. Temperatures behind the front were frigid, dipping as low as 36°, according to Hale's record, in the vicinity of Fort Kearny (Hale 1925, p. 66). Yet before the month was out, the entire pattern was once again repeated, bringing the total number of frontal passages to eight since the first argonauts had embarked on their trek to California.

By the beginning of June, the last of the stragglers had just passed Kansas Ferry. With every passing mile the opportunity for meteorological reconstruction was increasingly truncated along the eastern margin of this migration. The evidence clearly indicates that June was not abnormally wet. Following the intense frontal passage at the end of May, recognition of any but convective-type storms proves elusive. The polar front appears to have finally retreated northward. Winds became highly variant with the formation of daily convective buildup. There now becomes a distinct randomness in the spatial distribution of storms. Diarists begin to notice lightning on the horizon, often with the storm passing around their location. The frequency of storms cannot be generalized as increasing to the east, except that the locations from Fort Laramie to South Pass experienced no rain from mid-June to mid-July. Diarists in the Courthouse Rock vicinity mention no rain after June 20.

Examples of isolated rainstorms can be found at Ash Hollow on June 5, Independence Rock on the 6, Fort Laramie on the twelfth, and South Platte Ford on the fourteenth and twenty-seventh. In each case no rain is recorded in contiguous locales. To one traveler, compelled to stop on account of a storm

near Courthouse Rock, the violent storms of the locale were less than random. "Mr. Bryant observed today that he had camped within 5 miles of this rock some 4 times and that a violent storm blue [sic] up on each occasion. There is most probably some local cause for this fact" (Bieber 1928, p. 19). The record does not support his theory, however.

The days had now become "hot and sultry." The warmest temperature recorded while crossing the plains was by Dewolf, who, one day's travel east of Fort Laramie, cited a stifling 110 degrees combined with choking dust. In the same location, Major Cross encountered his "warmest day yet" much later in the month.

The only period of relief from the warm June days appears to have been fostered by the single cold frontal passage of the month. A severe storm track can be plotted, commencing in the evening of June 19. Accompanied by hail, a "fearful tempest" can be traced from Courthouse Rock and Ash Hollow to the South Platte Ford and Fort Kearny. The following day cool temperatures were reported at these locations, but by June 21, "oppressive heat" had returned. Captain Stansbury, to the east of Fort Kearny, noted both a wind shift and a drop in temperature following the rain (1852, p. 425).

Throughout June, and the short record for July, only rains accompanied by thunder and lightning are described by the pioneers in their diaries. It is perhaps of synoptic interest that the diurnal occurrence of these convective cells appears to vary. At western localities, scattered showers were almost always in the afternoon, often curtailing the day's travel. More to the east, at Fort Laramie and Courthouse Rock, all storms were nocturnal, whereas in the area of the Little Blue River the shortened tabulation for June indicates a higher number of morning showers.

One cannot assess the overall frequency of rain during June as anything more than average. The fort record at Kearny tends to reinforce this conclusion. The weather situations east of the available diary notations appear ostensibly to have been "monsoonal." It might be surmised that the meridional position of the jetstream in May, 1849, was predominantly over the central plains and then shifted eastward over the prairies by June, allowing more stable continental tropical air to dominate the western interior.

The record for July is primarily restricted to the region west of Fort Laramie. Gould passed the fort on July 6, with Stansbury following one week later. Now only the occasional shower broke the monotony of the heat and dust. Wind continued almost daily but was rarely the harbinger of the much-needed rain. Instead it brought unbearable dust storms. Stansbury relates these conditions as they pulled through deep, heavy white sand beyond La Bonta Creek.

Morning bright and pleasant—but at 9 A.M. the wind rose from the southwest, and blew almost a hurricane the whole day, tearing up the sand and gravel, and dashing it into our faces, as we rode, with such violence as to cause sensible pain. It was impossible to look up for a moment, as the eyes became immediately filled with sand, so that the teamsters were obliged to fasten their handkerchiefs over their faces to enable them to see where they were going. [1852, p. 63]

In the vicinity of the North Platte Ferry, rain clouds were now replaced by clouds of dust and sand. No rain fell at this location throughout the entire period of record (June 3 to July 17), making the region destitute of grass. At Independence Rock, July was similarly without moisture until the afternoon of the twenty-second, when an afternoon thundershower "settled the dust."

One must conclude from this climatic-systems analysis of weather conditions along the Oregon Trail east of the Rockies that the region cannot be pictured as having experienced ubiquitous heavy rains throughout the entire season of emigration. There is excellent evidence from the spatial tabulation of diaries that above-average precipitation resulted in May from a series of strongly developed cold fronts sweeping west to east across the eastern portion of the trail. With a weakening and northward displacement of the polar front by June, the frequency of storms decreased as their distribution similarly diminished. Primarily convective in origin, these storm cells generated as much intensity as the previous storms, but their extent was now restricted both temporally and areally. As the argonaut continued west, the roads that had been heavy because of rain now became clogged with sand. The grass that had been so luxuriant was now burned under the heat of the sun or trampled by the hooves of thousands of pasturing stock animals. So, having established the real meteorological experiences of the Forty-Niners, one is now in a better position to assess the impact of that reality on the attitudes of those experiencing it and, consequently, to attempt a reevaluation of the eastern imagery of the plains.

BIBLIOGRAPHY

Overland Narratives of the Oregon Trail, 1849

Armstrong, J.
1965. *Buckeye rovers in the gold rush.* Edited by T. Scamehorn. Athens: Ohio University Press.

Banks, E.
1965. *Buckeye rovers in the gold rush.* Edited by T. Scamehorn. Athens: Ohio University Press.

Benson, J.
1849. From St. Joseph to Sacramento. Typescript. Nebraska State Historical Society.

Berrien, J.
1960. Overland from St. Louis. Edited by T. and C. Hinckley, *Indiana Magazine of History* 56: 273–352.

Brown, J.
1908. Memoirs of an American gold seeker. *Journal of American History* 2: 129–54.

Bruff, J.
1944. *Gold rush: Journals, drawings, and other papers.* Edited by G. Read and R. Gaines. New York: Columbia University Press.

Clark, B.
1928. Diary of a journey from Missouri to California in 1849. Edited by R. Bieber. *Missouri Historical Review* 23: 3–43.

Clark, S.
1929. *How many miles from St. Jo?.* Edited by E. Mighels. San Francisco: Harr Wagner Publishing Co.

Cross, Major O.
1940. *The march of the mounted rifleman.* Ed-

ited by R. Settle. Glendale, Calif.: Arthur H. Clarke Co.

Day, G., and Day, E.
1895.   *Pioneer days: The life story of Gershom and Elizabeth Day.* Edited by M. Trowbridge. Philadelphia: American Baptist Publication Society.

Decker, P.
1966.   *The diaries of Peter Decker.* Edited by H. Giffen. Georgetown, Calif.: Talisman Press.

Delano, A.
1936.   *Across the plains and among the diggings.* New York: Wilson-Erickson, Inc.

DeWolf, Capt. D.
1925.   Diary of the Overland Trail and letters of Captain David DeWolf. *Illinois State Historical Society Transactions,* no. 32, pp. 185–222.

Farnham, E.
1950.   From Ohio to California . . . Edited by M. Mattes and E. Kirk. *Indiana Magazine of History* 46: 297–318; 403–20.

Foster, Rev. I.
1925.   *The Foster Family: California pioneers.* Edited by L. Sexton. Santa Barbara, Calif.: Shauer Printing Studio, Inc.

Geiger, V., and Bryarly, W.
1962.   *Trail to California.* Edited by D. Potter, New Haven, Conn.: Yale University Press.

Gibbs, G.
1940.   *The march of the mounted riflemen.* Edited by R. Settle. Glendale Calif.: Arthur H. Clarke Co.

Gould, C.
1849.   While crossing the plains 1849. Typescript. Nebraska State Historical Society.

Hackney, J.
1930.   Diary. In *Wagons west: A story of the Oregon Trail,* by E. Page. New York: Farrar & Rinehart, Inc.

Hale, I.
1925.   Diary of trip to California in 1849. *Quarterly of the Society of California Pioneers* 2: 61–130.

Johnston, W.
1948.   *Overland to California.* Oakland, Calif.: Biobooks.

Leeper, D.
1894.   The argonauts of 'Forty-Nine: Some recollections of the plains and the diggings. South Bend, Ind.: J. B. Stoll & Co.

Page, H.
1930.   Diary. In *Wagons west: A story of the Oregon Trail,* by E. Page. New York: Farrar & Rinehart, Inc.

Pearson, G.
1961.   *Overland in 1849: From Missouri to California by the Platte River and the Salt Lake Trail.* Edited by J. Goodman. Los Angeles.

Perkins, E.
1967.   *Gold rush diary.* Edited by T. Clark. Lexington: University of Kentucky Press.

Pritchard, Capt. J.
1924.   Diary of a journey From Kentucky to California in 1849. *Missouri Historical Review* 18: 535–45.

Ramsay, A.
1949.   Alexander Ramsay's gold rush diary of 1849. Edited by M. Mattes. *Pacific Historical Review* 18:437–68.

Scharmann, H.
1969.   *Scharmann's overland journey to California.* Translated by M. and E. Zimmerman. Freeport, N.Y.: Books for Libraries.

Searls, N.
1940.   *The diary of a pioneer and other papers.* San Francisco: Pernau-Walsh Printing Co.

Shaw, R.
1948.   *Across the plains in Forty-Nine.* Edited by M. Quaife. Chicago: Lakeside Press.

Stansbury, Capt. H.
1852.   *Exploration and survey of the valley of the Great Salt Lake of Utah.* Philadelphia: Lippincott, Grambo, & Co.

Stephens, L.
1916.   *Life sketches of a Jayhawker of '49.* Privately printed.

Webster, K.
1917.   *The gold seekers of '49.* Manchester, N.H.: Standard Book Co.

REFERENCES CITED

Bieber, R.
1928.   Diary of a journey from Missouri to California in 1849. *Missouri Historical Review* 23: 3–43.

Bieber, R., ed.
1937.   *Southern trails to California in 1849.* Glendale, Calif.: Arthur H. Clarke Co.

Barrien, J.
1960.   Overland from St. Louis. Edited by T. and C. Hinckley. *Indiana Magazine of History* 56: 273–352.

Brown, J.
1908.   Memoirs of an American gold seeker. *Journal of American History* 2:129–54.

Giffen, H., ed.
1966.   *The diaries of Peter Decker.* Georgetown, Calif.: Talisman Press.

Hale, I.
  1925. Diary of trip to California in 1849. *Quarterly of the Society of California Pioneers.* 2: 61–130.
Hannon, J.
  1969. *The Boston-Newton Company venture.* Lincoln: University of Nebraska Press.
Johnston, W.
  1948. *Overland to California.* Oakland, Calif.: Biobooks.
Martin, M., ed.
  1926. From Texas to California in 1849: Diary of C. C. Cox. *Southwestern Historical Quarterly* 29: 36–50; 128–46; 201–23.
Morgan, D.
  1962. The Significance and value of the overland journal. *El Palacio* 49: 69–76.
Oliphant, J., ed.
  1955. *On the Arkansas Route to California in 1849.* Lewisburg, Pa.: Bucknell University Press.
Page, E.
  1930. *Wagons west.* New York: Farrar & Rinehart, Inc.
Parker, W.
  1964. Wading to California: The influence of the Forty-Niners on the notion of a Great American Desert. *Great Plains Journal* 3: 35–43.

Potter, D., ed.
  1962. *Trail to California: The overland journal of Vincent Geiger and Wakeman Bryarly.* New Haven, Conn.: Yale University Press.
Powell, H.
  1931. *The Santa Fe Trail to California, 1849–1852.* San Francisco: Book Club of California.
Scamehorn, H.
  1965. *The buckeye rovers in the gold rush.* Athens: Ohio University Press.
Searls, N.
  1940. *The diary of a pioneer and other papers.* San Francisco: Pernau-Walsh Printing Co.
Settle, R., ed.
  1940. *The march of the mounted riflemen.* Glendale, Calif.: Arthur H. Clarke Co.
Stansbury, H.
  1852. *Exploration and survey of the valley of the Great Salt Lake of Utah.* Philadelphia: Lippincott, Grambo & Co.
Taylor, B.
  1862. *Eldorado; or, Adventures in the path of empire.* New York: G. P. Putnam.
Wyman, W.
  1952. California emigrant letters. New York: Bookman Associates.

Land of Plenty or Poor Man's Land

Environmental Perception and Appraisal Respecting Agricultural Settlement in the Peace River Country, Canada

C. J. Tracie

University of Saskatchewan, Canada

I saw enough, however, to satisfy me that the land was astonishingly rich, fit in fact to produce anything.

John Macoun, 1875

While the country that has been described should, in the opinion of the writer, not be settled by either the rancher or the grower of wheat until there is more satisfactory evidence that it is suited for either of these pursuits, it may be safely prophesied that after railways have been built there will be only a small part of it that will not afford homes for hardy northern people, who never having had much will be satisfied with little. It is emphatically a poor man's country.

James Macoun, 1904

These two assessments of the Peace River country point to the critical role of perception in the evaluation of what are assumed to be objective environmental "facts" about an unfamiliar area. The perception of these facts not only leads the observer to positive or negative conclusions about the suitability of the area for certain purposes, but may, through publication, exert an encouraging or retarding influence on later settlement of the area. Latitudinal anomalies of climate, soils, and vegetation in the Peace River region prompted sharply divergent perceptions and assessments of the environment and its capability for cereal agriculture. The environmental problems around which perceptions varied were somewhat different from those of the Great Plains

farther south. Paucity and variability of precipitation were not generally causes for concern in the Peace. Uncertainty revolved primarily around the occurrence of summer frosts as the northern limit to large-scale cereal agriculture was being questioned. At the time of the observations under consideration, the Peace lay some two hundred miles beyond the most northerly advance of agriculture.

The purpose of this paper is to note variations in the perceptions of a group of observers and the conclusions these perceptions prompted concerning the suitability of the Peace River area for agriculture. Further, some suggestions as to the reasons for these variations in perceptions are noted. The material is taken from the reports and accounts of a diverse group of scientists, travelers, and farmers who, for various reasons, published statements about the suitability of this area for agriculture. All made their observations in the period from 1870 to 1905, before any significant body of meteorological or pedological data had been collected; consequently their assessments were based primarily on their perceptions of environmental experiences and on their assessments of information from local informants.

VARIATIONS IN PERCEPTION

Among the observers there was general agreement on four environmental "facts": (1)

over much of the area, soils were good and were capable of supporting cereal agriculture; (2) there were extensive areas of grassland which offered the most immediate prospect for agricultural utilization; (3) the climate of the deeply incised valley of the Peace River differed from that of the upland; and (4) summer frosts were not uncommon. There was, however, considerable variation in the way these facts were perceived relative to the agricultural suitability of the area, particularly in the matter of the climatic variables.

Soils were generally perceived as satisfactory for cereal agriculture, although some diversity in observation is apparent. John Macoun noted that the soil over the entire region was consistently deep (averaging five feet in exposed sections) and fertile, and commented on the complete absence of stones and the limited amount of marsh and swamp (John Macoun 1874, pp. 93–94). In contrast to these assessments, other observers (his son among them) noted that soil depths were often greatly exaggerated, that in many sections of the Peace that soils were thin and stony, and that many sections were poorly drained (James Macoun 1904, p. 21E).

Again, while observers agreed on the existence of fairly extensive grassland areas and on the fact that these areas were the most immediately accessible for agriculture, statements

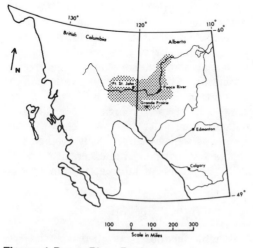

Figure 1 Peace River Region

concerning the size and quality of these grasslands varied considerably. For example, John Macoun was persuaded that "the whole country between Slave Lake and the Rocky Mountains is a continuation of the prairie" (John Macoun 1874, p. 95). Dawson's estimate of the grassland area was much more conservative. Not only were the grasslands confined in the main to the area west of the Smoky River, he reported, but the total area consisted of perhaps three thousand square miles of country "either perfectly open ... or dotted with patches of coppice and trees" (Dawson 1880, p. 114).

Most probably much of the exaggeration arose because surveyors and travelers generally followed Indian trails which were oriented so as to take maximum advantage of grassland openings. In this way, depending on the nature and enthusiasm of the observer and on his local sources of information, the character of the vegetation so encountered was ascribed to lesser or greater portions of the whole area.

The variations in perception relating to "facts" 3 and 4 above stem from a common concern about whether the length of the frost-free season was adequate to permit successful cereal production. Attention was directed to a consideration of climatic differences between valley and plateau not only because of the obvious contrasts in elevation (the valley being incised some 600 to 800 feet below the upland surface), but because cereal crops had been ripened successfully in the valley since at least 1809 (Harmon 1820, pp. 179–81). Quite clearly it was necessary to assess how representative of the general upland climate was this apparently favorable valley climate.

For several observers comparisons of conditions in the valley and on the upland indicated that growing conditions were more favorable on the plateau. Horetzky noted that the vegetation on the uplands did not appear to suffer so much from the effects of frost, a condition he attributed to "the air in these upper regions being constantly in motion, while in the deep and capacious valley of the river the winds have often no effect" (Horetzky 1874a, p. 44). Dawson's observations that shrubs and trees in the valley were tinged with frost to a much greater extent than those on the plateau appeared to corroborate these conclusions (Dawson 1881, p. 72B). In a later account, Horetzky substantiated his earlier assessments by reference to surface air drainage, arguing that the colder air, being heavier, would collect in the valley, thus increasing the dangers of frost there (Horetzky 1880, pp. 19–20).

Others had been convinced by their observations that the reverse was true; the climate in the valley was more favorable than that of the upland. James Macoun wrote (1904, p. 6E), "The fact that 'The Settlement' is in the bottom of a narrow valley should never be lost sight of. . . . When frosts are general throughout the country, the farms in the valley often escape, protecting fogs rising from the river as the temperature falls."

Bishop Clut gave evidence before a special Senate committee that the rivers exercised a great effect in preventing summer frosts and that away from their influence, the frosts were a good deal more common (Chambers 1908a, p. 56). Even John Macoun noted that the berries on the plateau ripened about a week later than those in the valley, although this observation did not appear to temper his enthusiastic claims for the upland (John Macoun 1876, pp. 155).

It seems curious, in the light of the interest in, and disagreement about, the climatic difference between the valley and upland, that few attempts were made to substantiate any difference by simple temperature comparisons. Horetzky (1880, pp. 19–20) appears to have at least considered the idea, but the closest to a consistent attempt to produce such evidence was Macdonnell's observations in 1905–1906. In comparing temperatures reported at Dunvegan (in the valley) and Spirit River (about 800 feet higher on the plateau) he noted a reasonably consistent difference of about eight degrees lower temperature at Spirit River (Macdonnell 1907, p. 5).

For the optimists, then, the evidence was clear; climatic conditions were at least as favorable on the plateau as in the valley, where long experience had proved that cereals could be ripened successfully. The success of the whole Peace area was thereby virtually assured. The pessimists were equally convinced by their observations that the climate in the valley was anomalously favorable; therefore, the success of agriculture in the valley could not be taken as a test of the capability of the upland.

Whether optimist, pessimist, or uncommitted observer, the frost hazard was one environmental fact which could not be ignored. Every observer either encountered or was given evidence of summer frosts, that is, frosts which occurred during the growing season. To some the occurrence of these frosts, particularly in June and July, ruled out the possibility of successful agricultural settlement. William Ogilvie commented on the positive features of the area but concluded that "the occurrence of severe frosts on the plateau when the grain is not far enough advanced to resist its effects may be as far as our experience goes considered a certainty in the majority of seasons" (Ogilvie 1893, p. 36). James Macoun noted the abundant evidence of severe frosts in June, July, and August which would either totally destroy the crop or at least make wheat unfit for flour-making purposes. (James Macoun 1904, p. 36E).

Other observers were merely dubious as to the agricultural potential of the area, reserving final judgment until more complete information was assembled. Cambie noted in 1880 that the area might be suitable for wheat "provided that varieties are used which come to maturity before the frosts in early autumn" (Cambie 1880, p. 56). Sandford Fleming's summary of the reports of a number of observers in the Peace prior to 1880 is representative of the assessments of those uncertain about the implications of frost for the agricultural settlement of the area. He noted that while the fertility of the soil was a recognized fact, there was not enough detailed information from which to generalize regarding the capability of the area for wheat culture (Fleming 1880, p. 10).

The occurrence of summer frosts did little to diminish the enthusiasm of some observers, however. While they could not and did not ignore their occurrence, they managed to diminish their significance as a hazard in several ways. Some argued that the frosts observed were "unusual" or "uncommon" and that in average years they could hardly be considered a detriment (Macleod 1880, p. 68). Others noted that most frosts were quite localized and, hence, not a wide-spread hazard (Dawson 1880, p. 118; Chambers 1908 *b*, p. 66). A "frost flees the plow" theory was invoked by some, acknowledging the danger of frosts, but confident that as soon as the land was cleared and cultivated the hazard would disappear (John Macoun 1874, p. 95; Chambers 1908*a*, pp. 53, 107). An effective counter to the occurrence of frosts was an emphasis on the evident *lack* of frost in several areas. John Macoun, for example, felt it wise to invoke the authority of the clergy in this matter, noting that the padre at Dunvegan had furnished him with a written statement to the effect that there were no spring frosts (John Macoun 1875, p. 94).

The variations in perception concerning soils and vegetation, it might be postulated, were not particularly significant in terms of the overall agricultural assessment of the Peace. The assessments, while variable, were positive; the soil and vegetative cover were conducive to agricultural settlement. The perception and assessment of the climatic elements—in particular, frost—were much more sharply contrasted and, it may be assumed, much more critical to the subsequent encouragement or retardation of agricultural settlement. Intending settlers would not be unduly concerned with minor variablity in the nature and areal extent of soils and vegetation since, on the whole, these were favorable. It is much more likely they would be concerned about the frost hazard, faced as they were with a two-hundred-mile, northward leap beyond an area where frost was already encountered as a significant hazard.

REASONS FOR VARIATIONS IN PERCEPTION AND ASSESSMENT

In analyzing the reasons for these divergent and often contradictory conclusions regarding the environment, one might suggest two points of view: that the environmental facts did indeed change or that the perception of these

facts varied. It would appear that both points of view have some validity in the present study. Variations in such factors as the route of the observer, the duration of the stay, and the year and season of the survey would have allowed for ample variation in the environmental conditions experienced (see fig. 2). On the other hand, it is evident from the accounts that certain consistent or similiar environmental elements were perceived and assessed quite differently. This suggests, then, that an important consideration is the differing frames of reference into which these "facts" were integrated. The query as to the reasons for differences in perception then becomes a quest for the factors involved in differing frames of reference. It is suggested here that major determinants would include the observer's personality, training, temporary dispostion, presuppositions, and prejudices.

A succinct example of the role of personality or temperament in perception is given by Frederick Niven in describing the reactions of a family first viewing the Red River Settlement in 1856:

As for the Settlement: each of them on arrival promptly observed it in a different way, and in that difference you have all three measured and weighed. Mrs. Munro saw the houses as alien, they being built of logs. Munro saw them as not altogether strange, they being thatched; and Angus saw them as romantic, they being log with thatch. The lack of a mountainside on which to rest their eyes was dreadful to Mrs. Munro, to Mr. Munro odd, to Angus novel and exciting. [Niven 1942, p. 17]

The differences in perception were an expression of, and modified by, differences in the observers' natures. This difference in nature or temperament is one element, perhaps a key one, in the observer's frame of reference.

In the present study, the contrasting views of John and James Macoun, a father-and-son team of biologists who often worked together but who visited the Peace on different occasions, point up the potential impact of personality on perception and assessment. Responding to a question concerning the rea-

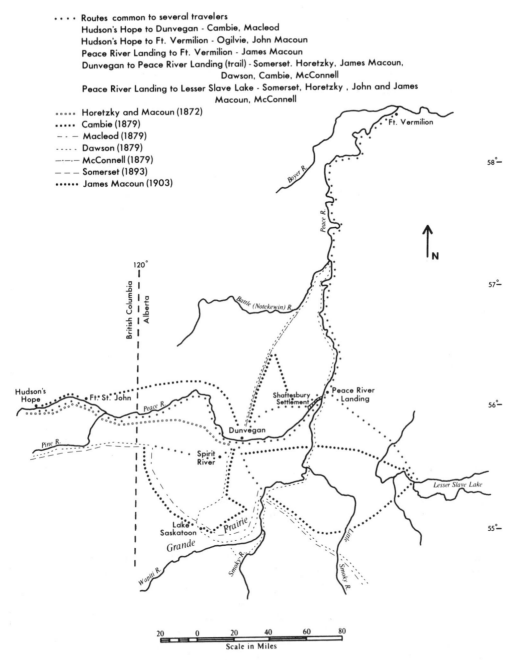

Figure 2 Routes of Selected Travelers. Source:
Travelers' published accounts.

son for their quite different conclusions about the agricultural potential of the Peace, the elder Macoun replied: "James was always the cautious sort" (Bowes 1952, p. 211). It is apparent from the enthusiastic descriptions and assessments not only of the Peace, but of Palliser's Triangle and the Yukon goldfields, that John Macoun was not. Horetzky described him as a man constantly in search of more acres, a commentary on Macoun's temperament rather than on his objectives, one might suggest (Horetzky 1880, p. 43). Macoun himself indicated he was constantly advised to temper his enthusiastic appraisals of new areas in order to avoid a backlash from exaggerated statements (John Macoun 1922, pp. 158, 164), and indeed it was for this reason that Horetzky took him to task for his intemperate application of the most favorable conditions he encountered to the whole Peace area (Horetzky 1880, p. 39). It appears that Macoun was possessed of an unusually optimistic nature, a fact which, it is reasonable to argue, greatly influenced his perceptions.

It appears that variations in training and experience had little to do with variations in the assessment of the Peace as suitable or unsuitable for agricultural settlement. Those who were prepared by their training and experience for sober and objective appraisals (i.e., scientists and surveyors) were markedly divided in their assessments. John Macoun and Dawson were optimistic, James Macoun and Ogilvie were pessimistic, while Cambie, McConnell, Macleod, and others were more or less uncommitted. The "untrained" visitors were also divided, Horetzky encouraging development, Pike and Somerset warning against it.

One might also note the effect of the temporary disposition of the observer, influenced by such factors as weather, travel conditions, and the like. Somers Somerset experienced many hardships in his travels through the Peace in the summer of 1893 and spoke of this "rain haunted land" and the "muskeg and sludgy swamp." Without attempting to establish the representativeness of these conditions, the temporary frame of mind that they engendered was probably not conducive to a sober appraisal of the agricultural potential of the Peace, and it is not surprising to find that his assessments were less than enthusiastic (Somerset 1985, pp. 93–96).

Finally, it is suggested that the observer's perceptions of the Peace area were influenced by what he *expected* to see (his expectations) and what he *wanted* to see (his prejudices). It is possible, for example, that the unexpected encounter with lush grassland, groveland, and parkland areas at 55° north latitude may have given Charles Horetzky and John Macoun a heightened sense of the fertility of the region, isolated as it was from similar areas to the south by 150 to 200 miles of forest and muskeg. The more critical appraisals of travelers after 1880 may reflect, in part, the fact that they were no longer overawed by this anomalous vegetation, having become familiar with it through the reports of earlier observers. In fact, it is possible that later travelers, being familiar with Macoun's descriptions, expected to see something really Edenic in the Peace, and when they encountered conditions that did not meet their inflated expectations, they became more critical than they might have been otherwise.

It is further suggested that perception often reflected what the observer *wanted* to see. Horetzky, for example, was obsessed with the adoption of the Pine Pass route for the Canadian Pacific Railway. His very positive assessment of the agricultural potential of the Peace may have been due to this desire; a sound agricultural base for future settlement in the area adjacent to the Pine Pass would do much to strengthen his argument. Resident farmers and local boosters also could be expected to perceive the environment through rose-tinted lenses, and indeed, almost all the statements by this group are unabashedly favorable. On the other hand, all the disparaging appraisals came from "disinterested" observers.

CONCLUSION

Variations in the assessment of the agricultural capability of the Peace River region by selected observers appear to be related to, or influenced by, two considerations: environmental conditions themselves varied because of differences in time, duration, and route of the observers' surveys; and/or *perception* of these environmental circumstances varied. While the times and routes of the surveys allowed for ample variation in the kinds of environmental circumstances encountered and assessed, it seems clear that certain consistent environmental constituents were perceived and assessed quite differently. This is particularly true of two environmental elements, the occurrence of summer frosts and the climatic differentiation between valley and plateau. It has been suggested that these variations in perception might be related to a combination of what the observer saw (influenced by his personality, training, and temporary disposition), what he expected to see (influenced by his presuppositions about the area) and what he wanted to see (influenced by the purpose of the observation and survey). This paper does not attempt to establish the relative importance of these factors in influencing perception, nor does it attempt to establish the constancy of their influence. It attempts only to document the existence and possible influence of these factors as they appear to have operated in the assessment of a new, potentially agricultural, area.

Assessing the impact of these varying perceptions on later agricultural settlement is a complex problem worthy of a separate study. That the "hardy northern people" that James Macoun mentioned did not wait for a railway, but pushed into the Peace in large numbers beginning in 1910 (some six years before the completion of such a line), would seem to underline the significance of the positive appraisals of the Peace. Certainly the bright prospects envisaged by John Macoun, Dawson, and others reached a fairly wide audience through such publications as Macoun's *Manitoba and the Great North-West* (1882), Horetzky's *Startling Facts* (1880), MacDougall's *Guide to Manitoba and the North West* (1880), and the simultaneous publication of the evidence heard before two special Senate committees (Chambers 1908*a* and 1908*b*). The Dominion government's own promotional literature made use of Macoun's Peace River observations as early as 1899 (Canada 1899, p. 61).

The earliest of a series of promotional booklets on the Peace area consisted almost wholly of quotations and paraphrases from John Macoun, Dawson, Brick, and other enthusiasts and was not above using favorable references made by such pessimists as Pike and Somerset (Canada 1916, p. 34).

On the other hand, it may be argued that the shortage of favorable land in the southern prairie provinces at about the same time (ca. 1910) *forced* the settlement of the Peace region —that this was done, in fact, with little, if any, evaluation of the statements published by earlier travelers. Thus it could be argued that the availability of Peace River land was much more significant to agricultural settlement than was the real or perceived attractiveness of such land. Whether one reasons that significant agricultural settlement was *pushed* into the Peace or was *attracted* to the Peace, by 1910 the beginning of a significant body of settlement was a reality. It was then up to the individual farmer to substantiate by experience the positive or negative assessments of earlier observers.

REFERENCES CITED

Bowes, G. E., ed.
  1952. *Peace River chronicles.* Edmonton: Institute of Applied Art.
Cambie, H. J.
  1880. Report. In *Canadian Pacific Railway report, 1880,* appendix no. 2, pp. 38–56. Ottawa: MacLean, Roger & Co.
Canada, Department of the Interior.
  1899. *Western Canada.* Ottawa: Queen's Printer.
  1916. *The Peace River country.* Ottawa: King's Printer.
Chambers, E. J., ed.
  1908*a.* *Canada's fertile northland; Evidence heard before a select committee of the Senate of Canada during the Parliamentary session of 1906–7, and the report based thereon.* Ottawa: Government Printing Bureau.
  1908*b.* *The Great Mackenzie Basin;* Reports of the select committee of the Senate, sessions 1887 and 1888. Ottawa: King's Printer.
Dawson, G. M.
  1880. Report. In *Canadian Pacific Railway Re-*

port, 1880, appendix no. 7, pp. 107–31. Ottawa: MacLean, Roger & Co.

1881.   Report. In *Canadian Geological Survey report of progress, 1879–1880,* pp. 1B–177B. Montreal: Dawson Brothers.

Fleming, S.
1880.   Report on explorations in Northern British Columbia and Peace River District. In *Canadian Pacific Railway Report, 1880,* pp. 1–12. Ottawa: MacLean, Roger & Co.

Harmon, D. W.
1820.   *A journal of voyages and travels in the interiour of North America . . .* Andover, Mass.: Flagg and Gould.

Horetzky, C.
1874*a*.   *Canada on the Pacific . . .* Montreal: Dawson Brothers.

1874*b*.   Report. In *Canadian Pacific Railway report of progress on the explorations and surveys up to January, 1874,* pp. 46–55. Ottawa: MacLean, Roger & Co.

1880.   *Some startling facts relating to the Canadian Pacific Railway and the north-west lands.* Ottawa: Free Press.

Macdonnell, J. A.
1907.   *Exploratory survey of 1905–1906 in connection with selection and location for the Dominion government of 3,500,000 acres in the Peace River District of British Columbia.* Ottawa: King's Printer.

MacDougall, W. B.
1880.   *MacDougall's guide to Manitoba and the North West.* Winnipeg: W. B. MacDougall.

Macleod, H. A. F.
1880.   Report. In *Canadian Pacific Railway report, 1880,* appendix no. 3, pp. 57–70. Ottawa: MacLean, Roger & Co.

Macoun, James M.
1904.   *Report on the Peace River region.* Geo-

logical Survey of Canada, no. 855. Ottawa: King's Printer.

Macoun, John
1874.   Report. In *Canadian Pacific Railway report of progress on the explorations and surveys up to January, 1874,* pp. 56–98. Ottawa: MacLean, Roger & Co.

1877*a*.   Report. In *Geological survey of Canada, report of progress for 1875–76,* pp. 110–232. Montreal: Dawson Brothers.

1877*b*.   Sketch of that portion of Canada between Lake Superior and the Rocky Mountains with special reference to its agricultural capabilities. In *Report on surveys and preliminary operations on the Canadian Pacific Railway up to January, 1877,* pp. 313–36. Ottawa: MacLean, Roger & Co.

1882.   *Manitoba and the Great North-West.* Geulph: World Publishing Co.

1922.   *Autobiography of John Macoun, M. A.* Ottawa: Ottawa Field Naturalists' Club.

Niven, F.
1942.   *The flying years.* Toronto: Wm. Collins Sons & Co. Ltd.

Ogilvie, W.
1885.   Report. In *Annual report for the Department of the Interior for the year 1884,* part 2, pp. 46–56. Ottawa: MacLean, Roger & Co.

1893.   Report on the Peace River and tributaries in 1891. In *Annual report of the Department of the Interior for the year 1892,* part 7. Ottawa: Queen's Printer.

Pike, W.
1892.   *The barren ground of northern Canada.* London: Macmillan & Co.

Somerset, H. S.
1895.   *The land of the Muskeg.* London: William Heinemann.

PART 5
The Desert and the Garden

The Influence of Ideology
on Changing Environmental Images
The Case of Six Gazetteers

David M. Emmons
University of Montana

There is a curious and, at times, confounding feature to the study of environmental image making. How, the student must inevitably ask himself, could two presumably rational men, separated only by time—and often not much of that—have traveled through the same region and come to such diverse conclusions regarding its appearance and value? Presuming no intervening improvements on the land and allowing for differences in personality, mood, scientific technique, and experience, it is still difficult to explain the often contradictory judgments rendered upon the same land over a span of, say, fifty years. The land is the same, and it remains passive; it does not create and transmit environmental images. Those observing obviously saw things differently and used correspondingly different environmental images to record their observations.

Nowhere is this feature clearer than when applied to the Great Plains. There, literally, one man's desert was another man's garden. For Stephen Long the plains were "tiresome to the eye, and fatiguing to the spirit . . . a sea of sand . . . wholly unfit for cultivation, and of course, uninhabitable by a people depending upon agriculture for their subsistence" (James 1819, in Thwaites 1904–1907, 15:232, 251, and 17:147; Pike 1805, 2:525; Bowden 1969, p. 17). Half a century later Ferdinand V. Hayden viewed many of the same scenes with considerably greater favor, insisting that constantly in-

creasing rainfall would correct what little there was of desert aridity and that the region had an "almost unlimited future" (Hayden 1872, p. 16; Hayden 1880, p. 87). To Long, and those who followed his lead, the plains region could only be described in desert images: "nomadic" Indians peopled its vastness; it was of no immediate or long-range use to a settled agricultural population. To Hayden and others of his persuasion, the plains were more properly categorized using Edenic images: in beauty and productivity the area was almost unmatched; it was a fit home for the highest expression of American culture, the yeoman farmer of settled and sober habits (Smith 1957, pp. 201–16).

The differences between Long and Hayden could be explained on the basis of individual personality—except for the fact that so many other observers and explorers could be similarly "paired." A more likely explanation would involve the political, economic, and social theories current in the societies that produced the observers. Granted, not all men perceived those theories in the same way; time, like most parents, produced divergent offspring. But for both the desert and garden theorists, recognizable external motives were at work, motives other than those of pure scientific observation. Those who traveled and commented upon the plains were, in subtle and often unconscious ways, programmed by the society from which they came and to which they reported (Goetzmann 1966; Goetzman 1963, p. 415; Bredeson 1968).

This argument applies with greater force to those who viewed the plains as gardenlike or nearly Edenic in its promise, but the desert theorists were certainly not immune to considerations other than scientific. Both Zebulon M. Pike and Stephen Long, for example, mentioned that desert aridity had at least the advantage of preventing, as Long put it, "too great an extension of our population westward" (James 1819, in Thwaites 1904–1907, 17:148; Pike 1805, 2:525). His fear, inspired by Montesquieu's earlier warning, was that a republic had to be restricted to certain limits lest the centrifugal force of its extension split it apart (Montesquieu 1748, 1:9, 130–31, 136, 194). No one can be certain, of course, that Pike and Long arrived at their desert theories because of this belief. The precise opposite is more likely the case. But this is not to say that theoretical considerations were unimportant: only that in this instance they were probably the result and not the cause of the environmental judgment. Should ideological considerations dictate, however, that environmental verdict could be—indeed, might have to be—reversed.

So, basically, did the matter stand. From 1820 until about 1850, theories of desert sterility in the American interior, if known at all, were of academic concern only (Bowden 1969). The American people did not yet need the plains in any immediate kind of way and deserts were, then, a tolerable part of their national landscape (White 1966, p. 73). Besides, such was the awesome power of American energies that, should the need ever arise, deserts could be brushed aside quite as easily as any other environmental obstacle. As one particularly sanguine spokesman put it, "That man must know little of the American people, who supposes that they can be stopped by any thing in the shape of . . . deserts" (Pilcher 1831, p. 19).

This threat of physical submission was not uncommon in the 1830s and '40s (Weinberg 1963, pp. 72–100; Marx 1964, pp. 171, 181–83, 201), but should it ever prove empty, Americans possessed another weapon: they could always change the environmental imagery and deny that there were deserts in need of conquest. The first approach, whatever it lacked in humility, at least involved a recognition that a problem of sorts existed. The second represented little more than an exercise in geographical sleight of hand. Two weapons, then, were available in the struggle against the desert—force and propaganda.

The second of the two was the first to be tried. It cannot be known with any degree of certainty why or when some Americans perceived a need to challenge the image of sterility on the plains. Larger social forces were obviously involved, and not of the romanticism-giving-way-to-realism sort. There was, in fact, an element of romanticism about both deserts and gardens (Goetzmann 1966, pp. 181–231, 303–4; Goetzmann 1959, pp. 18–19, 431). More to the point was that romanticism was itself being refined and modified by specific political and ideological forces. In the first place, a desert was an affront to America's Manifest Destiny—was, indeed, a denial of that secular faith. To capture land by military and diplomatic means, as in the Mexican War, and then dismiss that land as useless was to mock the entire effort (Weinberg 1963, p. 56; Frémont 1845, p. 48; Congressional Globe 1858, pt. 3, p. 2266). Secondly, to project a railroad linking the Mississippi River with the Pacific Ocean while condemning much of the region through which that road was to pass seemed to many an impossible and unnecessary undertaking. One might as well bridge the Atlantic as that "ocean" of grass and sage. The road, however, would be built; the image of the land would change (U.S. Senate 1854–55, pt. 7, p. 18; Bowles 1865, pp. 255–58). And then, too, deserts challenged that cosmological approach to natural science of which the mid-nineteenth century was so enamored. Most often associated with Alexander von Humboldt, this new vision sought, in an a priori kind of way, to find instances of environmental unity (Humboldt 1846, 1:2; Lewis 1966b, p. 35; Goetzmann 1966, pp. 303–4). Interior deserts in North America did not fit that pattern. They were alien, aberrant—and all too casually dismissed (Humboldt 1807, p. 32; Gilpin 1874, pp. 50, 61–62. See also Frémont 1845, p. 48, and Greene 1856, pp. 47–48).

Any of these developments, taken singly, might have occasioned a reevaluation of the desert image. Collectively, they all but compelled such a reevaluation. But the determining force, the most significant of the developments which caused or accompanied the changing environmental images of the Great Plains, were the political, social, and racial theories which preceded and followed the Civil War (Lamar 1961, pp. 34–35). The North-South conflict reshuffled ideas and reordered or redefined sectional priorities and ambitions. And since much of this sectional conflict centered around the "desert" West, environmental thinking about that region was unavoidably altered. From 1846 with the Wilmot Proviso until the election of Lincoln in 1860, North and South engaged in a rhetorical cold war in which each side attempted to gain a tactical, constitutional advantage in the contest for western lands. A common "imperial" struggle was in progress, except in this instance the lands in question had been condemned as uninhabitable. The desert theory was about to meet its first serious political test. It was not to survive the challenge. From the mid-fifties forward, Northerners would look out upon the plains and, where others had seen deserts, observe a great pasturage or, better yet, the future home of a thriving agricultural population (Lewis 1962, pp. 75–90; 1965, pp. 457–68; 1966a, pp. 135–50). The land was the same; the ideological perspective from which it was viewed was changing.

That new perspective was to receive its fullest expression from the early Republican party, and it is here that the influence of ideology upon environmental thinking is most clearly revealed. If a kind of shorthand version of Republican ideology can be found and if it can be shown that men acted upon that framework in rendering their environmental judgments on the plains, then a decent case can be made that the image of the plains changed in significant measure in response to felt ideological requirements.

The first task—that of constructing a working model of Republican philosophy—has been eased considerably by the recent studies of Eugene Berwanger, George Fredrickson, and Eric Foner. Each of these men is concerned with the ideological, as contrasted with the partisan, identity of the early Republicans. Their efforts, taken collectively, offer a kind of composite model of that political creed (Berwanger 1967; Fredrickson 1971; Foner 1970).

It is a complex model that emerges and one which must be used with care and restraint. In the first place, not all Republicans embraced each of its features with equal ardor. The party was too disparate for that kind of harmony (Foner 1970, pp. 103–226; Fredrickson 1965, pp. 7–53). Republicans ranged themselves from conservative to radical and they waged a kind of "inner civil war" among themselves (Fredrickson 1965). Speaking very generally, the radical and liberal factions were defeated in that struggle. The internal division, when it finally surfaced, was largely centered around abolition, race, and Reconstruction. For the radicals, the more perfect Union for which the North had fought was idealized in terms of both racial and sectional reconciliation; their war was, in important respects, a humanitarian crusade. For the conservatives, "more perfect" was defined in limited terms; their war involved principally the extension of the visible institutional features of Northern society to the backward and alien South (Stampp 1950, pp. 239–62; Warren 1961, pp. 29, 69–73; Fredrickson 1965, pp. 183–98; Woodward 1951, pp. 109–10; Foner 1970, pp. 40–72). It is to these postwar moderates and conservatives that most of the ideological generalizations refer.

In the second place, the Democrats, particularly in the North, both before and immediately after the war, did not choose to contest this Republican ideology in all its features (McKitrick 1960, pp. 67–76; Stampp 1950, pp. 46–63). Especially was this true where the conservative Republicans were concerned (McKitrick 1960, pp. 43–46). In other words, the model to be used was never employed for narrowly partisan purposes. Indeed, by the 1870s it had come to represent a near-consensus ideology, a national rather than partisan crusade (Warren 1961, pp. 46–49; Wiebe 1967, p. 11; McKitrick 1960, pp. 42–48).

Perhaps the best, certainly the handiest, expression of this Republican creed was the 1856 campaign chant, "Free Soil, Free Labor, Free Men" (Foner 1970, pp. 9–39). When applied to the lands of the Great Plains—and it often was—this theme had obvious and important implications for environmental imagery. Free soil would mean little if it was desert soil; free labor was more mockery than promise without fertile lands to which the working man could repair during hard times; and men were free only to the extent that they were supplied with the independence necessary to sustain and defend that freedom, an independence equated in the popular imagination with yeomanry and its attendant social virtues (Foner 1970, pp. 27–29, 30–36, 52–58; Morgan 1972, pp. 5–8). The expansion of slavery into the western lands obviously would disrupt this Republican vision, *but so would a desert.* Both evils had to be combatted, and though understandably greater emphasis was attached to the former, the denial of the desert in Kansas was as much a function of one's Republicanism as opposition to the admission of slaves into that same territory (Hale 1854, pp. 189, 222, 245–49; Boynton and Mason 1855, pp. 46–73, 139–41; Johnson 1954, pp. 19–23; Fredrickson 1971, pp. 130–64; Kansas Speeches 1860).

But there was more to this model than the promises made by that campaign theme. As George Fredrickson has shown, the more moderate Republicans, both before and after the war, were concerned with the wildly divergent forms the American Union had come to include. Theirs was a quest for homogeneity, an essential sameness of form which alone could provide for genuine union (Fredrickson 1971, pp. 130–64). Where the aberrant form violated Republican beliefs—as slavery so obviously and on so many levels did—they responded with a political ferocity unparalleled in this nation's history (Wilson 1962, pp. 59–99; Stampp 1950, pp. 239–62). These alien forms had to be reduced to a conforming (i.e., Republican) standard. The defeat and reconstruction of the South was the central part of that effort (Woodward 1951, pp. 109–10; Foner 1970, pp. 39–72).

But the Great Plains had to be similarly reduced and brought into conformity, and everything strange or alien, whether slaves, slaveholders, deserts, or "wandering aborigines," had to be denied entrance or be banished. American nationalism demanded a homogeneity at once institutional, geographical, and racial. When applied to the western territories before the war, this commitment meant that slavery, deserts, Indians, and blacks were to be attacked with a fine impartiality.[1] It was an ambitious undertaking, but the difficulty was eased considerably by the close associations which were immediately apparent. To prevent the advance of slavery was to block the entrance of the black and it remains impossible to determine which of those two goals was the more eagerly sought (Fredrickson 1971, pp. 130–32; Foner 1970, pp. 52–58; Berwanger 1967, pp. 123–37). Similarly, to deny the desert was by sophistic inference to deny the Indian his only proper home. The close association of Indian and desert dated at least as far back as Pike, and the removal of the former and his replacement with sturdy yeomen was a necessary first step in the denial of the latter (Pike 1805, 2:525; Smith 1957, pp. 204–7). In short, a very large measure of ethnocentrism was a part of the Republicans' ideological makeup.

For Americans so disposed, the West had come to assume enormous political and social significance. Opening that region to free, white settlement was part of a larger and grander plan of ensuring the continued tranquility and essential classlessness of American society. If access to the West were blocked, whether by slaveholders, Indians, or deserts, Americans would have to meet an entirely different and unwelcome set of problems. The labor safety valve, for one, would be closed; the settled harmony of the haves and the will-haves would be replaced by the discordant cries of the haves and the have-nots. It was a frighten-

1. It was suggested that desert sterility would block Southern as well as Northern ambitions, but after 1854 neither side took this argument seriously (Fredrickson 1971, pp. 146–47; Foner 1970, pp. 54–55; Genovese 1964, pp. 251–64. For the contrary view, see Ramsdell 1929, pp. 151–71).

ing specter, and for Republicans of conservative-to-moderate temperament the sin of the Southerners was not that some of them owned slaves but that all of them wished to see the West closed off to Northern settlement (Foner 1970, pp. 51–58; Fredrickson 1971, pp. 138–45). For these Republicans there was little room for abolitionist enthusiasms or sensibilities. This was a conflict of sectional interests; the future of white Americans, not that of black, was at issue. It was when these same Republicans came to believe that Great American Desert theorists were as pernicious in their influence as any slaveholder that the first movement toward changing environmental images began.

A civil war would be fought to "Yankeeize" the South, to correct and put straight Southern institutions. A similar, only slightly less significant, crusade would be mounted to ensure the extension of those same Northern-Republican ideals into the waste places of the West. As the Confederacy and slavery fell, so too would the desert—and for the same reasons, victims of the same near-irresistible forces. In both cases, orthodox Republican dogma played a major ideological role. The Northern victory was a vindication of Free Soil, Free Labor, Free Men; the full implementation of that ideology was a partial legacy of that victory (Wiebe 1967, p. 11). Again, not all Republicans joined equally in pursuing this particular spoil of war. Some of the more abolitionist-minded of them insisted that the legacy of the war was black freedom and equality and they meant to pursue both (Fredrickson 1971, p. 165). For most of them, however, the Civil War represented a victory for the free white man, not the enslaved black, and for that white victory to be fully realized the West had to be tamed and conquered (Smith 1957, pp. 193–94; Fredrickson 1965, pp. 183–99). The assault against the desert would be led, needless to add, by this second, more conservative group of Republicans.

Clearly this was not a partisan issue by the end of the Civil War. The identification of Republicanism with the denial of the desert does not mean that Democrats adopted a prodesert posture in order to preserve the adversary system. In fact, so persuasive was the Republican vision, so closely did it match the wishes of the American people, that partisanship on this issue was unthinkable. There were those who spoke of the plains in terms reminiscent of Pike and Long, but they acted from other than political motives (Hazen 1875; Powell 1878, pp. 33–34, 39, 42, 105–6; Beadle 1873, pp. 50–51, 233, 234). Republican ideology, on this issue at least, was immune from political attack (Wiebe 1967, p. 11; Fredrickson 1965, pp. 183–216). It should be pointed out, of course, that Republicans were more comfortable than Democrats in using that ideology. They were more practiced at it and had a more obvious claim on the sympathies of Union-minded Americans, but the significant point is not that the desert had been turned into a partisan issue —it had not. What is important is that environmental images would be changed in response to so unscientific a set of criteria.

In 1867 a Republican senatorial excursion party traveled to and through the Plains. The senators' reports on their observations provided a remarkably accurate indication of the kinds of attitudes that would accompany that environmental counterattack. The Northern victory, their accounts suggest, was more a triumph of organizational efficiency than of humanitarian commitment. The ideological legacy of that victory was not the elevation of civic sensibilities so much as the extension of the visible, institutional features of Northern society into the West and the South. The South would be reconstructed and revolutionized. The West would be similarly "civilized" (the word was a favorite of theirs) as it was cleansed of deserts, Indians, and any other barbaric remnants. "Our good 'Uncle Sam' has come here," Senator G. S. Orth explained, "and he brings with him science and civilization. He intends to plant permanently a part of his great family; for he is now founding empires, and his mission will not be fulfilled on this continent until every foot of its soil will acknowledge his dominion and his power" (Orth 1867, p. 49). This last reference involved more than just diplomatic posturing. Orth meant to see the addition of Canada to the American Republic, but he meant as well to witness the defeat of lingering desert images, the Americanization of the plains.

The best and most complete expression of this postwar mission came from the pens of a group of men given to western wanderings and determined to share their observations with as many people as they could reach. Their literary vehicle in this effort was the guidebook or gazette, a massive compendium of facts, figures, hearsay evidence, myth, lyrical promises, and a priori deductions. Their purpose was no less crusading than that announced by Senator Orth. They would expose the desert myth and in the process bring into conformity that last and most stubborn exception to America's geographical unity.

Their motives were neither scientific nor disinterested. These gazetteers were rather the advance agents of a political crusade. They brought to their tasks neither scientific skills nor the humility to recognize that such skills might prove useful. They brought instead an infectious enthusiasm and an abiding desire to promote the ideals and visions of Northern Republicanism. But these were no mere party hacks engaging in partisan contest with the Democrats; they were ideologues applying their political principles to a particular environmental problem or set of problems.

One of the first of these gazetteers was Albert Dean Richardson, a correspondent for Horace Greeley's *New York Tribune.* In 1865 Richardson made his first sojourn into the western regions. The immediate literary result was the publication a year later of a short booklet, *Our New States and Territories.* He was much impressed with the potential of the areas through which he traveled; they could look forward to a bright future, he wrote, not only as a result of the fertility of their soil and the salubrity of their climate but, and most significantly, by virtue of their participation in "our national civilization." All that was aberrant in the West, whether its geography, its racial characteristics, or its religious preferences, would "cease forever under contact with [that] national civilization." Deserts, Indians, and Mormons were obviously about to be converted or eliminated. No longer would they insult America's continental uniformity. "That stern policeman, civilization" demanded that they conform, just as it demanded a similar kind of conformity from the South. Richardson, in his own way, was a carpetbagger of sorts, engaged in a "reconstruction" quite as vital as that better-known effort in the South (Richardson 1866, pp. 22, 39, 66).

Politically, he was an ideal choice for the job. His commitment to the tenets of Republicanism spanned his entire adulthood, and working with Horace Greeley must have had its moments of political as well as journalistic education (Robbins 1933). In 1868 he put these skills to partisan use by preparing a campaign biography of U. S. Grant. It was a typical piece of campaign puffery, filled with predictable Republicanisms, and doing fitting honor to the man who, second only to Lincoln, had saved the Union and the vision of nationalism to which Republicans were dedicated. That vision was of a rugged and energetic people capable of wondrous acts of exploitation (Richardson 1868).

But this campaign tract, though a good example of his partisan zeal, did not reveal the fullness of Richardson's Republicanism. A year earlier, in 1867, he finished his *Beyond the Mississippi,* one of the first and certainly one of the best of the postwar gazettes. Breezier in style than some of the others, it was no less resolute in purpose. The defeat of the Confederacy had ushered in "the American era," and the West was to play host to its finest expression. "The Conquest of Nature," Richardson wrote "[was] moving toward the Pacific," and more to the point in terms of environmental imagery, nowhere did the conqueror encounter serious opposition. The West seemed everywhere productive. It offered to all who accepted its invitation "a clean page to begin anew the record of . . . life." Richardson even had a good word for sod huts, preferring them to the crude "log shanties and frame shells" of more forested regions (Richardson 1867, pp. i–ii, 38, 77, 79, 136, 559, 567). The desert theory was clearly being routed, but the choice of weapons was unfortunate. The projection of the garden image across the plains was a function of Richardson's patriotism, a test of his ideological loyalty, not his powers of observation.

Samuel Bowles was similarly motivated.

The respected and influential editor of the *Springfield (Massachusetts) Republican,* Bowles maintained an unwavering commitment to Republican principles. As early as 1851 he was referring to slavery as "an anomaly, . . . a gross imperfection" (*Springfield Republican,* April 14, 1851, in Merriam 1885, 1:86). It was always this anomalous nature of the institution that most concerned him. Whatever sympathies he may have possessed for the black slave (and they were few enough) were subordinated to his concern that so foreign an institution as slavery could have only destructive effects upon American life. When slaveholders began to demand the right to extend the institution into new areas his concern assumed a new and greater urgency. Such an extension would victimize the white working man, would mock the yeoman ideal, and would substitute for American middle-class values those of an alien and despised aristocracy (Merriam 1885, 1:148, 189, 319–20).

The war, as Bowles suspected it might, erased slavery, that "gross imperfection." Certainly that was cause for celebration, not because the black was now free but because abolition permitted North and South to consummate a genuine partnership, one in which all institutional obstacles to union had been removed. But Bowles made it clear that the sectional union of East and West was as important as that of North and South, and as deserving of attention (*Springfield Republican,* January 4, 1851, August 27, 1864, in Merriam 1885, 1:98–99, 348). The obstacle in this case was the desert theory, as alien to the American way as slavery, and as destructive. Bowles had written as early as 1854 that "it is good policy to Americanize everything resident in America," by which he meant the reduction of alien forms to one national standard (*Springfield Republican,* March 31, 1854, in Merriam 1885, 1:124). By 1865 what had been "good policy" was elevated to a near-divine calling. In his gazette, *Across the Continent,* he reminded the "men of the East" that they had expended a good many men and a good many dollars Americanizing one section of the Republic and "rescuing it from barbarism and from anarchy." Surely a percentage of those

sums could be spent to complete the nationalization process by funding the transcontinental railroad and rescuing the West from the same fate. Not to spend them, in fact, was to jeopardize those other and much larger sacrifices of the Civil War. But if the East responded generously and the road was completed, the West would provide final "payment of [the] great debt" of that war (Bowles 1865, p. 273; 1869a, pp. 116–17; 1869b, p. 8). The railroad would serve as the Union army had once served: a tool of conquest and a force for civilization. It would introduce Americans to their magnificent western empire and teach them how "all penetrating, all subduing was the power of their race." As for the Great American Desert, Bowles dismissed it as "the old nickname," assuring his readers that the "mark of America [was] over and upon all" now and that the geographical uniformity so much sought after was finally to be realized (Bowles 1869a, p. 77; 1869b, p. 115).

Racial uniformity must also be achieved. Bowles was uncertain about the fate of the free blacks; he doubted their ability, denying that they had the necessary "pluck" (Foner 1970, p. 297). But in regard to the Indian he was as certain as an unwavering belief in the triumph of civilization over barbarism could make a man. He was also blunt. "We know they are not our equals; we know that our right to the soil, as a race capable of its superior improvement, is above theirs. . . . The earth is the Lord's; it is given by Him to the Saints for its improvement and development; and we are the Saints." The Indian, then, like the "desert" in which he lived, was "a victim of that destiny" (Bowles 1869b, pp. 124–25). For Bowles, the denial of the desert was a function of the ethnocentrism he shared with many of his generation.

Frederick Goddard's gazette, *Where to Emigrate and Why,* is less notable in both style and substance. In fact, Goddard was more compiler than author, his book more a collection of random bits of western promotional literature than a sustained argument denying the desert in the name of national interest. His only other literary efforts consisted of uplifting guide books on the *Art of Selling* and *Giving and Getting Credit.* Yet Goddard's gazette belongs in the discussion for one significant reason. Alone among the gazetteers of the West, he included considerable information on the South. Freed by the Civil War from the obsolete institutional and social attitudes of the slaveocracy, the South, according to Goddard, "for the first time in our ... History," was a good field for immigrants (Goddard 1869, pp. 331, 333). It had been purified by the war, Americanized, and made fit to take its place as a refuge for "the down trodden millions of the Old World who would earn a nobler manhood." (Goddard 1869, p. 21). As for that other blasphemy, the Great American Desert, Goddard and those who contributed to his volume could find scarcely a trace. The Sandhills district of Nebraska was described as "a few patches of drift sand." Eastern Wyoming was declared as ready for the plow "as the fertile prairies of Illinois." And a good thing, too, for the weary and downtrodden of America's own cities stood in great need of "the broad fields and green pastures, the murmuring streams and long valleys of the West" (Goddard 1869, pp. 16, 177, 193).

For W. E. Webb, the wearier those downtrodden became, the more mutinous might become their intentions. Should they be offered only sterile deserts in place of murmuring streams and green pastures, he openly despaired for the future of the American Republic. But few were more convinced of the fertility of the Great Plains than W. E. Webb. As the former editor of the Kansas Pacific Railroad's promotional newspaper and later an official of the National Land Company, Webb had spent a number of years assailing deserts and desert theorists (Brainerd 1964, p. 15). His gazette, *Buffalo Land,* amply attests to his professionalism: it was filled with solicited testimony on the beauties and bounties of the plains (Webb 1872, pp. 194, 447, 476–80, 482, 485, and passim).

But in an appendix Webb drops his guard and reveals an ideological and social dimension which, one suspects, was more important in determining his environmental judgments than any past experience as a land promoter.

At issue was the question of labor and related unrest in the eastern cities. Webb wasted no charity on those "paupers" who petitioned for jobs or relief. Rather, he snorted out his contempt: these people were "idle and vicious"; they "brooded in the dark alleys, and bred vice to be flung out at regular intervals upon the civilized thoroughfares"; they were "germinators of disease and crime" and should be "dragged forth from their purlieus and hiding places and disinfected." Quite so! and the West, reclaimed from the desert theorists, was the proper place for this disinfection process (Webb 1872, pp. 436–37). For Goddard, then, and even more particularly for Webb, the denial of the desert was a vital first step in maintaining domestic peace and tranquility; it was a function of their fears and, in Webb's case, of his rancorous class prejudice.

Ferdinand V. Hayden offers yet another perspective on changing environmental images. The closest thing to a trained scientist among the gazetteers, Hayden diminished his scientific credibility by openly confessing other motives. William Goetzmann calls him "the businessman's geologist" and it is difficult to quarrel with that verdict (Goetzmann 1966, pp. 495–98; Smith 1957, p. 230). Hayden admitted that his "earnest wish at all times [was] to report that which will be most pleasing to the people of the West." As proof of his devotion he was prepared to spend "the remainder of the working days of my life [on] the development of its scientific and material interests" (Hayden 1871, p. 7).

He was true to his promise. In all his reports, in almost all that he did, Hayden viewed the West through that unscientific prism. He opened the pages of his reports to a number of undisguised land promoters; his principal assistant, Cyrus Thomas, used his official position to publicize his belief that rainfall was constantly increasing throughout the plains; he added the photographer William Jackson to his survey team largely that he might use Jackson's striking photographs to influence congressional appropriation committees; he published his *Sun Pictures* as a promotional lure (Elliott 1871, pp. 442–56; 1872, pp. 274–

79; Elliott, Letter Press Books; Thomas 1869, pp. 137–44; Goetzmann 1966, pp. 500, 522). And, finally, in 1880 he lent his name and his prestige to a massive gazette, *The Great West: Its Attractions and Resources.* There was nothing remarkable about the effort; the book was little more than a compilation of reports on the resources and opportunities of the western states and territories. The desert theory, needless to add, was given a severe, if quite unscientific, thrashing in its pages (Hayden 1880).

But then, science for Hayden was always of instrumental value; only as it advanced other and more significant ends did it command his respect. Hayden did write once that he "was obliged to speak the truth as I read it in the great book of nature," and though this hardly comported with his professed devotion to the interests of the West, he resolved the conflict by writing the book to fit this other and higher purpose (Hayden 1872, p. 7). To accuse him of duplicity, however, would be to misread him. He was the product of a society that looked to its explorers for comforting assurances, not scientific objectivity. Hayden shared that simple view (Goetzmann 1966, pp. 489–529).

Each of the men discussed spoke to one or two of the prevailing notions of his generation. Linus Brockett spoke to almost all of them. In this sense, if no other, he must be considered the dean of the gazetteers. His best-known effort, *Our Western Empire,* contains all the buoyant optimism, all the scientific hokum, all the ethnocentrism and racial conceit, and a fair sampling of the political fears of his generation. His Republican bias, moreover, was exactly what one would expect from a man whose literary credits included biographies of both Lincoln and Grant, plus three individual volumes on various aspects of the Northern victory in the Civil War (Brockett 1864; 1865; 1866; 1868; 1871).

Like Bowles, whom he closely resembled, Brockett was most impressed with the institutional consequences of the late war. The Northern victory had produced a Union; what passed for union in antebellum America was too badly marred by institutional heterogeneity truly to qualify. And this charge applied equally to the North. The transcendentalists and abolitionists were as foreign to his vision of American society as Jefferson Davis. It was not their humanitarian zeal which won the war, but the organized, disciplined actions of the men and women who peopled "the camps, the battlefields, and the hospitals," to borrow the title of one of his books. "The philanthropic results of the war," the title of another, were similarly interpreted. They were expressed most clearly not in abolitionism but in the *organized* Northern response to war and suffering. Brockett was a perfect representative of that class of Northerner who saw the war as a triumph of what George Fredrickson called "conservative nationalism," the reduction of all alien forms to the national, that is, Northern-Republican, standard (Fredrickson 1965, pp. 183–89). The blacks were obviously not the beneficiaries of this war and neither were the abolitionists. That honor must rightly fall to those who won it, the rigidly disciplined, institutionally organized middle-class Yankees. Their prize was the West.

The western empire was created for just such men—the kind of man who has "energy and pluck, who is not cast down because everything does not go just as he expected it would." On another occasion Brockett described this ideal Yankee as "industrious, enterprising, intelligent, moral, law-abiding, God-fearing, and brave" (Brockett 1881, pp. 192, 235). The Great Plains offered the perfect stage for the exercise of those virtues. Under the influence of the white man's higher civilization the final remnants of barbarism were being driven from the field. The rainfall was everywhere increasing, the climate was becoming more moderate, "the buffalo, the panther, and the prairie wolf" were being driven to extinction (Brockett 1881, pp. 42, 82, 98, 131, 208, 366, 730–36, 907).

More significantly, a similar fate must await the barbaric peoples who contested the white man's advance. The "indolent oriental" stood little chance against "our wide-awake, restless, impatient Yankees." Once his labors on the railroad were finished he was expected to return to his native China. As for the black and Indian populations, they were doomed to extinction "under the pressure of a higher civilization." The Mexicans, unfortunately, would probably survive, but "they are not aggressive and taking an inferior's position, they will be likely to be kept there." With the Indian and black gone and the Mexican cowering before "our more robust civilization," this western empire would be what God and destiny intended it: a white man's country (Brockett 1881, p. 234).

Brockett's indictment of past geographical errors was more general, more all-inclusive than that of the others, which is simply to say that his ethnocentrism was less restrained. There was no desert; there were, in fact, no environmental obstacles worthy of mention. The virtues that won the war would win the West. His beliefs were based not upon close reflection or observation, but upon what his political orthodoxy told him must be the case. Deserts involved alien, profane images. They clashed too obviously with the felt political and social needs of the postwar generation. Brockett and the others performed the necessary job of exorcising them.

Their tools were those their society provided: faith, energy, arrogance, and an overwhelming desire to impart some order and uniformity to the little-understood areas of the West. Deserts, however exotic and picturesque, were no longer an affordable luxury. The gazetteers set out, then, upon ideological, not scientific, quests, convinced and programmed to believe that the plains stood in need of "rediscovery." As one railroad promoter put it, the true discoverer of the region "was not Major Long, nor yet any of those wayfarers who beheld only its barrenness. Its true Columbus was he who ... first detected its latent capabilities" (Butler 1873, p. 10). The gazetteers here discussed believed that. But, believing it, they rendered themselves almost totally incapable of accurate description. Environmental images were changing; but useful environmental knowledge was not the result of that change. Nor would it be until political and social pressures remitted sufficiently to permit disinterested evaluation.

REFERENCES CITED

Beadle, J. H.
1873. *The underdeveloped West; or, five years in the territories.* Philadelphia: National Publishing Co.

Berwanger, Eugene.
1967. *The frontier against slavery.* Urbana: University of Illinois Press.

Bowden, Martyn.
1969. The perception of the western interior of the United States, 1800–1870: A problem in historical Geosophy. *Proceedings of the Association of American Geographers* 1:16–21.

Bowles, Samuel.
1865. *Across the continent.* Springfield, Mass.: Samuel Bowles & Co.
1869a. *The Pacific Railroad—open.* Boston: Fields & Osgood.
1869b. *The Switzerland of America.* Springfield, Mass.: Samuel Bowles & Co.

Boynton, Charles, & Mason, T. B.
1855. *A journey through kansas.* Cincinnati: Moore, Wilstach Keyes & Co.

Brainerd, John.
1964. William N. Byers & the National Land Company. MA thesis, University of Denver.

Bredeson, Robert.
1968. Landscape description in nineteenth century American travel literature. *American Quarterly* 20:86–94.

Brockett, Linus.
1864. *The philanthropic results of the war.* New York: Sheldon & Co.
1865. *The life and times of Abraham Lincoln.* Philadelphia: Bradley & Co.
1866. *The camp, the battlefield & the hospital.* Philadelphia: National Publishing Co.
1868. *Grant & Colfax.* New York: Richardson & Co.
1871. *The year of battles.* New York: G. Watson.
1881. *Our western empire.* Philadelphia: Bradley Garretson & Co.

Butler, James.
1873. *Nebraska: Its characteristics & prospects.* Omaha: Privately printed.

Congressional Globe.
1858. Speech of Andrew Johnson, May 20, 1858. 35th Cong., 1st sess.

Elliott, Richard Smith.
1871. Report on industrial resources of western Kansas & Colorado. In F. V. Hayden, *Preliminary report of the U.S. Geological Survey of Wyoming,* pp. 442–56. Washington, D.C.: GPO.

1872. Experiments in cultivating the plains along the line of the Kansas Pacific Railroad. In F. V. Hayden, *Preliminary report of the U.S. Geological Survey of Montana,* pp. 274–79. Washington, D.C.: GPO. [n.d.]. Letter Press Books, Missouri Historical Society, St. Louis.

Foner, Eric.
1970. *Free soil, free labor, free men.* New York: Oxford University Press.

Fredrickson, George.
1965. *The inner Civil War.* New York: Harper & Row.
1971. *The black image in the white mind.* New York: Harper & Row.

Frémont, John.
1845. *Report of the exploring expedition.* Washington, D.C.: Gales & Seaton.

Genovese, Eugene.
1964. *The political economy of slavery.* New York: Vintage Books.

Gilpin, William.
1874. *Mission of the North American people.* Philadelphia: J. B. Lippincott & Co.

Goddard, Frederick.
1869. *Where to emigrate & why.* Philadelphia: Peoples Publishing Co.

Goetzmann, William.
1959. *Army exploration of the American West.* New Haven: Yale University Press.
1963. The mountain man as Jacksonian man. *American Quarterly* 15:402–15.
1966. *Exploration & empire.* New York: Alfred Knopf.

Greene, Max.
1856. *The Kansas region: Forest, prairie, desert, mountain, vale, & river.* New York: Fowler & Wells.

Hale, E. E.
1854. *Kansas & Nebraska.* Boston: Phillips, Sampson & Co.

Hayden, F. V.
1871. *Preliminary report of the U.S. Geological Survey of Wyoming.* Washington, D.C.: GPO.
1872. *Preliminary report of the U.S. Geological Survey of Montana.* Washington, D.C.: GPO.
1880. *The great West: Its attractions & resources.* Philadelphia: Franklin Publishing Co.

Hazen, William.
1875. *Our barren lands: The interior of the U.S. west of the 100th meridian.* Cincinnati: R. Clarke & Co.

Humboldt, Alexander von.
1807. *Views of nature; or, contemplations on the sublime phenomena of creation.* Trans. by E. C.

Otte & H. G. Bohn, 1896. London: George Bill & Sons.
1845. *Cosmos: A sketch of the physical description of the universe.* Trans. by E. C. Otte, 1891–93. 5 vols. London: George Bill & Sons.

James, Edwin.
1819. Account of the Long Expedition, 1819–1820. In *Early Western Travels,* edited by Reuben G. Thwaites, 1904–1907. 39 vols. Cleveland: Arthur H. Clark Co.

Johnson, Samuel.
1954. *The battle cry of freedom.* Lawrence: Kansas University Press.

Kansas Speeches.
1860. Homesteads, the Republicans & settlers against democracy & aristocracy. Kansas State Historical Society, Topeka.

Lamar, Howard.
1961. *Dakota Territory.* New Haven: Yale University Press.

Lewis, G. Malcolm.
1962. Changing emphasis in the description of the natural environment of the American Great Plains area. *Transactions of the Institute of British Geographers* 30:75–90.
1965. Three centuries of desert concepts of the cis-Rocky Mountain West. *Journal of the West* 4:457–68.
1966a. Regional ideas & reality in the cis-Rocky Mountain West. *Transactions of the Institute of British Geographers* 38:135–50.
1966b. William Gilpin & the concept of the Great Plains region. *Annals of the Association of American Geographers* 56:33–50.

Marx, Leo.
1964. *The machine in the garden.* New York: Oxford University Press.

McKitrick, Eric.
1960. *Andrew Johnson & Reconstruction.* Chicago: University of Chicago Press.

Merriam, George S.
1885. *The life & times of Samuel Bowles.* 2 vols. New York: Century Co.

Montesquieu, Baron.
1748. *The Spirit of the Laws.* 2 vols., trans. by Thomas Nugent, 1905. London: George Hill & Sons.

Morgan, Edmund.
1972. Slavery and freedom: The American paradox. *Journal of American History* 59:5–29.

Orth, G. S.
1867. Speech of Senator G. S. Orth of Indiana. In *Proceedings of Meeting of Excursionists—1867 —Fort Harker, Kansas.* St. Louis: S. Levinson, Printer.

Pike, Zebulon M.
  1805. *The Expedition of Zebulon Montgomery Pike.* Edited by Elliott Coues, 1895. 3 vols. New York: Francis P. Harper.
Pilcher, Joshua.
  1831. Remarks to the U.S. Senate, *Executive Document 39,* 21st Cong., 2d sess.
Powell, John Wesley.
  1878. *Report on the lands of the arid region.* Edited by Wallace Stegner, 1966. Cambridge: Harvard University Press.
Ramsdell, Charles.
  1929. The natural limits of slavery expansion. *Mississippi Valley Historical Review* 16:151–71.
Richardson, Albert D.
  1866. *Our new states & territories.* New York: Beadle & Co.
  1867. *Beyond the Mississippi.* Hartford: American Publishing Co.
  1868. *A personal history of Ulysses S. Grant.* Hartford: American Publishing Co.
Robbins, Roy.
  1933. Horace Greeley: Land reform & unemployment, 1837–1862. *Agricultural History* 7:18–41.
Smith, Henry Nash.
  1957. *Virgin land.* New York: Vintage Books.
Stampp, Kenneth.
  1950. *And the war came.* Chicago: University of Chicago Press.
Stewart, Edgar I., ed.
  1968. *Penny-an-acre empire in the West.* Norman: University of Oklahoma Press.

Thomas, Cyrus.
  1869. Agriculture in Colorado. In F. V. Hayden, *Preliminary report of the U.S. Geological Survey of Colorado & New Mexico,* pp. 138–44. Washington, D.C.: GPO.
Tice, John.
  1872. *Over the plains; on the mountains.* St. Louis: Industrial Age Printing Co.
U.S. Senate.
  1854–55. Conclusions of the official review of the reports upon the explorations & surveys for railroad routes. *Senate Executive Document 78,* vol. 13, 33rd Cong., 2d sess.
Warren, Robert Penn.
  1961. *The legacy of the Civil War.* New York: Random House.
Webb, E. C.
  1872. *Buffalo land.* Philadelphia: Hubbard Bros.
Weinberg, Albert.
  1963. *Manifest Destiny.* Chicago: Quadrangle Paperbacks.
White, Lynn.
  1966. The legacy of the middle ages in the American Wild West. *American West* 3:69–77.
Wiebe, Robert.
  1967. *The search for order, 1877–1920.* New York: Hill & Wang.
Wilson, Edmund.
  1962. *Patriotic Gore.* New York: Oxford University Press.
Woodward, C. Vann.
  1951. *The origins of the New South.* Baton Rouge: Louisiana State University Press.

Mormon Perception and Settlement of the Great Plains

Richard H. Jackson
Brigham Young University

Although most people do not associate the Mormons[1] with the Great Plains, the plains play an integral role in Mormon folk and official history and historiography. The trek across the plains of some eighty thousand Mormons between 1847 and 1869 (when the railroad changed the method and meaning of the journey) symbolizes to all Mormons the faith, the sufferings, and the heroic magnitude of the accomplishments of the Mormon pioneers (Stegner 1964, p. 1). To the participants themselves it served as the literal rite of passage by which they proved their adherence to the new faith (Jackson 1972).

The general background of the Mormon colonization of the Great Basin is familiar to many. Driven from their homes in Independence, Missouri, they established Nauvoo, Illinois, on the Mississippi in 1840 (fig. 1). This city of twenty thousand people was in turn abandoned in January of 1846, when local mobs drove the Mormons out.

INITIAL APPROACH TO THE GREAT PLAINS

When they were driven from their homes in Nauvoo, it was the goal of Brigham Young and other Mormon leaders to move the Mormon population directly to the Salt Lake Valley (Arrington 1958). The exigencies associated with getting all of the Mormons out of Illinois in the winter prevented this and resulted in establishment of Winter Quarters (now Florence), Nebraska,[2] about five miles north of present-day Omaha, to prepare for the journey across the plains (fig. 1). Winter Quarters came into being almost instantaneously, as a city of 3,483 was created on Indian lands in a few months (Brigham Young University Library [3], December 24, 1846), and existed only until July 15, 1848, when it was abandoned by the Mormons (Journal History of the Church, July 15, 1848).

That this was to be a temporary settlement only was obvious from the first. Brigham Young indicated during the first weeks of its development that it was only to serve as a location where they could prepare for their migration to the Great Basin. Upon communicating a request to the president of the United States, Young was given permission to establish a location on the Indian lands on the condition that they left in the spring. A letter from the War Department to the superintendent of Indian Affairs in Saint Louis on September 2, 1846, stated that he should "impose upon [the

---

1. "Mormon" is the nickname given members of the Church of Jesus Christ of Latter-Day Saints because of their belief in the Book of Mormon.

2. The name Florence first appeared in 1854 after a non-Mormon company had established a town on the Winter Quarters site. See Donald F. Danker, "The Nebraska Winter Quarters Company and Florence," *Nebraska History* 37(1956), p. 30.

137

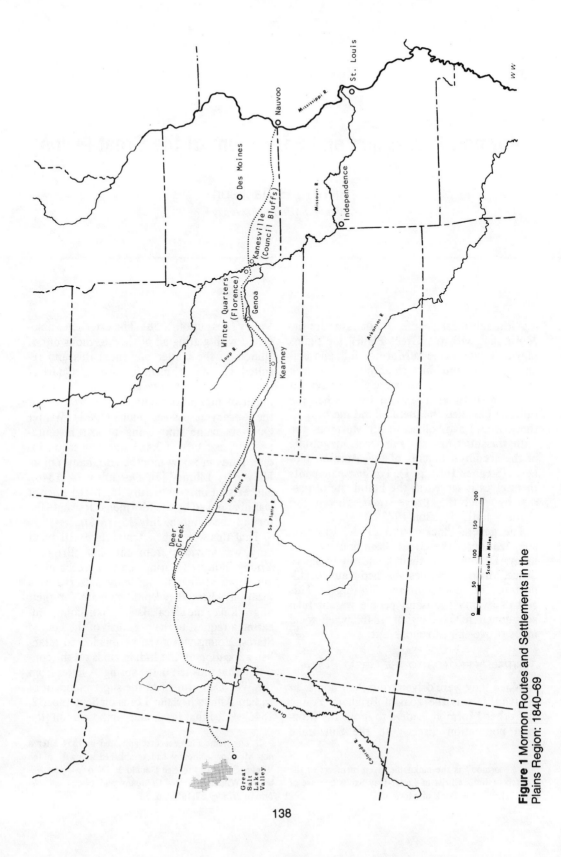

Figure 1 Mormon Routes and Settlements in the
Plains Region: 1840–69

Mormons] the necessity of leaving at the earliest moment their necessities and convenience will justify" (Journal History of the Church, September 2, 1846). If the residents had any illusions about staying on in the present-day Omaha area, they were disabused by Brigham Young's proclamation of April 16, 1847, as the pioneer company undertook its journey to the Great Basin.

The business of the Saints at Winter Quarters is to journey west until further instructions, and while some will have means to go forward at the springing of the grass, others will have to stop and raise grain to carry with them; and while some will come here prepared, others will have to stop and prepare for their journey, and in either case all preparation and organization is for journeying and not for permanent location at Winter Quarters. [Journal History of the Church, April 16, 1857]

The temporary nature of their stay, with the attendant lack of colonizing effort, affected the reaction of the Mormons to the environment. Rather than expressing interest in the potential for settlements, comments are restricted to those elements directly affecting their survival through the winter. Any and all factors which either supported or detracted from their goal of staying alive until spring received comment. Resources for accomplishing this end dominate the earliest records available for Winter Quarters (Jensen 1936, p. 5). Availability of clay for bricks, stone for well casings, forage for livestock, timber for fuel and construction, potential mill sites, and potable water are mentioned in all sources (Journal History of the Church, August–September, 1848).

Views of the environment beyond the availability of such necessities are few, however. Brigham Young reported that "we are located for the winter on a beautiful prairie, on the banks of the Mo. River" (Journal History of the Church, November 15, 1846). Such favorable comments are limited, possibly because of the sickness which struck the poorly provisioned group. Some members of the settlement referred to it as "Misery Bottoms," as six hundred inhabitants died during the one and one-

half years it existed (Reals and Merlis 1947, p. 46). The emigrants attributed the high incidence of disease to a variety of causes in the environment. Plowing the virgin soil was reported by some to release noxious vapors, others viewed the "rank vegetation and decaying organic matter at the bottom of the Missouri and its sluggish tributaries" as the cause, but the majority regarded the damp fog off the river as the problem. Young and other church leaders accurately viewed the high death rate as a natural consequence of inadequate food supplies (Reals and Merlis 1947, p. 47).

With the exception of the members' assessment of Winter Quarters as "Misery Bottoms," diarists did not categorize the environment favorably or unfavorably. Food availability, sickness and death, social interaction, and daily weather conditions preoccupied those few who kept diaries during the experience at Winter Quarters. They knew they were staying only temporarily, and leaders or members gave little attention to the suitability of the eastern margin of the plains for permanent settlements. They were aware, however, that the area around Winter Quarters would produce the normal crops of corn, potatoes, wheat, vegetables, and so forth. In the spring of 1847 Brigham Young encouraged the planting of crops to provision later arrivals and to provide food for the following winter for those remaining behind. The Mormons successfully produced these crops in the Winter Quarters area in 1847.

Winter Quarters ceased to exist as a Mormon settlement in 1848 as the Mormons moved the few remaining emigrants east of the Missouri to Kanesville (present-day Council Bluffs) (fig. 1.) This was done at the request of the Department of Indian Affairs to fulfill the original agreement to stay on Indian lands only temporarily. Kanesville served as the outfitting point for Mormons from 1848 until 1869. Until 1852, Kanesville had a sizeable Mormon population as the scattered members were brought together to prepare to journey west. By 1852 the bulk of the Mormons in the United States had gone west, and only a few leaders remained to organize future emigrant companies (Field and Reed 1907, pp. 8–10).

Perception of Kanesville was affected by the same factors mentioned for Winter Quarters. To those who lived there it was only a temporary residence, and comments about the environment beyond daily weather are limited. To the majority of Mormon emigrants it was simply a brief stopping point to outfit for the overland journey. These diarists commented on the layout of the town and pointed out that "idleness and dissipation were not tolerated. There was no jail nor need for one" (Babbitt 1916, p. 17). Weather conditions, availability of provisions, and other problems associated with camp life and the incipient overland journey were also noted. None of the writers assessed the suitability of the area for permanent homes and settlement. The Mormons were going west, and Kanesville was completely overshadowed by the journey ahead, the Mormon "Exodus."

Crossing the Plains

The Mormon perception of the rest of the Great Plains was restricted to a relatively narrow strip of land along the north bank of the Platte River. With the exception of the pioneer company in 1847,[3] who traveled under unique circumstances, the emigrants had no plans for ever settling the plains. They were important only as a barrier to be crossed en route to the Mormon mecca, Salt Lake City. As a result, appraisals of the general suitability of the region for settlements were restricted to diarists in the pioneer company of 1847 (Jackson 1970, pp. 124–25). The Mormon view of the plains was also colored by the manner in which they traveled. Unlike the Oregon and California immigrants, the Mormons were highly organized, and since they had fewer concerns for their safety, their diaries include more comments about the environment and fewer about day-to-day problems. After the first pioneer companies made the journey in 1847, every company had as leaders men who had made the trip at least once or, in many cases, several

3. The pioneer company was unique in that it was made up of picked men without families who were to locate a site for the Mormons to establish their settlement.

times. Each year, several hundred men and wagons were sent out from Utah to meet the immigrants at Winter Quarters or Kanesville. The guides had made the west-to-east journey only weeks prior to their east-to-west trips, so they were aware of the latest conditions on the trail. In addition, the Mormon companies had a strict military type of organization, with leaders of groups of ten, fifty, and one hundred (Utah State Historical Society [6], June 14, 1847). Once the journey commenced, immigrants were expected to adhere to the rules of their company. Consequently, they had few fears of the physical environment, and their perception of the plains reflects this. The trip itself was viewed as a semisacred experience. Members of the church were exhorted by their leaders to migrate to the Great Basin, and they approached the journey with varying levels of religious zeal. Consequently, any hardships the leaders could not prevent tended to be minimized, since devotion to duty in the face of such obstacles would only lead to some type of divine approval for their faithful obedience.

Perception

Materials for reconstructing the Mormon perception of the route across the plains are abundant. Church members were encouraged to keep a record of their experiences, and as a result, there are many diaries, letters, and recollections extant. These range from the phonetically spelled, unpunctuated diaries of individuals with little schooling to meticulous scientific expositions on botanical, astronomical, and meterological phenomena by college graduates. The vast majority of the Mormons, and their diaries, are intermediate between these. Unless otherwise indicated, it is the perception of these average immigrants which is detailed in the following pages.

The overwhelming response of individual immigrants to the plains was enthusiastic. One immigrant wrote to her parents in Leeds, England, that the journey, to her, "was the source of much enjoyment and pleasure. The varied scenery, the aspect of the country, so new to me and different from anything that I had ever seen, . . . combined to make the time pass swiftly along" (*Millenial Star,* December 6, 1862). Of 135 diaries examined for the period 1847–69, none contained a negative assessment of the Great Plains as a region. Individual weather events or localized areas were viewed unfavorably, but all diarists commented positively on the entire plains area they traversed.

Perhaps the most singular aspect of the Mormon perception of the plains is that *all* diarists who made any comment whatsoever on the environment include comments which can only be classed as superlative. Scarcely a day passed without the immigrants finding something that was "magnificent," "sublime," or "beautiful." This reflects the way the Mormons traveled across the plains. The high degree of organization in which decisions and problems were handled by the leaders reduced the difficulties of the trip to those of a tourist journey of the time. In the words of a correspondent for the *New York Tribune* (as quoted in the *Millenial Star* in 1855),

In every seaport of any consequence in this country and in Europe, emigration agents are located to give information to the inquiring and to those who desire to go to Utah, and arrange for their speedy transportation to that distant country. All along the line of travel, too, other agents are waiting with the necessary supplies for the journey, and under the auspices of Mormonism, the great land journey is now almost as safe as a journey from New York to Albany. [*Millenial Star,* January 20, 1855]

Landmarks and Scenery

Reflecting this tourist attitude, diaries of Mormon immigrants emphasize the unique and sensational encountered in the plains. Although many diaries are limited to terse comments about events within the camp, those which do include remarks about the plains describe phenomena common to all. Prominent among these were the landmarks along the trail, and the articulate diarists note that all travelers who were capable visited them. These landmarks were formalized for those

crossing the region, and served as mileposts against which to measure progress and as welcome interludes in the day's travel. Their importance to travelers is indicated by accounts of entire immigrant companies walking extra miles to visit a landmark, or of every member not confined to bed visiting Chimney Rock (Utah State Historical Society [4], September 8, 1850). The major landmarks were the erosional remnants along the Platte, the most famous being Court House Rock, Chimney Rock, and Scotts Bluff (fig. 1). In addition to those with names which were well known, other remnants were described by the more imaginative diarists. Table 1 indicates the incidence of diaries which note various aspects encountered along the trail.

The comments of the diarists concerning the "tourist attractions" of the plains range from a few brief words to effusive essays. Typical of the reticent diarists are those who confined themselves to reporting that there was "beautiful scenery on both sides" (Utah State Historical Society [2], August 11, 1853).

Others were more ecstatic in their view. "The Platt winding at our feet, the sun shining on it causing it to look like a ribbon of silver, the surrounding hills and masses of rocks in all shapes like ancient ruins form quite an interesting picture" (Brigham Young University Library [1], August 14, 1861). Sunsets, birds, changing patterns in the grass as it was rippled by the wind—all of these received attention. Even an invasion of grasshoppers, which were a scourge to later settlers, evoked a favorable response. "About 7 we had another heavy swarm of grasshoppers at this time everything is covered and millions in the air we never saw such a wonderful sight before" (Utah State Historical Society [2], August 19, 1853).

Such reactions illustrate the tourist nature of the Mormon journey but provide little insight into the Mormon view of the plains environment. Basic to understanding their perception of the broader elements of the plains is the assumption that when an individual or a group lives and travels for extended periods of time without adequate protection from the elements of the environment, those elements which most directly impinge upon

TABLE 1

Responses to Landmarks on the Great Plains

Number of Diarists by Year	Landmarks					
	Bluff Ruins	Court House Rock	Chimney Rock	Scotts Bluff	Scenic View and Panoramas	Curiosities[b]
1847 (22)[a]	17	8	15	12	17	18
1848 (13)	5	3	6	3	5	6
1849　(6)	3	2	3	1	3	2
1850　(6)	4	4	4	3	4	4
1851　(9)	3	2	3	1	2	2
1852 (14)	6	1	3	5	4	5
1853　(7)	3	–	3	2	3	3
1854　(6)	4	2	4	3	3	4
1855　(5)	2	1	3	1	3	2
1856　(7)	3	2	3	2	3	3
1857　(8)	4	3	4	3	5	4
1858　(5)	3	1	3	2	3	3
1859　(4)	1	1	3	2	3	2
1860　(7)	4	2	3	2	4	4
1861　(5)	2	1	2	1	1	2
1862　(2)	1	–	1	1	1	1
1863　(2)	–	–	1	–	2	2
1865　(4)	2	2	3	2	4	4
1866　(3)	2	2	2	2	3	3
Total 135	69	37	69	48	73	74

[a]The number in parentheses indicates the total number of diaries examined for the year.
[b]"Curiosities" was a term applied to miscellaneous items of the plains environment noted by the diarists. These range from "petrified bones" to grasshoppers.

them elicit the greatest amount of comment. In the case of the Mormon immigrants, the weather affected them directly. Storms with attendant phenomena, variations from anticipated temperatures, drought—such factors either facilitated or hindered the immediate problem of traveling. As would be expected, therefore, daily weather conditions are reported by nearly all diarists.

Weather Elements

The following was written west of Council Bluffs and represents entries on those days when the weather presented nothing untoward: "The weather is pleasant while it frosted a little at night" (Utah State Historical Society [6], April 7, 1857). If night tempera-

tures were low enough to cause serious discomfort, the immigrants included more specific information on the effect of such temperatures. Those immigrant companies departing in early spring were the only ones who mentioned cold on the plains. The bulk of the companies saw the plains in the summer months, yet high temperatures seldom received extended comment, presumably because the immigrant expected hot weather in the summer.

Precipitation was much more noteworthy to the diarists as they crossed the plains. The discomfort caused by rain-soaked clothing, bedding, and fuel was not easily alleviated. Each rainstorm encountered by a particular group is recorded, and the extent of the journal entry reflects the severity of the storm. A typical reaction to a convectional storm near Kearney was that "it has rained all night, with thunder and lighting [sic] the wind blew a perfect hurricane" (Utah State Historical Society [7], July 1, 1850). More severe storms often blew down tents, removed wagon covers, and otherwise inconvenienced the people. One diarist records that "in the afternoon a storm arose emitting very violent wind, thunder, lightning, rain and hail. Many tents blew over" (Clayton 1921, entry for May 6, 1846).

Wind unaccompanied by precipitation was of equal importance to the immigrants. The initial pioneer party in 1847 traveled on the north side of the Platte, where there had been little travel, yet the wind stirred up dust and had a generally desiccating effect upon their equipment. Clayton, the clerk of the first company, stated that "the wagons and everything else is shrinking up, for the wind is perfectly dry and parching; there is no moisture in it. Even my writing desk is splitting with the drought" (Clayton 1921, entry for April 29, 1847). In subsequent years, increased travel resulted in severe dust problems which were accentuated when the wind blew. An immigrant in 1850 described the trail through central Nebraska as "very dusty, a cold high wind makes it very unpleasant traveling" (Utah State Historical Society [7], August 11, 1850). Implicit and explicit in written comments about the wind is the fact that the wind made traveling uncomfortable or otherwise affected the diarists' physical comfort. There are no references to the psychological impact of the wind in the plains. No one indicated he was depressed or melancholy because of the wind. The wind was viewed only as a detraction from what might have otherwise been a reasonably enjoyable day's travel. The view of the wind and accompanying dust was summarized by one diarist, who stated "it has blown dust enough to choke us all to death" (Brigham Young University Library [2], May 3, 1847).

Another element of the environment which was of critical importance to the Mormons was the availability of grass. Its relative scarcity or abundance determined the speed with which they traversed the plains. The first group of pioneers, leaving in April of 1847,

were faced with a shortage of grass, as the Indians were burning the cured grass of the previous year to attract buffalo. "The Indians had set fire to the old grass which was among the new and all was burned together" (Utah State Historical Society [5], May 3, 1847). After a week of travel through such burned areas, another remarked that "the prairie is all burned bare and the black ashes fly bad, making the brethren look more like Indians than White folks" (Clayton 1921, entry for May 5, 1847).

That grass which escaped burning was in turn consumed by the migrating buffalo, causing the Mormons to compare the plains to a gigantic pasture. "In many places the grass is fed down by the Buffelows so that it has the appearance of an olde pasture onley the fence is missing" (Utah State Historical Society [5], May 2, 1847). The magnitude of the buffalo herds is indicated by another diarist, who said that "some think we have passed fifty, and some even a hundred thousand [buffalo] during the day" (Clayton 1921, entry for May 8, 1847). To another it seemed that they were crossing an "immense buffalo pasture" and that "the whole face of the earth is eat up here by the thousands upon thousands of buffalo" (Utah State Historical Society [6], May 8, 1847).

Succeeding companies left later in the spring and had no buffalo and fires to contend with, but they still commented on the presence or absence of grass. "We have traveled this forenoon over barren, sandy land being no grass," noted one (Clayton 1921, entry for June 20, 1847). More common in the plains were references to the abundance of grass. In eastern Nebraska one diarist remarked that "there is nothing to see but one boundless sea of grass, waving like the waves of the sea" (Utah State Historical Society [3], June 29, 1850). In the same area another noted, "This is a most delightful country of undulating prairie and the slopes covered with the richest kind of grass" (Utah State Historical Society [6], April 22, 1847). The grass in the plains near Kearney was described as buffalo grass: "It resembles blue grass it is fine and for common not more than from 4 to 6 inches high" (Utah

State Historical Society [5], May 2, 1847). The number and length of comments on grass or lack of it perhaps reflect the background of most immigrants.

Since they were originally from forested environments, the experience of traveling on the relatively treeless plains was a novel one. The appearance of any timber was dutifully noted by the immigrants. The pioneer company reported of the landscape west of present-day Omaha that the river bottoms were very broad, but "destitute of timber" (Utah State Historical Society [6], April 19, 1847). The group "had come up the Platt and Loup Fork about 130 miles through as fine a contrey [sic] as I ever saw for farming or grazing. The great difficulty was the lack of timber" (Utah State Historical Society [5], April 23, 1847). Near present-day Ogallala the soil was "rich," but there was "no timber" (Clayton 1921, entry for May 15, 1847). The appearance of some trees near Scotts Bluff was noteworthy. "Today we could see a fue trees on the outher side of the [Platte] River which was a new thing to us for we had not seen such a sight for a long time" (Utah State Historical Society [5], May 28, 1847). Had they been more familiar with the plains environment, it is doubtful that the lack of trees would have drawn such extensive remarks. The appearance of occasional trees or groves made the landscape seem more familiar and seemingly reduced the feeling of alienation the immigrants felt in crossing the Great Plains.

Other than grass and trees, the vegetation of the Great Plains was not perceived as important, if diary entries represent a valid sample of the immigrants' view. Of 135 diaries, only one contains anything beyond an occasional remark to the effect that they had seen some flowers that day. The exception was William Clayton, clerk of the pioneer company of 1847. He was charged with the responsibility of keeping an accurate record of events on the journey, and he evidently regarded his duties seriously (Clayton 1921). In one instance he noted that they had encountered "a great variety of shrubs, plants and flowers all new" to him. On another occasion he dutifully reported that "about one quarter of a mile from

where we camped is one of the prettiest beds of nettle I have seen for some time" (Clayton 1921, entry for April 21, 1847). Of the diaries examined, Clayton's is the only one which indicates the use of any apperceptive sense other than visual. Clayton systematically sampled herbs, reporting that they tasted the same as those grown in gardens. He also commented on the texture and odor of plants encountered. Clayton's diary is of value because of his attempt to catalog every item encountered in the Great Plains.

Climate

From their observations concerning weather phenomena and vegetation, the Mormons drew conclusions concerning the climate of the plains. The eastern margin was viewed as a "well-watered country," but in western Nebraska they noted "the country here is evidently getting drier" because the grass was shorter (Utah State Historical Society [6], May 22, 1847). The Mormons did not view the plains as a desert. None of the 135 diaries have any reference to the idea of a "Great American Desert" or any other large expanse of desert. Only three use the term *desert* in referring to any part of the plains, and then it is restricted to a specific day's journey. A typical entry from one of these three refers to western Nebraska and states that they "travelled aboat 15 and a half miles and about 6 miles was over a Dessert and barren except what they call Devils tonges which grows on a Desert" (Utah State Historical Society [1], May 28, 1847). According to the definition of the diarist, if grass did not grow it was a desert. He notes that they traveled "over a Dersert 4 miles and came to where there were grass" (Utah State Historical Society [1], May 30, 1847). One diarist reacted strongly to a particularly trying day's journey. "We roll over a bad road in a desolate country that would remind any-one of the Deserts in Arabia (we read about)" (Brigham Young University Library [1], September 16, 1861). The later immigrants, as in this case, used *desert* or *desertlike* to refer to sections of the overland trail which were particularly hard to traverse. The vast majority of the Mormons were utilitarian in their view of the plains environment. Grass was sufficient for their oxen, water was available at least once a day, and the land had enough vegetation that it did not warrant being called a desert.

Suitability for Settlement

Realistic appraisal is never more evident than in their assessment of the suitability for settlement and agriculture of the Great Plains region. The entire area from Winter Quarters to Fort Laramie was viewed as being replete with suitable settlement sites. The first 150 miles west of present-day Omaha was through "as fine a contrey [sic] as I ever saw for farming or grazing," wrote one immigrant (Utah State Historical Society [5], April 23, 1847). Of the same region the company clerk said, "The soil looks black and no doubt would yield a good crop of corn" (Clayton 1921, entry for April 22, 1847). Farther west in the Sandhills area one immigrant noted that "we have passed through a fine boatom Country of good land for sum days. The interior is too broaken for cultivation" (Utah State Historical Society [5], May 1, 1847). North of the eastern border of Colorado another said that "the soil on this prairie looks good and rich but there is no timber" (Clayton 1921, entry for May 15, 1847). The key indicator of soil fertility and, hence, suitability for agricultural settlement was soil color and texture. Sections of the trail with sandy soil were regarded as unsuited for crops, but these were few in number compared to the numerous choice agricultural sites found on the plains of Nebraska. The attitude of the Mormons concerning the suitability of the plains for agricultural settlements was summed up by one immigrant who pointed out that those who viewed the plains of Nebraska as sterile and forbidding were simply misinformed.

This is the most delightful country of undulating prairie and the slopes crowned with the richest kind of grass. . . . This country is so beautifully adapted to cultivation that there is driven from the

mind all idea of its being a wild waste in the wilderness. The fields . . . and habitations of men one is continually looking out for. [Utah State Historical Society (6), April 22, 1847]

It should be noted that the appraisal of the plains in terms of potential for settlement was restricted to the pioneer company of Mormons. Subsequent immigrants were concerned in getting to their homes in the Great Basin settlements, and they paid little attention to the suitability of the plains for occupation. The optimistic view of the pioneer company points out, however, that the plains in the vicinity of the Platte were not viewed as an area unsuited for agriculture. Evidence that the diarists' comments quoted above were serious appraisals is afforded by Mormon settlements established on the plains in 1857. Although only two were settled, the Mormon leaders planned more (Journal History of the Church, June 10, 1857).

One of the two established was located in Wyoming where the trail crossed Deer Creek, and the other was at the crossing of the Loup River in Nebraska (fig. 1). The former was called Deer Creek and the latter was designated the Beaver Creek Colony, or more formally, Genoa City. Judging from the activity, these were seemingly viewed as permanent settlements. Deer Creek was established in the spring of 1857, and a fort containing forty-two houses was constructed. Seventy-two men were engaged in the labors, which also included digging a canal for irrigation and cutting hay for the winter. (Jensen 1941, pp. 177–78). Genoa City was established in May of 1857, and by July it had ninety-seven men, twenty-five women, forty children, a sawmill, a brickyard, a four-hundred-acre village which had been surveyed into blocks and lots, and one thousand acres planted to corn, wheat, and other crops (*Millenial Star,* September 19, 1857). Allegations by anti-Mormons in 1857 led the federal government to send a military force to put down a purported rebellion in Utah, and these settlements, along with all Mormon settlements outside of the core area of what is now the Mormon cultural region, were abandoned (Meinig 1965). Had this not occurred, some of the earliest permanent villages on the Great Plains might have been those of the Mormons.

CONCLUSION

The preceding pages have demonstrated the overwhelmingly positive view of the plains held by the Mormons. But the question as to why the Mormons ignored them as a settlement site until 1857 remains. The Mormon immigrants had a goal fixed in their minds which they believed their religion commanded them to attain. In crossing the plains between 1847 and 1869 the Mormon was embarked on perhaps the most unique experience of his life. For most, this was a one-way journey and represented a break with their past life. They did not plan to settle the plains but only passed through them. Their resultant perceptions reflect this, with dairy entries which emphasize the scenic aspects of the trip rather than assessment of settlement suitability. But the diary entries also point out that the Mormons did not view the plains as a desert and that the reaction of immigrants who were properly outfitted for the journey was highly favorable. The suggestion from this is that the plains remained unsettled not because they weren't recognized as suitable, but because those crossing them were already committed to a different site. As a result, the plains, no matter how attractive, offered no serious alternative as a place to settle. When church leaders did authorize settlements in the plains rather than in Utah, the Mormons quickly established villages because of their favorable perception of the region. The Mormons, as suggested earlier, presumably had an easier journey across the plains than other immigrants, but the California and Oregon immigrants were similar to the Mormons in that they had committed themselves to a goal before entering the plains. As a result, it is hypothesized, they also passed over the plains without seriously considering establishing a permanent residence. The California and Oregon immigrants were less likely to return and settle in the plains after reaching their destination because they were more isolated from them. The hardest part of their journey had been after they had crossed the plains, and they were loath to repeat it.

The significance of this hypothesis is that it indicates that the plains were settled at a relatively late date not because of inaccurate perception, or lack of experience or technology (Webb 1931, p. 149), but only because the alternative goals of those crossing the plains exerted a stronger attraction, for assorted reasons, than the plains. Martyn Bowden has pointed out that immigrants did not view the plains as a desert (Bowden 1969, p. 21), but if the Mormon immigrant's reaction to the plains is representative, then overland immigrants were actually enthusiastic about opportunities for settlement in the region. It is anticipated that future research on non-Mormon immigrants will establish the validity of this statement.

REFERENCES CITED

UNPUBLISHED SOURCES

Brigham Young University Library, Provo, Utah.
  (1) Sixtus E. Johnson, Journal, MS.
  (2) Mary Elizabeth Lightner, Journal, MS.
  (3) Hosea Stout, Diary, MS.
Jackson, Richard H.
  1970. Myth and reality: Environmental perception of the Mormons, 1840–1865, an historical geography. Unpublished Ph.D. dissertation, Clark University.
Journal History of the Church.
  Church Historian's Office, Church of Jesus Christ of Latter-Day Saints, Salt Lake City, Utah.
Utah State Historical Society, Salt Lake City, Utah.
  (1) William A. Empey, Journal, MS.
  (2) James Farmer, Diary, MS.
  (3) Sophia Hardy, Journal, MS.
  (4) Martha Heywood, Diary, MS.
  (5) Levi Jackman, Journal, MS.
  (6) Norton Jacob, Diary, MS.
  (7) Mary Ann Maughan, Journal, MS.

NEWSPAPER

Millenial Star (Liverpool, England). 1840–1870.

PUBLISHED MATERIAL

Arrington, Leonard.
  1958. *Great Basin kingdom.* Cambridge: Harvard University Press.
Babbitt, Charles A.
  1916. *Early days at Council Bluffs.* Washington, D. C.: Byron S. Adams Press.
Bowden, Martyn.
  1969. The perception of the western interior of the United States, 1800–1870: A problem in historical geography. *Proceedings of the Association of American Geographers* 1: 16–21.
Clayton, William.
  1921. *William Clayton's Journal.* Salt Lake City: Clayton Family Association.
Field, Homer H., and Reed, Joseph H.
  1907. *History of Pottawattamie County* [Iowa], Chicago: S. J. Clarke Publishing Co.
Jackson, Richard H.
  1972. Myth and reality: Environmental perception of the Mormon pioneers. *Rocky Mountain Social Science Journal* 9: 33–38.

Jensen, Andrew.
  1936. *Tragedy at Winter Quarters.* Salt Lake City: Deseret News Publishing Co.
  1941. *Encyclopedic history of the Church of Jesus Christ of Latter-Day Saints.* Salt Lake City: Deseret News Publishing Co.
Meinig, Donald.
  1965. The Mormon culture region: Strategies and patterns in the geography of the American West, 1857–1964. *Annals of the Association of American Geographers* 55: 191–220.
Reals, William J., and Merlis, Sidney.
  1947. Mormon Winter Quarters: A medical note. *Bulletin of Creighton University School of Medicine* 4: 46–49.
Stegner, Wallace.
  1964. *The gathering of Zion.* New York: McGraw-Hill Book Co.
Webb, Walter P.
  1931. *The Great Plains.* New York: Ginn and Co.

The Desert Goes North

John Warkentin
York University, Canada

Common observation has it that physiographically Canada is an extension of the United States. In the 1930s this view was contested by scholars such as H. A. Innis and Donald Creighton, and more recently it has been questioned by geographers. Nevertheless, the idea of a north-south continuity of physical features exists and has been applied to the interior plains. In this paper I want to look at movements of selected concepts of the geographical nature of the plains across the line of the Canada–United States boundary, especially during the nineteenth century.

Along the 49th parallel the international border dates from the Convention of 1818, although the actual demarcation on the ground was not accomplished until the 1870s. Much more important than the line of the boundary itself in the years before agricultural settlement was the fact that the divide between two strategic transportation systems, along the Missouri and the Saskatchewan rivers, diverged in the vicinity of the 49th parallel (fig. 1). East-west movements of men have tended to prevail during the historic times which concern us here, and our task will be to see how a north-south interaction of ideas was accomplished against this flow.

Different types of information on the plains were recorded and transmitted, including empirical observations of topographic features, climatic impressions and statistics, and evaluations of resources involving speculation and interpretation. I will be selective and concentrate on the transfer of a few ideas, particularly the idea of the Great American Desert. By way of introduction I provide a very brief perspective on earlier perceptions and interpretations of the interior, going back to the first reports by Europeans.

I

The penetrations of Coronado (1540–42) and Kelsey (1690–92) make striking contrasts (fig. 2). Each man entered territory which was new to Europeans. So little general attention was given to the interior at that time that we tend to forget that they made their journeys 140 years apart. Each conveys an impression of plains, treelessness, and short grass, expressed tersely by Kelsey as barrenness.

Twenty years before Kelsey, Frenchmen were already traveling from the Saint Lawrence to Lakes Superior and Michigan (fig. 2) and describing the tall prairies of the modern Middle West. And from then right until the 1750s the French moved along the eastern side of the interior within a wide front (fig. 3). They were not circumscribed traders, but explorers who wanted to travel and report on new discoveries. Consequently their approach to exploration was encompassing; they prepared comprehensive reports on the land, many of which were published. Present-day Minnesota became a nexus of information, a central clear-

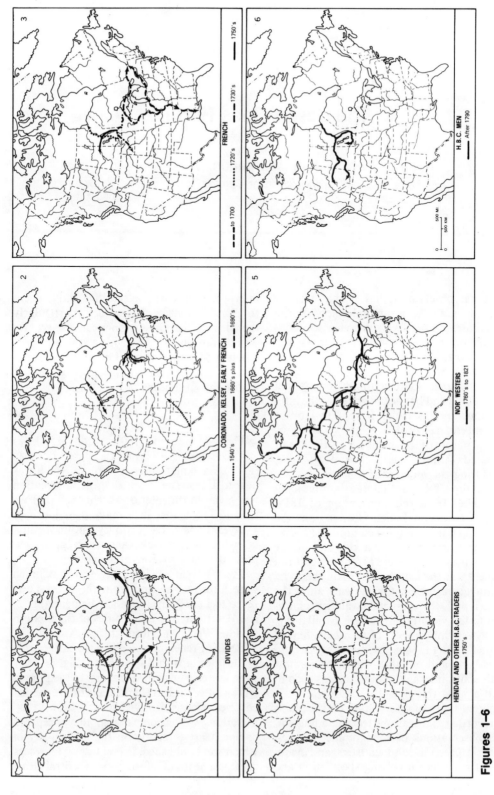

Figures 1–6

inghouse for observations from south, west, and north. To the north, Frenchmen were active as well. Information on the meadows near Lake Winnipeg went north to Hudson Bay in the 1720s, and in the 1730s La Vérendrye bridged the very zone which concerns us in this paper by traveling overland from the Assiniboine River to the Missouri. But his descriptions were not printed at that time. In all the French reports, published or unpublished, there was no differentiation of the interior into northern and southern tracts. Prairies and plains were reported lying westward whether the observers were at the mouth of the Missouri or on the Lower Saskatchewan. In the English translations of their reports, prairies sometimes become plains, meadows, or grasslands, depending upon the translator, so the translated material must be used with care.

In the 1750s Henday, succeeded in following years by other Hudson's Bay Company men, renewed the thrust from the bay into the plains immediately south of the North Saskatchewan. The concept of barren plains, but with the association of rich food resources in the herds of bison, began to emerge (fig. 4). The information garnered by these men, who were literally branch managers working under central direction, was carried to London and largely remained buried there in the offices of the Hudson's Bay Company.

The Nor'Westers who soon followed were a very different breed of fur trader. They came from Montreal; entrepreneurs in their own right, they possessed a much greater drive for exploration than the Hudson's Bay Company men, resembling the French in this regard, and ranged over a vast territory (fig. 5). The earliest had known the Minnesota nexus and had been in contact with men who traded there. Some of the Nor'Westers wrote and published. In their writings they gave their impressions of what the plains were like and noted the great north-south dimension of the plains in the interior of the continent, extending from the Gulf of Mexico to the far northern lakes. David Thompson, originally a Hudson's Bay Company man, also wrote in continental terms. Thus the great latitudinal sweep of the plains was made explicit by these men. Few

remarked on the potential of the land for agriculture, except in passing, but they gave indications of variations in vegetation and moisture from north to south, and the area along the 49th parallel was spanned by some of these generalizations. Thus, south of the North Saskatchewan the interior no longer was considered to be one uniform plain.

These Nor'Westers faded away in the third decade of the nineteenth century after their operations were absorbed by the Hudson's Bay Company, whose men did not have the same continental breadth of vision (fig. 6). Superb subregional observers, they curbed wider generalizations. They stopped short in their internal reports at the Saskatchewan-Missouri watershed, and made no extraregional comparisons with the area to the south where the Americans were becoming active. The Hudson's Bay Company's base of operations, the aspen-grove park belt along the North Saskatchewan River, was a very special area to these traders and became a foundation of their perception of the interior. They were only too aware of a change in the face of the country away from the park belt toward the south. However, they did not define this change beyond continuing to use the term *barrens* for grasslands. But it must be emphasized that barren was a topographic term. The grassland, inhabited by bison on which the traders depended for food, was not a wasteland to them in the sense of its resources. However, the watershed between the Saskatchewan and the Missouri had begun to assert itself as a conceptual border, and we will now have to look at how this barrier was broken.

II

The Americans did not have as well-watered and well-treed an avenue across the plains as the British had found the North Saskatchewan River and the park belt to be. But they did have promised lands in California, Oregon, and Utah to draw them in considerable numbers across the grasslands. The contrasts in perception of the country which emerged south of the 49th parallel were more clearly longitudinal than latitudinal, culminating in the concept of the existence of the Great American Desert east of the Rockies in the early decades of the nineteenth century (fig. 7). In the 1840s and '50s, scientific reporting received considerable emphasis. This included general speculations on climate and resources by Dr. Joseph Henry (Henry 1857) and very precise reports on geology and vegetation by Ferdinand Hayden (Hayden 1857) and by James Hall and Josiah Whitney (Hall and Whitney 1858) (fig. 8). Concurrent resource evaluations by the United States Railroad Surveys included an attempt by Governor Isaac Stevens to demonstrate the agricultural potential of the Missouri country, using analogies with Russia and the Red River Colony to substantiate his claims and thus breaking the bounds of the 49th parallel here as well (Stevens 1860, pp. 319–25). In the 1850s Professor H. D. Rogers (Johnston 1856) and Lorin Blodget (Blodget 1857) produced important "think pieces" on a continental scale on topography and geology and on climate and resources, respectively (fig. 8). Both extended their ideas across the border. This was no gradual transfer of ideas northward, but an encompassing of entire continental areas within their generalizations, on the order of the French or the Nor'Westers when those men, too, had looked at the continent in the round. As a result of these varied activities of the Americans, a cadre of knowledge and prejudices on the plains was built up south of the border within a few decades. All the information was published and waiting to be picked up by anyone who might want to start to apply some of the insights in evaluating the potential of the Saskatchewan basin, just across the gentle watershed.

For a while there was little interaction. In British North America the Hudson's Bay Company calmly went about its business, unperturbed about distant perceptions of the area it was administering. Despite meager data, grand generalizations about the interior plains were made in Europe on a continental scale. Alexander von Humboldt described a plain extending from the Gulf of Mexico to the Polar Seas (Humboldt, 1850, p. 39), and so did some British geographers (fig. 9). The border

was ignored, the "Desert" in the United States might be mentioned in such references, but of course nothing new of factual significance could be possibly added. Railroad dreamers were the worst offenders because they even took away what little was known of the area, largely obliterating variations in topography whenever they carried their imaginary railroads across the interior of British North America (fig. 9).

Essentially, the decades from the twenties to the fifties were a holding period in British North America. But the breakthrough of American ideas into Rupert's Land was coming. This was foreshadowed by the fact that Lorin Blodget and Dr. Joseph Henry were being read in Canada. Their ideas on the nature of the climate of the Northwest and the existence of the Great American Desert in the United States began to register in Toronto and elsewhere. However, people living in the plains north of the border—Indians, métis, fur traders, Red River colonists, and missionaries—gave no indication that they thought that any part of the area in which they lived was a desert (fig. 10). If such a novel idea was to be transferred northward it would have to be done by outsiders. And the intriguing question is, When would the banked-up American ideas cross the divide to the Saskatchewan basin, and who would be instrumental in doing this?

III

The men chiefly responsible for bringing about an interaction of American and British North American ideas about the plains in mid–nineteenth century were H. Y. Hind, a scientific explorer from Toronto, and Thomas Blakiston and James Hector, scientific explorers from Britain on an expedition led by Captain John Palliser.

Hind's successive views on the nature of the plains can be read in at least eight different sources, written between 1857 and 1862 (Hind 1857, 1858a, 1858b, 1858c, 1859, 1860a, 1860b, 1862). His thinking is transparent in that the quotations he carefully cites clearly show how many of his ideas originated and developed. Hind took ideas from all available

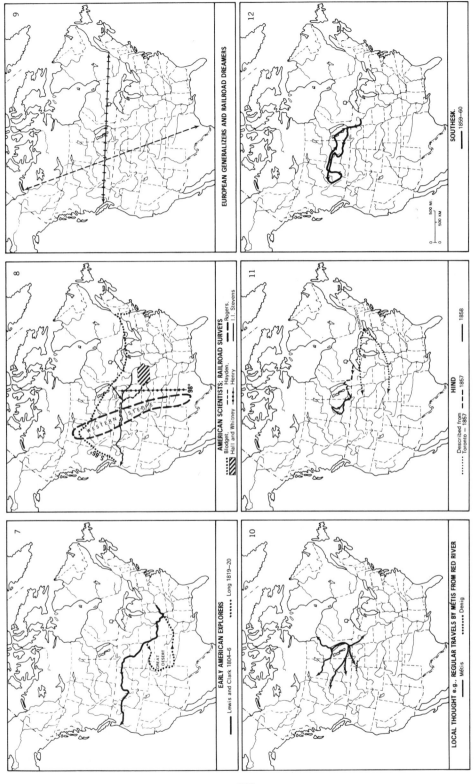

7 EARLY AMERICAN EXPLORERS
— Lewis and Clark 1804–6 ••••• Long 1819–20

8 AMERICAN SCIENTISTS; RAILROAD SURVEYS
Blodget, ⫶⫶⫶⫶ Hayden, —·— Rogers,
⫽⫽⫽ Hall and Whitney, ↑↑↑ Henry, ······ I.I. Stevens

9 EUROPEAN GENERALIZERS AND RAILROAD DREAMERS

10 LOCAL THOUGHT e.g., REGULAR TRAVELS BY MÉTIS FROM RED RIVER
— Métis ••••• Denig

11 HIND
······ Described from ——— 1857 ——— 1858
Toronto — 1857

12 SOUTHESK.
——— 1859–60

500 MI.
500 KM

Figures 7–12

153

sources, mixed them with his own field observations without thoroughly digesting the two kinds of material, and then quickly published this conglomeration. Thus he became a very active agent in disseminating a variety of ideas.

Even before Hind first went to Red River in 1857, he had read about the Great American Desert, as is revealed in an article he wrote in the *Canadian Almanac* (Hind 1858*a*) quoting Dr. Joseph Henry and others. On that initial exploration he traveled only as far west as Portage la Prairie (fig. 11), and in his reports of interviews with residents he unconsciously demonstrated that there was no local conception of a Great American Desert lying somewhere toward the Missouri. He mentions the Desert, but with no apparent intent of applying the concept to British North America. Size obviously was a factor; the interior plains were big enough to hold a desert in the United States without it necessarily protruding into British North America.

Next year Hind traversed the country extending from the Assiniboine to the South Saskatchewan (fig. 11), and from his letters written in the field before traveling west of the Assiniboine it is evident that he did not anticipate entering a desert (Hind 1859). He reports a considerable number of showers on the trip, so he did not see the country in a particularly dry year. The notes in Hind's field diary indicate that he believed that he was proceeding through a country where fertility increased northward, but there is no mention of a desert to the south (Hind 1858*c*). This apprehension quickly changed upon his return to Toronto when he began preparing the general report of his explorations. While writing up his own observations he apparently continued to consult American sources.

In the general report of his expedition in the Saskatchewan country (Hind 1859), Hind began to juxtapose quotations on the Great American Desert with his own descriptions of arid conditions in British North America, without as yet making an explicit connection between them. However, in a map drawn by John Arrowsmith which accompanied the British Parliamentary version of the same report, issued in August, 1860 (Hind 1860*a*), the

"Great American Desert" is clearly shown extending into British North America and a transition parkland zone to the north, between the grasslands and the forested areas, is marked "Fertile Belt" (fig. 14). In rapid succession many strands were thus brought together: (*a*) Hind's own impressions, (*b*) knowledge gained from reading American sources, and (*c*) information from Palliser on the location of arid areas in British North America and the territorial limits of the grasslands and the parklands (on the map but not as yet in the letterpress). The latter information may have come via Arrowsmith, who was drawing maps for both Hind and Palliser in London in the summer of 1860.

Hind, meanwhile, was preparing an account of his two expeditions for the general public, published late in October, 1860 (Hind 1860*b*). The additional time available to Hind in the summer and early fall of 1860 gave him the opportunity to write up some of his ideas on the resource zones of the interior which had not appeared in the *General Report* (Hind 1859) and to incorporate material from Palliser's first two parliamentary papers (Palliser 1859, 1860*a*). There are new explicit analyses of the characteristics of the Great American Desert and Fertile Belt, and the possible significance of each in the future development of the interior is considered. The transfer northward of the Desert was thus quickly completed in the summer and fall of 1860. In his *Narrative* (Hind, 1860*b*) and in other publications, Hind made effective use of a great many other American sources. He applied Hall and Whitney's definitions of prairie and plain (Hall and Whitney 1858, pp. 18–19) and Hayden's geological classifications on the Missouri area to British North America (Hayden 1857, pp. 109–16).

Hind made no careful analysis of the midcontinental interior and of the validity of transferring most of these ideas, particularly that of the Desert, northward. A model was simply plucked from the south and applied to a seemingly similar area in British North America, where it took on a new life of its own. Of course, there were physical similarities which induced Hind to do this, but nevertheless, such an uncritical comparison was hazardous. It seems unlikely to me, after reading Hind's field notebook and his first two published field reports, that he would have identified a desert in British North America and mapped it in the way he did had he not been exposed to American ideas and Palliser's field reports describing some of the arid areas. In this regard it is worth pointing out the reactions to the environment of two other observers who were on the British North American plains at this time. S. J. Dawson of Toronto, also a member of the Canadian expedition but working separately from Hind, traveled as far west as the Assiniboine in 1858. In his report (Dawson 1859) he does not appear to have used American sources and does not speak of a desert in the interior. He did not, it is true, travel into the extensive grasslands along the Saskatchewan River. However, the Earl of Southesk, representative of British big-game hunters who visited the interior occasionally, reached the South Saskatchewan in 1859–60 (fig. 12). He thought the country was barren prairie, scarcely even suitable for grazing purposes (Southesk 1875, pp. 78, 332), and it appears that it would not have taken much to convince him that it was a desert. But he stopped short of making that generalization.

IV

I turn next to the most famous scientific exploration of the British North American plains of all, the Palliser expedition of 1857–60. The British explorers made extended field observations over a vast territory (fig. 13), were influenced by American ideas, and interacted with Hind, although at a distance. Incredibly, there does not seem to have been a direct and thorough comparison of the observations and conclusions of the two expeditions through personal contact or even by letter—only a limited mutual exchange of ideas through printed reports.

Thomas Blakiston, the magnetical observer on the Palliser expedition, wrote a separate report on his activities, going well beyond recording his magnetic observations (Palliser, 1860a, pp. 29–75). His is an excellent recon-naissance account of the interior, with incisive and apt generalizations on physical geography. Unlike Hind, Blakiston does not indicate where he got his ideas, but it is evident that he had done considerable reading in American sources. He uses the American classifications of dry and arable prairie. The desert beyond the Missouri is mentioned, and Blakiston very elusively indicates that the country on the South Saskatchewan River may be similar in character. This report was written in 1859 and appeared in print in 1860. It clearly indicates an exposure to American ideas, independent of Hind, and a limited application of them to British North America. However, the references are so vague that it is up to us to disinter them from Blakiston's report, and they seem not to have made an impression on contemporary readers. Blakiston's fine document, however, is worth close study for its clear presentation of data on the interior.

James Hector, the geologist on the Palliser explorations, wrote most of the scientific reports issued by the expedition. It is possible to trace the growth of his ideas beginning with his first report from the field in 1857 (Palliser 1859, pp. 19–23) to the final culminating account of the work of the explorers in 1863 (Palliser 1863). Hector's results and interpretations are really the touchstone for assessing the scientific work of the expedition.

Hector uses information based on the writings of other men in a way very different from Hind's. New ideas are more carefully integrated into his own observations and not just rafted in, and fewer sources are cited. This makes it difficult to tell which thoughts are his and what ideas have been derived from others.

Before he left for North America, Hector was given an intensive exposure in London to all available scientific materials on the interior, including American publications. We know he had copies in the field of D. D. Owens's *Report of a Geological Survey of Wisconsin, Iowa, and Minnesota* (Owens 1852), and Professor H. D. Rogers's "Geological Map of N. America." In his first geological report written in December, 1857, Hector cites Jules Marcou on the Cretaceous (Palliser 1859, p. 22), but it is almost certain that he did not see Hayden's articles on the geology of the Missouri country until he returned to Britain in 1860. Once back in London he made full use of Hayden's classic work on the Cretaceous, as Hind had done, in interpreting his own field observations.

One of Hector's original contributions to the physical geography of the plains is his separation of the surface of the interior of British North America into three great relief levels, rising to the westward and separated by gentle scarps. In 1857 he referred to them as the three "prairie levels" (Palliser 1859, pp. 19–23), and then four years later he used the term "prairie steppes" (Hector 1861a, pp. 391–92). It is an intriguing problem why a careful man such as Hector should have adopted a vegetation term for a relief feature, and there is some evidence that his usage may have an American origin. On February 8, 1856, Professor H. D. Rogers, in a talk to the Royal Institution, London, England, "On the Geology and Physical Geography of North America" (Rogers 1971, pp. 69–89), applied the term "steppe" to the elevated tablelands extending from latitudes 28° to 60° immediately east of the Rockies. These remarks were expanded by Rogers in the article accompanying a map of North American relief features in A. K. Johnston's *Atlas of Physical Phenomena* (Johnston 1856). The map showed "Western Steppes" extending far into British North America (fig. 8). My surmise is that Hector got the term from Rogers, either from the talk to the Royal Institution, printed in the *Proceedings* of the institution for 1856, or from the material in Johnston's *Atlas.* He apparently did not use "steppe" until 1861, by which time he had returned to London and would have had access to Rogers's map of North American surface features in Johnston's *Atlas,* in case the map or the commentary had not been available to him before the expedition left Britain.

In time Hector also came to adopt the idea that a desert existed in the British North American interior. It is almost inconceivable that a man in Hector's position would not have been aware of the concept of a Great American Desert before he left Britain, but even if he knew of it he does not appear to have applied it to British North America on the basis of his own reading of American sources. The trigger, I think, was Hind.

In their first reports on the interior (Palliser 1859, 1860a), Hector and Palliser recognized an arid grassland country in the southern part of the interior and a parkland containing patches of rich land sweeping around it in a great arc. In June, 1860, shortly after returning to Britain, Palliser and Hector addressed the British Association for the Advancement of Science in Oxford, and in his paper Palliser explicitly compares those two major types of country (Palliser 1861). These generalizations, publicly presented, were based on the expedition's own field evidence. Later in 1860, as we have seen, Hind introduced the terms "Great American Desert" and "Fertile Belt" in both the map in his British Parliamentary report and in his *Narrative.* This terminology was available to Hector by the last half of 1860 when he began preparing botanical and geological papers for publication and writing the final account of the Palliser explorations in collaboration with J. W. Sullivan, the secretary of the expedition. Hector uses the terms "fertile belt" and "desert" in papers he published in 1861 (Ashburton 1861, pp. 200–201; Hector 1861c, p. 264) and they appear in the final report of the explorations (Palliser 1863). Despite his customary apparent care in generalizing, Hector does not critically assess the validity of the terms as resource evaluations, and his use gave them added credence and circulation.

Palliser is a special case in this examination of transfer of ideas. He was on the Missouri and Yellowstone rivers in 1847–48 hunting bison (Palliser 1853), and thus was in a good position in 1857–60 to compare the land on both sides of the 49th parallel (fig. 13). In his book describing his 1847–48 journey there is no indication that he is aware of a desert, nor is there any mention of it in his early letters and reports written in the course of the 1857–60 explorations. But in the short introduction to the final report (Palliser 1863), for which Palliser must bear responsibility, although he may not have written it himself, the idea of a thrust of the "Central American Desert" into British North America, in the form of a triangle extending to the 52nd parallel, is adopted (Palliser 1863, p. 7), and the "fertile belt" is referred to as well (Palliser 1863, pp. 8–13) (fig. 14). The references to a desert and a fertile belt are not emphasized nearly as much as in Hind's works, and even more significantly, the terms do not appear in the great map of 1865 intended to accompany the report, although there are numerous remarks on the face of the map praising the parklands and indicating that the southern country is not suited to agriculture (Palliser 1865).

To me it seems likely, although I cannot prove this, that the members of the Palliser expedition must have known about the Great American Desert but were not ready to transfer the idea northward without a great deal of deliberation, and perhaps not until they were pushed by Hind's aggressive generalizing. This reluctance may have been partly a matter of scale. The interior is huge. If one doesn't know too much about an area and is a dreamer it is easy to generalize, as railroad promoters did. But if one knows something about the dimensions of a region and its topography and has only a limited knowledge of climate, soils, and vegetation, one is more reluctant to make grand interpretive generalizations on future resource potential. This was the case with the British explorers. It did take a leap of the "informed imagination" to attribute the qualities of the alleged Great American Desert to the British North American plains; the men on the Palliser expedition did it only with hesitation and reservation and, except for Blakiston's tentative suggestion, only after Hind had led the way. The paradoxical thing is that they eventually got tagged with the prime responsibility for moving the Desert northward, because the comprehensive nature of the final Palliser report and the splendid map that went with it made their work more widely known and used in a more sustained way than Hind's vividly expressed but areally limited field observations.

V

In the 1860s the new information and interpretations on the West stemming from Hind and Palliser were used in different ways. Some writers, advocating the exploitation of the potential agricultural resources of the interior, saw only the Fertile Belt and applied terms such as "Rainbow of Rupert's Land" (Dodds, 1866, p. 5), "ordained garden" (Rawlings 1866, p. 7), and "Paradise of Fertility" (Waddington 1868, p. 13) to that favored area. Those were publicist's ravings. A few men scrutinized the Hind and Palliser evaluations closely and questioned some of their assumptions. A. J. Russell, writing in 1869 from Ottawa (Russell 1869) (fig. 15), is obviously against a cavalier adoption of selected American generalizations on the character of the interior plains, although he does not say so directly. He does show how a closer study of the characteristics of the region might be advisable before sweeping generalizations are made (Russell 1869, pp. 43–46, 65–67). To drive this point home in another way he cites generalizations on the productivity of the Russian steppes (Russell 1869, p. 32), which he probably was led to in Governor I. I. Stevens's accounts of the Missouri country in the United States Railroad Survey Reports where analogies are made with Russia (Stevens 1860, pp. 322–23) (fig. 15). One might almost say that Russell was turning the tables on Hind and Palliser by using American reports against them, but that is putting it too strongly. He also quotes, with telling effect, empirical observations made by Hind in the field which contradict the Hind and Palliser generalizations on the quality of the land in the southern interior (Russell 1869, pp. 43–46).

Russell stood virtually alone in arguing the need for caution before judging and generalizing. Once Hind and Palliser were on record with certain grand interpretations, others responded with their own sweeping evaluations. In 1869, Bishop Taché, who had a quarter century of experience in the West, and in 1873, William Butler, who made two winter journeys from Fort Garry to the North Saskatche-

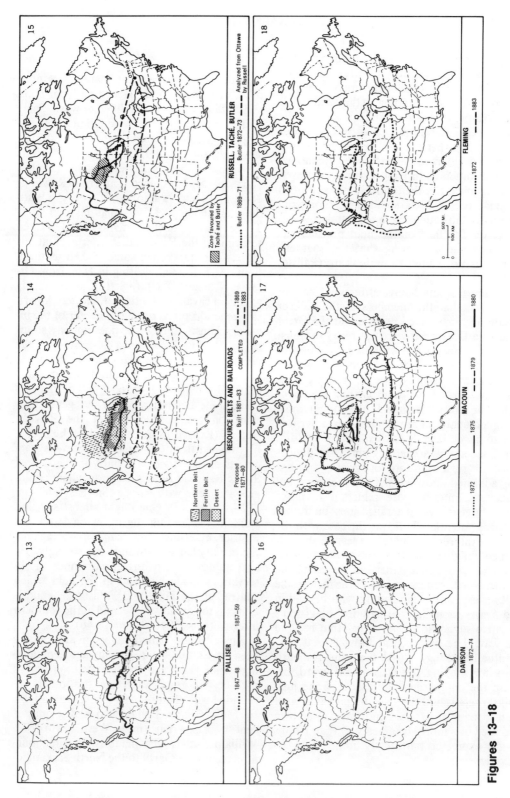

13

PALLISER

•••••• 1847–48 ──── 1857–59

14

RESOURCE BELTS AND RAILROADS

Northern Belt
Fertile Belt
Desert

COMPLETED { ─·─· 1869   ─── 1883 }

Proposed •••••• 1871–80 ──── Built 1881–83

15

RUSSELL, TACHÉ, BUTLER

Zone favoured by Taché and Butler

•••••• Butler 1869–71   ─── Butler 1872–73   ─·─· Analyzed from Ottawa by Russell

16

DAWSON

──── 1872–74

17

MACOUN

•••••• 1872   ──── 1875   ──── 1879   ──── 1880

18

FLEMING

•••••• 1872   ──── 1883

0   500 MI.
0   500 KM

Figures 13–18

158

wan in the early 1870s, urged that the best areas for settlement lay to the north of the parklands, that is, beyond the Fertile Belt of Hind and Palliser, in the forested zone (Taché 1870, pp. 19–20, 28; Butler 1896, p. 357) (fig. 15). Taché dismissed the southern country as desert (Taché 1870, pp. 10–16), corroborating the thinking of Hind and Palliser in that regard.

More field observation was needed. This started to come with the International Boundary Survey of 1872–75. An important new scientist, G. M. Dawson, entered the scene with that survey. Dawson closely examined the geology and topography of the country along the 49th parallel from Lake of the Woods to the Rockies (fig. 16). He was aware of the various ideas presented by Palliser, Hind, Hector, Hayden, and the U.S. railroad surveyors and compared their observations to his own on a carefully surveyed transect along the 49th parallel, not over a vast diffuse realm in the middle of the continent. His east-west comparisons of the ecology of the land along the 800-mile length of the border raised questions about the assumption that the arid conditions presumed to be characteristic of the alleged Great American Desert covered an extensive area in the central and western part of the zone investigated by the boundary survey (G. M. Dawson 1875, p. 299). Dawson followed Hayden, suggesting that the arid soil conditions in parts of the third prairie level were due to the special quality of the Cretaceous shale parent material, not to climate (Dawson 1875, pp. 144–45). His work began the dissolution of the idea of a continuous desert in interior British North America.

Dawson's reassessment of the extent of the desert and the agricultural potential of the southern Canadian plains did not bear fruit until an active resource appraisal of the land was undertaken by the Canadian Pacific Railway in the 1870s at the time it sought to establish a route across the plains to the Pacific Coast. Already in 1872, the chief engineer of the CPR, Sandford Fleming, had proposed that the main line go through the Fertile Belt (Fleming 1872), but the investigation of the resources of the entire prairie region for settle-

ment purposes continued. The CPR, of course, was anxious to promote settlement of the land, and this meant that the objectivity of any favorable revisionist findings might be suspect, especially if they were of the southern area still regarded as desert.

Many men reported on the resources of the interior at this time, but the chief interpreter was a botanist, John Macoun, who first worked for the CPR and then later for the Department of the Interior. Macoun's first journey to the plains, in 1872, was westward through the Fertile Belt, Peace River Country, and then on to the Pacific Coast, returning to Ontario via the United States on the Union Pacific Railway (fig. 17). In 1875 he visited the same areas again, roughly reversing his itinerary, but this time he journeyed right to Lake Athabaska. Then in 1879, and again in 1880, he was expressly sent into areas tagged arid by Palliser in order to find out if Palliser's judgment of the land was correct (Macoun, 1882, provides a review of Macoun's opinions on the resources of the interior). Macoun's reports were generally optimistic, and since both the CPR and the government wanted to settle the prairies, the impartiality of his views has been questioned (Roe 1946, pp. 131–49), especially at the point when he began to directly refute Palliser's generalizations on aridity and declared the southern lands to be fertile.

Macoun was influenced by the opinions of Dawson, trusted to his own knowledge of plants as indicators of fertility, and had some basis for making north-south comparisons from his quick look at the American plains when he had passed through by train. His observations must have been affected as well by the fact that he visited the western interior in relatively moist years. In the late 1870s and early '80s he bluntly attacked the idea that the Great American Desert extended on a broad front into Canada (Macoun 1882, pp. 105, 141–42), and a close study of his work indicates to me that he genuinely held these views, even though I doubt that he had the evidence to be as emphatic in his position as he tended to be. He was somewhat reckless in his optimism. His ideas had influence because he was in contact with and advised railroad men and politicians who were making decisions on the strategies to be followed in exploiting the West and because he wrote much and lectured widely. Some of his views appeared in the reports on land surveys issued by the Department of the Interior (Macoun 1881), giving his position added weight. Macoun's career bears very close study in order to investigate fully how his ideas developed and by whom he was influenced, but no scholar has done this yet. In any event, in the early 1880s the concept of the presence of a desert in the Canadian interior was being substantially criticized by Macoun and by others who followed his lead.

VI

When the task of constructing the CPR was transferred in 1880–81 from the government to a private company, the decision was quickly made to shift the route of the railroad from the Fertile Belt to the southern plains. The railroad was put through this more arid country in 1881–83 (fig. 14), even before there was a final consensus on what the potential for agriculture in most of that area might be. In the decision to follow a southern route, general strategic considerations on railroad routing probably overruled any apparent qualms about the possibilities for agricultural development in that drier zone.

In Canada in the 1880s there still was a belief that the Great American Desert existed in the United States, and some writers continued to say that a similar desert existed in Canada, despite the efforts of Macoun and others to counteract this, simply because the inertia of ideas is strong. But there was little exact debate on the matter. Perhaps the best example of how the relationship between the American and Canadian plains had come to be viewed by the time the CPR was being built is embodied in the writings of Sandford Fleming. He had been chief engineer of the CPR during the years it was a government undertaking, and after his departure in 1880 he continued his association through consulting. In the course of his work Fleming made four crossings of the interior plains, all in different latitudes—two in 1872 and two in 1883 (fig. 18).

In a book he wrote in 1884, Fleming suggested that on the plains there was a gradient of increasing fertility from south to north, culminating in the Fertile Belt (Fleming 1884, pp. 409–13). This idea of a gradual transition in agricultural resource potential makes sense when contrasted to the sharp distinctions implied in polarized terms such as desert and garden.

After the railroad was in operation, talk of a desert receded, despite the fact that settlers faced many handicaps in those drier grasslands through which the railroad passed and where great adjustments had to be made in agricultural operations. This quick abatement in attention to the desert reveals something of the mythic quality of the earlier discussions on the desert.

I have seen little evidence to indicate that the idea of a desert was widely held or even well known by the local population, although this matter requires further research. To a considerable degree, the image of a desert had its real existence on the printed pages of scattered publications, read by what must have been a limited number of readers, most of them far removed from the scene. The concept did have some practical importance, however, when the route of the railroad was debated in the Canadian Parliament and also affected government attitudes with respect to resource development.

As a measure of experience in trying to farm the land was acquired, the easy generalizations and ready south-to-north flow of desert perceptions based on the Long–Joseph Henry–Hind–Palliser sequence in transferring such ideas fell away. Desert images had to meet the touchstone of reality and new evaluations took place. Local experience became paramount in making assessments of aridity and potential productivity, and comparisons with the United States faded into irrelevance.

Since the 1880s, new conceptions of a desert have emerged whenever arid conditions have ruined farming. These are regionally produced ideas, which may apply to a wider international spatial context if there are concurrent dry conditions in the United States, or may even be projected back into the temporal context of the erstwhile desert of Hind and Palliser. The important thing, however, is that any current desert images arise out of Canadian conditions during times of drought and crisis and are not derived by transfers across the border. The fact that the earlier desert images are well known naturally makes it all the easier to resurrect conceptions of such a desert when circumstances warrant.

The fear of arid conditions is part of the continuing reality of living on the plains. By and large the plains are a proven area for settlement, but a residuum of caution and an awareness of hazard for arable farming remains. The climate of the plains is not consistent from year to year; therefore the geographer must recognize that any valid climatic images of the region must span and accommodate the experiences of a generation and more. Memory on the plains is important, and the image of an interior desert has been part of the regional history of the plains since the 1850s. The clearly enunciated British North American desert of the 1860s and '70s had American roots, but since the 1880s any desert imagery is largely home grown.

BIBLIOGRAPHY

The earlier source material used in this paper is well known, so complete references are not given. For those interested, most items are mentioned in my article "Steppe, Desert and Empire," in *Prairie Perspectives*, vol. 2, edited by A. W. Rasporich and H. C. Klassen (Toronto: Holt, Rinehart & Winston of Canada Ltd., 1973), pp. 102–36. Below are listed sources for the period after 1850.

The sequence of the H. Y. Hind material is:
Hind, H. Y.

1857.   Our railway policy: Its influence and prospects. In *Canadian Almanac and Repository of Useful Knowledge, for the Year 1857*, pp. 30–33. Toronto: Maclear & Co.

1858*a*.   The Great North-West. In *Canadian Almanac and Repository of Useful Knowledge, for the Year 1858*, pp. 27–30. Toronto: Maclear & Co.

1858*b*.   *Report on the exploration of the country between Lake Superior and the Red River Settlement.* Toronto: Printed by Order of the Legislative Assembly.

1858*c*.   "Rough Notes" by H. Y. Hind, July 19 to August 6, 1858. In Henry Yule Hind Note Books, 1858. Public Archives of Manitoba, Winnipeg, Canada.

1859.   *North West Territory: Reports of progress, together with a preliminary and general report on the Assiniboine and Saskatchewan Exploring Expedition made under instructions from the provisional secretary, Canada.* Toronto: Printed by Order of the Legislative Assembly.

1860*a*.   *British North America: Reports of progress, together with a preliminary and general report, on the Assiniboine and Saskatchewan Exploring Expedition.* London: Presented to both Houses of Parliament.

1860*b*.   *Narrative of the Canadian Red River Exploring Expedition of 1857 and of the Assiniboine and Saskatchewan Exploring Expedition of 1858.* 2 vols. London: Longman, Green, Longman and Roberts.

1862.   *A sketch of an overland route to British Columbia.* Toronto: W. H. Chewett & Co.

The sequence of the Palliser Expedition material is:
Palliser, John.

1853.   *Solitary rambles and adventures of a hunter in the prairies.* London: J. Murray.

1859.   *Papers relative to the exploration by Captain Palliser.* London: Presented to both Houses of Parliament. (Includes Hector's first geological report with its reference to levels.)

1860*a*.   *Further papers relative to the exploration by the expedition under Captain Palliser.* London: Presented to both Houses of Parliament. London. (Includes Lt. Blakiston's report.)

1860*b*.   Latest explorations in British North America: By Captain J. Palliser, with Dr. Hector and Mr. Sullivan. Read June 25, 1860. *Proceedings of the Royal Geographical Society* 4 (1859–60): 228–34.

1861.   On the course and results of the British North American Expedition, under his command in the years 1857, 1858, 1859. By Captain J. Palliser. In *British Association for the Advancement of Science, Report of the 30th Meeting, Oxford, June, July 1860*, pp. 170–74. London.

Ashburton, Lord.

1861.   Lord Ashburton's anniversary address, read by Sir Roderick Murchison, May 27, 1861. *Proceedings of the Royal Geographical Society* 5(1860–61): 202–3. (This contains material on the Palliser explorations prepared by Hector.)

Hector, James.

1861*a*.   On the geology of the country between Lake Superior and the Pacific Ocean. *Quarterly*

Journal of the Geological Society of London 17: 388–445.

1861*b*. Physical features of the central part of British North America, with special reference to its botanical physiognomy. *Edinburgh New Philosophical Journal,* n.s. 14: 212–40.

1861*c*. On the capabilities for settlement of the central part of British North America. *Edinburgh New Philosophical Journal,* n.s. 14: 263–68.

Palliser, John.
1863. *The journals, detailed reports, and observations relative to the exploration, by Captain Palliser . . . during the years 1857, 1858, 1859, and 1860.* London: Presented to both Houses of Parliament.

1865. *A general map of the routes in British North America explored by the expedition under Captain Palliser, during the years 1857, 1858, 1859, 1860.* London: Stanford's. (This map was intended to accompany the preceding *Report.*)

OTHER REFERENCES

Blodget, Lorin L.
1857. *Climatology of the United States . . .* Philadelphia: J. B. Lippincott & Co.

Butler, William.
1896. *The wild north land.* 10th ed. London: Sampson Low, Marston & Co. (First edition, 1873)

Dawson, George M.
1875. *Report on the geology and resources of the region in the vicinity of the forty-ninth parallel.* Montreal: Dawson Brothers.

Dawson, S. J.
1859. *Report on the exploration of the country between Lake Superior and the Red River Settlement, and between the latter place and the Assiniboine and the Saskatchewan by S. J. Dawson, Esquire C. E.* Toronto: Printed by Order of the Legislative Assembly.

Dodds, James.
1866. *The Hudson's Bay Company: Its position and prospects.* London: Edward Stanford.

Fleming, Sandford.
1872. *Progress report on the Canadian Pacific Railway Exploratory Survey.* Ottawa: Department of Public Works.
1884. *England and Canada.* London: Sampson Low, Marston, Searl & Rivington.

Hall, James, and Whitney, James D.
1858. *Report on the geological survey of the State of Iowa.* Vol. 1, part 1. Published by Authority of the Legislature of Iowa.

Hayden, F. V.
1857. Notes explanatory of a map and section illustrating the geological structure of the country bordering on the Missouri River, from the mouth of the Platte River to Fort Benton, in lat. 47°30' N., long. 110°30' W. *Proceedings of the Academy of Natural Sciences in Philadelphia,* May, 1857, pp. 109–16.

Henry, Joseph.
1857. Meteorology in its connection with agriculture. In Report of the Commissioner of Patents for the year 1856. 34th Cong., 3d sess. *Executive Document 65,* pp. 455–95.

Humboldt, Alexander Von.
1850. *Views of Nature.* London: Henry G. Bohn. (First edition, 1807)

Johnston, A. K.
1856. *The physical atlas of natural phenomena.* Edinburgh and London: William Blackwood & Sons. Plate 7 is a map entitled "The Physical Features of North & South America showing the Mountains, Table-Lands, Plains & Slopes. By A. K. Johnston, F. R. S. E. with original sections by Prof. H. D. Rogers." The accompanying text is: "The Physical Features of America: Its Mountains, Table-Lands, Plains, and Slopes. I. North America. By Henry Darwin Rogers, Boston."

Macoun, John.
1881. Annual report of the Department of the Interior for the year ended 31st December, 1880. *Canada: Sessional Papers 1881* (no. 3), pt.1, pp. vii–viii. Ottawa. (Summary account of John Macoun's findings.)
1882. *Manitoba and the Great North-West.* Guelph: World Publishing Co.

Owens, David D.
1852. *Report of a geological survey of Wisconsin, Iowa and Minnesota.* Philadelphia: Lippincott, Grambo & Co.

Rawlings, Thomas.
1866. *What shall we do with the Hudson's Bay Territory? Colonize the "Fertile Belt," which contains forty millions of acres.* London: A. H. Baily & Co.

Roe, F. G.
1946. Early opinions on the "Fertile Belt" of western Canada. *Canadian Historical Review* 27: 131–49.

Rogers, Henry D. 1971. On the geology and physical geography of North America. Lecture given Friday, February 8, 1856. Reprinted in *The Royal Institution Library of Science, Earth Sciences,* edited by S. K. Runcorn, vol. 1, pp. 69–89. London: Applied Science Publishers Ltd.

Russell, A. J.
    1869.   *The Red River Country, Hudson's Bay &*
    North-West Territories, considered in relation to
    Canada. Ottawa: G. E. Desbarats.
Stevens, I. I.
    1860.   *Reports of explorations and surveys, to as-*
    certain the most practicable and economical route
    from the Mississippi River to the Pacific Ocean.
    36th Cong., 1st sess. *Senate Executive Document,*
    vol. 12, book 1.
Southesk, Earl of.
    1875.   *Saskatchewan and the Rocky Mountains:*

A diary and narrative of travel, sport and adven-
ture, during a journey through the Hudson's Bay
Company's territories, in 1859 and 1860. Edin-
burgh: Edmonston & Douglas.
Taché, A.
    1870.   *Sketch of the North-West of America.*
    Translated from the French by Capt. D. R. Cam-
    eron. Montreal: John Lovell.
Waddington, Alfred.
    1868.   *Overland route through British America.*
    London: Longmans, Green, Reader, & Dyer.

Early Visitors to the Canadian Prairies

Irene M. Spry

University of Ottawa, Canada

On the evening of August 10, 1859, a Scottish nobleman, the earl of Southesk, "sat up late reading 'Much Ado about Nothing'. . . . The wolves howled, the night was very cold." His tent was pitched "on a knoll a few hours from Edmonton [then a fur trading post of the Hudson's Bay Company], from which there was a beautiful view over a circle of wooded plain, perfectly level except where the steep north bank of the river was discernable." After a heavy thunderstorm had cleared, "there was a lovely effect caused by the setting sun; on one side all was orange and gold, beneath a black cloud which melted into misty grey as it met the bright tints of the sunlight, and on the opposite side moved the dark departing thunder-cloud with a perfect rainbow enamelled on its face." This characteristic entry from the peer's diary was published in 1875 in a travel classic, *Saskatchewan and the Rocky Mountains* (pp. 145–46), one of many diaries, letters, articles, and books written by early visitors to Rupert's Land and the Indian Territories, which in 1870 became the Canadian West. In these writings—and, no doubt, in conversation, as well as in public lectures—they described exciting adventures amid scenes of exquisite beauty among picturesque savages. Their accounts abundantly reinforced the idea that the "Great Lone Land" (Butler 1872) was a land of adventure and romance, an idea which thousands upon thousands of juvenile readers imbibed from the works of R.

M. Ballantyne and other writers of children's books about the Great West.

At the time of Lord Southesk's visit, the Hudson's Bay Company was facing mounting opposition to its monopoly and proprietary rights in Rupert's Land, held under the charter that Charles II had given the company in 1670, and to the exclusive license of trade it held in the adjoining Indian Territories—opposition both economic and political. From the time of its merger in 1821 with the North West Company until the early 1840s, the western plains of British North America had been virtually the fur-trading, buffalo-hunting domain of the "Honourable Company." The plains were connected with the outside world only—or almost only—by the company's vessels sailing each year into Hudson Bay and by the brigades of boats that made the annual journey from the bay to the inland posts. The North American governor of the company and other rare passengers and express packets still used the canoe route from the Saint Lawrence. Occasional travelers on special missions traversed the wilderness between the Red River and the outlying settlements of the westward-moving frontier of the United States. Otherwise, the vast country drained by the rivers that flow to Hudson Bay, stretching from the Red River Settlement (where modern Winnipeg stands) to the Rocky Mountains, from the unsurveyed and unmarked international border between British and American terri-

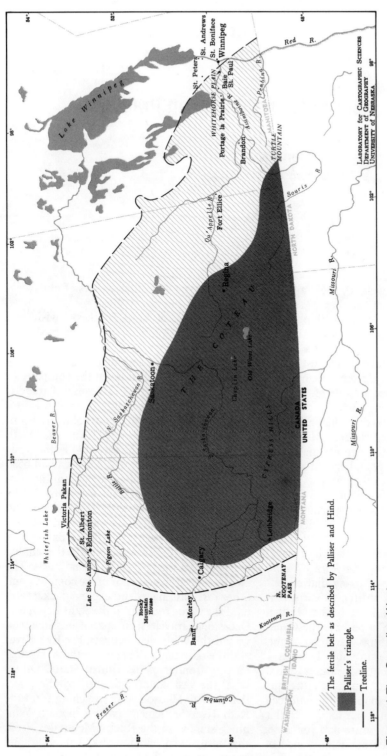

The fertile belt as described by Palliser and Hind.

Palliser's triangle.

Treeline.

Figure 1 The Canadian West

tory to the sub-Artic forest, was virtually isolated.

The boundaries of this prairie country, to quote Lieutenant (later General Sir William) Butler, were "on the north a huge forest, on the west a huge mountain, on the south an immense desert, on the east an immense marsh" (Butler 1872, p. 230). Apart from the officers and servants of the company and the handful of Selkirk settlers at Red River, the immense stretch of country so enclosed was inhabited only by wandering bands of Indians and by the mixed-blood descendants of fur-trade personnel and Indian women, the "new nation" of Bois Brûlés, who had developed a way of life well suited to their own special character and to the character of the western plains that were their familiar home.

The custom of the country, tribal usage, and the company's paternalistic sway—to say nothing of the force of character of the governor of Rupert's Land, Sir George Simpson—maintained tolerable order, seldom disturbed except by the customary horse-raiding and skirmishes among tribes traditionally hostile to one another.

The economy of the country was based on the great buffalo herds that provided the basic subsistence of the Plains Indians and Bois Brûlés and provisions for the fur-trade posts and voyageurs who manned the boat and Red River cart "brigades" that carried furs outward and trade goods inward, year after year. The fur trade was the tenuous link that tied the economy of the country to the commercial system of Europe and to its price system, through a complex chain of credit, culminating in "debt" accorded season by season to the Indians who hunted and brought in the pelts and pemmican. The isolation of this fur-trading, buffalo-hunting preserve was breached first by a trickle and then a swelling stream of newcomers from the outside world.

The Honourable Company was early "disposed to countenance and promote" (Church Missionary Society Proceedings, 1838–39, cited in Boon 1962, p. 46) missions of a number of rival denominations, partly by reason of the philanthropic benevolence of some influential members of the governing committee and partly by way of refuting accusations of indifference to the moral well-being, Christianization, and civilization of the aborigines, to say nothing of the company's own servants. At first Protestants and Catholics alike found plenty to occupy them in the Red River valley, on the Assiniboine River immediately to the west, and in the forest and lake country that fringed the prairies; but by the 1840s missionaries were moving westward across the plains. By 1841 the pioneer Wesleyan missionary, the Reverend Robert Terrill Rundle, was so far west that he saw the Rocky Mountains on his way from Edmonton to Rocky Mountain House (Rundle 1840–48). He was followed, after an interval, by his Methodist colleagues, the Reverend Thomas Woolsey (Glenbow Institute, 1855–64) and the Reverend George McDougall and his son John, who established mission settlements at Pigeon Lake, Whitefish Lake, Victoria Pakan, and Morleyville. Records of their impressions and adventures were disseminated through the Methodist church and John McDougall's prolific and lively writings found a wide audience (McDougall 1888, 1895, 1896, 1898, 1903, 1908, 1911; MacLean 1927; Nix 1960).

The Catholic church in 1818 established its western base on Red River at Saint Boniface (Provencher 1836) where the cathedral, with its "turrets twain" celebrated in Whittier's poem, was built in the 1830s. Later the "black robe" missionaries moved out across the plains. The need to keep in touch with their roving Métis flock took the priests onto the prairies as chaplains to the great biannual buffalo hunt (Belcourt 1847; Laflèche 1853). Mission settlements were founded on the Assiniboine at White Horse Plain (Saint François Xavier) and Saint Paul; in 1841, in the far Northwest at Lac Ste. Anne, some sixty miles northwest of Edmonton; at Ile-à-la-Crosse; and, in 1861, at Saint Albert. Work among the Métis was readily established, but it proved more difficult to Christianize the Indians. The great Oblate missionary Father Albert Lacombe moved from the Métis settlement at Lac Ste. Anne to work among the Plains Cree and Blackfoot Indians (Hughes 1911; Une Soeur de la Providence 1916).

A long succession of devoted missionaries reported back to their bishops and archbishops. Some of their ideas and observations were published in the *Rapports du Diocèse de Québec* and *Annales de la Propagation de la Foi de Québec,* as well as in such books as Mgr. Taché's *Vingt années de missions dans le nord-ouest de l'Amérique* (1866), which he described as "vingt années de dévouement et de sacrifice," and his *Esquisse sur le nord-ouest de l'Amérique* (1869). The great Jesuit missionary Father Pierre-Jean de Smet made his way eastward across the Rockies to the plains along their eastern edge in the hope of finding and converting the Blackfoot Indians—a hope which was not fulfilled (1905).

The Anglican church in 1820 sent a chaplain to the Hudson's Bay Company at Red River, the Reverend John West, but apart from a trip he made to Fort Ellice, the church concentrated most of its efforts in the valley of the Red River and in the northern country of rock and forest. The pioneer Archdeacon William Cockran (or Cochrane) extended his activities from Saint Andrew's Parish to the Indian mission lower down the Red River at Saint Peter's Dynevor. Later he established a settlement at Portage la Prairie. Work among the Plains Cree was initiated in the 1840s by two native catechists, James Settee (later ordained) and Charles Pratt. It was not until the '70s that such men as the Reverend Samuel Trivett and the Reverend John William Tims went to work among the tribes of the Blackfoot confederacy in the southwestern plains. By then work was spreading among scattered groups of settlers and ranchers. Indeed, the Anglicans felt that the "broad prairie lands, through which the Saskatchewan River flows," were destined for agricultural development; they were "lands to be farmed by settlers of perhaps many nationalities but certainly not to any extent by native Indians" (Boon 1962, pp. 102–3).

Mammon as well as God brought early visitors from the outside world. News of the discovery in 1857 of gold in the Fraser River, in what is now British Columbia, brought several groups of prospectors across the prairies in 1858 and 1859 in the hope of finding an easy route through the Rocky Mountains in British territory. These were followed by a second spate of gold seekers on their way to the Cariboo in 1862. In one of the parties from Minnesota, in 1859, John W. Jones kept a careful diary (Newberry Library). Many of the overlanders of '62 kept journals (Wade 1931; McNaughton 1896), and one of them, W. G. R. Hind, sketched his way across the prairies and mountains, taking home a lively collection of drawings and paintings and probably inspiring his explorer brother, Professor Henry Youle Hind of Trinity College, Toronto, to write a small book about alternative routes across the British prairies and through British passes to the "diggings" west of the Rocky Mountains (H. Y. Hind 1862; Harper 1969).

Perhaps still more influential was the group of "pleasure seekers" with whom this paper is especially concerned: the numerous young men of fortune and high social position who came to the prairies "in search of adventure and big game" (Spry 1968, p. lxxxvi). The earliest recorded visitors of this sort traveled to the prairies with Sir George Simpson in 1841, when he was starting out on his journey round the world. He wrote:

The Earls of Caledon and Mulgrave were to be my fellow-travellers all the way to Red River settlement, whence they intended to proceed to hunt the buffalo. . . . About ten days after my arrival, I despatched Lords Caledon and Mulgrave to the plains, under the escort of Mr. Cuthbert Grant, an influential native of mixed origin, and a party of hunters. Being desirous of encountering as many of the adventurers [*sic*] of the wilderness as possible, these young noblemen had determined on passing through the country of the Sioux to St. Peters on the Mississippi; and for this purpose they had provided themselves with guides, &c. Lord Caledon succeeded in carrying his intentions into effect, gaining golden opinions among the hunters by his courage, skill, and affability; but Lord Mulgrave, from indisposition, retraced his steps, first to Fort Garry and thence to Sault Sainte Marie. [Simpson 1847, vol. 1, pp. 13, 47–48]

Their journey started an epidemic of "prairie fever" that by 1861 had spread so that the Council of the Northern Department of the Hudson's Bay Company was constrained to pass a resolution providing that all travelers not connected with the fur trade were to be charged ten shillings a day for board and lodging when staying at company posts, while their servants and "retainers" were to be charged five shillings a day.

Eminent adventurers, some of whom came to the West on official missions, included several earls, at least two viscounts, half a dozen baronets or baronets-to-be, and a cosmopolitan sample of counts from France, Italy, Denmark, and Germany, besides plenty of young gentlemen without titles, but with some means and leisure, many of them soldiers on leave. Several of them also traveled in the American West—for example, Lieutenant (later General Sir Henry) Warre, who was sent in 1845 with Lieutenant M. Vavasour, R. E., on a secret mission—ostensibly a hunting trip—to report on the possibility of sending troops overland to the Oregon Territory (Public Record Office [1]). Warre had earlier been on a buffalo-hunting expedition to the "Grand Prairies of the Missouri" with some fellow officers, including the future brother-in-law of John Palliser, the explorer (Fairholme 1840). Warre kept a diary of his journey across the plains in 1845 and made charming sketches of the country through which he passed (Public Archives of Canada [1]). His sketches were published with a brief text on his return to Britain (Warre [1848]).

Still more notable was John Palliser himself, the Irish sportsman who became an explorer. He spent the best part of a year in the American West in 1847–48 and published a best seller about his adventures, *Solitary Rambles and Adventures of a Hunter on the Prairies* (1853). Charles Dickens spread his fame with a lively account of his prowess in an article in 1854 called "Mighty Hunters" in his weekly journal, *Household Words.* Palliser's example brought more than one friend and a brother to western British North America—just as William Fairholme's example had taken him to the West in the first place. A friend, Captain

Arthur Brisco, joined him at Edmonton in 1858 with still another friend, W. R. Mitchell. They spent the winter of 1858–59 and the summer of 1859 with the exploring expedition. The fourth earl of Dunraven, as a boy at Adare Lodge, County Limerick, was taken camping by Palliser in the deer park, and, as a man, emulated the exploits of his mentor, making hunting trips in the American West and Canada and crossing the Atlantic in sixteen consecutive years. His book, *The Great Divide* (1876), was illustrated by the artist Valentine Bromley, whom Lord Dunraven took with him to the Yellowstone country. For a time he had a hunting lodge or ranch at Estes Park, Colorado (Dunraven 1922). Edward Palliser, a younger brother of the explorer, spent some time with the CPR near Calgary and served in the Alberta Field Force in 1885. He submitted to the British government a project for teaching emigrants to western Canada the essentials of what they needed to know before they began life as prairie farmers (Public Record Office [2]).

Other "travellers west" included Frederick Ulric Graham, later a baronet, in 1847 (Graham 1898); Sir Edward Poore, who hired as a guide, but soon dismissed, the artist Paul Kane, who had himself earlier crossed the plains and mountains on a notable painting expedition (Harper 1971; Kane 1859); Count de la Guiche, who went right to the Rocky Mountains and was back in Red River in 1851 (Rich and Johnson 1956); Lord Robert (or, perhaps, Richard) Grosvenor, a member of the family of the marquess (later duke) of Westminster, who went hunting on the plains in 1858, as did Lord Frederick Cavendish, son of the duke of Devonshire, with several friends (Devonshire MSS; Hudson's Bay Company Archives [1], [2]).

In 1860 Lieutenant Dunn of the Royal Canadian Rifles, then posted at Fort Garry, went off with the Métis hunt to the Souris River for six or seven weeks. (*Nor'Wester,* October 9, 1860). A Mr. Malcolm from Argyleshire went the same year as far as the Cypress Hills to hunt grizzly bear, attracted by John E. Harriott's account of the game, but "more from a love of adventure" (*Nor'Wester,* August 14,

1860). Dr. John Rae, of Arctic fame, the next
year led a party across the southern prairies,
renaming the Old Woman's Lakes after his
companions, Sir Frederick Johnstone, Bt., and
Henry (later, Viscount) Chaplin (Royal Geographical Society). Chaplin Lake is still so-
called, but Lake Johnstone is now again Old
Wives Lake.

Young Viscount Milton, after an earlier
buffalo-hunting trip, spent the winter of
1862–63 with his attendant mentor, Dr. Walter B. Cheadle, at the edge of the prairies, as
did their chance-met associate, Charles A.
Messiter (who figures in their book as "Tree-
miss"). Much later, Messiter published his
own book, *Sport and Adventure among the
North-American Indians* (1890), to let the
Britons, who by then were going "west every
year," know what life once was on the prairies.
He returned to England while Milton and
Cheadle went on to the Pacific Coast. An account of their adventures and impressions appeared in their *North-West Passage by Land*
(1865), while Cheadle's day-by-day record of
the journey—frank and unexpurgated—was
published in 1931. At the same time Lord
Dunmore and some fellow officers of the Scots
Fusilier and Grenadier Guards started out on
a hunting trip from Red River to the Cypress
Hills but turned back to the Souris River to
avoid Cree-Blackfoot hostilities (Dunmore Papers), while Count Arrigo di Castiglione Mag-
giore, the chamberlain of the King of Sardinia
(otherwise, aide-de-camp to His Majesty the
King of Italy), led a "Royal Italian Expedition" across the prairies and over the Rocky
Mountains. Alleged to have been "organised
by command of His Majesty the King of Italy," this expedition was undertaken partly
"to fulfil a mission entrusted to the Count by
his Sovereign" and partly "to enjoy the plea-
sures of the chase" (Hudson's Bay Company
Archives [3]). The nature of the "mission" remains a mystery to this day, but the recorded
result was "a most valuable collection of both
the animals and mineralogical productions" of
the country through which it passed and a
catch of fifty live wapiti (elk) shipped to a
royal park of the king of Italy
(*Nor'Wester,* May 31, 1864). With the count

traveled his aide-de-camp, Major de Vecchi;
two English officers, Captain William Bromley
Davenport and Lieutenant Arthur Lake; two
foreign servants; and twelve Red River men,
including the noted plainsmen Joe Macdonald
and Joseph McKay. The latter reported that
the four gentlemen "were most excellent travellers and sportsmen, and had plenty to shoot
in the way of buffalo, jumping deer, and cabris.
The entire harmony and good feeling which
prevailed in our party, all the way through,
added much to the pleasure of the journey. I
wonder that gentleman travellers do not frequent this Far West more than they do"
(*Nor'Wester,* December 7, 1863).

In fact, an astonishing number of "gentlemen travellers" and even a few ladies continued to frequent the western plains. Dr.
Thibodo mentions two Scottish ladies on their
way north to the Mackenzie River from Saint
Paul as the "Fraser Gold Hunting and Saskatchewan Exploring Expedition" started on
the journey that took it across the plains and
across the Rocky Mountains in 1859
(Thibodo, 1859), while there are tantalizing
references in the Innes papers in the Saskatchewan Archives to a trip made in November,
1878, by Lord and Lady Percy on horseback
from Edmonton to Red River (Saskatchewan
Archives [1]).

Not all the early visitors to the prairies were
rich and distinguished. A surprising number
of "stragglers" (as Sir George Simpson considered them) found their way to the western
wilderness. The Palliser expedition encountered a young man called Vidler living with the
Indians in a state of destitution. He had sold
his commission in the British army and used
the proceeds to get to Rupert's Land (Spry
1968). Then there were John McDougall's
traveling companions, the Connors—the father, a former minister turned "floater," and
his young son—as well as a Scot intent on
crossing the Rocky Mountains (McDougall
1895). There was a Mr. Gilbert Parker of West
Tennessee who was believed to have drowned
in the Rockies. There was Henry Head Alexander, a painter who had worked his passage
round the world from New York to India and
who was going back to settle at the McDougall

Mission—his legs tarred and feathered to keep off the mosquitoes (Saskatchewan Archives [2]). Other "refuge seekers" turned up at the mission, among them the egregious "Mr. O'B" (McDougall 1895), who later hitchhiked across the mountains with Milton and Cheadle spouting philosophy larded with classical tags and studying Paley's *Evidences of Christianity,* but not doing a hand's turn of work to help himself or anyone else on the arduous journey (Cheadle 1931).

Besides missionaries, miners, tourists, and stray wanderers, there was an increasing inflow of scientists, explorers, and surveyors, many of them on official missions. The basic work of exploration had, of course, been carried out by fur traders, and until the middle of the nineteenth century, official British expeditions were concerned with problems that took them to the far North, notably Franklin's search for the Northwest Passage and J. H. (later Sir Henry) Lefroy's search for the magnetic north.

The first official journey across the southern plains seems to have been that of Warre and Vavasour, already mentioned. In 1857 the Palliser expedition set off on its great prairie journey. Palliser's taste of the "noble sport" of buffalo hunting in the American West had kindled in him a determination to return to the plains. From this interest developed the idea of exploring the British prairies. With the help of the undersecretary of state for the colonies, John Ball, and the Royal Geographical Society, he persuaded the British government to finance and sponsor an enterprise that was transformed from a personal journey into a full-blown scientific expedition. Its members were a geologist-naturalist (Dr., later Sir, James Hector, M. D.); a magnetical observer (Lieutenant, later Captain, T. W. Blakiston, R. A.); a botanical collector (Eugene Bourgeau, from the French Alps); and an astronomical observer and secretary (John W. Sullivan, from the Greenwich Naval School). For three seasons they traveled on the prairies and in the mountains, collecting specimens and data, making observations, and drawing conclusions as to the capability of the country for settlement and agriculture and the possibil-

ity of establishing communication through British territory with the settlements of the East and the Pacific Coast. The results of their work were published in four Blue Books (Palliser 1859, 1860, 1863, 1865; Spry 1968). While Palliser was in the field, Professor Henry Youle Hind of Trinity College, Toronto, followed up a season's study in 1857 of the country between Lake Superior and the Red River settlement by making, on behalf of the Canadian government, a survey of the country between the Red River and the Elbow of the South Saskatchewan. He supplemented his formal report with a two-volume popular work (Hind 1860).

There had been some American visitors, too —for example, Governor Alexander Ramsey of Minnesota, who visited Red River in 1851 (Bond 1853). James Doty, assistant to Isaac I. Stevens, traveled north from Fort Benton to the neighborhood of modern Gleichen, Alberta, to bring "American" Indians to the treaty negotiations of 1855 (Doty 1855). Colonel W. H. Nobles set out in 1859 on behalf of the citizens of Saint Paul, with John Wickes ("Consul") Taylor as secretary to the expedition, to test the possibility of finding a route to a mountain crossing. Nobles turned back at Fort Ellice, but some of his colleagues continued across the plains, eventually crossing the mountains successfully (Thibodo 1859).

The Riel Rising of 1870 brought a small army of visitors in the Red River Expedition led by Sir Garnet Wolseley. Some of them stayed on; others traveled still further west. For example, Charles Napier Bell made a long journey in 1872–73 through the Saskatchewan country (C. N. Bell 1872–73). The best known of the 1870 visitors was Lieutenant Butler. He had earlier taken leave to go buffalo hunting on the Platte River, in what was then the territory of Nebraska, and now he came to Red River as an intelligence officer in advance of the Red River Expedition. Afterwards, he was sent west across the plains to examine and report on two threatening problems: the growing disorder and violence in Canada's newly acquired North-West Territory and the virulent smallpox epidemic. The year after Butler had made his report, Colonel Robertson-Ross, commanding officer and adjutant general of the Militia of Canada, was also sent across the plains. He penetrated to the southwestern prairies, then the scene of the trade across the border, at Fort Whoop-Up and other points, in whisky, which was proving so destructive to the Indians (Robertson-Ross 1872).

Butler and Robertson-Ross were only two of a multiplying succession of public servants who now began to visit the Canadian prairies on a variety of official and semiofficial assignments that prepared the way for settlement. Between 1872 and 1876 the border was surveyed and marked, with members of the boundary commission producing not only the commission's formal report, but also a variety of personal records (see, for example, Dawson 1875; Millman 1928; and Anderson 1876).

Sandford (later Sir Sandford) Fleming, engineer-in-chief of the Canadian Pacific Railway, in 1872 made his first great journey across the prairies and mountains. George M. Grant, secretary to the expedition, published his best seller, *Ocean to Ocean* (1873), about its adventures and later contributed sections on the Northwest to *Picturesque Canada*. Meanwhile, the Geological Survey was sending out teams to make a systematic examination of the country, much of which had not yet even been mapped. Notable reports were published by such geologist explorers as Robert Bell (1873–74), George Mercer Dawson (1883), and J. B. Tyrrell (1886).

Perhaps the most important of all the official groups was the North-West Mounted Police, whose centennial was celebrated in 1973. Their famous march across the southern plains in 1874 is well recorded not only in reports, diaries, letters, and books, but also in pictures by the artist Henri Julien, who accompanied the great march west (*Canadian Illustrated News*). The force attracted many adventurous young men to the western plains. Some of them stayed on to become residents; others, such as Constable Count Rosencrantz of Denmark (McCook 1953), returned home after a term of service. Several published widely read accounts of their adventures. The first such account, by Jean d'Artigue, was translated from the French and published in English in 1882 as *Six Years in the Canadian North-West.*

Other public servants who traveled the plains in advance of the main influx of settlers included land commissioners, such as the redoubtable William Pearce, Indian agents, and farm instructors, following the seven Indian treaties that between 1871 and 1877 extinguished the Indian title to traditional hunting grounds on the prairies and established the reserve system (Morris 1880). Three lieutenant governors took part in the negotiation of these treaties, and a governor general later met the Blackfoot Indians in conference. This was Lord Lorne, who visited the West in 1881. His predecessor, the marquis of Dufferin, had earlier made a memorable trip to the West in 1877 with his wife, who recorded their adventures in her charming volume, *My Canadian Journal* (1891).

Such VIP visits heralded a new order of things, as did the visits of scouts for prospective immigrants; for example, Jacob Shantz was sent out to reconnoiter land for the Russian Mennonites, who subsequently settled in southern Manitoba (Shantz 1873). Other visitors were those interested in ranching and other new types of enterprise. The Oxley Ranch brought Lord Lathom out to the foothills country (Craig 1903). A fox-hunting settlement was established at Cannington Manor. The Canadian Coal and Agricultural Colonization Company brought back Lord Dunmore to the Lethbridge area in 1883 (Geographic Board of Canada 1925).

In the seventies and early eighties, the last adventurous travelers and big-game hunting parties overlapped with the arrival of pioneers of settlement out on the plains, as is well illustrated by an advertisement (fig. 2) inserted in an early immigration pamphlet (Spence 1879) by the Hon. James McKay, "that prince of travellers" (*Nor'Wester,* July 1, 1861), and, by general agreement, "the ablest guide in the country" (Royal Geographical Society).

Even before Rupert's Land had become part of Canada, parties had been sent to survey the road that was to be a section of the Dawson Route connecting Red River with Canada, and to start the land survey which would be

FROM MANITOBA

—TO THE—

ROCKY MOUNTAINS.

THE SASKATCHEWAN EXPRESS

Carrying Passengers and Mails on the Royal Mail Route, between

WINNIPEG, BATTLFORD, EDMONTON,

And all intermediate points *en route.*

Special arrangements made with IMMIGRANTS and parties visiting the Interior, with a view to settlement, as also for HUNTING and PLEASURE PARTIES.

COMPLETE OUTFITS FURNISHED, including *Experienced Hunters and Guides.* Horses and Conveyances, &c.

AT REASONABLE RATES!

Freight forwarded to all Points in the North-West Territories between WINNIPEG and the ROCKY MOUNTAINS.

☞ For further particulars and information apply or address

HON. JAS. MACKAY,

PROPRIETOR SASKATCHEWAN EXPRESS

AND

Contractor North-West Royal Mail Line,

ST. JAMES, MANITOBA.

Figure 2

needed before settlers could take up farm land —both initiatives that helped to precipitate the Riel Rising. In the survey party was one Donald Codd, who, after fleeing with P. G. Laurie from Red River during Riel's regime, compiled the great Laurie map of 1870 (Public Archives of Canada [2]) "to meet numerous requests for information about the west."

Once an organized government had been set up, land surveyors fanned out across the western plains, sending back in their reports, year by year, descriptions and maps of the country they examined. Once again, a clash over the river lots claimed by the mixed-blood native population and the new, systematic thirty-six-section township survey played a part in creating unrest that led to the second Riel Rising in 1885.

This uprising brought a second army of outsiders into the country in the North-West Expedition under the command of Major General Frederick Middleton, whose chief of staff, Lord Melgund (later, as Lord Minto, a governor general of Canada), had an aristocratic orderly, the Hon. Mr. Fiennes, son of Lord Saye and Sele (McCook 1953).

The completion, also in 1885, of the Canadian Pacific Railway spelled the end of the old adventurous, free, nomadic order. It was already doomed by the disappearance of the buffalo at the beginning of the 1880s, though more than another decade was to pass before the first seepage of settlers out onto the prairies beyond Red River swelled, after 1896, to the flood that transformed the open plains into farms and settlements.

In this process of transformation the impressions of the pre-1885 visitors played a part. Letters and diaries were certainly passed round a circle of family and friends. The splendid series of letters, for example, sent home by Palliser's fellow traveler, W. R. Mitchell, whose family were neighbors of the Barretts of Wimpole Street, have been cherished by his son. How wide such circulation may have been cannot, of course, be established, but there seems to have been a chain reaction of emulation among adventurous young "society" sportsmen. They appear not only to have read one anothers' letters and diaries and studied one anothers' sketches, but to have sent each other trophies of their prowess in the chase in the form of buffalo and elk heads and grizzly bear skins. Some even brought back live beasts, such as Palliser's buffalo, bear, and Indian dog (Palliser, 1853) and Castiglione's wapiti. The lively books that so many of them produced went through numerous editions (Peel 1956), while articles in periodicals—such as Charles Gay's "Le Capitaine Palliser et L'exploration des Montagnes Rocheuses, 1857–1859," Hind's articles in the *Illustrated London News* (1858), and Julien's drawings in the *Canadian Illustrated News*—gave a still wider currency to accounts of life and adventure in the "Great Lone Land." In addition, on their return to England many travelers to the western interior lectured both to learned societies, such as the British Association for the Advancement of Science and the Royal Geographical Society, and also to numerous church and other local groups. Newspaper reports of such lectures multiplied their impact, as in the case of Milton and Cheadle, evidenced by clippings among the Cheadle Papers (McGill University, McLennan Library).

About one thing all the travelers were unanimous and eloquent—the mosquitoes were a torment beyond imagination! They all had stories of hardship and privation—of agonizing cold, of parching heat, of drenching rain, of waterless camp sites, of shortages of food, of weary plodding through swamps and mud, and of danger in crossing rivers, especially at break-up and freeze-up. For example, Butler lost his favorite horse on the Saskatchewan River when the animal broke through ice that proved not to be strong enough to bear his weight. Yet most of them, despite discomfort, exhaustion, illness, danger, and periods of misery and gloom, found their western travels exhilarating and enlivening; they came back again if they had the chance. The excitement of the chase; the risk of short commons if the hunt was not successful; the wonderful taste of crude camp meals to a palate whetted by hunger, a delight that no epicure could know; the dangers of travel on uncertain trails, sometimes with equally uncertain guides; the difficulties presented by deep and swift rivers, sometimes with half-formed ice along the banks, or by sudden blizzards; the unrelenting rigors of journeys by dog-train or with horses —all these were challenges to courage, resourcefulness, and strength, a test of manhood. There was zest in overcoming dangers and difficulties. Besides, there was a glorious sense of freedom on the wide plains, under the huge vault of brilliant sky; in the vast wilderness there was escape from "life rusting routine" and the "servitude of civilization" (Butler 1872, p. 324).

Many boys dreamed of the Great West; how many fed their dreams on Ballantyne's *Young Fur Traders* (1856) or on Butler's *Great Lone Land* (1872) we cannot tell. Some, such as Henry Moberly (1929) and Matthew McCauley (Blower 1972) followed their dreams from Ontario to the western plains. The late George Pocaterra of Calgary was inspired by tales of adventure he read while at school in Switzerland to leave a well-to-do home in Italy for adventure in the West (CJOC Broadcast). At least one family of settlers arrived with an arsenal of firearms, no doubt inspired by romantic reading (Shepherd 1965, p. 20).

Narratives of missionary exploits also made lively reading, notably the writings of John McDougall and E. R. Young. The heroic tone of the latter may be illustrated by a comment on one of his "most loved and trusted guides": "We have looked death in the face together many times, but I never knew him to flinch or play a coward's part." (Young 1890, p. 133).

Accounts of hardship and heroism attracted the adventurous—as well as generous contributions to missionary funds; but on occasion they may have deterred possible settlers from moving West. A. I. Silver suggests that the "dark picture of Red River life" spread in Quebec by the Catholic missionaries making appeals for help played a part in convincing many *Québécois* that this "territoire aussi dangereux que peu fertile" should not be annexed to Canada. The pessimistic view of the prairies "inspired charity" and "discouraged immigration." When, after 1870, immigration to the West from Quebec became desirable, a predicament was created: "Quand on a tant décrié une contrée, le sol, le climat, les moyens d'existence, etc., etc., on ne doit pas être surpris de voir le courant se diriger d'un autre côté" (Lacombe, cited in Silver 1969, p. 17). Relatively few immigrants from Quebec joined the colonists who came to the Canadian West in search of new homes after 1870, though the reason may not have been only the picture of hardship painted by the missionaries but the fear that the French-speaking, Catholic element in the Red River Settlement had already been overwhelmed by Orangemen from Ontario.

Whether, in fact, the country was suitable for settlement remained a vexed question. Travelers' impressions depended at least in part on whether their route lay through Palliser's semiarid "Triangle" in the south or through the parklands further north; on whether the plains they traveled were gay with a springtime carpet of flowers or grazed bare by buffalo herds; on whether they saw the prairies at the low point of a period of drought or in the verdure of a period of relatively high precipitation. Butler, with his gift for dramatic summary, wrote, "The Saskatchewan country has its poles of opinion; there are those who paint it as a paradise, and those who picture it as a hell. It is unfit for habitation, it is to be the garden-spot of America. . . . In reality, what is it? . . . It is rich; it is fertile; it is fair to the eye. Man lives long in it, and the children of his body are cast in manly mould" (Butler 1872, p. 231).

With this, compare Sir Edward Poore's laconic "This country is not what it is cracked up to be" (Harper 1971) and Dr. Rae's careful judgment, south of modern Qu'Appelle Fort: "Nearly all the country through which we have travelled from Fort Garry is well watered, moderately well wooded and fit for cultivation"; and his subsequent comment, while passing near modern Regina: "On the 13th of July we had a long day's ride over a dry, parched, and barren country in a south wester[l]y direction towards the Dirt Hill" (Royal Geographical Society). The distinction is clear between the Fertile Belt described by Palliser and Hind and the semiarid area of the Triangle.

This distinction was lost sight of in the Deed of Surrender accepted by the Hudson's Bay Company in 1869. This includes in the Fertile Belt all the country from the North Saskatchewan to the border, an extension which was carried over into the land grant to the CPR in 1881.

Controversy continued about the agricultural capabilities of the prairies. John Macoun, the botanist who had traveled west with Sandford Fleming and George Grant in 1872 and who had since explored the Peace River country and, later, the plains between the Qu'Ap-

pelle and the Rocky Mountains, "fearlessly announced that the so called arid country was one of unsurpassed fertility and that it was literally the garden of the country." Such statements involved him in a furious altercation with Hind, neither man, apparently, allowing for the fact that Macoun's visit was made, as he himself indicates, in a period when a "series of wet years" had "set in" (Macoun 1883, pp. 469, 611).

Immigration pamphlets and tracts on the importance of opening up the rich prairie lands to settlement cited freely the writings of early travelers who had been favorably impressed. Notable examples are Rawlings's *What Shall We do with the Hudson's Bay Territory?* (1866) and Thomas Spence's spate of immigration literature, beginning with his *Manitoba and the North-West of the Dominion* (1871).

The direct impact of enthusiastic best sellers was probably even greater than quotations from them in promotional literature. Butler's writings, for example, played a part in the migration of the McClung family to the West (McClung 1935). John McDougall saw "thousands of homesteads and countless acres of rich grass and soil, verily homes for the millions; but as yet the units of men were not here, doubtless because there was a Providence in all this, and the time had not come for settlement" (McDougall 1896, pp. 176–77). Milton and Cheadle had much the same idea, except that they attributed the emptiness of the land not to Providence, but to the Hudson's Bay Company: "This glorious country, capable of sustaining an enormous population, lies utterly useless, except for the support of a few Indians, and the enrichment of the shareholders of the Last Great Monopoly" (Milton and Cheadle 1865, p. 41).

The Honourable Company in 1869 surrendered its proprietary rights and privileges to the imperial government, which in 1870 transferred Rupert's Land and the North-West Territory to Canada. The Indians and their mixed-blood cousins remained to come to terms with the new order. The wanderers of the plains, Indian and Métis alike, had deeply impressed early visitors. Warre, for example, wrote: "I can imagine nothing more picturesque and more perfectly graceful than a Blackfoot Indian in his war costume, decorated with paint and feathers, floating wildly in the wind, as he caracolles on his small but wonderfully active barb, in the full confidence of his glorious liberty" (Warre [1848], p. 2). Southesk, Lady Dufferin, and others paid glowing tribute to the great plainsman James McKay (Southesk 1875; Dufferin 1891). Now the day was fast coming when the buffalo would be gone; the red man would lose his "glorious liberty"; and the Métis buffalo hunt would come to an end. Butler wrote with sensitive sorrow of the "last despairing struggle" of the Blackfoot against "the ever increasing tide that hems them in." The Indian's freedom would come to an end—the freedom which made it impossible for him to understand why the white man should "put sticks over the land and say, Between these sticks this land is mine; you shall not come here or go there" (Butler 1872, pp. 241–45, 268, 272). Surveyors and settlers were coming to tame and farm the plains, to transform the wild, exciting sportsman's paradise in which the early visitors had rejoiced. Neither the image nor the reality of the old free, wandering life of adventure on the open prairie could survive. Railways, real estate deals, homesteads, and cash crops would soon overwhelm the old life in an untamed wilderness.

BIBLIOGRAPHY

Unpublished Material

Bell, C. N.
    Diary, 1872–73. In the possession of Mrs. F. C. Bell.
Devonshire Manuscripts, Chatsworth, Derbyshire, England.
    Lord Frederick Cavendish. "Letters from the Prairies, 1858."
Dunmore Papers.
    Lord Dunmore. "Log of the Wanderers on the Prairies in Search of Buffalo, Bear, Deer, &c, North American Prairies, August, September, October, 1862." In the possession of Lord Dunmore.
Fairholme, William.
    Diary of an expedition to the Grand Prairies of the Missouri, 1840. In the possession of Mr. Ian Fairholme.
Glenbow Institute, Calgary, Alberta.
    The Reverend Thomas Woolsey's Journal, 1855–64.
Hudson's Bay Company Archives.
    (1) Correspondence in D. 4/78 and D. 5/47.
    (2) Fort Ellice Journal, B. 63/a/4.
    (3) Thomas Fraser to Governor A. G. Dallas, February 19, 1863, D. 8/1.
    This material is used by kind permission of the Hudson's Bay Company.
McGill University, McLennan Library, Montreal, Quebec.
    The Cheadle Papers.
Mitchell, William Roland.
    Letters, 1857–60. In the possession of Commander H. K. B. Mitchell, R. N., Retired.
Newberry Library, Chicago.
    John W. Jones. "Across the plains: My trip from Faribault, Minn., to Oregon, via Saskatchewan-route, British America—Account of the country, our sufferings and trials, etc., 1858–59."
Public Archives of Canada.
    (1) Henry J. Warre. Diary and Sketches.
    (2) [P. G.] Laurie. "Map of the North-West Territories showing the surveys now made, and the railway and other routes thereto." Montreal: Roberts, Reinhold & Co., Lithographers, 1870.
Public Record Office, London.
    (1) Henry J. Warre and M. Vavasour, R. E. Correspondence and reports, FO5/457 and WO1/552.
    (2) Edward Palliser to the Under-Secretary of State for the Colonies, April 3, 1886, and subsequent correspondence, CO384/159, 162, 163.
Royal Geographical Society, London
    Dr. John Rae's Manuscript. "A visit to Red River and the Saskatchewan, 1861."
Rundle, Rev. Robert Terrill.
    Diary, 1840–48. Copy in the possession of the National Parks Office, Banff, Alberta: February 21, 1841.
Saskatchewan Archives, Saskatoon.
    (1) Innes Papers. Biographies of Lawrence Clarke and Thomas McKay.
    (2) Innes Papers. Biographies of George, Jerry, and Angus McKay.

Newspapers and Broadcasts

Canadian Illustrated News.
    1874.   July 25; August 8, 15, 29; September 19, 26; October 3; November 7, 28.
    1875.   February 6, 13, 20, 27; March 6, 13, 20,

27; April 3, 11, 17, 24; May 8, 15, 22, 29; June 5; July 3, 14.

CJOC Broadcast, Calgary, Alberta.
1956. George W. Pocaterra. "Here's Alberta: People and places." February 5, 1956.

Illustrated London News.
1858. "The Canadian Red River Exploring Expedition," October 2, pp. 318, 620. "The Assiniboine and Saskatchewan Exploring Expeditions," October 15, pp. 366–67.

Nor'Wester.
1860 August 14; October 9.
1861. July 1.
1863. December 7.
1864. May 31.

BOOKS AND ARTICLES

Anderson, Captain Samuel.
1876. The North American Boundary from the Lake of the Woods to the Rocky Mountains. *Royal Geographical Society, Journal* 46: 228.

Artigue, Jean d'.
1882. *Six years in the Canadian North-West.* Toronto: Hunter, Rose & Co.

Ballantyne, Robert Michael.
1848. *Hudson's Bay; or, Every-day life in the wilds of North America, during six years residence in the territories of the Honourable Hudson's Bay Company.* Edinburgh: William Blackwood & Sons.
1856. *Snowflakes and sunbeams; or, The young fur traders, A tale of the far north.* London: T. Nelson & Sons.

Belcourt, Rev. Georges-Antoine, A. M. C.
1847. Lettre, 1845. In *Rapport sur les Missions du Diocèse de Québec,* no. 7. Quebec: Fréchette et Frère.

Bell, Robert.
1873–74. *Report on the country between Red River and the South Saskatchewan.* Geological Survey of Canada.

Blower, Jim.
1972. Matthew McCauley. *Alberta Historical Review* 20:11–17.

Bond, John Wesley.
1853. *Minnesota and its resources, to which are appended camp fire sketches; or, Notes of a trip from St. Paul to Pembina and Selkirk Settlement on the Red River of the North.* New York: Redfield.

Boon, T. C. B.
1962. *The Anglican church from the bay to the Rockies.* Toronto: Ryerson.

Butler, General Sir William Francis.
1872. *The great lone land: A narrative of travel and adventure in the north-west of America, 1870.* London: Sampson, Low, Marston, Low, & Searle.
1911. *Sir William Butler, an autobiography.* London: Constable & Co.

Canada, Geographic Board of.
1925. *Place-names of Alberta.* Ottawa: Department of the Interior.

Cheadle, Walter Butler.
1931. *Cheadle's journal of a trip across Canada, 1862–1863.* Ottawa: Graphic Publishers Limited.

Craig, John R.
1903. *Ranching with lords and commoners.* Toronto: William Briggs.

Dawson, George Mercer.
1875. *Report on the geology and resources in the vicinity of the forty-ninth parallel, from the Lake of the Woods to the Rocky Mountains . . .* Montreal: Dawson Brothers.
1883. *Preliminary report on the geology of the Bow and Belly river region, N. W. territory.* Geological Survey of Canada.

De Smet, Father Pierre-Jean, S.J.
1905. *Life, letters and travels of Father Pierre-Jean De Smet, S. J., 1801–1873.* Edited by Hiram M. Chittenden and Alfred T. Richardson. 4 vols. New York: Francis B. Harper.

Dickens, Charles.
1854. Mighty hunters. *Household words: a weekly journal conducted by Charles Dickens* 8, no. 198:446–49.

Doty, James.
1855. A visit to the Blackfoot camp [s]. Edited by Hugh A. Dempsey. *Alberta Historical Review* 14, no. 1 (1940): 17–26.

Dufferin and Ava, The Marchioness of.
1891. *My Canadian journal, 1872–8.* London: John Murray.

Dunraven, Wyndham Thomas Wyndham-Quin, Earl of.
1876. *The great divide: Travels in the upper Yellowstone in the summer of 1874.* With illustrations by Valentine W. Bromley. London: Chatto & Windus; New York: Scribner. Reprint edition. Lincoln: University of Nebraska Press, 1967.
1922. *Past times and pastimes.* 2 vols. London: Hodder & Stoughton.

Frémont, Donatien.
1935. *Monseigneur Provencher et son temps.* Winnipeg: Editions de la liberté.

Gay, Charles.
1860. La Capitaine Palliser et l'exploration des Montagnes Rocheuses, 1857–1859. *Le Tour du Monde* 1: 273–94.

Graham, Frederick Ulric.
  1898. *Notes of a sporting expedition.* Printed for private circulation. Copy at Glenbow Institute, Calgary, Alberta. Microfilm copy, Simon Fraser University.

Grant, George M.
  1873. *Ocean to ocean: Sandford Fleming's expedition through Canada in 1872.* Toronto: James Campbell & Son.

Harper, J. Russell.
  1971. *Paul Kane's frontier.* Toronto: University of Toronto Press, for the National Gallery of Canada; and Fort Worth: for the Amon Carter Museum.
  1969. *Painting in Canada: A history.* Toronto: University of Toronto Press.

Hind, Henry Youle.
  1859. *North-West Territory: Report on the Assiniboine and Saskatchewan Exploring Expedition.* Toronto: John Lovell.
  1860. *Narrative of the Canadian Red River Exploring Expedition of 1857, and of the Assiniboine and Saskatchewan Exploring Expedition of 1858.* London: Longman, Green, Longman, & Roberts. 2 vols. Reprint edition. Edmonton: Hurtig, 1971.
  1862. *A sketch of an overland route to British Columbia.* Toronto: W. C. Chewett & Co.

Hughes, Katherine.
  1911. *Father Lacombe, the black-robe voyageur.* Toronto: William Briggs.

Kane, Paul.
  1859. *Wanderings of an artist among the Indians of North America from Canada to Vancouver's Island and Oregon through the Hudson's Bay Company's Territory and back again.* London: Longman Brown, Green, Longmans, & Roberts.

Lacombe, Rev. Father Albert, O. M. I.
  1890. *Un nouveau champ de colonisation, la vallée de la Saskatchewan, branche nord, districts d'Alberta et de Saskatchewan, Territoires de l'Ouest.* [n. p.]
  1910. *Memoirs on the half breeds of Manitoba and the territories of the Canadian North West.* [n. p.]

Laflèche, Rev. Louis-François Richer
  1853. Lettre de M. Richer Laflèche à un de ses amis, le 4 septembre, 1851. In *Rapport sur les Missions du Diocèse de Québec,* no. 10. Quebec: Fréchette et Frère.

McClung, Nellie.
  1935. *Clearing in the West.* Toronto: Thomas Allen Ltd.

McCook, James.
  1953. Peers on the prairies. *The Beaver,* outfit 284 (June 1953): 10–13.

McDougall, Rev. John.
  1888. *George Millward McDougall, the pioneer, patriot, and missionary.* Toronto: William Briggs.
  1895. *Forest, lake, and prairie: Twenty years of frontier life in western Canada, 1842–62.* Toronto: William Briggs; Second edition, Toronto: Ryerson, [n. d.].
  1896. *Saddle, sled, and snowshoe: Pioneering on the Saskatchewan in the sixties.* Toronto: William Briggs; Second edition, Toronto: Ryerson, [n. d.].
  1898. *Pathfinding on plain and prairie: Stirrring scenes of life in the Canadian North-West, 1865–1868.* Toronto: William Briggs.
  1903. *In the days of the Red River Rebellion: Life and adventures in the Far West of Canada, 1868–1872.* Toronto: William Briggs.
  1908. *Wa-pee Moos-tooch, or White Buffalo, the hero of a hundred battles: A tale of life in Canada's great West during the early days of the last century.* Calgary: Printed for the author by the Herald Job Printing Co., Ltd.
  1911. *On western trails in the early seventies: Frontier life in the Canadian North-West.* Toronto: William Briggs.
  1970. *Opening the Great West.* Calgary: Glenbow-Alberta Institute.

Maclean, John.
  [1927]. *McDougall of Alberta: A life of Rev. John McDougall, D. D., pathfinder of empire and prophet of the plains.* Toronto: Ryerson.

McNaughton, Margaret.
  1896. *Overland to Cariboo: An eventful journey of Canadian pioneers to the gold fields of British Columbia in 1862.* Toronto: William Briggs.

Macoun, John
  1883. *Manitoba and the Great North-West.* London: Thomas C. Jack.

Matheson, Rev. Canon E. K., D. D.
  1927. The Mathesons of Red River. *Canadian North-West Historical Society Publications* 1 (no. 3): 14–15.

Messiter, Charles Alston.
  1890. *Sport and adventure among the North-American Indians.* London: R. H. Porter.

Millman, Dr. Thomas.
  1928. Journal of 1873. *Transactions of the Women's Canadian Historical Society of Toronto* 26.

Milton, Viscount, and Cheadle, Walter Butler.
  1865. *The North-West Passage by land: Being the narrative of an expedition from the Atlantic to the Pacific, undertaken with the view of exploring a route across the continent to British Columbia through British territory, by one of the northern*

passes in the Rocky Mountains. London: Cassell, Petter, & Galpin.

Moberley, Henry J.
1929. *When fur was king.* In collaboration with William Bleasdell Cameron. Toronto: J. M. Dent.

Morris, Alexander.
1880. *The treaties of Canada with the Indians of Manitoba and the North-West Territories; including the negotiations on which they are based, and other information relating thereto.* Toronto: Bedfords, Clarke Co.

Nix, James Ernest.
1960. *Mission among the buffalo.* Toronto: Ryerson.

Palliser, John.
1853. *Solitary rambles and adventures of a hunter on the prairies.* London: John Murray. A paperback "mini" edition is in the holdings of the Nebraska State Historical Society. New York: Robert M. De Witt: [n. d.].
1859. *Papers relative to the exploration by Captain Palliser of that portion of British North America which lies between the northern branch of the River Saskatchewan and the frontier of the United States; and between the Red River and Rocky Mountains.* London: Eyre & Spottiswoode for Her Majesty's Stationery Office.
1860. *Further papers relative to the exploration by the expedition under Captain Palliser of that portion of British North America which lies between the northern branch of the River Saskatchewan and the frontier of the United States; and between the Red River and the Rocky Mountains and thence to the Pacific Ocean.* London: Eyre & Spottiswoode for Her Majesty's Stationery Office.
1863. *The journals, detailed reports, and observations relative to the exploration by Captain Palliser of that portion of British North America, which in latitude lies between the British boundary line and the height of land or watershed of the northern or frozen ocean respectively, and in longitude, between the western shore of Lake Superior and the Pacific Ocean during the years 1857, 1858, 1859, and 1860.* London: Eyre & Spottiswoode for Her Majesty's Stationery Office.
1865. *Index and maps to Captain Palliser's reports* . . . London: Eyre & Spottiswoode for Her Majesty's Stationery Office.

Peel, Bruce Braden.
1956. *A bibliography of the prairie provinces to 1953.* Toronto: University of Toronto Press, in cooperation with the Saskatchewan Golden Jubilee Committee and the University of Saskatchewan.

Picturesque Canada.
1880. London: Cassell.

Provencher, Bishop J. N.
1836. Memoir or account on the establishment of the Red River Mission and its progress since 1818: Presented to the Propaganda of the Faith in the Vatican in Rome, March 12, 1836. *The Beaver,* outfits 303–4 (Spring 1973): 16–23.

Rae, Dr. John.
1861. A visit to Red River and the Saskatchewan. *Proceedings of the Royal Geographical Society* 7 (April 13, 1863): 102–3.

Rawlings, Thomas.
1866. *What shall we do with the Hudson's Bay Territory? Colonize the fertile belt, which contains forty millions of acres.* London: A. H. Baily.
1865. *The Confederation of the British North American Provinces: Their past history and future prospects including also British Columbia and Hudson's Bay Territory* . . . London: Sampson Low, Son, & Marston.

Rich, E. E., and Johnson, A. M.
1956. *London correspondence inward from Eden Colvile, 1849–1852.* London: Hudson's Bay Record Society.

Robertson-Ross, Colonel P.
1872. Robertson-Ross' diary, Fort Edmonton to Wildhorse, B. C., 1872. *Alberta Historical Review* 9 (Summer 1961): 5–22.

Russell, Alex[ander] J [amieson].
1869–70. *The Red River Country, Hudson's Bay and North-West Territories, considered in relation to Canada with the last report of S. J. Dawson on the line of route between Lake Superior and the Red River Settlement.* Ottawa: C. E. Desbarats.

Shantz, Jacob Y.
1873. *Narrative of a journey to Manitoba* . . . Ottawa: Robertson, Roger & Co.

Shepherd, George.
1965. *West of yesterday.* Edited by John Archer. Toronto: McClelland & Stewart.

Silver, A. I.
1969. French Canada and the Prairie frontier. *Canadian Historical Review* 50 (March 1969): 11–36.

Simpson, Sir George.
1847. *Narrrative of a journey round the world during the years 1841 and 1842.* 2 vols. London: Henry Colburn.

Southesk, The Earl of.
1875. *Saskatchewan and the Rocky Mountains, 1859–1860.* Edinburgh: Edmonston & Douglas.

Spence, Thomas.
1871. *Manitoba and the North-West of the Dominion: Its resources and advantages to the*

180 THE DESERT AND THE GARDEN

emigrant and capitalist as compared with the western states of America ... Toronto: Hunter, Rose & Co.

1876. *Manitoba and the North-West of the Dominion.* Second edition, revised. Quebec: S. Marcotte.

1877. *The Saskatchewan Country of the North-West of the Dominion of Canada.* Montreal: Lovell Printing & Publishing Co.

1879. *The prairie lands of Canada; presented to the world as a new and inviting field of enterprise for the capitalist and new superior immigrants compared with the western prairies of the United States* ... Montreal: Gazette Printing House.

1881. *Useful and practical hints for the settler on Canadian prairie lands and for the guidance of intending British emigrants to Manitoba* ... Montreal: Gazette Printing House. Revised edition, 1882. St. Boniface, Manitoba.

1886. *Canada: The resources and future greatness of her great prairie North-West lands.* Ottawa: Department of Agriculture.

Spry, Irene M., ed.
1968. *The papers of the Palliser expedition.* Toronto: Champlain Society.

Taché, Rev. Father Alexandre Antonin, O. M. I.
[1861]. *Lettre de Mgr. Taché évêque de St. Boniface donnant à Mgr. de Montréal le récit des malheurs de son diocèse depuis deux ans.* Montreal.

1866. *Vingt années de missions dans le nord-ouest de l'Amérique.* Montreal: Typographie du Nouveau Monde.

1869. *Esquisse sur le nord-ouest de l'amérique.* Montreal: Typographie du Nouveau Monde.

1870. *Sketch of the North-West.* Translated by D. R. Cameron. Toronto: J. Lovell.

Thibodo, Dr. Augustus J.
1859. Diary of Dr. Augustus J. Thibodo of the Northwest Exploring Expedition, 1859. Edited by Howard S. Brode. *Pacific Norwest Quarterly* 31 (1940): 287–347.

Tyrrell, J. B.
1886. *Report on a part of Northern Alberta, and portions of adjacent districts of Assiniboia and Saskatchewan.* Ottawa: Geological Survey of Canada.

Une Soeur de la Providence.
1916. *Le Père Lacombe.* Montreal: Imprimeur au Devoir.

Wade, Mark Sweeten.
1931. *The overlanders of '62.* Edited by John Hosie. Victoria: C. F. Banfield, by order of the Legislative Assembly.

Warre, Captain H.
[1848]. *Sketches in North America and the Oregon Territory.* London: Dickenson & Co.

Young, Rev. Egerton Ryerson.
1890. *By canoe and dog-train among the Cree and Salteau Indians.* London: Charles H. Kelly.

1893. *Stories from Indian wigwams and northern camp fires.* London: Charles H. Kelly.

[n. d.]. *On the Indian trail: Stories of missionary work among the Cree and Saulteaux Indians.* London: Religious Tract Society.

Constructing the British View of the Great Plains

John F. Davis
Birkbeck College, London

Before 1865 few of the reports about or descriptions of the Great Plains were written by English visitors; indeed, few Britons had traveled in the area west of the Missouri and then returned to Britain to write of their experiences. During the last few decades of the nineteenth century, however, an increasing number of descriptions of the Great Plains written by British people became available. Travelers for business and pleasure as well as settlers came and then wrote of their experiences and impressions.

Some travelers, used to a very different way of life in Europe and indeed in the eastern United States, were somewhat taken aback by the frontier nature of the plains and its lack of "civilized" facilities and graces and commented at length on these matters and on Indians, cowboys, and similar topics. Whether or not such comments were critical, condescending, or complimentary depended partly upon the educational and social background of the visitors, partly on the amount and source of the background reading they had done before arrival, and partly, of course, on the actual areas that were visited and the time of visit. To an extent the travelers were further conditioned by their purpose in visiting the region. Thus, businessmen, farmers, and such were far more observant of economic and climatic details and were more practical in their outlook, while the ordinary traveler was more concerned with the quality of the lodging and food

along the stagecoach routes, the station restaurants, and similar matters. Britons also came to the area on scientific expeditions and as hunters.

Each group was seeking and often expecting something different. Some sought out the new, while others tried to find the familiar. The variety and extent of the preconceived needs and desires were reflected in the response each made to the actual environment as it was seen. To this environment the responses were often not only at least partially predetermined, but were also expressed in terms with which the travelers were familiar. An explanation or description of the landscape and living conditions for people who had not seen them for themselves was made more meaningful by the use of analogies, comparisons, and similes with which not only the writer but also the reader was familiar. Obviously, what might have seemed tedious country to the tourist could convey important detail to the hunter or hint of great potential to the farmer.

The majority of early descriptions of the Great Plains which the visitor was likely to have had the opportunity of reading were those which referred to the wilderness and desert nature of much of the region. This concept had gained wide credence in the United States and was further copied by British writers such as Farnham, who wrote of "the Great Plains Wilderness occupying the area between Louisiana and Arkansas and Missouri and the upper Mississippi in the east; and the Black Hills and Rockies in the west" (Farnham 1843, p. 22). Also, a number of the American books dealing with the area would have been available to the more inquiring British traveler. Later, however, the realities of the region were described by those who made journeys through the plains by wagon train and these more accurate descriptions were amplified by the travelers by railroad. Inevitably the destruction, or at least modification, of the Great American Desert myth was encouraged by the major railroad companies. These companies, having received large land grants as indirect financial inducements to build across the plains to the Pacific Coast, were in great need of selling these lands to settlers. Such sales would obviously go better if the desert idea could be refuted. As a result, many railroads prepared books and pamphlets extolling the virtues, qualities, scenery, and physical attributes of the regions through which they passed or intended to pass. On occasion, direct refutation of the desert hypothesis was put forward, but often the attack was indirect. Much of this literature, at least in brief form, found its way to Britain, either through the advertisements in daily or weekly papers and various journals or through the activities of the railroad land office agents and private land companies who set up offices in various large cities in Britain. The major railroads not only prepared their own pamphlets but sometimes used other people's work; for example, a Mr. Curley, a free-lance journalist, traveled to the United States on an assignment from *The Field* and received nearly £300 to send back explanatory letters to his journal, and some letters of his were also published in newspapers, for example, the *Belfast Journal* and the *London Free Press.* This journalist also wrote a volume entitled *Nebraska: Its Advantages, Resources and Drawbacks,* published in London in 1875, of which the Union Pacific Railroad bought over four hundred copies. Another journalist from Britain who exhorted his readers, especially the poorer people, to hasten to the plains, calling it a land of opportunity, was Joseph Hatton. He wrote for the *London Standard* and was the author of a two-volume

book called *Today in America,* published in 1881, based on his visit to the West and other parts of America, both in 1876 and again four years later.

Before sailing westward across the Atlantic, the traveler had the possibility of getting information about the Great Plains from a variety of sources. However, what is virtually impossible to ascertain is what each visitor had learned of the area before departure; only in a few cases is this possible, and then the evidence is frequently only partial. It is important to remember also that although books, travelogues, newspaper articles, and similar items had been written, there is no guarantee that the visitor would have either known about them or consulted them. It is even more difficult to discover the extent of preconceived knowledge of the plains in the case of the settlers. This study of approximately one hundred letters and reports from settlers is inconclusive. Admittedly, in some cases there is evidence of a background concept of the area gained before arrival in the West, but on the other hand, from various reports it can be gathered that some Britons, especially the settlers, were abysmally ignorant of the areas to which they were going and where they hoped to settle.

It seems valid to divide the descriptions of the plains into two categories: first, those of a general nature, normally provided by the educated traveler who later wrote of his or her experiences, and second, the writings, usually letters, of settlers, whose descriptions and information had a specific and immediate purpose—either to extol the virtues of the area and so encourage more people to come out and join them or to warn would-be settlers of the hazards or problems of the particular area.

Descriptions are inevitably expressed in terms of experience; all visitors, permanent or transitory, had reached the plains by crossing the Atlantic Ocean, and most Englishmen, too, were familiar with the sea. Thus it is not surprising that many of the descriptions of the region should use maritime terminology:

We were at sea—there is no other adequate expression—on the plains of Nebraska. . . .

It was a world almost without a feature; an empty sky and an empty earth; front and back, the line of the railway stretched from horizon to horizon, like a cue across a billiard board; on either hand, the green plain ran till it touched the skirts of heaven. [Stevenson 1915, p. 40]

Occasionally comparisons were made with scenery with which they were familiar back in Britain. Writers like Kipling (1889), Stevenson (1915), Vivian (1878) and Lester (1873) were most likely to have been read by only a small number of the people who moved to the plains region to settle. They were much more likely to have been read by other travelers and possibly the businessmen who visited the plains. Those intending to migrate would, if they had read very much at all, have been much more likely to have studied the emigrant promotion literature put out by railroads, land companies, and states through the agencies of newspapers and journals and also through British-based agents, many of whom were British and not American. These agents used as their means of disseminating information the addressing of public meetings, lecturing, and numerous inserts in local newspapers.

It should not be forgotten that the plains region was looked upon essentially as a farming area, both arable and for raising stock, and that in spite of hope expressed by some of the more ardent visitors and guidebook writers, there was never any real belief in widespread industrialization except insofar as industry servicing agriculture and processing its products would be established. The emphasis was largely upon getting farmers and their families and those who would service their needs to come to the plains and settle. Therefore, while on the one hand the main centers of population might prove to be fruitful sources of quantities of emigrants, it was the rural areas that were most likely to supply emigrants with the necessary aptitudes and skills. For this reason a very large number of the advertisements by the various settler-seeking organizations were placed in local papers serving the rural regions. As a result it is in such newspapers that much of the material providing descriptions of

the region is to be found; and it is such descriptions that frequently provided the only information the potential settler had, other than the settlers' guides. The major daily newspapers also carried material but are probably less likely to have been read in country areas.

One example of the descriptions to be found in immigrants' letters is contained in that of a former resident of Kelso, William Kennedy, whose letter written from Plain Creek, Dawson County, Nebraska, was published in the *Kelso Courier* on July 26, 1872. His aim, he stated at the beginning of the letter, was to tell readers something of the area:

Soil is of a rich mixture of siliceous alluvial mould and clay, from 1–6 feet in depth, sometimes impregnated with carbonate of lime, just sufficient to pulverise easily, but leaving the surface free from stone and gravel. . . . Lands that have been cultivated for 15 years in corn, small grain and root crops show no falling off in the quantity or quality of their production.
Through the wise liberality of the State, the provision for common schools is magnificent, one eighteenth part of the whole soil having been donated for educational purposes, and is available for immediate benefit. . . . No village or community remains long without its school churches and other public institutions. . . . Although [Nebraska's] development has but just begun, her natural advantages are such that the most casual observer cannot fail to see the great and glowing future that awaits her when all her rich lands shall be under cultivation, and when within her vast borders are gathered together the brain and talent, the muscle and sinew, of the hardy industrious emmigrant from the too thickly populated regions of our country and Europe.
Stock raising in Nebraska is delightful work and yields the largest profit. . . . All the fruits of the temperate zone find a congenial home on our bright sunny prairie lands, which bring them forth in rare profusion, all of most delicious quality. . . . Our market facilities are many and of easy access [via Burlington and Missouri, Union Pacific, and Missouri Valley railroads].
Such large rivers as the Platte, Elkhorn,

Loup, Big and Little Blue and their tributaries, furnish ample inducements to bring among us the foreign capitalists and call for the erection of mills factories etc. which will produce a demand for skilled labour in mill shop and factory, and offer an inducement for the mechanic and artisan to settle amongst us.

He says that soon the place will be dotted with farms and that "thriving towns and cities have sprung up on all sides," and concludes by offering all the advice he can to all those who intend to go out to settle.

Although it cannot be proved, there is little doubt that some of the material finding its way to the press in the form of letters and reports from particular towns and places could have been instigated by or written with the help of the organizations who were so keen on a good image being provided of the area or town in question. This does not necessarily mean that every letter or report which wrote in only good terms of places should be considered suspect. In a number of instances, railroads and others found that in their more detailed literature there were advantages in giving a more balanced view with some warnings; they saw the advantage of not painting a completely rosy picture. On the other hand, the brief advertising literature carried none of these more sobering elements. It was the latter which the would-be settler saw first and sometimes the only thing that was seen of "official" literature. Newspaper material in the form of letters therefore built up much of the rest of the picture. The letter quoted above was all in favor of the area, others struck a warning note. The following selections make this point clear:

We had no difficulty in taking up 80 or 160 acre lots. . . . The first year no crop can be put in; the sod is so much affected by summer heat that everything put on it would be parched up. May, June, and July are the only months in which prairie can be ploughed. . . . It takes 18 months to get first crop. [They could not raise stock because of the cost of fencing.] Had to haul grain 300 miles to Omaha and sell at 60 cents a bushel. Because of cold winter we had to

dig a sod cave for the winter. My object in penning these lines is that they may act as a warning to farmers.[1]

Tarpy Co. in Nebraska is inhabited principally by Canadians, the great majority of whom would return had they the money to do so. Twenty families to my own knowledge have returned to Canada, and will be followed by more. . . . The Pacific Railroad runs within 15 miles of my farm and while it was being built prosperity reigned all round, but now there is no sale of grain, and you cannot think of raising stock.[2]

The picture of the plains provided by the newspapers of the latter half of the nineteenth century did not consist only of the perceptual views of particular writers. It was, on many occasions, supplemented by a considerable amount of factual material relating to land costs, costs of raw materials and fuel, transportation costs, prices for farm products, and wage rates, thus giving an accurate picture of conditions at a particular time—information which could be interpreted clearly in the same way by all readers.

A Nebraska commissioner had told one emigrant by letter before he left England that the climate in Nebraska was like England and carpenters earned at least fourteen to twenty shillings a day. The settler wrote, however, that the winters were "fearfully cold, wages low—8–12 shillings a day if you can get work as a carpenter. . . . cloths dear, food from outside dear—we consider a dollar here . . . goes as far as a shilling in England."[3] Another letter reported that passage money for one man from Scotland to Kansas was £10 and that £700 would buy and stock a 160-acre farm.

1. Letter from a farmer in Nebraska and published in *People's Journal for Perth and Stirling,* July 20, 1872.

2. Letter signed "A British subject who cares" and contained within one signed by a Mr. J. Kirkland saying that the first appeared in a Canadian newspaper. Mr. Kirkland's letter was published by *Daily Standard,* June 27, 1871. It is interesting that the letter quoted from a Canadian newspaper is very similar to ones quoted by other local Scottish and also Lincolnshire papers.

3. Letter signed by E. Storer and published in *People's Journal for Perth and Stirling,* February 7, 1872.

[It is] a very good policy for emigrants to combine into colonies for the purpose of coming to this country as thereby they can get cheaper rates and other facilities than by coming singly, although, after getting to their destinations, it is best for every man to "paddle his own canoe" as I have never . seen colonies work well together yet after they get located.[4]

The national and local newspapers and various journals such as *The Field* and the *Methodist Recorder* provide a fruitful source of material on the subject of the British view of the plains: it is a field in which as yet relatively little work has been done. From the numerous letters and reports flowing back to Britain and published in these papers a picture of the plains region can be formulated. The image is one which quickly dispels the concept of the plains as a desert or a region of savage landscape, people, and manners. "I arrived in Solomon City a year ago and found myself not in an uncivilised country as we were led to believe from many reports but surrounded by my own countrymen," writes one emigrant. He goes on to name some ten people, including one "Mr. Baxter, a well known farmer from Meigle, Perthshire, [who] purchased about 2 months ago, 640 acres of our Scotch Colony lands, and is, with his family, busily engaged improving the same." The writer continues that he has a good farm, a herd of cattle, a fine team of horses, wagons, and other implements and that the "climate is second to none, I believe, our winters are short and not severe." He continues by saying that the soil is good and the land cheaper than in the East.[5]

At the same time it is a picture which changes because of fluctuating economic and physical conditions in the region with their effect on economic propserity and life in the area as a whole. The changes and differences are also in part related to the scale of region perceived by the writers. Whereas Kipling, Hutton, and others traveled widely and could, as a result, generalize their views to a degree, the farmers, clergymen, and other settlers usually spoke of the area in which they were settled, so that the observations of the plains were limited to a particular county within a particular state. It was the travelers who commented most on the limitless plains (Stevenson 1915, p. 40), although some settlers did allude to the scale and associated loneliness of the plains.[6]

It is important to bear this difference of scale in mind when considering the general field of the British image of the plains. Then these views of the region are of great value in deepening our knowledge as to the processes of colonization and settlement and the adaptation and adjustment of the settlers to an environment so very different from their original homeland.

REFERENCES CITED

Curley, G.
  1875. *Nebraska: Its advantages, resources and drawbacks.* London.
Farnham, T. J.
  1843. *Travel in the great western prairies, the Anahuac and Rocky Mountains, and in the Oregon Territory.* London.
Hatton, J.
  1881. *Today in America.* 2 vols. London.
Kipling, J. R.
  1889. *From sea to sea: Letters of travel.* 2 vols. London.
Lester, J. E.
  1873. *The Atlantic to the Pacific and what to see and how to see it.* London.
Stevenson, R. L.
  1915. *Across the plains: With other memories and essays.* London.
Vivian, H. H.
  1878. *Notes on a tour in America.* London.

---

4. Signed by Mr. Louis McKenzie of Markerville, Morris County, Kansas, and published in *People's Journal for Perth and Stirling,* April 27, 1872.

5. Another letter published in same number of the newspaper from Mr. D. Andrews of Springfield, Solomon City, Kansas, who was a blacksmith by trade in Meigle, Perthshire, before he emigrated initially to Virginia in 1868 and then moved west in 1871.

6. A letter from Sterling in Blue Earth County, Minnesota, published in *People's Journal for Perth and Stirling* on August 11, 1872, refers to loneliness, long winters, and snow. Similar references occur in Lincolnshire and Manchester newspapers in the late 1860s and early 1870s.

PART 6
Adaptations to Reality

Desert Wheat Belt, Plains Corn Belt

Environmental Cognition and Behavior of Settlers in the Plains Margin, 1850–99

Martyn J. Bowden

Clark University

The changing conceptions of most new lands, as revealed in literature and art, describe the course of a pendulum in a clock winding down. At first the amplitude of the swings is wide. The first clear American image of the Great Plains was an agricultural Eden, yet within a decade all was sandy Saharan desert. Narrowing swings brought the literary image closer to reality. Sahara contracted before expanding steppe. Short-grass plains gave way in turn to tall-grass prairie, which bloomed to prairie garden of the world in the 1880s before the pendulum swung back to reveal a problem region (Bowden 1969, 1971; Allen 1971). Semiarid short grass advanced and some desert patches reappeared in the 1890s before moderate-to-good rainfall years and Turner's charisma and frontier hypothesis had the subhumid prairie pulsing westward again. During the 1930s the short-grass plains and even deserts were on the march again, led by Webb (1931) and symbolized in the Dust Bowl. Halted and perhaps set back in the war years, the desert specter returned as Webb's "desert-rim" in the 1950s, only to be halted again in the sixties (Bowden 1975).

Such a gross scheme obviously conceals variations in the amplitude and the timing of the swings. Among the well-educated, images of the plains varied according to sectional background, cultural values, and political affil-iations of individuals. For instance, New Englanders held the desert conception longest, and the Great American Desert was largest and most barren for certain Federalist-Whigs in New England. Southerners saw a desert beyond the Missouri for a shorter period, and many better-educated Missourians may not have thought of the region west of them as a desert (Bowden 1971).

There are indications also that the plains images of the poorly educated and of the illiterate were different from those of the well-educated before 1900. What were the nineteenth-century plains images of the settler and frontiersman? How different were they from those of the literati outlined in the first paragraph? How rapidly did behavior respond to these image changes and to changes in the literary image? Conversely, did the literary image respond to the changing imagery and behavior of the settlers?

This essay is a beginning in answering these questions in the case of the settlers of the plains margin of Nebraska and bordering Kansas. A representative county was chosen, and the attempt was to reconstruct the environmental images of farmers (newcomers and residents), to pinpoint the agents of image change and the interaction between image makers, and to assess the effects of plains images of various groups on agricultural behavior in the plains margin.

Jefferson County: Representativeness and Sources

The plains margin between the 96th and 100th meridians in Nebraska and northern Kansas is a level-to-undulating country dissected by the tributaries and main courses of the Kansas, Platte, and Niobrara. It is covered in the east by drift, by loess in the west, and in the valleys by bottomland alluvium. There are mantle-rock areas throughout. The area is transitional between Prairie and Chernozem soils, with the latter dominant. The median rainfall of constituent counties ranges from twenty-three to thirty inches. The incidence of extreme drought and the frequencies of drought differ little in the area (Lawson 1971).

Jefferson County is admirably representative of the area. Lying west of the 97th meridian on the Nebraska-Kansas border, it is undulating-to-level tableland, dissected sometimes deeply. It is dominantly a loess plain, with a dissected drift plain occupying the second largest area. Sizable mantle-rock areas and alluvial bottomlands are present (fig. 1). The main soil associations were classified by the Soil Survey (1921) as Prairie but reclas-

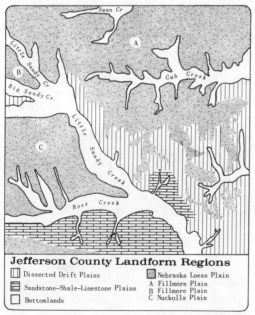

Jefferson County Landform Regions

- Dissected Drift Plains
- Sandstone–Shale–Limestone Plains
- Bottomlands
- Nebraska Loess Plain
  - A Fillmore Plain
  - B Fillmore Plain
  - C Nuckolls Plain

Figure 1 Jefferson County Landform Regions

sified in the 1930s as Chernozem. The median rainfall is twenty-eight inches (1876–1957), two to three inches above the average on the plains margin; but as summer temperatures are 2° to 5°F higher in Fairbury than in the counties of central and northern Nebraska, evapotranspiration is higher in the south and precipitation effectiveness is similar in both areas (Bowden 1959, pp. 13–45).

Throughout this century the plains margin has been transitional between the corn and winter wheat belts, with corn (and oats) increasing in wet periods and wheat (and sorghum) in drier periods. Alfalfa is the major legume and hay is also important. These six crops constitute the bases of the crop combinations of the plains margin. Between 1919 and 1949, Jefferson County reflected the larger region in both combinations and ranking of major crops (Weaver 1954a, 1954b, 1954c). Jefferson and its northern neighbor, Saline, were the only two counties in Nebraska and Kansas in Marple's corn–winter wheat transition zone for all cross sections drawn this century. Furthermore, in 1889 and 1899, when the transition zone was fingering into the High Plains, eastern Nebraska and northeastern Kansas were part of the corn belt, as was Jefferson County (Marple 1958, 1969).

Clearly, the county epitomizes the plains margin in physical characteristics and agriculture. As a case study it has other attributes. All plains-margin counties were covered by the U.S. Land Survey, but Jefferson, lying on the Base Line and on the 6th Principal Meridian, was described by more surveyors and covered earlier than most counties. Moreover, most counties lack the literary records afforded by the accounts of Oregon Trail travelers who crossed the uplands in the 1850s and 1860s, and by the plat books (1871 and 1886)[1] and loan records (1880–1926) of the Security In-

1. The plat books described in detail and evaluated the land and activities, providing in 1871 a valuable view of the settler in the uplands, and in 1886 an inestimable record of the state of occupation of the upland grass. Although other counties were surveyed by the company, Jefferson was one of the few in which the survey did not consider alternate sections.

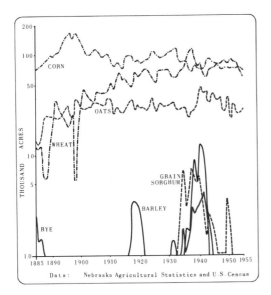

Data: Nebraska Agricultural Statistics and U.S. Census

vestment Company (Bowden 1959, pp. 2–3, 50–66, 215–17).

Agricultural Behavior in Jefferson County, 1854–1956

Analysis of land use changes on a yearly basis for Jefferson County reveals that agricultural behavior falls into two phases: equilibrium after 1909 and experimentation and adjustment before that date. In the second period, farmers showed a sensitivity to short-period changes in rainfall, in price levels, and, to a lesser extent, in related federal legislation. The sensitivity is reflected particularly in the acreages of corn and oats as against wheat and sorghum; and four reciprocal cycles are easily recognized (fig. 2). In the average-to-wet and wet years of the 1920s and 1940s, the acreages of corn and oats were up while those of wheat and sorghum were down; and the opposite was true in the very dry and dry periods of the 1930s and 1950s (Bowden 1959, pp. 130–97).

Before 1909 no similar and predictable relationships were apparent between price levels and rainfall periods and the ratio of corn to wheat. This was the phase of adjustment in which farmers were less responsive to the complex factors of change operative in the twen-

tieth century. Land use trends reflected more the beliefs of people of varied background—the geosophical factor—and the expansion of cultivated acreage as a product of population influx and availability of land—the historical factor. The people were adjusting to what they thought the environment was rather than to what it actually was, and, as individuals, to their understanding of the agricultural potential of different ecological situations, notably of the bottomland and upland.

Pioneers' Images of the Plains Margin

What were the settlers' conceptions of the land they occupied in the 1850s and 1860s? Webb believed that they saw the Great American Desert. This was, he wrote, a reality in the American public mind in some quarters until after the Civil War, reaching its peak in the decade from 1850 to 1860 (Webb 1931, pp. 152–60). Webb's view is an *idée fixe* that pervades the writings of social scientists and literary historians (Bowden 1975).

Ralph Brown (1948) cited the desert as the "classic example" of the importance of belief, as against actuality, in the occupancy and settlement of regions. He suggested that a succession of imagery, ranging from the plains as desert to the region as garden more fertile than the humid East, occurred in the 1870s. This perceptual change and the process behind it was perhaps expressed best by Henry Nash Smith, who accepted Webb's construct of the durability of the desert image in concluding that it was as "settlement moved up the valleys of the Platte and Kansas rivers" (in the 1860s and 1870s) that "the myth of the desert was destroyed and in its stead the myth of the garden of the world was projected out across the plains" (Smith 1950, p. 208). In this view the desert notion was current among settlers who came into Nebraska between 1850 and 1870, and it was part of the consciousness of those who followed in the 1870s and 1880s.

A rereading of Oregon Trail diaries in 1966 revealed that at the time when the desert idea was supposedly most prevalent, few, if any, diarists mentioned the Great American Desert or used the word *desert* either in preparation for or in the crossing of the plains. Lawson (1973) found the same in his search of 31 diaries, as did Jackson (1970, 1972) in his reading of 160 Mormon diaries. Travelers' letters and accounts in newspapers told the same story—few of the populace and none of their media cognized a vast desert east of the Rockies between 1845 and 1870. Conclusions published elsewhere suggest that the desert image of the plains was an idealized conception of the well-educated. Among them it took hold in New England in the 1820s, and it became common among the well-educated of the Eastern Seaboard in the early 1840s. Later, in the 1850s the desert either contracted in the elite view or was rejected for a concept of grassland plains or prairie (Bowden 1969).

In the newspapers, diaries, letters, and elementary textbooks of the lesser-educated majority, there is much to confirm a popular image of the lands beyond the Missouri as grassland plains, with an increasingly broad expanse of prairie in the east, and little to suggest a desert image, at least from the middle 1840s onward (Bowden 1971, pp. 58–69). The desert of the well-educated, thus, had no direct effect on the behavior of the comman man from 1850 to 1870.[2]

If the trans–Missouri West was dominantly short grass with expanding prairie in the east, was the plains margin regarded as prairie or plains in the 1850s? No contemporary records of settlers' appraisals of Jefferson County exist for the 1850s, but an answer to this and other questions is given by the surveyors of the Original Land Survey—frontiersmen reflecting popular western values who operated in the area between 1855 and 1857. Apart from

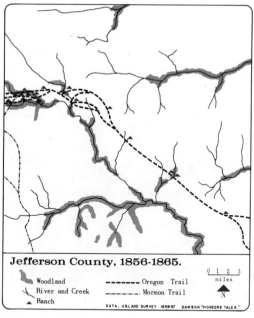

Figure 3 Jefferson County, 1856–65

2. This is not to say that well-educated officials did not act in response to the desert in their cognized world after 1850: Jefferson Davis's camels are an example. Clearly also the trans–Missouri West was not as favorably regarded by the populace in the 1850s as it was to become in the wheat uplands phase in the late 1870s or in the years of overassessment during the 1880s. In a ranking of priorities of most Americans, the High Plains and plains margin would probably have been rated the lowest in agricultural productivity in the area between the Appalachians and the Rockies between 1840 and 1860, and lower than California and Oregon.

the restricted wooded bottomland (figs. 1 and 3) the county was characterized by all seven of them as prairie. What to the surveyors was the agricultural potential of this "prairie" and bottomland? In the Illinois and Iowa they had just left, the first full onslaught was being made in the mid-1850s on the high, treeless, upland prairie hitherto avoided by settlers (Dodge 1932; Bogue 1963, pp. 8, 72). Thus, in the early fifties there was still doubt about the agricultural qualities of prairie uplands east of the Missouri. The same was true in Jefferson County, where upland prairies were most often judged by the surveyors as second-rate and sometimes third-rate. Not all the surveyors commented on farming potential, but at least one did so in the six upland townships in the east. In five of them, one or two surveyors remarked either on some potential for agriculture or saw the township as capable of sustaining a good or large population (Division of Educational Lands [1, 4, 5]). In the sixth case, Osborn, the subdivision surveyor (1856), found the township "first rate rolling prairie" but felt that "the soil is good but too dry to be useful for agricultural purposes," while Withrow (1856) found it "rolling and soil second rate" but "admitting of a large settlement" (DEL [1, 3]).

Surveyors of similar situations in the west were less optimistic. Three upland townships were thought to have farming potential by one surveyor but not by another: Caldwell, the surveyor of the subdivisions (1857) found them broken third-rate prairie not fit for cultivation, while Withrow, surveyor of the township lines (1856), felt they would "sustain a good settlement" and were "good second rate farming land" (DEL [1, 5]). In two other upland townships, Caldwell (1857) found one "below the common average . . . uplands are rolling. Soil third rate, poor for cultivation," and Doyle found the contiguous township "averaged as first and second rate. It cannot [but] be valued only for stock graising as the township is destitute of timber" (DEL [2, 3]).

A similar contrast between east and west existed in the assessment of bottomland. Only in the southeast townships in the Little Blue bottomlands was the land judged by two surveyors as of "first quality" (DEL [4, 5]). Elsewhere the bottomland was regarded as second-rate, and occasionally as third-rate and suitable only for grazing. Obviously, three of the five surveyors of upland prairies projected assessments of the Illinois prairies and bottomlands of the early 1850s to the uplands of eastern Nebraska, and two of the three, troubled by the absence of surface water, the poor timber, and greater dryness, saw the bottomlands at best as suitable for "general farming purposes" and the uplands as suitable mainly for grazing.

Initial Adjustment to Dry Prairie: Bottomland Hay and Open Upland Range

The initial adjustment to this dry prairie was made by subsistence ranchers, most of whom catered to travelers on the Oregon Trail. They were largely located where the trail crossed wooded bottomland (fig. 3). Bottomlands were valued for the rich wild hay that could be cut (Lemmon 1907, p. 131; Dawson 1912, p. 109), while upland was used as open range for the recuperating livestock acquired from, and often sold back to, the passing emigrants (Morris 1864, pp. 43–48). The census (Nebraska State Historical Society [4]) for 1859 reveals that a William McCanless had about forty acres of corn and ten of potatoes in perhaps the one good rainfall year in a dry phase and in the one bottomland area described by surveyors as of "first quality." There may have been an earlier cultivator (Dawson 1912, p. 269), but few, if any, of the other ranchers cultivated during the first decade of settlement. Certainly most ranchers were located in the western upland townships judged by the surveyors Caldwell and Doyle to be suitable mainly for grazing. Possibly the bottomlands remained uncultivated because of the dry phase or because of the belief among the majority of the ranchers that the lands were at best second- and third-rate and not worth cultivating, as Doyle and Caldwell had implied. The Oregon Trail ranchers may have shared the surveyors' assessments, and the two ranchers there during the survey may have helped shape their views. Perhaps because of these assessments (as the trail rancher Helvey noted), "in these years most of the corn had to be bought and hauled from points along the Missouri River" (Dawson 1912, p. 109).

Homesteaders and Bottomland Corn

By the mid-1860s, attitudes toward bottomlands were no longer equivocal, and homesteaders, favored by good rainfall years, surged in. "During 1865–66," noted the Rose Creek settler Avery, "many old soldiers filed on the rich bottomlands along the valley which, coupled with the other newcomers dotted the whole valley with cabins and dugouts of settlers" (Dawson 1912, p. 367). The bottomland pattern of occupance was so marked in 1869 and '70 that the deciduous forest man's practice in Illinois of avoiding the prairie and settling on the wooded bottomlands may have become more rigid in the later 1860s and early 1870s as the frontier moved into the dry prairie beyond the Missouri River (fig. 4). At this time, 1869–70, the bottomlands were used for growing corn (also wheat), while most of the uplands were considered as suited for

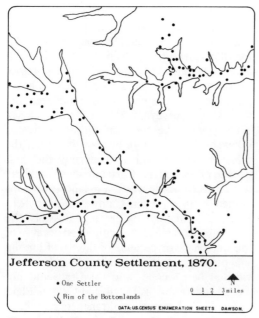

Figure 4 Jefferson County Settlement, 1870

grazing. Thus, although a bread grain was needed for subsistence and rainfall conditions favored wheat, the localization of farming in the bottomlands meant that the acreage in corn in this second phase was always as extensive as that of wheat and generally more extensive (particularly in the early seventies) (Bowden 1959, pp. 83–84).

How the old families appraised the open prairie upland we have some indication, for they told the newcomer Chirnside, who ventured onto the uplands in 1869–70, that his "open high prairie [was] unfit for settlement" (Dawson 1912, p. 356). It was, of course, in the interests of bottomland owners like the Helveys to keep the upland range open as long as they could, and their warnings to prospective uplanders may have reflected this self-interest. But it seems just as likely that they had adopted a traditional belief in the uncultivability of the uplands or rationalized their own failure to cultivate the uplands into a belief that uplands would not produce good crops.

Immigrants' Wheat Belt in the Uplands

The next cognitive change, with implications for agricultural behavior in the uplands,

occurred in the early seventies. It was felt at first that "the uplands were fit for wheat only for a limited section along the Missouri" (Porter 1882, p. 359). But in the plains margin a few farmers like Chirnside first tested this assumption by moving into the uplands of Cub Creek Township in northeast Jefferson County and cultivating wheat there successfully in 1870. The test was successful enough that wheat acreage surpassed that of corn in this predominantly upland precinct (NSHS [5]; Bowden 1959, pp. 210–11). But the achievement of Chirnside and others did not receive instant recognition in Jefferson County, for Peter Jansen (1921, p. 41), who came with the Mennonites in 1873, recounts that "farmers at that time had mostly settled along the creeks on the bottomlands and I well remember how they cautioned us not to try farming the table or uplands saying that we could not raise crops on them." The scale of the Mennonite operation—25,000 acres of upland—(Miller 1953) and the success in planting their traditional crop, wheat (Jansen 1921, p. 50), made old-timers believe in the cultivability of the upland. Looking backward to the mid-seventies, Jansen (1921 p. 46) concluded: "We had proven that farming in the tablelands could be made a success." The cognitive change was more dramatic in Jefferson County than elsewhere, but by 1876 experiments by Mennonites and non-Mennonites had dispelled the belief in the uncultivability of the uplands throughout the plains margin.

Attitudes toward the upland changed quickly in the mid-seventies, but there was no corresponding rise in wheat acreage in the uplands, because land sales there were frozen following the crisis of 1873 (Diller 1941, pp. 18–20), and this kept the farm population in the bottomlands. There, following the arrival of the railroad in 1872, most farmers maintained the production of the crop they felt best suited to their bottomland farms—corn. In Jefferson County as a whole, corn was probably more extensive than wheat in the mid-seventies (fig. 5).

By 1877 those who had occupied the uplands in the early seventies were beginning to grow wheat on a commercial scale (the ratio of wheat to corn in Cub Creek was 3:2) (*Fairbury*

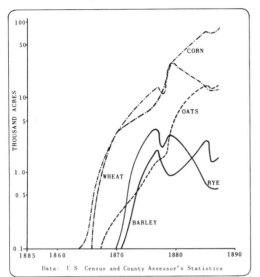

Data: U.S. Census and County Assessor's Statistics

Figure 5 Jefferson County Grain Acreages (1856–87)

Gazette, 1878), and settlers were coming into the uplands in large numbers again (NSHS [1, 2]). Some undoubtedly emulated the Mennonites in their wheat cultivation, but the majority, like Hamlin Garland's father in Iowa, had probably said, "We are wheat raisers, and we intend to keep in the wheat belt" (Garland 1937, p. 234). By 1879 wheat acreage in Cub Creek had tripled in two years and the ratio of wheat to corn was 3:1 (NSHS [6]). In a period of excellent rainfall (predictably corn years) there is thus a paradox: for two years only in the nineteenth century, wheat displaced corn as the dominant crop in Jefferson County (fig. 5). Even in the bottomland townships, the acreages of corn and wheat were equal (Paine 1948).

After 1873, therefore, there was in the Midwest a general belief promoted by boomers that the trans-Missouri uplands were fit for wheat cultivation (Baltensperger 1974). At this time half the textbooks were still presenting a plains image of a contracted desert in short-grass plains. Thus the well educated still greatly underestimated the plains (Bowden 1971). It was not this source that inspired wheat farmers in Iowa and emigrants from Europe to commit themselves to the uplands of the plains margin. Encouraged by the early boomers, the successful newcomers in the up-

lands in the early seventies added extra fuel to the boomers' fire by the mid-seventies, thereby inspiring further emigration of wheat farmers from the Midwest, convincing residents of the cultivability of the uplands, and finally removing the plains desert from the textbooks.

Newcomers' Corn Belt on the Far Border

The phenomenal and sudden rise in corn acreage in the eighties and the virtual abandonment of wheat after 1879 are difficult to explain (figs. 2 and 5). Both trends indicate a characteristic response to the occurrence of a wet period (1876–1886). The magnitude of the trends, however, suggests that other factors were more significant (Bowden 1959, 106–11). Perhaps the critical factor was the timing of the reappraisal of the agricultural potential of the uplands, the Great Dakota Boom (1879–1886) which diverted prospective Midwestern wheat farmers from Nebraska (Brown 1948, p. 425), and the synchronous influx of Midwestern corn farmers into the upland precincts (NSHS [3]). In the Midwest the attitudes of potential plains settlers were being changed markedly by the boomers (Baltensperger 1974). They exaggerated the potentialities of the region to counteract what they thought was a lingering popular desert notion, convincing many and perhaps themselves that the trans–Missouri West was the prairie garden of the world (Smith 1950, pp. 210–13; Emmons 1971). Unlike the promoters of the early seventies, the boomers had little support for their claims, contending that rain followed the plow and that soils were inexhaustible.

The belief that corn was the best crop on the trans-Missouri uplands gained currency in the corn belt just as conditions became favorable for migration (Austin 1936, pp. 85, 105), and after 1879 settlers from this agricultural region flooded into the uplands of the plains margin and of Jefferson County (NSHS [2, 3]). Encouraged as they were to believe that these uplands were prime corn lands, richer than those they had left, it is not surprising that these settlers with the "corn belt mentality" (Spencer and Horvath 1963, pp. 80–82) favored corn so strongly that the corn acreage was five to ten times that of wheat throughout the eighties. After the remarkable early success with corn due to wet years, these settlers judged the amount of rainfall as typical and made eastern Nebraska part of the core area of the corn belt (Marple 1958, 1969).

With the onset of a dry period, 1887–95, there came the gradual realization that the uplands and their climate had been overassessed (Bowden 1959, pp. 112–13). The painful but necessary adjustment was delayed until this century both because farmers had overcommitted themselves and become locked into the corn belt economy and because of an initial and optimistic reluctance to admit their overassessment. Between 1887 and 1892, bad crop years, poor corn yields, and the declining price advantage of corn over wheat encouraged diversification (Sweedlun 1940, pp. 97, 165). Yet during this period wheat never occupied more than one-third of the acreage devoted to corn, and there was continued and optimistic extension of corn acreage in an attempt by farmers to hang on to their livestock (Diller 1941, p. 27; Sweedlun 1940, p. 146). But the very dry years from 1893 to 95 finally convinced the farmers that diversification was needed. They realized that the lands were best suited to the mixed cash grain–feed grain economy that by 1909 became the equilibrium adjustment, but they felt they could do nothing about it. During the remaining moderate-to-dry years of the 1890s, farmers planted every acre to corn despite excessively low corn prices, for they were intent on subsistence, on saving a few stock, and on building up their exhausted feed stores (Warren 1909, p. 312). Corn acreage therefore increased rapidly while that of wheat remained steady and very low, even though climate and price conditions favored wheat.

In 1899, the year of maximum cultivated acreage in Jefferson County, the ratio of corn to wheat reached an unparalleled 30:1. But if this year saw the ultimate in the gamble for survival of the corn belt economy, it also saw a major increase in the acreage of the spring link crop, oats (Bowden 1959, p. 114). Plains margin farmers were about to swing away from corn to winter wheat. Nineteen hundred was thus the first year that agricultural behavior as expressed in land use adjusted obviously to the cognitive change that had occurred in the middle nineties. It was another ten years before the adjustment was complete, but the steady increase in winter wheat acreage despite relatively wet years reveals that farmers had a new environmental image of the plains margin (fig. 2).

Conclusion

So little is known about the images of the plainsmen that this study of image change in the plains margin is but a first approximation. Yet two conclusions can be drawn. (1) The plains imagery of the literati of the Eastern Seaboard in the nineteenth century always lagged behind that of the plainsmen and had no influence on the plains imagery of ordinary frontiersmen, as exemplified in the desert notion. (2) There were two sets of images held by plains settlers that affected agricultural behavior in the plains margin—those of residents and those of newcomers.

The desert notion admirably illustrates the gap between the literati and the poorly educated or illiterate frontiersmen. With possible qualifications in the 1820s, it is unlikely that the latter looked west and saw a desert east of the Rockies at any time in the nineteenth century. Thus for the populace there could have been no direct behavioral implications of the desert image, by definition. Many of the well-educated, particularly on the Eastern Seaboard, believed in the existence of a Great American Desert east of the Rockies, particularly between 1825 and 1845, and some minor governmental acts resulted from this belief. But as far as can be determined, neither the course and character of settlement and migration in America nor the sequence of economic activities in the plains were affected either directly or indirectly by this desert conception of the well-educated.

The desert image of the plains seems to have affected settlers' images and related behavior *only after 1875,* and only then indirectly, when the fable of the conquest of the desert by the sturdy yeoman was one of many themes used by boomers to establish the plains as the garden of the world and to promote the overextension of the farming frontier and of the corn belt in particular. The fable was present

TABLE 1

Cognition of the Plains and Behavior of Settlers
on the Plains Margin, 1850–1910

	COGNITION				BEHAVIOR (MAJORITY)	
	Trans-Missouri West		Plains Margin		Plains Margin	
Year	Literati	Boomers	Residents	Newcomers		Year
1850	Desert and plains			Prairie, with rich hay bottomland (cultivable); uncultivable upland	Subsistence ranching along Oregon Trail, bottomland haying, occasional cultivation; upland grazing	1850
1860	Western desert and eastern plains					1860
	Contracting western desert with plains and prairies	Eastern 2/3 prairie, western 1/3 plains for grazing	Hay bottomland, upland grazing	Prairie, with rich, prime corn bottomland		
1870			Prairie with rich, prime corn bottomland	Prairie, prime wheat upland (wheat belt)	Bottomland corn (and wheat), upland grazing	1870
		All prairie garden of the world	Prairie, prime corn bottomland, prime wheat upland		Upland wheat, bottomland corn (and wheat) (wheat belt)	
1880	"Desertless" western plains, eastern prairies		Prairie, prime corn upland and bottomland	Prairie garden; prime corn upland and bottomland (corn belt)		1880
					Corn monocrop in bottomland and upland (corn belt); occasional increases in wheat	
1890	Rich prairie garden with western plains	Prairie garden with drier High Plains				1890
1900	Eastern prairie, middle plains, western desert		Prairie diversified: wheat and corn upland (depending on climate phase), bottomland corn		Corn and winter wheat upland, corn bottomland; transition zone	1900
1910	Subhumid prairies, semiarid plains in Far West				Wheat (with corn) upland, corn (with wheat) bottomland; transition zone	1910

in perhaps one-quarter to one-half of the millions of pamphlets distributed between 1868 and 1892 (Baltensperger 1974). Paradoxically, the popular image of a conquered desert proved an incentive to plains settlement and to agricultural occupancy.

The two sets of images of the plainsmen (in the plains margin) can be seen in Table 1. Five behavioral responses (as reflected in land use) were made before 1910 and were preceded by five conceptions of the environment. Of the four cognitive changes involved, the first three were effected directly by newcomers who had a more optimistic assessment of the environment than did the residents. The latter had come earlier when the lands were assessed more conservatively and often had settled because the initially projected optimal activity suited them. The reluctance of the resident to change practices without outside stimulus may well have stemmed from satisfaction with a way of life; it may also have come in part from experience with an environment that was no longer idealized.

During the first four decades of settlement, people came to Jefferson County (and the plains margin) in three bursts: in the mid-to-late sixties (Dawson 1912, p. 367; Bowden 1971), the early seventies, and the early eighties. In each case, outsiders quickly tended to outnumber residents, and as each group of newcomers had a higher evaluation of the environment than did the residents, the result was a behavioral change as soon as a critical threshold was reached, that is, when newcomers outnumbered residents.[3]

Behind the environmental cognition of the

---

3. In some cases, therefore, the threshold was reached so quickly, as in the early eighties, that the behavioral response was practically instantaneous; in other cases, when population increase was more gradual or was faced with setbacks, as in the middle seventies, the obvious behavioral response (as measured in acreage totals) to the qualitative change in population took about five years from the onset of immigration of the new group. Although some locals were clearly experimenting in the direction of the future change, it was the newcomers who, in the first forty years of settlement, effected the changes in agricultural behavior. The residents either adapted their behavior and, presumably, their images or moved out.

dominantly Midwestern and European newcomers were the boomers, particularly in the eighties, but also in the early seventies. Where the literati and the politicians before the Civil War had failed, the boomers were very successful with their millions of pamphlets that reached the minimally and moderately literate. The boomers' images strongly influenced the newcomers from the Midwest.

There were, of course, other influences upon Midwesterners. From the passage of the Kansas-Nebraska Act onward and possibly earlier, the evaluations of all groups viewing the plains were increasingly favorable. Furthermore, from the 1820s to the early 1860s, Midwestern environments were being favorably reassessed, and these views were projected westward by a people bent on the westward course of empire, obsessed with and attracted to new lands. The boomers addressed potential emigrants who were willing to listen.

In the mid-sixties, old soldiers had heard much about the West, had the right to homestead, preferred the bottomlands, and knew that such locations were taken up east of the Missouri. The boomers were hardly needed. But their voices were audible by the late sixties and early seventies; much of what they wrote about the eastern uplands was based on proven facts, and their appraisals were surprisingly accurate (particularly when it is remembered that settlement was still largely in the plains margin). Their appeals to "wheat belters" in the early seventies were far less misleading than they were to be to "corn belters" bound for the High Plains and the uplands of the plains margin in the late seventies and early eighties. Nevertheless, the boomers' images of the plains margin were rosier than those of the plains margin residents; they strengthened and exaggerated those of migrating Midwesterners and thus contributed indirectly to the behav-

---

In the early years when there was much land available, the residents were able to continue their early practices with only little modification, for example, the Helveys in the late sixties. In such a situation the threshold level of newcomers to residents was much higher and less important than in the seventies and eighties, when land was being taken up rapidly and many old practices, such as open-range ranching, could not survive alongside the new.

ioral change in the plains margin in the seventies.

It was in the third phase, however, that the boomers had their greatest influence. Without strong evidence of the suitability of the uplands in the east and of the High Plains in the west for corn, they moved wholeheartedly and irresponsibly into the realm of myth and deceit, claiming that there were no differences between west and east, no limits to crop production in Nebraska, that rain followed the plow and tree culture, and that irrigation was unnecessary (Baltensperger 1974). The vast numbers who read their pamphlets in the Midwest probably knew the boomers were exaggerating, but had no idea of the scale of the misrepresentation. As a result they swarmed in with the first popular overassessment of the plains in the nineteenth century and, supported by good years, dragged more skeptical residents some way with them in their agricultural practices.

The final cognitive change, in the middle nineties, and the behavioral response after the turn of the century do not seem to have been affected directly by either newcomers or boomers. Both the delay and the gradualness of the cognitive response to the dry years and of the behavioral response to the cognitive change suggest that residents were responsible on the basis of local experience for both changes. Pressures for diversification from agricultural experts and the scientists of the agricultural college were common throughout the "corn belt" years, and these pressures had been heeded after bad corn years, as reflected in the increased plantings of spring and winter wheat in the plains margin. Yet these responses were only temporary, until the succession of disasters in the mid-nineties. A new agricultural system was perhaps seen by the farmers who had been appraised through local channels of the success of the Kansas Mennonite accident—Turkey red wheat. But the farmers' dire straits, as well, perhaps, as the conservativeness of the emerging agricultural establishment and of milling interests, prohibited a rapid response (Malin 1944).

In the plains margin, the boomers did much to mold the preconceptions and expectations of incoming plainsmen, who were responsible directly for the major cognitive and behavioral changes of the plainsmen as a whole during the 1870s and 1880s. It was the wealth of local experience among tenacious residents, aided as well as curbed by science and industry, that checked the optimistic excesses of the boomers' garden and the newcomers' corn belt and established the plains margin as the transition zone from corn and oats to winter wheat and sorghum. Through all these behavioral changes, the well-educated of the East were distant, time-lapse observers.

REFERENCES CITED

ARCHIVAL SOURCES

Division of Educational Lands (DEL).
(1)   Field Notes of the Original Land Survey, vol. 14
(2)   Field Notes of the Original Land Survey, vol. 29.
(3)   Field Notes of the Original Land Survey, vol. 37.
(4)   Field Notes of the Original Land Survey, vol. 45.
(5)   Field Notes of the Original land Survey, vol. 53.
Nebraska State Historical Society (NSHS).
(1)   Nebraska State Census of Population, 1874.
(2)   Nebraska State Census of Population, 1875–79.
(3)   Nebraska State Census of Population, 1881–82, 1884.
(4)   Enumeration Sheets of the Census of Agriculture, 1859.
(5)   Enumeration Sheets of the Census of Agriculture, 1869.
(6)   Enumeration Sheets of the Census of Agriculture, 1879.

NEWSPAPER.

Fairbury Gazette (Nebraska). 1878.

OTHER REFERENCES

Allen, John L.
1971.   Geographical knowledge and American images of Louisiana Territory. *Western Historical Quarterly* 2: 151–70.
Austin, Milan D.
1936.   Trends in acreage, of important cultivated crops in Nebraska, 1879–1934. Master's

thesis, Department of Rural Economics, University of Nebraska.

Baltensperger, Bradley.
1974. Plains promoters and plain folk: Premigration and post-settlement images of the central Great Plains. Ph.D. diss., Department of Geography, Clark University.

Bogue, Allan G.
1963. *From prairie to corn belt: Farming on the Illinois and Iowa prairies in the nineteenth century.* Chicago: University of Chicago Press.

Bowden, Martyn J.
1959. Changes in land use in Jefferson County, Nebraska, 1857–1957. Master's thesis, Department of Geography, University of Nebraska.
1969. The perception of the western interior of the United States, 1800–1870: A problem in historical geosophy. *Proceedings of the Association of American Geographers* 1: 16–21.
1971. The Great American Desert and the American frontier, 1800–1882: Popular images of the plains. In *Anonymous Americans: Explorations in nineteenth century social history,* edited by Tamara K. Hareven, pp. 48–79. Englewood Cliffs, N.J.: Prentice-Hall.
1975. The Great American Desert in the American mind, 1890–1972: The historiography of a geographical notion. In *Geographies of the mind: Essays in historical geosophy in honor of John K. Wright,* edited by Martyn J. Bowden and David Lowenthal. New York: Oxford University Press and American Geographical Society.

Brown, Ralph H.
1948. *Historical geography of the United States.* New York: Harcourt, Brace & Co.

Dawson, Charles.
1912. *Pioneer tales of the Oregon Trail and of Jefferson County.* Topeka: Crane & Co.

Diller, Robert.
1941. *Farm ownership, tenancy, and land use in a Nebraska community.* Chicago: University of Chicago Press.

Dodge, Stanley D.
1932. Bureau and the Princeton community. *Annals of the Association of American Geographers* 22: 159–200.

Emmons, David M.
1971. *Garden in the grasslands: Boomer literature of the central Great Plains.* Lincoln: University of Nebraska Press.

Garland, Hamlin.
1937. *A son of the middle border.* New York: Macmillan Co.

Jackson, Richard H.
1970. Myth and reality: Environmental perception of the Mormons, 1840–1865, an historical geosophy. Ph.D. diss., Department of Geography, Clark University.
1972. Myth and reality: Environmental perception of the Mormon pioneers. *Rocky Mountain Social Science Journal* 9: 33–38.

Jansen, Peter.
1921. *Memoirs of Peter Jansen: The record of a busy life.* Beatrice, Nebr.: By the author.

Lawson, Merlin P., et al.
1971. *Nebraska droughts: A study of their past chronological and spatial extent with implications for the future.* Occasional Papers No. 1, Department of Geography, University of Nebraska.
1973. The climate of the Great American Desert. Ph.D. diss., Department of Geography, Clark University.

Lemmon, J. H.
1907. Early days on the Little Blue. *Proceedings and Collections of the Nebraska State Historical Society* 15: 127–33.

Malin, James C.
1944. *Winter wheat in the golden belt of Kansas.* Lawrence: University of Kansas Press.

Marple, Robert P.
1958. The transition zone between the corn belt and the hard winter wheat belt. Ph.D. diss., Department of Geography, University of Nebraska.
1969. The corn-wheat ratio in Kansas, 1879 and 1959: A study in historical geography. *Great Plains Journal* 8: 79–86.

Miller, D. P.
1953. An analysis of community adjustment: A case study of Jansen, Nebraska. Ph.D. diss., Department of Sociology, University of Nebraska.

Morris, M. O'Connor.
1864. *Rambles in the Rocky Mountains with a visit to the goldfields of Colorado.* London: Smith, Elder & Co.

Paine, Clarence S., ed.
1948. The diaries of a Nebraska farmer, 1876–1877. *Agricultural History* 22: 1–31.

Porter, Robert P.
1882. *The West: From the Census of 1880.* Chicago: Rand McNally & Co.

Smith, Henry N.
1950. *Virgin Land: The American West as symbol and myth.* New York: Vintage Books.

Spencer, J. E., and Horvath, Ronald J.
1963. How does an agricultural region originate? *Annals of the Association of American Geographers* 53: 74–92.

Sweedlun, Verne S.
1940. A history of the evolution of agriculture in Nebraska, 1870–1930. Ph.D. diss., Department of History, University of Nebraska.

Warren, Joseph A.
1909. An agricultural geography of Nebraska. In *Annual Report of the Nebraska State Board of Agriculture,* pp. 271–351. Lincoln.

Weaver, John C.
1954a. Changing patterns of cropland use in the Middle West. *Economic Geography* 30: 1–47.
1954b. Crop-combination regions in the Middle West. *Geographical Review* 44: 175–200.
1954c. Crop-Combinations for 1919 and 1929 in the Middle West. *Geographical Review* 44:560–72.

Webb, Walter P.
1931. *The Great Plains.* Boston: Ginn & Co.

The Great Plains
One Hundred Years After Major John Wesley Powell

Leslie Hewes
University of Nebraska

John Wesley Powell in his *Report on the Lands of the Arid Region,* published in 1879, urged that land in the United States west of the 100th meridian be reserved primarily for grazing, with limited areas to be irrigated. Dryland farming was conceded as a possibility for some northern parts of the Great Plains. As late as 1889, in an address to the North Dakota constitutional convention, he categorically restricted farming without irrigation to the eastern third of the state. In the original report, Powell also urged strongly that fundamental changes be made in the manner of settling the West and of using its resources (Powell 1879, 1969).

Nearly a century after Powell, it is amazing how often the 20-inch-rainfall line or the 100th meridian is said to mark the western limit of farming without irrigation in the Great Plains. Supporters of Powell have claimed that although his proposals were not accepted at the time, events have vindicated his ideas. "Scientific prophecy . . . experimentally proved," according to De Voto. In the words of Hafen and Hollon, "In the end, the agricultural West had to be settled approximately as he had foretold." Stegner wrote, "On any composite map showing the modern use and management and reclamation of western lands . . . it would appear as if about every suggestion Powell made has been adopted and every type of western land is being put to the kind of use Powell advocated" (De Voto 1954, p. xvii; Stegner 1954, p. 357; Hafen, Hollon, and Rister 1970, p. 472).

Although the events vindicating Powell form a list of some length, total preservation of the semiarid grassland of the plains is not one of them. Inability to see that dry-land farming exists is a blind spot, a very large one. Dry-land farmers did not stop at the 100th meridian or at the 20-inch isohyet. Recent maps of cropland show little relation to rainfall lines in the Great Plains (Marschner 1959, inside front cover; National Atlas 1970, pp. 158–60). Instead, they indicate favorable appraisal of glacial till and of loess more faithfully than respect for any isohyet. Those who broke and farmed the dry grassland either did not know of Powell's warning or percived the plains differently.

RETROSPECT

The advances into the semiarid grasslands have been costly, especially when stemmed and thrown back. At least three of the retreats have been on such a scale and so spectacular as receive wide notice. These included the disastrous flight from the central Great Plains of Kansas, Nebraska, and Colorado in the 1890s, which Barrows called the "first great crushing defeat" of the American farmer (1962, p. 231). Johnson, after conducting field work in the stricken area, was convinced that the defeat was permanent and that the only proper use of most of the High Plains was grazing (1901, pp. 609–744). A second major retreat took place in northern Montana in the very early 1920s after an especially deep penetration of the dry plains between 1910 and 1920, a few years after the passage of the 320-acre homestead law. The considerable pullback of the 1930s, especially the late thirties—which might have been a rout over a much larger area than before, but for gigantic governmental intervention—is known to most as an aspect of the Dust Bowl period.

Gleanings from the Montana Triangle

As far as I have been able to determine, Wilson's study of the Montana Triangle (bounded approximately by the towns of Havre, Great Falls, and Cut Bank) in the north central part of that state is the most illuminating account of what happened in a newly settled area under drought (Wilson 1923). A brief summary follows.

This contemporary account, based on conditions of 1922, showed that less than one-half of the homesteaders in an extensive sample had been farmers; less than one-half were married, and 30 percent had started with "no capital." Many had come from grassland areas, the leading sources being Minnesota, North Dakota, western Canada, and Washington. Farm abandonment averaged 49 percent, running much higher among nonfarmers, single men, and those starting with no capital. It was not clear that small size of farms was a major condition making for failure or that emphasis on livestock was protection against failure. However, gardens, often planted alongside windbreaks that caught snow or placed near windmills, aided persistence, and dairy cattle were called "sticking plaster." A close-up study showed that successful farmers obtained higher wheat yields than their neighbors.

Certainly, many of the homesteaders were experienced in living in a dry grassland, and there were exceptions to the Webb-Kraenzel thesis that farm practices introduced to the Great Plains were unsuitable (Webb 1931; Kraenzel 1955). A number of instances of introductions that did fit can be recognized: the

equipment and practice of summer fallowing for wheat by subtillage (plowless) methods, imported from Canada; the drilling of wheat in corn stubble, as in western Kansas; the practice of making corn silage from early corn, including Dakota white flint corn, brought in, presumably, from North Dakota; the putting up of Russian thistle as silage, although the source area of the settlers acquainted with it was not identified; the use of trench silos, as in western Canada, Kansas, and Nebraska; and the use of tillage equipment, introduced from eastern Washington.

Experimentation and flexibility were demonstrated, as shown in the references to the development of new tillage devices in the area; the trying out of new methods of subtillage; the use of grain hay, especially when it appeared that the crop would not "make"; working with brome grass for hay; and the realization of the need for a cloddy surface rather than a dust mulch on fields in a windy area.

Seed was as new to the area as farmers were. In this contemporary study of the triangle, the only reference to source of seed noted was to Dakota flint corn. Elsewhere, as in Colorado, Turkey red wheat and other introductions from Russia were among the crop varieties considered adapted. There only locally produced corn proved suitable, although "Mexican" corn, possibly local, was referred to in the early 1900s as the most drought resistant (Cottrell 1909, p. 25).

The claim made for the Montana Triangle, "Had the profits of 1915–16 been husbanded and saved, the country could have tided it over the years of adversity," was an exaggeration, considering that the newcomers were buying land and equipment and, with a homesteading peak in 1917, many came too late to share in the bountiful crops. Perhaps it is important that of 130 successful farmers operating in 1921, 21 had begun as early as 1912, taking advantage of the good crop of that year, and 80 had begun as early as 1915, presumably benefiting from the good crops of 1915 and 1916. Although the report does not emphasize the fortuitous circumstance of the time at which the homesteader began, this seems a point of major importance, having a great deal

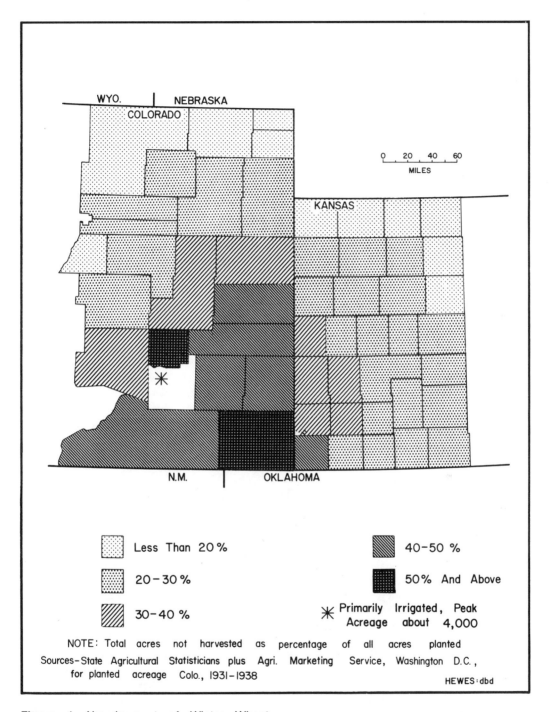

Figure 1 Abandonment of Winter Wheat (Weighted): Eastern Colorado and Western Kansas, Average, 1931–68

to do with his financial condition.

After the great drought and depression were well along, it was pointed out that the maximum number of farm bankruptcies in Montana occurred in 1924, far more than in either the drought period of the teens or of the 1930s. The area hit hardest was the dry-farming country, including the triangle. The heavy outlays of settlement in 1910 to 1918, when farm prices were high, the decline of farm prices that followed, and depressed land values contributed importantly to the bankruptcy of the farmers (Renne 1938).

The Montana Triangle study did not identify any foreign group settlement. However, an on-the-ground report from northeastern Colorado after the pullout of the 1890s included attention to a Mennonite group that stuck. This group, as was common, was carrying on a diversified operation, with cattle, feed, and wheat, although some localities emphasized wheat (Payne 1900, pp. 5–16). Some of the Mennonites are still there.

Risk

Although each advance and each retreat was probably different in a number of ways, it may be generalized that the advances came largely at times of average or better rainfall and wheat prices, and of technological improvements, and that retreats have usually followed soon after, at times of reduced rainfall, lower prices, and poorer economic conditions. The common allusion to three generations of homesteaders or other farmers implies great wasted effort and resources and blasted hopes, although it is claimed that many planned to dispose of their cheaply obtained land early.

Drought has been—and is—a major hazard, but one compounded by unfavorable economic conditions. The first severe drought in a newly settled area was enough to dislodge many, sometimes most, of the pioneer farmers, who were commonly in debt and without reserves. The evidence is insufficient to include inadequate size of farms as a major cause of failure on the frontier. In fact, in Montana around 1920 and in the central Great Plains then, and earlier, there were authoritative contemporary

references to farmers attempting to farm too many acres. The planting of wheat without prior preparation of the land was common (Wilson 1923, p. 31; Payne 1904, p. 27; Arnold 1919, p. 135).

The argument that wheat failure is an important index of risk in dry farming has been presented elsewhere. High variability in wheat yields is, of course, partly an expression of failure (Hewes and Schmieding 1956; Hewes 1958; Barber 1951). The map of long-term weighted abandonment of wheat in eastern Colorado and western Kansas (fig. 1), much of which was Dust Bowl country, should provide a red flag of danger to even those wheat farmers having reserves. It is not surprising that Crowley County, in south central Colorado, at over 50 percent abandonment, has gone back to grass; that Baca, at the extreme southeastern corner of the state, is still wheat country must mean that failure and production figures (Nanheim, Bailey, and Merrick 1958, p. 82) do not tell the whole story. For one thing, wheat is commonly pastured. More important, grain sorghum, the chief crop on sandy land, is often a catch crop on hard lands after wheat has failed. In good years, there is profit on wheat; in poor years, losses may be cut or wiped out by grain sorghum.

It is a curious notion that grazing is adapted to the semiarid grassland but that dry farming is not. After all, both pasture and crops depend on the uncertain and often inadequate precipitation. True, it is harder to measure risk in ranching and livestock farming and to map it, but the evidence of high risk is abundant. Nor has the irrigation farmer gotten off scot-free, as shown by references by the Colorado State agricultural statistician to water shortages and resulting crop damage in several years, both in the 1930s and 1950s. A study of irrigation along the North Platte in western Nebraska, one of the few efforts to measure risk in irrigation farming, shows that in five consecutive years (1937–1941), more than 40 percent of the irrigated acreage was deprived of canal water for periods of over six weeks in the summer season (Brandhorst 1968, p. 495). Well irrigation is more dependable—until the wells run dry.

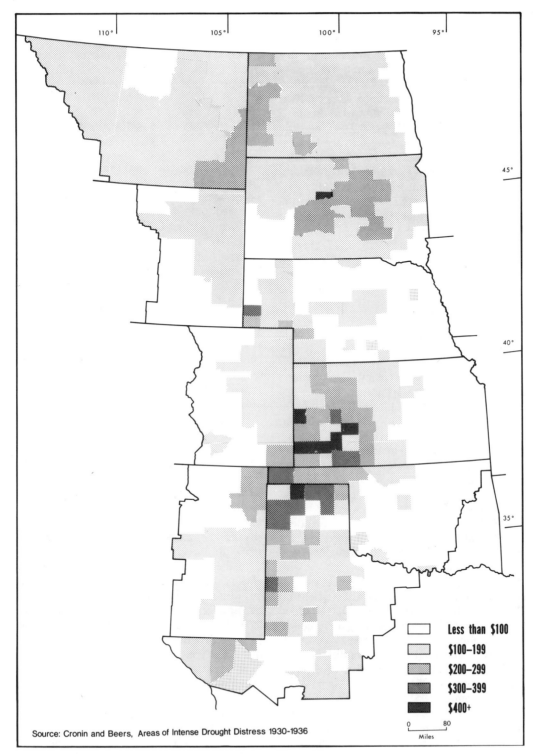

Source: Cronin and Beers, Areas of Intense Drought Distress 1930-1936

Figure 2 Federal Aid Per Capita, 1933–36, in Great Plains Area.

Records from the 1930s show that many dry farmers were hit hard. Per capita relief payments in the early thirties in the plains ran highest in the dry-farm country, especially in southwestern Kansas, as shown in figure 2 (Cronin and Beers 1937, pp. 41–54), and the percentage of farms mortgaged to the Federal Land Bank was especially high in a belt of dry farming from west Texas into North Dakota (Great Plains Committee 1936, p. 55).

Severe shortages of water, feed, and pasturage on the Great Plains received official notice in the form of emergency purchases of cattle in 1934 (Kifer and Stewart 1938, p. 27). Figure 3 shows that over 40 percent of all cattle in most of North Dakota, South Dakota, and extreme eastern Montana were bought by the government. The southwestern margin of the plains was the second largest such area.

It is not clear that dry farming has had a poorer record than stock raising since the 1930s. The major increase in summer fallowing and its increasing efficiency have provided important short-term insurance to the dry farmer against wheat failure. It is doubtful that an equivalent cushion has been afforded the grazier.

The 1950s provide an instructive lesson. According to former secretary of agriculture Ezra Benson, although the drought was as severe as in the thirties in the central and southern Plains, areas that blew badly before did not this time, and there was less abandonment of farms and less human hardship. He credited greater financial reserves, increased know-how and equipment to cope with drought and dust, and the remembrance of recovery from the earlier disaster ([Benson] 1955, pp. 26–29). He should have added higher prices and improved economic conditions as important considerations.

Maps of crop and pasture conditions as of July 1 are available for a number of drought years, including 1952–57 (Great Plains Agricultural Council 1953, pp. 59a and 59b; 1954, f. p. 10; 1956, pp. 4 and 5; 1957, p. 13 and f.). As might be expected, crops and pastures were hit hard in about the same places. If the abandonment of winter wheat acreage is a reliable index of failure of dry-land farming, 1954 was

the worst year for the dry farmer in the central Great Plains. Figures 4 and 5 confirm that both crops and pasture failed there.

The Testimony of Events: Dry Farming Tested

The fact that cash grain farms continue as the chief type in both the northern and central wheat belts shows that the dry farmers have occupied and continue to hold large parts of the Great Plains. Both dry farmers and their land have shown remarkable recovery from the crisis conditions of the 1930s. The dire conclusions of *Deserts on the March, The Plow That Broke the Plains,* and the Joel report have had to be changed (Sears 1935; Resettlement Administration 1936; Joel 1937, p. 53). The latter recommended that over 4 million acres, or 52 percent, of the cultivated and idle land in the heart of the Dust Bowl be returned to grass. However, as of about 1950, it was stated authoritatively that 90 percent of the land plowed in the 1920s in the Dust Bowl was then in crops, including 60 percent of the land that had been abandoned in the mid-1930s (Finnell 1951, p. 96; 1949, p. 4).

The wheat farmers did not stop with the reoccupation of partially lost territory. By 1950 several million more acres in both the central and northern plains had been added. In the Dust Bowl, this was new wheat country in advance of earlier wheat frontiers (Hewes 1973, pp. 97–120).

In the late 1950s, farmers and land owners of the nation were given the opportunity to get out of farming for a period of up to ten years by, in effect, "leasing" their cropland to the federal government under the Conservation Reserve Program of the Soil Bank. In most of the wheat country, farmers elected to stay in farming rather than collect the sure payments. Participation was high in only a few parts of the dry-farm country—most notably at the southwestern margin, then recently plagued by drought and crop failure; to a smaller degree, along the Oklahoma-Texas border; and at the eastern margin in the northern Plains (Hewes 1967, pp. 331–46). Figure 6 shows the

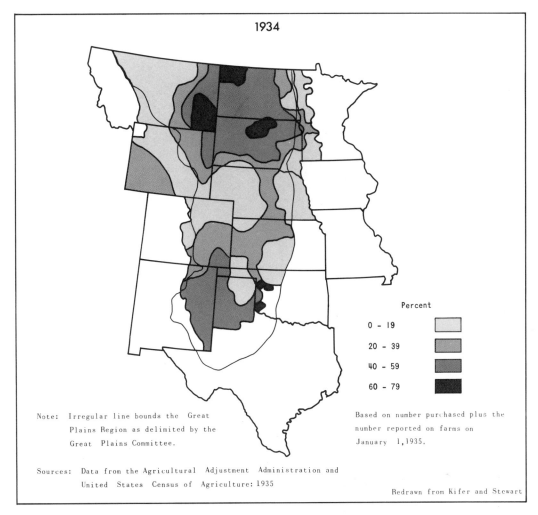

1934

Percent

0 - 19

20 - 39

40 - 59

60 - 79

Note: Irregular line bounds the Great
       Plains Region as delimited by the
       Great Plains Committee.

Based on number purchased plus the
number reported on farms on
January 1,1935.

Sources: Data from the Agricultural Adjustment Administration and
          United States Census of Agriculture: 1935

Redrawn from Kifer and Stewart

Figure 3 Percentage of Cattle Purchased under
the Emergency Livestock Purchase Program of
the Agricultural Adjustment Administration

percentage of cropland placed in the conservation reserve.

Generally, the turnover of farmers on the
dry margin of wheat farming in southeastern
and east central Colorado at this time was high
—another sign of insecurity there. Of 882
farmers included on the wheat lists for 1954 in
ten communities, only 488 were listed in the
same communities in 1961 or 1962. Nearly
400 had dropped out. A large percentage of
the farmers who dropped out had only 320
acres of cropland or less—60 of 135 suitcase

farmers and 126 of 259 local farmers. In 1961–
62, only 13 percent of the persisting local
farmers had 320 acres or less of cropland. The
percentage for persisting suitcase farmers remained at 28, but many nonresidents operate
farms in more than one locality (Hewes 1973,
table 30, p. 153). By this time, small farms
were commonly uneconomical, whether in
drought or average times.

The dry, southwestern edge of dry farming
appears to be an area of uncertain future. In
four counties in southern Colorado near the

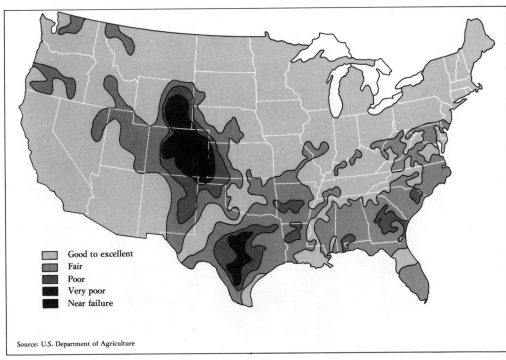

Figure 4 Crop Prospects, July 1, 1954

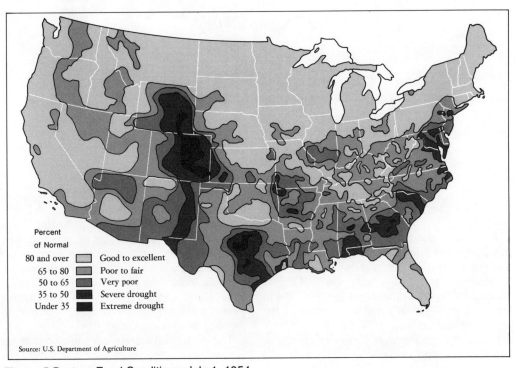

Figure 5 Pasture Feed Conditions, July 1, 1954

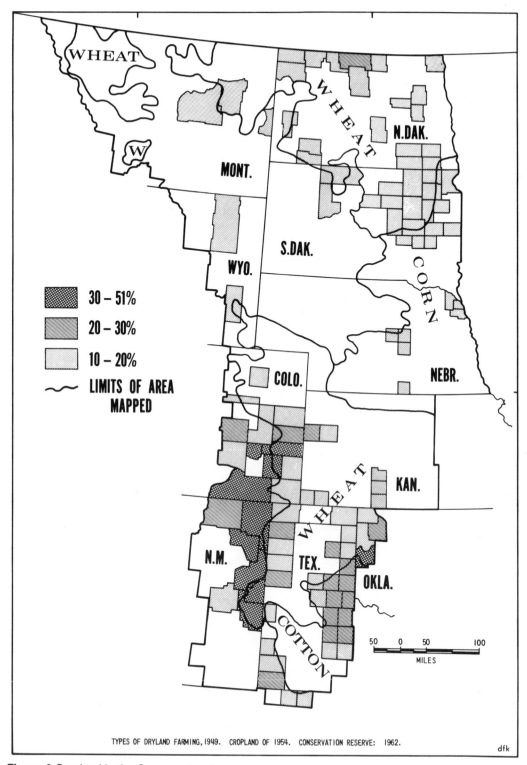

Figure 6 Cropland in the Conservation Reserve

211

212   ADAPTATIONS TO REALITY

Arkansas River, most notably in Bent and Crowley, wheat acreages have been cut by more than half. However, most farmers in the Kansas and Colorado portions of the Dust Bowl are still committed to wheat. In most of the counties in the wheat country of western Kansas and eastern Colorado, 90 percent or more of all farms have wheat allotments. Overplanting of allotments is frequent—as a hedge against failure in poor years and "for real" in good years.

The wheat country has made a notable comeback from the reverses suffered. This includes the land itself, which is in amazingly good condition after the dust storms of the thirties and fifties. In at least two cases the soil surveyors noted specifically only slight damage to soil or to soil productivity (U.S. Department of Agriculture 1961, p. 8, and 1963, p. 9). At the western, drier edge, the shorter period of wheat farming is reported to have done substantial damage to the thin soil there. Some older men in the Soil Conservation Service dispute the conclusion that damage was slight elsewhere. The long-predicted shortage of organic matter and associated nitrogen is not yet a common limitation to wheat yields in the central Great Plains. Twenty years ago, it was generalized that nitrogen was seldom a limiting factor in the Great Plains (Salmon, Mathews, and Leukel 1953, p. 41). This is still the case in the central Great Plains (Smika 1970, p. 16, and Greb et al., in press, p. 55).[1] The protein content of wheat is reported to have decreased in irregular fashion but still to be at apparently acceptable levels (Kansas State Board of Agriculture 1953–54, p. 56; 1961–62, p. 42; 1971–72, p. 39 f.).[2]

PROSPECT

Presenting the Great Plains one hundred years after Powell calls for looking ahead a few years. Recent trends must be considered as generally favorable to dry farming. Among the favorable circumstances—which have become stabilizing influences—are more experience and, doubtless, larger reserves in the hands of the farmers. Other conditions are reductions in crop failures and higher yields, particularly in good years. Both changes in varieties and improved methods have contributed to higher yields (Greb et al., in press).[3] Wind damage has been reduced. Also important to the dry farmer are price floors under wheat, and government payments, including built-in crop insurance; considerable dependence in some areas on catch crops, whose yields are commonly up; and some integration with irrigation and with stock raising. For many, commercial grain farming is as specialized as ever, although additional cash crops may have been added. Few now place any dependence on dairy cattle or chickens.

Except for possible changes in government programs, a prediction of continued dependence on wheat with supplementary use of catch crops and, in some localities, of irrigation seems reasonable for the present wheat country of the semiarid Great Plains. The wheat economy and its dry-land base promise to have a more secure future than more intensive uses of the land based on the overuse of underground water. West Texas is a case in point. It is predicted that in what is the chief irrigation area in the Great Plains, extending

1. At North Platte, Nebraska, at the eastern edge of the semiarid belt, the response to nitrogen over a nineteen-year period averaged less than 7 percent, while at Akron, Colorado, it was reported "there has been no evidence of significant N-responses to fallowed wheat in Colorado except on sandy soil."
2. In west central Kansas, the average protein content of wheat has varied from 14.9 to 11.9 percent from 1948 to 1971. Eleven of the thirteen years having less than 13 percent occurred in the fifteen-year period beginning in 1957.

3. According to Roy E. Gwin, Jr., superintendent of the Kansas Agricultural Experiment Station, Tribune branch (personal communication, February 1, 1973), the average yield for varietal wheat tests at Tribune for the years 1970–72 was 39 bushels as compared with 11 bushels for 1924–29, although the average precipitation for both periods was less than 15 inches. At Akron, Colorado, the percentage of the precipitation saved by summer fallowing increased from 19 percent for 1910–35 to 35 percent for 1967–70, according to B. W. Greb, soil scientist at the Great Plains Field Station, Akron, Colorado (personal communication, November 20, 1968), and Greb, et al. (in press).

from just south of Amarillo to beyond Lubbock, the 3.5 million acres irrigated in 1966 will be reduced to less than 125,000 acres by the year 2015 (Hughes and Harman 1969, pp. 5 and 31).

REFERENCES CITED

Arnold, J. H.
1919. Farm Practices in Growing Wheat. In *USDA Yearbook, 1919,* pp. 123–50. Washington, D.C.: GPO.

Barber, E. Lloyd.
1951. Variability of wheat yields by counties in the United States. Mimeographed. USDA Bureau of Agricultural Economics.

Barrows, Harlan H.
1962. *Lectures on the historical geography of the United States as given in 1933.* Edited by William A. Koelsch. University of Chicago, Department of Geography Research Paper no. 77.

[Benson, Ezra Taft].
1955. Interview, from the dust country: Secretary Benson reports on the big blow of 1955. *U.S. News and World Report,* May 6, pp. 26–29.

Brandhorst, L. Carl.
1968. The panacea of irrigation: Fact or fancy. *Journal of the West* 7: 491–508.

Colorado Department of Agriculture.
1932. *Colorado agricultural statistics.* Denver: Colorado Department of Agriculture with the USDA.
1954. *Colorado agricultural statistics* (final). Denver: Colorado Department of Agriculture with the USDA.
1955. *Colorado agricultural statistics* (preliminary). Denver: Colorado Department of Agriculture with the USDA.

Cottrell, H. M.
1909. *Dry land farming in eastern Colorado.* Agricultural Experiment Station of the Colorado Agricultural College Bulletin 145. Fort Collins.

Cronin, Francis D., and Beers, Howard W.
1937. *Droughts: Areas of intense drought distress, 1930–1936.* Works Progress Adminstration, Division of Social Research Bulletin, series 5, no. 1. Washington, D.C.: GPO.

De Voto, Bernard.
1954. Introduction to *Beyond the hundredth meridian: John Wesley Powell and the second opening of the West,* by Wallace Stegner. Boston: Houghton Mifflin Co.

Finnell, H. H.
1949. *Land use experience in southern Great Plains.* USDA Circular no. 820. Washington, D.C.: GPO.
1951. The plow-up of western grasslands and its resultant effect upon Great Plains agriculture. *Southwestern Social Science Quarterly 32: 94–100.*

Great Plains Agricultural Council.
1953. *Proceedings of the Great Plains Agricultural Council,* Fort Collins, Colo. Maps in this volume by Bureau of Agricultural Economics, USDA.
1954. *Proceedings of the Great Plains Agricultural Council,* Sylvan Lake, S.D. Maps in this volume by the Marketing Service, USDA.
1956. *Proceedings of the Great Plains Agricultural Council,* Fort Collins, Colo. Maps in this volume by the Marketing Service, USDA.
1957. *Proceedings of the Great Plains Agricultural Council,* Sylvan Lake, S.D. Maps in this volume by the Marketing Service, USDA.

Great Plains Committee.
1936. *The future of the Great Plains.* Report of the Great Plains Committee. Washington, D.C.: GPO.

Greb, B. W.; Smika, D. E.; Woodruff, N. P.; and Whitfield, C. J.
In press. Summer fallow in the central Great Plains. In *Summer fallow in western United States,* USDA Conservation Research Report, no. 17. Washington, D.C.: GPO.

Hafen, LeRoy Reuben; Hollon, W. Eugene; and Rister, Carl Coke.
1970. *Western America: The exploration, settlement, and development of the region beyond the Mississippi.* 3rd ed. Englewood Cliffs, N.J.: Prentice-Hall.

Hewes, Leslie.
1958. Wheat failure in western Nebraska, 1931–54. *Annals of the Association of American Geographers* 48: 375–97.
1967. The conservation reserve of the American Soil Bank as an indicator of regions of maladjustment in argiculture, with particular reference to the Great Plains. In *Festschrift Leopold G. Scheidl Zum 60. Geburtstag,* vol. 2, pp. 331–46. Vienna: Institute of World Trade.
1973. *The Suitcase Farming Frontier: A study in the historical geography of the central Great Plains.* Lincoln: University of Nebraska Press.

Hewes, Leslie, and Schmieding, Arthur C.
1956. Risk in the central Great Plains: Geographical patterns of wheat failure in Nebraska, 1931–1952. *Geographical Review* 46: 375–87.

Hughes, William F., and Harman, Wyatte L.
1969. *Projected economic life of water resources,*

subdivision number 1, High Plains underground water reservoir. Texas Agricultural Experiment Station Technical Monograph 6. College Station, Texas.

Joel, Arthur M.
1937. *Soil conservation reconnaissance survey of the southern Great Plains wind erosion area.* USDA Technical Bulletin no. 556. Washington, D.C.: GPO.

Johnson, W. D.
1901. *The High Plains and their utilization.* Part 4, Hydrography. In U.S. Geological Survey, 21st Annual Report, 1899–1900, pp. 609–741. Washington, D.C.: GPO.

Kansas State Board of Agriculture.
1953–54. *Thirty-ninth biennial report of Kansas State Board of Agriculture.* Topeka: Kansas State Printing Plant.
1961–62. *Farm facts.* Topeka: Kansas State Board of Agriculture.
1971–72. *Farm facts.* Topeka: Kansas State Board of Agriculture.

Kifer, R. S., and Stewart, H. L.
1938. *Farming hazards in the drought area.* Works Progress Administration, Division of Social Research Monograph 16. Washington, D.C.: GPO.

Kraenzel, C. F.
1955. *The Great Plains in transition.* Norman: University of Oklahoma Press.

Marschner, J. F.
1959. Major land uses in the United States (map). In *Land use and its patterns in the United States,* USDA Agriculture Handbook no. 153. Washington, D.C.: GPO.

Nanheim, Charles W.; Bailey, Warren R.; and Merrick, Della E.
1958. *Wheat production, trends, problems, programs, opportunities for Adjustment.* USDA Agriculture Research Service, Agricultural Information Bulletin 179. Washington, D.C.

National Atlas of the United States of America.
1970. U.S. Department of the Interior Geological Survey. Washington, D.C.: GPO.

Payne, J. E.
1900. *Investigation of the Great Plains: Field notes from trips in eastern Colorado.* Colorado Experiment Station Bulletin 59. Fort Collins.

1904. *Wheat raising on the plains.* Colorado Experiment Station Bulletin 89. Fort Collins.

Powell, J. W.
1879. *Report on the lands of the arid region of the United States, with a more detailed account of the land of Utah.* U.S. Geographical and Geological Survey of the Rocky Mountain Region. 2d ed. Washington, D.C.: GPO.
1969. Address at the North Dakota Constitutional Convention, August 5, 1889, Bismark. Edited by James E. Sherry. *North Dakota History* 36: 369–76.

Renne, R. R.
1938. *Montana farm bankruptcies.* Montana State College Extension Service, Bulletin 360. Bozeman.

Resettlement Administration.
1936. *The plow that broke the plains.* Documentary film.

Salmon, S. C.; Mathews, Q. R.; and Leukel, R. W.
1953. A half century of wheat improvement in the United States. *Advances in Agronomy* 5: 3–151.

Sears, Paul B.
1935. *Deserts on the march.* Norman: University of Oklahoma Press.

Smika, D. E.
1970. Summer fallow for dryland winter wheat in the semiarid Great Plains. *Agronomy Journal* 62: 15–17.

Stegner, Wallace.
1954. *Beyond the hundredth meridian: John Wesley Powell and the second opening of the West.* Boston: Houghton Mifflin Co.

United States Department of Agriculture.
1961. *Soil Survey, Greeley County, Kansas.* USDA Soil Conservation Service and Forest Service, series 1958, no. 12. Washington, D.C.
1963. *Soil Survey, Morton County, Kansas.* USDA Soil Conservation Service and Forest Service, series 1960. no. 8. Washington, D.C.

Webb, Walter Prescott.
1931. *The Great Plains.* New York: Ginn & Co.

Wilson, M. W.
1923. *Dry farming in the north central Montana "Triangle."* Edited by R. B. Bowdsen. Montana State College Extension Service Bulletin 66. Bozeman.